Consultation
Practice and Perspectives

A. Michael Dougherty

Western Carolina University

Brooks/Cole Publishing Company
Pacific Grove, California

Brooks/Cole Publishing Company
A Division of Wadsworth, Inc.

Printed in the United States of America
10 9 8 7 6 5 4 3 2 1

Library of Congress Cataloging-in-Publication Data
Dougherty, A. Michael, [date]
    Consultation: practice and perspectives / Michael Dougherty.
        p.   cm.
    Bibliography: p.
    Includes indexes.
    ISBN 0-534-10362-6
    1. Psychological consultation. I. Title.
BF637.C56D68 1989
    158'.3—dc20   89-9724
                                                      CIP

Sponsoring Editor: *Claire Verduin*
Editorial Associate: *Gay C. Bond*
Production Editor: *Marjorie Sanders*
Manuscript Editor: *Alan Tiche*
Permissions Editor: *Carline Haga*
Interior and Cover Design: *Sharon L. Kinghan*
Art Coordinator: *Sue C. Howard*
Interior Illustration: *Sue C. Howard*
Typesetting: *Execustaff*
Printing and Binding: *Arcata Graphics, Fairfield*

(Credits continue on p. 337.)

Dedicated to my parents,
Arthur and Cecilia,
with love

Preface

One of the roles increasingly demanded of and performed by members of the helping professions is consultation. The need for a book on this subject became increasingly apparent to me over the past few years. What I felt I needed in teaching my course on consultation was a readable text that provided the basics of the consultation process, surveyed various consultation models, used case-study illustrations, discussed the nature of organizations, and dealt with ethical and professional issues. I therefore designed this book to be a thorough introduction to consultation practice. It is an attempt to gather into one place the information necessary for a comprehensive overview of consultation. A great deal of information from the two main fields that influence human services consultation—the helping professions and business and industry consultation—has been compiled here.

This book, then, presents an overview of what students and practicing consultants in the human services professions need to know about consultation practice and theory. I have attempted to structure the book in such a way that the reader can begin to develop the basic rudiments of a personal model of consultation. Students of the subject can then refine the development of their personal model at a later date through supervised practice and field experiences.

Consultation: Practice and Perspectives is based on the assumption that consultation is first and foremost a human relationship. It is my opinion that consultation cannot be effectively conducted by people whose practice does not flow from respect for themselves and others, genuineness in their attempts to be of assistance, and empathy for those with whom they work. Although consultation should not be mistaken for counseling or psychotherapy, it should be seen as a relationship emanating from the human qualities of the parties involved.

This book is intended for graduate students in counseling, psychology, social work, human resource development, and other helping professions. It can be used as the primary text in consultation courses or as a supplemental text in courses in the helping relationships. In addition, it can be a useful resource in courses or for topics such as introduction to community agency counseling, introduction to human resource development, organization of school counseling services, the role and function of school psychologists, introduction to social work, and organization of student development services. Practicing consultants can find a wealth of practical and theoretical information to help guide their practices.

OVERVIEW

What does this book contain? What will you discover as you read it? This book is divided into three parts. Part One: Consultation and Consultants sets the stage for understanding what consultation is and what consultants do. Chapter 1 is an orientation to the practice of consultation. It contains an introduction, a definition of consultation, a brief historical overview, and a glossary of the key terms used throughout the text. Chapter 2 presents a discussion of the characteristics of effective consultants, as well as the roles in which consultants engage. The effects on the consultation process of the people with whom the consultant works (consultees) are also described.

Part Two: A Generic Model of Consultation describes in detail the ins and outs of the consultation process. It presents a model of consultation that involves four stages: entry, diagnosis, implementation, and disengagement. You will read about such things as how to negotiate a contract and how to follow up and terminate, and you will also become familiar with some of the ethical, legal, and professional issues that consultants face. Chapter 3 is about the entry stage; it discusses how the consultation process gets started. Chapter 4 discusses diagnosis, which includes a sense of how the consultant can assist in determining the problem to be solved during consultation. Chapter 5 describes the implementation stage, in which consultants and the people with whom they work attempt to solve the problem defined in the diagnosis stage. Chapter 6 examines the ending of the consultation process, including the difficulties consultants have in determining the degree to which consultation was successful and how consultants say "good-bye" in a personal yet professional manner. Chapter 7 focuses on the ethical, legal, and professional issues encountered by consultants in their practices, such as dual relationships, malpractice, and confidentiality.

Part Three: Popular Models of Consultation surveys organizational, mental health, and behavioral types of consultation, and some of the different approaches these models can take. Chapter 8 examines the nature of organizations in general. I have included this chapter because almost all consultation takes place within some type of organization. In addition, I found that many students felt a need for more formal education concerning organizations and how they operate. Chapter 9 deals first with a general discussion of organizational consultation, followed by a discussion of four particular types: education/training, program, doctor/patient, and process. Chapter 10 reviews mental health consultation; because of the traditional popularity of Caplan's (1970) model, I have made it the central focus of the chapter. Chapter 11 explores how behavioral consultation uses behavioral technology to help with cases, organizations, and the training of human services professionals and others in its use. The last chapter, Chapter 12, presents a case study application of most of the consultation approaches and includes my own views on how I would proceed in the given situation.

WAYS TO USE THIS BOOK

You may want to take special note of the questions at the beginning of each chapter. They are designed to stimulate thought about each chapter's main points as you read it. In addition, the questions at the end of each chapter are designed to assist you in applying what you have learned through your reading. I hope you will take the time to reflect on these questions after you have completed each chapter.

I suggest that you look over Chapters 8 and 12 after you read Chapters 1 and 2. Chapter 8 covers the nature of organizations and will reinforce the point that almost all consultation takes place in some organizational context. By skimming through this chapter you can appreciate how complex organizations and, consequently, consultation can be. Chapter 12 presents the case of ACME Human Services Center and illustrates how various consultation approaches can be applied to that case. By looking through this chapter you can get a feel for the "nuts-and-bolts" of the various ways in which consultation can proceed in real life. Once you have obtained a perspective on how consultants actually consult, you can more readily see the critical importance of such procedures as creating relationships with the people with whom you are going to consult.

This is a book about consultation: what it is, how it is effectively practiced, and the different forms it can take. I sincerely hope that after reading this book you will be motivated and empowered to perform consultation in a confident and effective manner.

Acknowledgments

I would like to thank the many graduate students in counseling, psychology, and human resource development at Western Carolina University who contributed indirectly yet significantly to the development of this text. Their feedback on the consultation course I teach was an invaluable asset in determining the final form this text would take.

I particularly thank Diane Purcell, who as a graduate assistant contributed innumerable hours to library research on consultation. In addition, she kept me well organized and provided feedback on the manuscript from a student's perspective. Thanks, Diane!

Many thanks to the manuscript reviewers for their helpful comments: Stanley Baker, Pennsylvania State University; Gordon L. Berry, University of California, Los Angeles; Joseph Brown, University of Louisville; Cheryl Carmin, Kent State University; John H. Childers, University of Arkansas; and Jane L. Winer, Texas Tech University. I would also like to thank Gerald Corey of California State University at Fullerton for his suggestions concerning the organization of the text.

To my wife and life partner, Leslie, a special thanks for the love, support, and understanding shown during the preparation of this manuscript. She also helped me keep the perspective that "work is always there and love is not always as accessible."

Finally, to the talented people at Brooks/Cole, my gratitude for being able to work with a first-class group of professionals. It was a pleasure to work with Claire Verduin, Ellen Brownstein, Marjorie Sanders, Gay Bond, Carline Haga, Alan Tiche, and the many others who helped this book become a reality.

A. Michael Dougherty

Contents

Chapter 6
Disengagement Stage   109

Chapter 7
Ethical, Professional, and Legal Issues   134

PART 3
Models of Consultation   156

Chapter 8
The Nature of Organizations   159

Chapter 9

Organizational Consultation 182

Chapter 10

Mental Health Consultation 219

Chapter 11

Behavioral Consultation 254

Chapter 12
Case Study Illustrations   285

Consultation and Consultants

"Who me? Be a consultant? Are you kidding? I can't do that stuff! Why, I don't even know what it is. *Consultants* don't even know what it is!" These famous last words reflect my views of consultation as an aspiring human services professional 15 years ago. I now spend a substantial amount of my professional life performing consultation. As a human services professional you'll spend a great deal of your professional time performing consultation, too.

Consider the following example:

CASE STUDY:
Chris Gonzolez is the head counselor at a large urban secondary school that has a severe substance-abuse problem among its student body. The counseling department of the school has a well-defined procedure for referring substance-abuse cases to community resources. Chris has been studying several drug-prevention programs but is uncertain about which one would be best for the school. Chris contacts Leslie Green, who is a substance-abuse counselor at the mental health center in the community. Leslie is quite familiar with a number of substance-abuse programs for schools and has consulted with counselors in other schools about how to choose an appropriate substance-abuse program. Chris and Leslie meet for three two-hour sessions over a three-week period. During the first meeting they explore the school's substance-abuse problem in detail and Leslie observes the overall operation of the school. In the second meeting, Leslie provides Chris information on possible substance-abuse programs with which Chris was not familiar. In the final meeting, Leslie assists Chris in deciding which program would be best for the school.

This example is typical of the many types of situations about which human services professionals are called upon to consult. Consultation is becoming an increasingly powerful force in the helping professions (Kurpius, 1978). Whereas a decade ago consultation was an "emerging role" (Kurpius, 1978, p. 335), today it is an accepted role of human services professionals. In the work settings of almost all human services professionals, consultation is becoming a "specialized professional process" (Kurpius, 1986, p. 58). A tremendous social demand for this kind of professional service has developed (Parsons & Meyers, 1984). Some authors even call consultation an "emerging profession" (Gallessich, 1982, p. 1) or an "independent field of study" (Mazade, 1985, p. 7).

If you aspire to be a human services professional or are already a practicing one, you will be faced with opportunities to consult with other human services professionals, caretakers (for example, parents), or human services organizations.

Part One of this book introduces you to the world of consultation, provides a frame of reference for its practice, and focuses on what consultants do and the skills they need. In addition, it discusses the ways consultees—the people to whom consultants provide services—affect the consultation process.

Chapter

1

Introduction and Overview

PREVIEW

Consultation is practiced by most human services professionals in a variety of settings for a variety of reasons (Meyers, Alpert, & Fleisher, 1983). Consider the following list of examples:

- A psychologist helps a therapist deal with problems she is having with one or more clients in her caseload.
- A counselor works with a school teacher to improve classroom management techniques.
- A social worker consults with a special-education teacher about dealing with a student's family.
- A family therapist trains school counselors in family systems theory.
- A professor of human services assists a job corps center staff in increasing its morale.
- A human resource development specialist helps her organization survey employee satisfaction.
- A psychologist diagnoses the reasons for high turnover in a social services agency.
- A counselor assists the staff of a counseling center in identifying its major work concerns and in making plans to solve them.
- A mental health worker assists a Head Start program in evaluating its parent training program.

These examples illustrate how consultants in the human services provide a variety of services under the rubric of "consultation."

Because of the many types of services that can constitute consultation, this human services function is difficult to define. Little agreement exists about what consultants do, although some consensus exists concerning the personal traits and professional skills consultants need to perform their work well.

This chapter will introduce the concept of consultation, define consultation, show how it is different from other functions in which human services professionals engage, and provide a glossary of key terms used throughout the book.

3

Here are five questions to consider as you read this introductory chapter:

1. What does a consultant actually do?
2. What are the differences among consultation and other activities, such as counseling and psychotherapy, supervision, and education?
3. How would you define consultation?
4. Why would you ever want to perform consultation in the first place?
5. In what activities do each of the parties involved in consultation tend to engage?

INTRODUCTION

Human services professionals (such as counselors, psychologists, social workers, and educators) provide consultation to individuals, groups, and human services organizations as one of their functions. Consultants usually perform their services in one of three organizational settings (MacLennan, 1986). One setting is some type of mental health organization whose mission in part is to provide consultation services to the community. A community mental health center is an example. A second setting is a private firm or independent practitioner offering consultation services to the community. For instance, a professor of human services might provide stress management training to the employees of a job corps center. In the third setting consultants work "in-house" and consult within the organization that employs them. An example is a school counselor consulting with a teacher about a student's behavior.

Organizations hire consultants for several diverse reasons common to many agencies and organizations (Gattiker & Larwood, 1985; Matthews, 1983):

1. Consultants can have more expertise to solve a given problem than have any of the members of the organization in which consultation is needed.
2. Consultants can provide expert opinions about the possible alternatives an organization may take to combat a given set of problems.
3. Because consultants are frequently outsiders, they can provide organizations with a fresh view of themselves and their problems.
4. Consultants are usually more objective about problem situations than are the people facing those situations.
5. Consultants can handle tasks that would cause work overloads for existing personnel.
6. Organizations often need the expertise in problem solving that consultants can provide.
7. Having a consultant come in to examine a problem can enhance the credibility of an organization's attempt to deal with a problem.
8. Consultants can constitute "instant staff" to help an organization meet its special needs.
9. Consultants can provide needed training for personnel in organizations.

10. Consultants can provide impartial assessment of an organization's programs.
11. Consultants can provide external justification of organizational decisions or strategies.

In order to fulfill any of these consulting functions effectively, you need to possess an understanding of the various views of how consultation is practiced. The first step is to obtain a generic model of consultation, which provides a general framework for understanding and practicing consultation. It helps you develop a cognitive map and a sense of direction for performing consultation. The second step is to become familiar with the various consultation models that are available. Familiarity with the types of consultation—usually categorized as organizational, mental health, and behavioral—provides you with models that have limited, quite specific applicability in particular situations (Mazade, 1985). As you will see, there are several approaches to each of these types of consultation.

In addition to understanding models of consultation, five other facts must be understood before you can effectively practice consultation:

1. Consultation is a unique helping activity.
2. The effects of different models vary according to the emphasis of each model.
3. A body of theory provides direction for consultation and guides change toward solutions of problems.
4. The context and setting in which consultation occurs affect its outcome.
5. There is a wide range of possible interventions that can be used in consultation (Kurpius, 1987, p. 495).

Understanding these facts provides you with the basic rudiments from which you can develop your own personal model of consultation. I strongly recommend that you start to develop your own personal model of consultation because you will consult most effectively when you have integrated your knowledge with your unique personality. For example, I am a very social person; I need people around me. One way I use this trait in my own personal model of consulting is by appreciating the importance of relationships in the context of consultation.

I make five very basic assumptions in this book. The first assumption is that *how* a consultant performs consultation is as important as *what* a consultant does in consultation. This concept leads to a very important point: the perceptions of the consultation process by the parties involved are critical in determining the success of consultation. For example, as a consultant I might know what I need to do to help a person with whom I am working. But if I don't know how to do it in a way that the other person sees as helpful, then the consultation is less likely to be successful. It is not the creation of a working relationship with the people who will receive consultation that is most significant, but rather how that working relationship is established. I hope you will seek out situations in which you can consult under the supervision of well-trained consultants, for such supervision is essential in helping you understand how you do what you do when you consult and the impact your behavior has on the effectiveness of the consultation process.

The second assumption is that consultation is a human relationship. Consultants do not consult *to* the people with whom they are working, but rather they consult *with* those people. When consultation is viewed as a human relationship, its personal side becomes as important as its professional side. Consultants need to identify and clarify their values about both life and consultation so that they do not fall into the trap of inadvertently imposing those values during consultation. Such an imposition can restrict the professional growth of those with whom the consultant is working. In addition, lack of self-knowledge about values can in effect place "blinders" on the consultant, which can cause a type of tunnel vision and lead to mistakes during the course of consultation. For example, some consultants with tunnel vision develop and use only certain "pet" interventions. However, when consultation is viewed as a human relationship, the respect, dignity, and welfare of the parties involved become paramount. The consultant then attempts to objectively provide the most needed services, whether they are "pet" ones or not. Effective consultants excel by behaving in ways that demonstrate respect, that recognize the dignity, and that protect the welfare of their consultees.

The third assumption is that consultants need to know about the nature of consultation. Many people "consult" without ever having a course or any kind of training in consultation; these people have learned to consult through a series of consulting experiences alone. Only by chance do they develop a frame of reference for approaching consultation. "Flying by the seat of one's pants" is dangerous in consultation, for the professional (and sometimes the personal) aspects of other peoples' lives are involved. Consequently, consultants need to be well grounded in consultation models and interventions. This knowledge creates an objective frame of reference for consultants. Further, only such knowledgeable and skillful consultants lend credibility to consultation as a legitimate role for human services professionals.

The fourth assumption is that there is no one best way to consult. Relative to other functions that human services professionals deliver, such as counseling, psychotherapy, and teaching, consultation is not well researched. In addition, consultation tends to occur within organizations, which adds a tremendous amount of complexity to the process and makes consultation itself very difficult to evaluate. Consequently, the best resources available to consultants are some limited empirical research, a few adequately developed models, their knowledge about people and organizations, an ethical and professional attitude, and their skills related to consulting.

Maintaining an open mind about the various approaches to consultation is very important. Some readers are turned off by the term *behavioral* because it reminds them of horror stories about the misuses of behavior modification. Others are prejudiced against the term *mental health* because they automatically identify it with "shrinking someone's head" or using psychotherapy on someone. Some readers may not like the term *organization* because it leads them to think of a bureaucratic structure in which rules and regulations are more highly valued than the people within it. But because being effective in consultation depends on the context in which the consultation occurs, an effective consultant develops a broad repertoire of skills and a large knowledge base from which to consult. Then, depending upon the situation, the consultant is able to use the most pertinent knowledge and appropriate skills available.

The fifth assumption relates to whether consultation is a science, an art, or a craft. I believe that what one author (McKeachie, 1986) noted about teaching applies to consultation: consultation is more than a science, more than an art, more than a craft. It is all of these, along with commitment—commitment to oneself, commitment to the persons with whom one consults, and commitment to the challenging endeavor of getting ideas and concepts out of the consultant's mind and into the minds of those with whom consultation is occurring.

CONSULTATION DEFINED

What is consultation? This very simple question does not have a simple answer. In one wit's view, consultation is a lot like pornography: you can't define it but you know it when you see it! There is no widespread agreement on the definition of consultation (Mannino & Shore, 1986). Some authors (for example, Schmidt & Osborne, 1981) argue that consultation and counseling are basically the same process. They are in the minority, however. The term *consultation* has been used to mean a variety of things and to encompass a variety of functions that provide it with its own identity (West & Idol, 1987).

Consultation tends to be defined in terms of the role and function of the consultant (Kurpius & Robinson, 1978)—that is, in terms of what consultants actually do. A variety of generic definitions of consultation have been suggested (for example, Gallessich, 1982; Parsons & Meyers, 1984; Brown, Wyne, Blackburn, & Powell, 1979; Brown, Pryzwansky, & Schulte, 1987). These definitions generally agree about the role of consultation, but they differ on such issues as whether the consultee must be a human services professional or whether the consultant must be from "outside" the system in which consultation is occurring.

General agreement does exist on several aspects of consultation that can be used in formulating an acceptable definition. Most authors consider consultation to be a problem-solving process; the goal of all consultation is to solve a problem. What constitutes a "problem" can, of course, vary significantly. An organization could seek a consultant to assist in such problems as alleviating poor staff morale or determining how best to evaluate the effects of a substance-abuse program. Hence, consultation can occur in a very broad range of problem-solving situations.

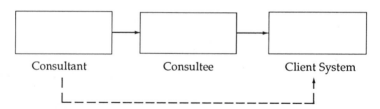

FIGURE 1.1   **Relationships of the Parties in Consultation**

A second commonly accepted aspect of consultation is that it is tripartite in nature (Mannino & Shore, 1986); that is, consultation usually involves three parties: a consultant, a consultee, and a client system. The consultant delivers direct service to a consultee, who delivers direct service to a client system. The client system receives indirect service from the consultant through an intermediary—the consultee. Thus, the consultant provides assistance to the consultee that can positively affect the consultee's work with the client system. Figure 1.1 shows the relationships among the parties involved in consultation. The solid lines represent direct service; the broken line represents indirect service.

In human services consultation, the consultant is typically a human services professional, such as a counselor, a psychologist, a social worker, or a human resource development specialist. The consultee is typically another human services professional. In some cases, the consultee may be a person with some caretaking role (for example, a parent, work supervisor, administrator, or teacher). There can be one or more consultees involved in consultation, and the client system can consist of one person, a group, an organization, or a community.

A third aspect of consultation on which there is substantial agreement is that the goal of consultation is to improve in some way both the client system and the consultee. The term *improve,* of course, can mean many things, and hence a large number of approaches to consultation and a great many interventions become available to consultants. Thus, for example, a consultant might help a consultee not only to work more effectively with a given moderately depressed client, but also to improve the consultee's ability to work with moderately depressed clients in the future.

Agreement on these aspects of consultation leads to a general, yet widely accepted definition: *consultation is a process in which a human services professional assists a consultee with a work-related (or caretaking-related) problem with a client system, with the goal of helping both the consultee and the client system in some specified way.*

COMMON CHARACTERISTICS OF CONSULTATION

Can consultation be identified by certain common characteristics? A survey of the literature (for example, Gallessich, 1982; Brown, et al., 1987; Mannino & Shore, 1986; Gutkin & Curtis, 1982; Mazade, 1985; West & Idol, 1987) on the nature of consultation suggests an affirmative answer. In addition to the three aspects discussed above, some general agreement seems to exist on the following characteristics of consultation:

1. Either the consultee or the client system may be given priority over the other at a given time, depending on the approach to consultation that is taken.
2. The consultant provides indirect service to the client system by providing direct service to the consultee.
3. A consultant can be either separate from or part of the system in which consultation is to occur. Consultants who are not part of the system in which consultation is to occur are termed *external consultants;* those who are part of the system are called *internal consultants.*
4. Participation in consultation is voluntary for all parties involved.
5. Consultees are free to do whatever they wish with the consultant's suggestions and recommendations. They are under no obligation to follow the consultant's recommendations.
6. The relationship between the consultee and consultant is one of peers, of two equals. Although the consultation relationship is equal in terms of the power of the consultant and consultee, it is unequal in terms of need; that is, the consultee needs help with a problem and the consultant does not, at least as far as the consultation relationship is concerned.
7. The consultation relationship is temporary. Depending on the type, consultation may range from a single session to weekly sessions for more than a year. Whatever its length, however, the relationship is always temporary—the consultant does not replace the consultee.
8. Consultation deals exclusively with the consultee's work-related or caretaking-related problems. Consultation, by definition, never deals with the personal concerns of the consultee.
9. The consultant can take on a variety of roles in consultation, depending on the nature of the problem, the skills of the consultee, the purpose and desired outcomes of consultation, and the skills of the consultant.
10. Consultation tends to be collaborative in nature; that is, consultants and consultees work together to complement each other in solving the problems defined in consultation. Typically, consultants do not do for consultees what consultees can do for themselves. One exception is when consultees have the skills but not the time to do a given task. For example, a consultee might ask a consultant to lead an in-service workshop on substance-abuse counseling for the consultee's organization, even though the consultee is skilled in that task.

In summary, consultation is a tripartite, voluntary, and temporary relationship among peers. The consultant, whether internal or external, provides both direct service to the consultee in a variety of capacities and indirect service to the client system by assisting the consultee in problem solving. The focus of consultation is a work-related or caretaking-related problem of the consultee, and the goal is to improve both the consultee's and the client's situation through collaboration. The consultee is assumed to have a willingness to cooperate and is free to do whatever he or she wishes with the consultant's assistance and recommendations.

CONSULTATION COMPARED TO OTHER HUMAN SERVICES ACTIVITIES

Consultation can be compared to the three other common human services functions—counseling and psychotherapy, supervision, and teaching—as a way of making the concept of consultation clearer. Such comparisons were popularized by Caplan (1970).

Consultation is different from *counseling and psychotherapy* in two fairly obvious ways. First, counseling and psychotherapy are dyadic in nature—they involve two parties, the therapist and the client—whereas consultation is triadic. Second, counseling and psychotherapy deal with the personal problems of the client, whereas consultation deals with work-related or caretaking-related concerns only. This is not to say that the effects of resolving a work-related problem cannot be therapeutic to the consultee. Still, consultants, even if they are trained therapists, never provide counseling or psychotherapy to consultees, even if the work-related or caretaking-related problem being solved in consultation is determined to be due to a personal problem of the consultee. In such cases, the consultant brings up his or her concerns and then refers the consultee for assistance. A final point: when the consultant is trained in counseling and psychotherapy, it is quite easy to inadvertently turn the consultation session into a therapy session. Such consultants should take care to monitor their consultation behaviors carefully.

Another human services function that is different from consultation is *supervision*. Supervision tends to be performed in dyads and implies an ongoing relationship, whereas consultation is typically considered a temporary, tripartite relationship. More significantly, supervision implies the power of one person over another. If I am your supervisor, I typically have the power to perform ongoing evaluations of your effectiveness on the job. These evaluations will be used in personnel decisions that affect you in many possible ways at work and thus create inequality in the relationship. Therefore, consultants do not become supervisors of consultees; in fact, consultants act in such a manner that consultees become better "self-supervisors."

Teaching is also different from consultation. Traditional teaching involves a predetermined, detailed lesson plan, whereas events in consultation often dictate more spontaneous behavior by the consultant. Further, teaching is an unequal relationship in which teachers have power over and evaluate students, typically by some grading process. Consultants may assess consultee learning, but in a manner different from that used by a teacher in a university.

A consultant may, however, take on a teaching role on occasion. For example, a mental health consultant might teach a consultee how to perform a behavioral counseling technique with a client, or an organizational consultant might teach a consultee the basics of survey design. Later in this text you will read about a special approach to consultation called education/training consultation; it is one of the most commonly requested approaches to consultation.

In summary, then, consultation differs from counseling/psychotherapy, supervision, and teaching in one or more of the following ways: it is tripartite, it does not deal with the consultee's personal problems, it does not evaluate the consultee, it typically is not planned in great detail, and it is a relationship among equals.

HISTORICAL OVERVIEW

Like any other human services function, the roots of consultation go back to ancient times, when two prototypical roles of consultation emerged: the healer and the technological advisor (Gallessich, 1982). The healer had the power to improve well-being, and the technological advisor could tell someone how to fix something or how to proceed to the next step in solving a problem. As human knowledge expanded, so too did the need for people who could help solve problems and provide technical expertise.

The field of medicine provided the model that consultation used as it developed into a tool of human services professionals. This model is the familiar medical consultation. If a physician noticed something about a patient that might require the attention of a specialist, that physician consulted with the specialist. Frequently, that meant "turning over" the patient to the specialist (consultant). The physician who originally handled the case frequently did not treat the patient again. Hence, in the original form of consultation, the consultant saw and treated the patient.

Such was the state of consultation around the turn of the 20th century. Then it became increasingly apparent to medical professionals that the referring personnel could benefit from participating in treating the patient further. This change in perspective created the conditions that fostered the emergence in the human services professions of consultation as we now know it. Consultation today, common in such human services professions as psychology, counseling, social work, education, and human resource development, has developed into three broad types: organizational, mental health, and behavioral. The historical development of each of these types is covered in later chapters.

GLOSSARY OF KEY TERMS USED IN THE BOOK

Because consultation is neither well defined nor has adequately developed its own identity, many of the terms used in the consultation literature are vague and confusing. Therefore, the glossary that follows contains some key terms used throughout this book. It is very important that you familiarize yourself with these terms so that you can avoid confusion as you read.

Behavioral consultation: One of the three major types of consultation. It attempts to assist consultees and their client systems through a systematic, problem-solving approach based on behavioral technology.

Client: In some approaches to mental health and behavioral consultation, the person with whom the consultee is having a work-related or caretaking-related problem; in this instance the client constitutes the client system (see below). One of the goals of consultation is to improve the functioning of the client.

Client system: The person, group, organization, or community with whom the consultee is having a work-related or caretaking-related problem. One of the goals of consultation is to improve the functioning of the client system.

Collaboration: The type of approach most consultants use when working with their consultees. This approach allows both parties to pool their strengths and resources in their efforts to solve the work-related or caretaking-related problem about which consultation is taking place. This approach minimizes the danger of too much dominance by the consultant.

Consultant: A person, typically a human services professional, who delivers direct service to another person (consultee) who has a work-related or caretaking-related problem with a person, group, organization, or community (client system).

Consultation: A type of helping relationship in which a human services professional (consultant) delivers assistance to another person (consultee) in order to solve a work-related or caretaking-related problem the consultee has with a client system.

Consultee: The person, often a human services professional or a caretaker (for example, a parent, teacher, or supervisor), to whom the consultant provides assistance with a work-related or caretaking-related problem. One of the goals of consultation is to improve the current and future functioning of the consultee.

Diagnosis: The second of the four stages of the consultation process. In this stage the problem to be solved in consultation is defined. Thus, in its simplest form, diagnosis is the equivalent of problem identification. In its more complex form, it is an ongoing process in which the target problem is continually redefined and worked on by gathering, analyzing, interpreting, and discussing data.

Direct service: By definition, assistance a consultant provides a consultee or that a consultee provides a client system. When consultants work with consultees they are providing direct service to them. When consultees work with client systems, they are providing direct service to them. This term is frequently contrasted with indirect service.

Disengagement: The last of the four stages in the consultation process. It typically involves the winding down of consultation, including evaluation of consultation, postconsultation planning, reduced contact, follow-up, and termination.

Entry: The first of the four stages of the consultation process. It involves perceiving the presenting problem, formulating a contract, and physically and psychologically entering the system in which consultation is to occur.

Generic model of consultation: That model of consultation that contains those characteristics common to the various types of consultation and the approaches to these types. It is what distinguishes consultation as a unique helping relationship from other helping relationships.

Human services organization: A broad term describing an organization that as its major mission provides some form of contact with clients and has as its aim the improvement of the well-being of those clients, and therefore of society. Counseling centers, mental health centers, Head Start programs, homes for the mentally retarded, and social services departments are all examples of human services agencies.

Implementation: Third of the four stages of the consultation process. It is the "action" or "doing" stage, the one in which some action is taken on the problem. It begins with formulating and choosing a plan to solve the problem that has been diagnosed, and it includes implementing and evaluating that plan.

Indirect service: That type of service provided to the client system by the consultant. The consultant affects the well-being of the client system by helping the consultee help the client system more effectively. It is one of the characteristics of consultation that differentiates it from other helping relationships.

Mental health consultation: One of the three major types of consultation. It attempts to focus on the "psychological" well-being of all the parties involved in consultation. Its ultimate goal is to create a mentally healthier society.

Organization: A group of people put together for a common purpose. Almost all consultation, regardless of the type, occurs within some type of organization. It is one of the factors that influence the processes and outcomes of consultation. Throughout this book this term is used synonymously with the term *agency.*

Organization contact person: That person in the organization in which consultation is being considered who initially contacts (or is contacted by) the consultant. This person is often a mid-level administrator who may or may not become a consultee. This person usually paves the way for the consultant's entry into the organization.

Organizational consultation: One of the three major types of consultation. Its primary goal is the enhancement of an organization's effectiveness. The organization itself is the client system, and the members of the organization involved in consultation are the consultees. Consultants frequently work together in teams when performing organizational consultation.

Parties-at-interest: Those people (who usually belong to the organization in which consultation is occurring) who are not directly involved in consultation but are affected by the consultation process in some way. Parties-at-interest typically include contact persons and administrators. If the consultant belongs to an organization (for example, a mental health center), then those members of the consultant's organization indirectly affected by the consultation are also parties-at-interest.

Tripartite: Composed of three parts. With respect to consultation, it refers to the three parties involved: consultant, consultee, and client system.

Work-related problem: The kind of problem considered to be suitable for the primary focus in consultation. In the case of consultation with people such as parents, the term *caretaking-related* is sometimes used instead. This term is often contrasted with *personal problem,* a type of problem not dealt with in consultation.

QUESTIONS FOR REFLECTION

1. How do the roles of consultant, consultee, and client differ from one another?
2. What is the basic difference between indirect and direct service that consultants provide?
3. In what ways can consultation be called a "problem-solving" process?
4. Why is it important for consultants to have a personal theory of consultation?
5. Why is *how* consultants do what they do as important as *what* they do?
6. Many consultants are technological experts with little training in consultation theory and practice. What are some of the potential problems that such consultants can encounter when performing their work?
7. How can consultation have the goal of improving the consultee and the client system at the same time?
8. Because consultants, by definition, work with consultees who have work-related problems, how can the consultation relationship be one among equals?
9. How would you as a consultant determine which roles to take on during consultation?
10. How is consultation similar to counseling and psychotherapy, to teaching, and to supervising? How is it different?

SUGGESTED SUPPLEMENTARY READINGS

The journal *Consultation*, published by the Human Sciences Press, New York. This excellent journal is not widely distributed, so you may have some trouble locating it. If necessary, ask for help from the interlibrary loan department of your local university library. This journal covers a variety of topics related to consultation, its processes, and its variations. Articles in this journal tend to be timely and on the "cutting edge" of consultation, and they cover not only a variety of topics but also a variety of settings. Many of the articles, however, assume prior knowledge of consultation. In short, it is worth the trouble to find this journal.

Mannino, F. V., Trickett, E. J., Shore, M. F., Kidder, M. G., & Levin, G. (Eds.). (1986). *Handbook of mental health consultation*. Rockville, MD: National Institute for Mental Health. This book provides 810 pages of "everything you wanted to know about consultation." The authors consider the terms *human services consultation* and *mental health consultation* to be basically synonymous. One of the most valuable parts of this book is the annotated reference guide to the consultation literature for 1978–1984. If you need to look up something on consultation or need to find some articles of interest quickly, I strongly suggest that you consult this annotated reference guide first.

Chapter

2

Consultants and Consultees

PREVIEW

If you were looking for a consultant to work with people in your human services organization, what type of person would you hire? What kinds of professional skills would be needed in such a consultant, and how would you be able to tell if the consultant truly possessed those skills? What roles would you want this person to take during his or her consultation activities? What would be the most critical factor for you in determining whether or not to hire this prospective consultant?

This chapter provides some answers to these questions—it discusses the characteristics that effective consultants possess, the skills critical to successful consultation, and the various roles that consultants play. In addition, we will examine three important factors that influence the outcome of consultation: consultee characteristics, the consultant's position (internal or external) to the organization in which consultation is to occur, and the role of stress in consultation.

As you read this chapter, consider the following questions:

1. How are the personal characteristics of a consultant likely to influence the consultation process?
2. What skills seem necessary for consultants, regardless of the role they take during consultation?
3. Do any of the roles of consultants tend to contradict one another?
4. In what ways can the characteristics of the consultee affect the consultation process?
5. How can the stress that is part of consultation affect the consultation process, positively as well as negatively?

INTRODUCTION

CASE ONE:
Dale Jones, a psychologist, and Jackie Cheng, a social worker, work together in a community mental health center. Jackie approaches Dale for consultation

16

regarding a migrant family that is part of Jackie's caseload. It seems that the family is having difficulty adjusting to the community, which consists primarily of retirees who have their summer homes there. When Jackie asks Dale for help in facilitating the family's adjustment, Dale makes light of the request by noting that by late fall both the retirees and the migrant family will be long gone.

CASE TWO:
Terri Brodski, a psychologist, and Jamie Stewart, a social worker, work together in a community mental health center. Jamie approaches Terri for consultation regarding a migrant family that is part of Jamie's caseload. It seems that the family is having difficulty adjusting to the community, which consists primarily of retirees who have their summer homes there.

When Jamie approaches Terri about the family's problems, Terri asks her to present her concerns about the family in detail, and she listens to and clarifies Jamie's concerns. When she shares discouragement about the possibilities of helping the family, Terri offers encouragement and support, and she asks how Jamie's work with the family ties into their agency's role and mission. Finally, they establish a verbal contract between them and agree to meet twice more about how Jamie can work more effectively with the family.

First, Terri observes Jamie working with the family. During the next consultation session, they exchange their impressions about the family, divide the family's adjustment problem into three smaller, more specific problems, and set goals to solve each problem. Terri then leads Jamie through a brainstorming session during which possible interventions for solving each of the defined problems are generated. Once they agree on an intervention for each problem, Terri assists Jamie in formulating their ideas into a feasible plan, which Jamie agrees to carry out.

During their final consultation session one month later, Terri and Jamie formally evaluate the degree to which each problem was solved and the effectiveness of the consultation process itself (that is, how well Terri and Jamie worked together). They plan additional follow-up strategies for Jamie to use in later contacts with the family, and they agree that within 30 days Terri will make a follow-up call to Jamie concerning the family's progress. Then they say their good-byes.

Who, in your opinion, is the more effective consultant, Dale Jones or Terri Brodski? Terri clearly spent much more time and used a much larger number of skills with Jamie than Dale did with Jackie.

Terri displayed many of the characteristics of effective consultants. She used interpersonal skills when offering support and encouragement to Jamie. When Terri listened to and clarified Jamie's concerns, she used effective communication skills. She used several problem-solving skills with Jamie in order to identify ways to help the migrant family. Terri showed skill in working with organizations when she asked how Jamie's work with the family tied into the agency's role and mission, and she displayed ethical and professional behavior skills by spending the time and effort needed to help Jamie. As you can see from these two cases, there are characteristics and skills that differentiate effective consultants from less effective ones. Let's examine these characteristics next.

CHARACTERISTICS OF EFFECTIVE CONSULTANTS

Because consultation is demanding, the requirements to perform it successfully are also demanding (Kelley, 1981). Effective consultants have a personal and professional growth orientation, knowledge of consultation and human behavior, and consultation skills. Figure 2.1 illustrates the makeup of an effective consultant.

| Effective Consultant | = | Personal and Professional Growth Orientation | + | Knowledge of Consultation and Human Behavior | + | Skills in Consulting |

FIGURE 2.1 Three Characteristics of an Effective Consultant

A *personal growth orientation* involves the willingness of a consultant to grow and change as a person. Because consultation typically involves problem solving and because solving problems involves change on the part of the consultee, consultants need to be willing to model that change. Personal growth orientation does not necessarily mean that consultants must experience personal growth counseling or therapy, although such experiences can be quite beneficial. Rather, the concept of personal growth orientation entails any aspect of a consultant's life in which the consultant endeavors to "stretch." For example, one consultant might decide to accomplish the feat of hiking to every waterfall in a national park within a certain time frame. Another consultant might volunteer ten hours a week of free consultation services to a church group, whereas another consultant might participate in a personal growth group to improve his interpersonal effectiveness. In short, personal growth orientation is an attitude toward life that helps consultants become more effective human beings by periodically "stretching" themselves in some way.

A *professional growth orientation* refers to consultants' participation in activities that enhance the effectiveness of their consultation practices. Consultants often participate in workshops, training programs, academic courses, and supervised practice in order to remain current in their fields. In addition, many consultants seek additional training and knowledge in order to expand the parameters of their consultation practices. For example, a consultant, a university professor by training, might take a series of management and organizational behavior courses in order to be able to expand her consultation services to include consultation with human services agencies.

Thus, a personal and professional growth orientation helps consultants to "practice what they preach" more effectively. By experiencing growth in their own lives, consultants are better able to empathize with consultees about the barriers to growth that consultees normally experience and to be more authentic role models for those with whom they work.

Effective consultants, of course, also possess *knowledge of consultation* and a basic *knowledge of human behavior* (Levinson, 1985). Even though it seems obvious that consultants need to be knowledgeable about consultation, the fact remains that many practicing consultants have had no formal training in consultation other than any on-the-job training they may have received. This lack of any systematic means for acquiring knowledge about consultation creates issues concerning the professional limitations of consultants and the ways they assess their effectiveness. Regardless of how they acquire their knowledge, effective consultants know the "ins and outs" of consultation; that is, they possess a generic model of consultation and are knowledgeable about the various types of consultation. Such knowledge provides them with a sense of meaningfulness and adds direction to their practices.

Effective consultants must also possess knowledge about human behavior—including both individual and group behavior—for consultation is first of all a human relationship. Because consultants spend much of their time working with individual consultees, they need to know the basics of personality theory, normal and abnormal behavior, interpersonal relationships, and human communication. Knowledge of these topics is essential for maximizing the effectiveness with which each stage of consultation is accomplished. Further, a basic knowledge of group dynamics and organizational theory and behavior is quickly becoming a necessity for almost all consultants because most consultation occurs in and is affected by an organizational setting. Therefore, consultants need a working knowledge of organizations in order to maximize the effectiveness of their interventions.

Even when consultants have a personal and professional growth orientation and a knowledge of consultation and human behavior, if they are to be effective they need a third characteristic: *skills in consulting.* Consultants must be able to "do" as well as "know." Effective consultants have a broad repertoire of consultation skills that range from basic communication skills to sophisticated problem-solving intervention skills.

In summary, then, the three general characteristics of effective consultants—a personal and professional growth orientation, knowledge of consultation and human behavior, and skills in consulting—combine to make a professional who consults with a sense of authenticity, expertise, and functional ability.

CONSULTANT SKILLS

Many skills are required of effective consultants. Many authors (for example, Lippitt & Lippitt, 1986; Hunsaker & Alessandra, 1980; Conoley & Conoley, 1982; Dustin & Ehly, 1984; Parsons & Meyers, 1984; Kurpius, 1986) point out the importance of competent interpersonal and communication skills. Competence in problem-solving skills is also essential for effective consultants (Kurpius & Robinson, 1978; Maris, 1985; Schindler-Rainman, 1985). Skills in working with organizations are increasingly needed by consultants (Schein, 1969, 1987; Egan, 1985). Finally, well developed ethical and professional behavior skills are essential to competent consultants (Gallessich, 1982; Corey, Corey, & Callanan, 1988).

Interpersonal and Communication Skills

Attitudes

Consultation is a human relationship that involves extensive communication. Interpersonal and communication skills, which are related to creating and maintaining effective human relationships, are essential for a consultant. Further, the attitudes from which these skills flow are as important as the skills themselves (see Medway, 1982).

The desirable underpinnings for these skills are unconditional regard, empathy, and genuineness (Rogers, 1961). These attitudes form the core conditions upon which an effective consultation relationship can be built. Without these attitudes in the consultant, the development of rapport with the consultee may take longer to achieve or may not occur at all. These attitudes exist on a continuum; their presence in a person is not an all-or-nothing thing. However, to the degree that consultants possess these attitudes, the conditions for successful consultation will be established.

Unconditional regard (often referred to as acceptance) refers to the willingness of the consultant to respect and accept the consultee as a human being who is worthwhile, has dignity, and can be liked or cared for by the consultant, in spite of the consultee's imperfections. Regard is often manifested by the consultant as nonjudgmental and nonpossessive behavior toward the consultee.

Empathy is a form of understanding that refers to the consultant's ability to tune in to and accurately perceive the consultee's subjective experience at a given moment during consultation, without losing his or her objectivity. It is a posture of putting oneself in another person's shoes to understand that person's experiences at a given moment. Empathy helps in establishing rapport, trust, open communication, and a common ground from which consultation can proceed.

Genuineness is demonstrated when consultants are free to be themselves in the consultation relationship—when they need not hide behind roles, become defensive, or play games with the consultee. When consultants are being genuine they are open, not closed; authentic, not phony; spontaneous, not overly controlled; flexible, not rigid; and "together," not fragmented. When consultants are genuine they are aware of what they are experiencing in the relationship and within themselves. Perhaps one of the greatest contributions of genuineness to successful consultation is the modeling effect it can have for the consultee. When consultees view consultants as genuine, they too can become more genuine.

Other attitudes that appear to be related to effective interpersonal and communication skills are a positive outlook about oneself and others, a willingness to take risks, a commitment to creativity (Schindler-Rainman, 1985), and a desire to be trustworthy (French & Bell, 1978). Whenever consultants possess and manifest these positive attitudes, they create the conditions from which their interpersonal and communication skills can flow naturally and in which effective consultation can occur.

Interpersonal Skills

Interpersonal skills are the skills of creating, maintaining, and terminating relationships; they refer to our ability to get along with other human beings. Because consultation is a helping relationship, consultants need relatively high levels of these skills. The creation and maintenance of consultation relationships require several major interpersonal skills, many of which are:

1. putting the consultee at ease (for example, making small talk);
2. setting expectations about the relationship (for example, contracting behaviors);
3. creating an environment conducive to collaboration (for example, determining early on what the consultee can and cannot do);
4. creating an environment conducive to change (for example, talking implicitly and explicitly about how consultation is related to change);
5. creating an appropriate consultant's image in the eyes of the consultee (for example, explaining early on who the consultant is and what he or she can do for the consultee);
6. developing a social influence base built on prestige, trustworthiness, and similarity (for example, making explicit use of expertise, benign intent, and similarities to the consultee);
7. locating the proper physical environment in which consultation can occur (for example, procuring a private office);
8. making efficient and valuable use of time during consultation (for example, being prepared);
9. being comfortable with "oneself as consultant" (for example, exuding confidence);
10. taking spatial factors into consideration (for example, seating arrangements);
11. considering any cross-cultural factors or issues (for example, identifying a consultee's possible values differences that result from a different cultural background);
12. using conflict resolution interventions when necessary (for example, assisting a consultee to express and deal with disagreement about some issue that emerges in consultation);
13. noting and responding not only to consultee verbalizations, but also to emotions and nonverbal behaviors (for example, noting not only what is said, but also the feelings accompanying the statement);
14. having the ability to deal with the "here and now" issues in the relationship (for example, inviting consultees to express their true perceptions about the helpfulness of consultation); and
15. using appropriate humor (for example, having the willingness to laugh at oneself).

Interpersonal skills assist consultants in developing and sustaining strong relationships with their consultees. The strength and outcome of the consultation relationship are often directly related to consultee motivation, a commitment to change, and a positive attitude toward consultation (see West & Idol, 1987).

Communication Skills

Communication skills refer to peoples' ability to send and receive meaningful messages. Such skills tend to be more specific than relationship skills. As we know from our experiences with others, communicating is sometimes quite difficult. Consultants need to use a broad repertoire of communication skills to increase the probability of a successful outcome to consultation.

There are many "basic" communication skills. Many books (for example, Okun, 1976; Pietrofesa, Hoffman, Splete, & Pinto, 1978; Cormier & Cormier, 1985) provide detailed discussions of communication skills. The more important ones for consultants are:

1. nonverbal attending (for example, keeping an open body posture);
2. listening (for example, actively discerning a consultee's intended meaning);
3. expressing empathy (for example, understanding the consultee's experience at a given moment and accurately communicating that understanding back to the consultee);
4. questioning (for example, asking consultees to expand on or be more specific about their communication);
5. clarifying/paraphrasing (for example, putting consultees' expressions into the consultant's own words to demonstrate understanding or to help consultees understand themselves better);
6. summarizing (for example, putting together the main points of discussion in order to determine the next step in the consultation process);
7. confrontation (for example, pointing out, in a nonthreatening manner, discrepancies a consultee is making);
8. feedback (for example, providing consultees with information about themselves for the purposes of examination and change);
9. information giving (for example, informing the consultee of the possible ways a given client might be helped effectively);
10. "speaking the same language" (for example, choosing plain language that avoids jargon); and
11. self-sharing (for example, sharing by consultants of their experiences that are similar to those of their consultees).

Communication skills such as these are related to successful consultation outcome in that they allow the consultant and consultee to exchange meaningful and accurate information, which facilitates more effective problem solving and aids relationship maintenance throughout the consultation process.

Problem-Solving Skills

Because consultation is by nature a problem-solving activity, consultants need to be highly skilled in problem solving (Kelley, 1981). Some of the many problem-solving skills available to consultants are:

1. setting the stage for problem solving (for example, defining consultation as a problem-solving activity);
2. formulating objectives (that is, determining what is to be accomplished);

3. defining the problem to be examined and solved during consultation (that is, isolating "what is to be fixed" during consultation);
4. examining the conditions surrounding the problem (for example, noting antecedents and consequences);
5. gathering, analyzing, and interpreting data pertinent to the problem (for example, surveying organizational personnel and providing feedback on the results);
6. diagnosing the problem (for example, analyzing data to shed light on the problem);
7. formulating a plan (that is, putting together the steps to solve a problem);
8. generating alternatives (that is, identifying ways to solve the problem);
9. identifying facilitating and restraining forces (that is, determining which forces are working for and against a given plan);
10. selecting alternatives (for example, choosing the best plan);
11. designing interventions for a particular situation (for example, identifying consultee strengths that increase the likelihood of successful plan implementation);
12. identifying available resources (for example, determining the strengths of a selected plan);
13. performing interventions (that is, actively attempting to solve the problem);
14. evaluating problem-solving attempts (that is, determining the degree to which a selected intervention worked);
15. determining who will do what, how, and when during the problem-solving process (that is, arranging the responsibilities involved in carrying out the plan); and
16. predicting the ramifications and implications of solving the problem (that is, examining how change can affect other parts of the system).

Consultants use problem-solving skills such as these to assist their consultees in solving work-related problems. Many consultants attempt to facilitate the development of more sophisticated problem-solving skills in their consultees. The critical implications of these skills for successful consultation will become apparent in later chapters (Chapters 4 and 5) that discuss specific problem-solving skills.

Skills in Working with Organizations

As the cases presented at the beginning of this chapter indicate, almost all consultation occurs within some organizational context. Because of this, consultants need to have some basic skills—specific behaviors—in working with an organization as a whole. When successfully demonstrated, these skills increase the likelihood of a successful outcome of consultation. Some of the more important skills consultants need when they work with organizations are:

1. becoming accepted by the members of the organization in which consultation is to occur (for example, creating working relationships with prospective consultees);

2. using organizational analysis (for example, determining who talks to whom under what conditions);
3. providing feedback (for example, giving the consultee objective information about some aspect of the organization's functioning);
4. gathering information (for example, using surveys to determine the attitudes of the organization's members);
5. using a repertoire of organization-wide interventions (for example, providing a stress management program);
6. determining the climate of an organization (that is, determining the type of working atmosphere within the organization);
7. determining the culture of the organization (that is, understanding the norms and standards that operate within the organization);
8. using program planning (for example, assisting consultees in executing effective programs); and
9. determining how to utilize human resources within the organization (for example, assisting consultees in improving managerial styles).

As the list suggests, human services consultants need not have all the skills required to give the organization with which they consult everything it needs. However, such consultants do need selected skills that allow them to operate at an optimal level within the organization and assist with selected organization-wide changes. The importance of a repertoire of skills for working with organizations will become even more apparent in Chapter 8, which provides an orientation to organizations and how they function.

Ethical and Professional Behavior Skills

In order to be successful, consultants need to be able to behave ethically and professionally. The necessary skills are often associated with internal feelings or beliefs that are explicitly demonstrated in consultants' behavior. Throughout their careers all consultants encounter professional situations that require a set of skills based on sound ethical judgment. For example, what would you do if as a consultant you were "over your head" in trying to help a consultee work with a difficult client? Some of the myriad of important skills that can enable consultants to act in an ethical and professional manner are:

1. acting with integrity (for example, maintaining confidentiality);
2. adhering to an ethical code (that is, adhering to accepted guidelines for professional behavior);
3. acting with confidence (for example, doing what one does well with a sense of personal power);
4. engaging in consultation only within one's professional limits (that is, declining consultations for which one is not qualified);
5. maintaining personal and professional growth (for example, engaging in professional development activities);
6. having the intent to help (for example, being as thorough as possible);

7. effectively coping with the stress of consulting (for example, using stress management skills during consultation activities);
8. avoiding manipulation of others (for example, maintaining basic respect for others);
9. using effective writing skills (for example, writing high-quality reports);
10. putting forth one's best effort (for example, providing all the services at one's disposal);
11. avoiding self-aggrandizement (for example, taking only appropriate professional credit for one's accomplishments); and
12. using power for legitimate purposes only (that is, using one's skills to influence others appropriately).

Acting in an ethical, professional manner creates positive perceptions among the consultant's coworkers and contacts. Such perceptions contribute to the successful outcome of consultation because consultees are able to attribute to the consultant the social influence necessary for maximum effectiveness during consultation. Chapter 7 of this text deals extensively with the ethical and professional behavior of consultants.

Possessing all the skills discussed above seems a tall order. The extent of a consultant's skills is best understood if the skills are seen as part of a continuum; no consultant either lacks or completely possesses each skill. And although it is important to note that effective consultants are not expert in all of these skills, they possess most of these skills to a moderate or higher degree. Developing the skills to be even more effective is a process that continues for the entire career of every consultant.

In summary, effective consultants have highly refined interpersonal and communication skills built on attitudes of positive regard, empathy, and genuineness; a large repertoire of problem-solving skills with which to help their consultees; a set of basic skills for working with organizations; and a set of ethical and professional standards that guide their actions.

CONSULTANT ROLES
The Nature of Consultant Roles

Consultants use the skills described in the preceding sections in a variety of consultation roles or functions performed at any given time during the consultation relationship. Just as consultation is not easily defined, neither are the roles in which consultants function.

Consultants can take on any number of roles during a particular consultation relationship. The nature of the roles is usually defined in the consultation contract, although some authors (for example, Argyris, 1976) suggest that the real role is more often determined by the consultant through trial and error. Effective consultants are able to determine which roles are necessary, define them to the satisfaction of all parties involved, and then perform those roles.

The primary role a consultant takes on during consultation depends on several factors, including the consultant's abilities and frame of reference, the consultee's expectations and skill levels, the nature of the problem that consultation is attempting to solve, and the environmental context in which consultation is occurring (Lippitt & Lippitt, 1986; Schindler-Rainman, 1985; Brown et al., 1987). In addition to the primary roles they take on, consultants frequently have the indirect goal of developing their consultees' consulting skills for future consultations.

The Categorization of Roles

Most categorization schemes put consultation roles on some sort of continuum. The most popular categorization approach is that of Lippitt and Lippitt (1986), in which consultants' roles lie on a continuum ranging from directive to nondirective. In directive roles the consultant is something of a technical expert, whereas in nondirective roles consultants tend to facilitate the consultee's expertise. Another approach to consultants' roles, that of Margulies and Raia (1972), includes task roles (roles related to expertise) at one end of a continuum and process roles (roles related to facilitation) at the other. Matthews (1983) proposed a continuum of consulting roles ranging from standard (expert) consulting to process (facilitative) consulting. Brown and others (1987) described a system that categorizes consulting roles according to both a task/process dimension and a consultant's degree of active involvement.

Regardless of how consulting roles are categorized, the bottom line is that categorization schemes tend to reflect the consultant's degree of involvement in the consultation process relative to that of the consultee. They guide the consultant in determining who is responsible for what tasks and how the consultant should proceed in consultation. For most human services professionals, the directive/nondirective categorization scheme of Lippitt and Lippitt (1986) seems most appropriate; the terms are familiar to most human services professionals and they provide a very helpful rule of thumb because they imply the amount of control the consultant should have over the consultation process. The following discussion of common consultation roles is grounded in the categorization scheme of Lippitt and Lippitt (1986), but it also reflects my thoughts and those of other authors (for example, Margulies & Raia, 1972; Gallessich, 1982; Matthews, 1983; Brown et al., 1987).

Common Consultation Roles

Consultants can engage in the consultation process in a broad range of roles that vary in terms of how much the consultant directs the activity occurring in consultation (Lippitt & Lippitt, 1986); that is, some roles are more directive than others. Next we'll consider six consultation roles: advocate, expert, trainer/educator, collaborator, fact finder, and process specialist.

Advocate

The most directive consulting role is that of *advocate.* As an advocate the consultant attempts to persuade the consultee to do something the consultant deems highly desirable. For example, a consultant, relying on her superior knowledge about data collection in organizations, might advocate the use of several data-gathering methods in addition to the method the consultee thinks is necessary. Another consultant might advocate the rights of the handicapped when consulting with a group of mental health specialists concerning a day treatment program for the retarded.

Because it may involve improper use of power by the consultant and hence would violate the peer nature of the consultation relationship, advocacy can be a high-risk role. Further, consultants may place themselves in an advocating position because of values and/or needs of which they are wholly or partially unaware. The use of power, politics, and influence to induce change in the advocacy role (Conoley & Conoley, 1982), can jeopardize the peer relationship between the consultant and consultee.

Some authors (for example, Conoley & Conoley, 1982) promote a very positive view of advocacy, even to the point of calling it a type of consultation in and of itself. However, to get a feel for the possible turmoil in which an advocacy role might place a consultant, consider the following:

CASE STUDY:
A school counselor is an advocate for a student (client system) identified as a possible dropout. Some school personnel (consultees) feel strongly that because the student can't be adequately educated in the system as it stands, the student is better off in some setting other than the school. The counselor agrees that the system cannot meet the student's needs but maintains that it should obtain the resources to do so.

This advocacy position places the counselor in a lose-lose situation. By attempting to change the system to benefit the client, the consultant risks losing consultee support. If the consultant does not attempt to change the system, the client may drop out.

There are times, situations, and issues for which advocacy is the most appropriate role for a consultant. One common example of an appropriate advocacy role is when the consultant detects within an organization a discrepancy between the way an organization is supposed to treat its clients and the way it actually treats them. Consultants can avoid misusing the advocacy role by maintaining a high level of self-awareness and a collaborative relationship with the consultee.

Expert

The most common role that consultants take on is that of *expert* or technical advisor (Gallessich, 1982). In this circumstance the consultee needs some knowledge, advice, or service that the consultant can provide upon request. When consultants are retained as experts over a long period of time, it seems apparent that the consultees (or organizations) retaining the consultants know what they need from the consultants. However, this is often not the case (Schein, 1969).

Consultants who consult with agencies about their programs—perhaps they are asked to make a diagnosis of what is wrong with an agency's client system—typically act in the role of expert. Consultants also function as experts when they are asked to recommend solutions to previously defined problems. For example, a consultant might recommend a training program in stress management for the members of the counseling department at a large secondary school. As in any other consulting role, the consultant does not treat the client system directly.

Consultants who engage in the role of expert need to be aware of the possibility that they could create dependence on the part of their consultees (Lippitt & Lippitt, 1986). The consultee can "get used to" having the consultant do the work and can effectively "give the problem away" to the consultant. Consultants engaging in the expert role need to be aware that under such circumstances their consultees may not improve their own problem-solving abilities, especially if the consultant does not take the time and energy to help them to do so.

Trainer/Educator

Very closely related to the role of expert is that of *trainer/educator.* Whereas the role of "technological advisor" does not imply change in the professional functioning of consultees, the role of a trainer/educator does. Consultants can engage in both formal and informal training and/or educating. Some authors (for example, Conoley & Conoley, 1982) contend that formal education/training activities such as workshops are not truly consultation because of the amount of preplanning involved. Others (for example, Lippitt & Lippitt, 1986) see the trainer/educator role as a legitimate and distinct approach to consultation itself (West & Idol, 1987). Perhaps these differences in viewpoint result because education is compared to consultation as if it were a different human service. One way to reconcile these different perspectives is to take the view that whereas consultants frequently train and educate, both formally and informally, this role is only one of a great variety of roles in which they engage.

Consultants are frequently asked to act in the capacity of trainer/educator. The role of trainer implies that the consultant has both the expertise in certain skills and the ability to create the conditions under which consultees can acquire those skills. The role of educator implies that the consultant possesses a body of knowledge that consultees desire and has the ability to teach them that knowledge. Formal training and education sessions usually take the forms of workshops and seminars. For example, a consultant might train a group of program leaders in a human services agency in methods of motivating subordinates. Informal training/educating usually occurs between the consultant and the consultee during some other aspect of and within the context of the consultation relationship. Thus, a consultant might teach a consultee how to gather baseline data on certain client behaviors.

One advantage of the trainer/educator role is that the consultee receives skills and/or knowledge that can be used perhaps repeatedly in the future, and thus the consultee's professional development is enhanced in some specific way. However, it is possible to erroneously assume that the consultee will actually use the newly acquired skills and knowledge in some way. Unless the consultant incorporates into the training the context in which the skills and knowledge are most useful, there is a strong likelihood that they will not be adequately put into practice in the future.

Collaborator

Consultants generally take a collaborative approach to consultation in that the consultant and consultee pool their resources and work together on the task of creating a successful consultation experience. When used to describe consultants, *collaborator* refers to that role in which the consultant engages the consultee in a joint endeavor to accomplish a particular task at a particular time. The concept of complementarity is important in the collaborator role. Consultants do not perform for consultees tasks that the consultees could perform for themselves, but rather consultants contribute expertise to accomplish those tasks with which consultees need assistance. Collaboration is frequently needed in identifying alternative solutions to a problem, in determining the positive and negative forces operating on various alternatives, and in making decisions about how to approach a given problem.

In one example of collaboration, a consultant and a consultee might compare their observations of a client and come to a mutually agreed upon diagnosis of the client's problem. In another case a consultant and a consultee might mutually agree upon how much and what kinds of data need to be gathered about the consultee's organization.

Among the relatively few risks involved in engaging in the collaborator role is that consultants may not realize that they are affected by consultees' behavior during collaboration. Perhaps the most common mistake human services professionals make in the role of collaborator is that they overestimate their consultees' abilities and consult in such a way that consultees' knowledge and skill inputs hinder effective consultation. To avoid this pitfall, consultants need some assessment of consultees' problem-solving abilities before assuming the collaborator role.

Conditions to enhance consultees' professional development are built into the role of collaborator. By participating in consultation in which consultants act as collaborators, consultees' problem-solving skills are enriched for the future. In addition, consultees' confidence is likely to increase because they feel a sense of contribution to the consultation process.

Fact Finder

The role of *fact finder* is one every consultant takes on frequently. In its simplest form it merely involves obtaining information. In the typical fact-finding role, the consultant gathers information, analyzes it, and feeds it back to the consultee (Lippitt & Lippitt, 1986). The consultant often takes on the fact-finding role in order to collect information needed to clarify or diagnose a problem. Methods for gathering information include reading records, interviewing, observing, and surveying. (We will discuss several ways to gather information in Chapter 4.) In the role of fact finder, the consultant determines what facts are needed, how best to gather and analyze them, and the best approach to interpreting them.

Consultants can gather information on a consultee's client or on an entire organization. Fact finding can range from a simple, quickly accomplished task to a very complex, time-consuming one. A school psychologist (consultant) might administer an individual intelligence test to a student (client system) who is being seen by a school counselor (consultee) and report the findings back to the counselor. In another example, a consultant might design and send out a survey to an organization's members to determine the level of morale within the organization.

One question the consultant should ask before beginning fact-finding activities is, "Why am I (and not the consultee) gathering this information?" If the answers relate to lack of consultee expertise, political sensitivities, time constraints, or the consultant's need to learn more about the environment in which the problem is occurring, then the role of fact finder is a legitimate one. If the answer is, "Because it's the consultant's job, not that of the consultee, to gather the facts," then the consultant should reexamine whether or not that role is appropriate.

Process Specialist

The least directive role of the consultant is that of *process specialist*. When consultants take on the role of process expert, they focus more on the "how" than on the "what." Instead of asking "What's going on?", the process specialist asks "How are things going?" When a problem is being solved, the consultant as process specialist does not examine the content but rather the problem-solving process itself. The focus is not so much on the nature of the problem-solving steps, but on how those steps are accomplished. One approach to consultation with organizations, called process consultation, has as its major goal enhancement of the consultee's understanding of the process events that affect everyday behavior (Schein, 1969). We will discuss process consultation again in Chapter 9.

In one example of a process specialist role, a consultant might sit in on a school's faculty meeting. At the end of the meeting the consultant might ask the faculty questions to assist them in analyzing their interpersonal behavior relative to what was accomplished in the meeting. In this example the consultant merely puts into exploratory questions what he or she observed. In another case a consultant might help an administrator learn how to have more effective meetings by using agendas. In this instance the consultant assists the consultee in making an intervention designed to allow people to have more time to participate in meetings.

Because consultants typically focus on structure and content, they are often uncomfortable in the process specialist role. And because the role of process specialist frequently requires the consultant to work with more than one consultee, group process skills are necessary. One common mistake consultants make in the process specialist role is to assume they have permission to bring up interpersonal issues (Schein, 1969). Consultees should ask for feedback or raise questions concerning interpersonal issues first.

INTERNAL AND EXTERNAL CONSULTANTS

Consultants may or may not belong to the system in which consultation is to occur. An *internal consultant* is a person who is already a part of the organization in which consultation is occurring. An *external consultant* is not already a part of the organization but consults within it on a temporary basis. The entire consultation process remains the same regardless of the locus of the consultant.

Some authors (for example, Alpert & Silverstein, 1985; Brown et al., 1987) recommend that the concepts of internal and external consulting be viewed as ends of a continuum rather than as discrete entities. For example, an itinerant elementary school counselor may serve three different schools. Depending on one's viewpoint, the consultant can be seen as internal or external. A staff member at the school system's central office may note that because the school counselor is employed by the system that runs the three schools and because everyone involved in the consultation also belongs to the school system, the counselor functions as an internal consultant. But consider another point of view: because the counselor is at a given school only infrequently, he or she is not really a part of that school. Thus, to most of the school's staff—those at the school every workday—the counselor is seen as an "outsider," an external consultant. Therefore, whether the consultant is internal or external is determined to some degree by the perceptions of the members of the organization in which consultation is occurring (Brown et al., 1987). Still other authors (for example, Bell & Nadler, 1979c) suggest that the internal/external distinction receives too much attention. They note that a consultant is always external to the problem to be resolved by consultation whether or not the consultant is external or internal to the organization itself.

Can being either an internal consultant or an external consultant be considered more effective than being the other? The little empirical research investigating such a differential effectiveness reveals no differences (Brown et al., 1987). One empirical study (Dekom, 1969) supports the contention that internal consultants can be effective. It seems reasonable to suggest that effective consultants are effective whether or not they are permanently attached to the system receiving consultation. This contention is further supported by the fact that internal consultants are taking on many of the functions historically reserved for external consultants (Kelley, 1981). External consultants do, however, seem to be characterized by marginality; that is, external consultants are only marginally admitted into the organization. They are likely to be objective, neutral, and comfortable with conflict, ambiguity, and stress (Goodstein, 1978).

Many organizations with internal consultants hire external consultants with the expectation that the two work as a team (Swartz, 1975; Kelley, 1981). Such a team approach can blend the objectivity, expertise, and "newness" of the external consultant with the knowledge of the organization, expertise, and continuity provided by the internal consultant (Margulies & Raia, 1972).

MYTHS ABOUT CONSULTANTS

Many human services professionals who function as counselors, psychotherapists, educators, and supervisors have some myths concerning their work. Consider the following examples:

Counselors and psychotherapists must be mysterious to be effective.
A supervisor must meet behind closed doors with the supervisee's coworkers; the supervisee must not be present.
An educator's workday is over when class is dismissed.

Many myths about consultants also exist. Here are several of them and the realities that dispel them:

Myth	Reality
1. As a human services professional I will rarely be called upon to consult.	There is an increasing demand for services of all types, including consulting.
2. Most human services professionals can't perform consultation.	Most human services professionals who say they can't consult mean they won't consult.
3. It is more difficult to be a consultant than a counselor or therapist.	The more intimate nature of counseling or therapy makes them riskier and more difficult than consulting.
4. Some human services professionals don't have enough confidence to consult.	The issue here is confidence, not consulting.
5. Some human services professionals are too inexperienced to consult.	In the matter of experience, everyone has to do a new thing for the first time sometime; why not now?
6. Because no one really knows what consultation is, no one should be expected to perform it.	There is a growing consensus on what consultation is and human services professionals should be expected to perform it.

So consultants have their own mythology with which to deal. By dispelling these myths in their own minds, they are less likely to pass them on inadvertently to those with whom they work. Such myths lead to jokes about consultants by the public, by consultees, and by organizations, including defining a consultant as anyone who is 50 miles away from home and has a suitcase, or as someone who asks you for your watch and then tells you the time of day, or as someone who makes a living by telling you to try the impractical things you've already discarded. Consultants can enhance their image by acting professionally at all times, by educating the persons with whom they work about consultation, and by putting forth their best efforts when consulting.

CONSULTEE CHARACTERISTICS

The presence of effective consultants alone does not guarantee that consultation will be successful. Consultee characteristics also affect consultation at every point (Swift & Cooper, 1986) and are very powerful in determining the success of consultation (West & Idol, 1987). Several authors have reviewed the literature on the effects of consultee characteristics upon consultation (see Swift & Cooper, 1986; Brown et al., 1987; West & Idol, 1987). The amount of empirical research is limited and the results mixed. Demographic variables (for example, age) and cultural variables (for example, world view) seem to affect consultation the most (Swift & Cooper, 1986; Smith & Corse, 1986). Published empirical research and reviews of research indicate that race (Gibbs, 1980), ethnic identity (Smith & Corse, 1986), gender (Gallessich, 1982), personality type (Pryzwansky, 1986), readiness for consultation (Cherniss, 1978), professional experience (West & Idol, 1987), cultural frame of reference (Swift & Cooper, 1986), familiarity with the role of consultee (Sandoval, Lambert, & Davis, 1977), level of anxiety (Medway, 1982), and expectations about consultation (Brown et al., 1987) can affect the outcome of consultation.

Thus relatively little is known, although much is speculated, about how consultees' characteristics affect consultation. Consultants may be able to increase the probability of successful consultation by considering their consultees' unique qualities during the course of their relationship.

THE IMPACT OF STRESS
ON CONSULTANTS AND CONSULTEES

Engaging in consultation is a stressful activity for both consultant and consultee. This section discusses the ways stress can affect consultation, a way of examining response patterns to stress in terms of personality type, and methods for effectively handling stress during consultation.

Stress in Consultation

Simply because it is part of the consultant's work, consultation is a stressful activity (Haney & Boenisch, 1982). Specifically, consultation is stressful for consultants because of their attempts to create conditions that are effective for problem solving and because of their efforts to engage in that process. Many consulting activities—building relationships, entering new settings, being observed, trying to determine what information is needed and how to get it— can be sources of stress for the consultant. In addition, the consultee's perception that the consultant is an expert in some subject creates the stress of having to provide adequate services that meet the expectations of others.

Consultation is stressful for consultees because of the implication that they will somehow have to change as a result of consultation. Although the consultation relationship is an equal one in terms of status, it is unequal in terms of need because the consultee needs some kind of help from the consultant. This need places the consultee in a vulnerable position, which causes stress. Within the consultation relationship stress can be generated for the consultee because of trying out new behaviors, going through new types of problem-solving procedures, having concerns over confidentiality, and changing perceptions of the consultant's competence.

Whether the effect of stress in consultation is positive or negative for consultants and/or consultees depends a great deal on how they view that stress (Meichenbaum, 1985). Stress is the rate of wear and tear on our organism (Selye, 1975). It does not have to be negative; it can have positive effects. For example, stress can motivate the consultee to develop an action plan for a client.

Consultants and consultees who take care of themselves in all aspects of their lives (for example, by staying physically fit) are less subject to the negative effects of stress. The more effectively consultants and consultees can manage the stress involved in consultation, the more likely they are to have a successful experience. One key to successful management of the stress in consultation is awareness of how one responds under stress. Such awareness provides the ability to have more control over stress.

Response Patterns to Stress

One way of conceptualizing how people respond to stress considers a person's personality type; stress can make people either more active or more passive (Chandler, 1985). In addition, a person's degree of introversion and extroversion affects people's responses to stress (Chandler, 1985). Introversion refers to a reflective personality who thinks and reflects on experience before acting. Extroversion refers to a personality who seeks excitement first and then reflects later. The personality traits of introversion and extroversion have been combined with the tendencies toward activity or passivity to create a pattern for conceptualizing response patterns to stress (Chandler, 1985). Although this model was developed for understanding stress reactions in children, it also applies to adults.

According to Chandler (1985), there are four response patterns to stress: dependent (passive-extroverted), impulsive (active-extroverted), passive-aggressive (active-introverted), and repressed (passive-introverted). The discussion of response patterns that follows is based on Chandler's views. Although these patterns might sound "mentally unhealthy," they simply identify the ways in which individuals tend to respond to stress. No one response is any healthier than any other; they cause an individual problems only when they are extreme. Because the response patterns to stress are coping mechanisms, they have advantages and disadvantages in actual use.

The dependent response pattern to stress is typified by lack of independence and initiative. Consultants and consultees who respond to stress in this manner tend to be thorough, good listeners, and good learners. They tend to be non-judgmental, will not jump to conclusions, and gather data adequately well. The disadvantages of this response pattern include a tendency to avoid taking responsibility, too much reliance on facts and numbers, excessive data collection, a tendency to extend consultation longer than necessary, and the tendency to irritate the other party, who feels trapped into doing all the work involved. Clearly, this response pattern can cause annoyance in others.

The impulsive response pattern is characterized by acting without thought or by overactivity. Persons with this pattern can create a dynamic work atmosphere, produce quick results, and appear to function well under pressure. They are action-oriented, typically possess high energy levels, and are willing to take risks. The disadvantages of this pattern include making poor plans, operating on a trial and error basis, being disorganized and making unnecessary mistakes. People with the impulsive response pattern may not gather enough or the appropriate information and may suffer from tunnel vision. This response pattern can cause others to feel on edge because they can neither accurately predict nor keep up with the rapidly paced behavior of such people.

The passive-aggressive response reflects overcompliance or lack of cooperation. People with this pattern appear successful, are not overly concerned about being right or wrong about things, and accept responsibility for the correct things they accomplish. They are typically determined and scrutinize details, and they perform tasks at their own pace. The disadvantages of this pattern are the possibility of a negative attitude, procrastination, a tendency toward manipulation of others, and difficulty in building and maintaining trusting relationships. This response pattern can cause others to become angry.

The repressed response can be typified either by anxiety or the tendency to withdraw. Persons with this pattern tend to be sensitive, aware of emotions, good listeners, and empathetic. They tend to be methodical, to think before they act, and to have nervous energy that can provide momentum. The disadvantages of this pattern are tendencies that can include lack of willingness to take risks, avoidance of change in oneself, avoidance of taking action, becoming immobilized about what to do next, and obvious physiological manifestations of anxiety. This response pattern can cause others to feel sorry for or pity the other person.

What Consultants and Consultees Can Do About Stress

Stress within the consultation process is best managed if the consultant and consultee have effective stress management skills in the first place. Consultants can minimize the negative effects of stress in consultation by being aware of when they are under stress, by understanding how they typically respond in stressful situations, and by taking coping action.

Because consultation is first and foremost a human relationship, the stress of consultation can be effectively managed to the degree that the relationship is based solidly on trust. Consultants and consultees can continuously examine and work to enhance their relationship throughout its duration. Consultants and consultees can be aware of their response patterns to stress and take measures to avoid excessive responses.

Consultants or consultees with dependent response patterns can break tasks down into smaller units, develop increasingly independent behaviors, collaborate whenever possible, and seek out feedback frequently.

The impulsive response can be maintained within proper limits by taking the time to write out plans in detail, by using brainstorming activities, by practicing coping self-statements when engaging in tasks, and by thinking through situations before taking action.

Passive-aggressive responders can benefit by dealing openly with trust issues in the consultation relationship, by taking measures not to identify too strongly with their role as consultant or consultee, and by remembering to take responsibility for all of their actions.

Consultants or consultees with the repressed response pattern can create a mutual support system, break tasks down into small steps, seek outside sources of encouragement, and engage in activities that bolster their sense of self-esteem.

SUMMARY

The characteristics of effective consultants result from their desire to grow personally and professionally, to acquire knowledge in consultation and human behavior, and to enhance their consulting skills. Consultants need interpersonal and communication skills that flow from a genuine attitude based on respect, as well as problem-solving skills and skills in maintaining ethical and professional behavior.

Consultants take on a variety of roles during any given consultation. These roles can range from nondirective ones, such as process specialist, to directive ones, such as advocate. The role a consultant takes is a result of the consultant's abilities, the consultee's needs, and the nature of the problem.

There are many myths about consultants, ranging from "human services practitioners do not consult" to "consultation is more difficult than other human services activities such as counseling or psychotherapy."

Consultee characteristics can play a large role in consultation. The amount of empirical research on consultee characteristics is inadequate, but what there is indicates the importance of demographic variables such as race and culture.

Consultation is a stressful activity for the parties involved. Like everyone else, consultants and consultees respond to stress in certain patterns. By being aware of their response patterns to stress, consultants and consultees alike can more effectively control the stress inherent in the consultation process.

QUESTIONS FOR REFLECTION

1. Which criteria indicate that you have an adequate personal and professional growth orientation as a consultant?
2. The basic attitudes from which a consultant's interpersonal and communication skills flow are critical to effective consulting practice. Why?

3. Why are interpersonal skills as important for the consultant as communication skills?
4. What are the most essential problem-solving skills for a consultant to possess? Why?
5. With which of the consultant roles discussed in this chapter do you feel most comfortable? Why?
6. What are the basic differences in consultant and consultee behavior when a consultant changes from a directive to a nondirective role?
7. What are the factors that determine the role a consultant will take on?
8. Review the six myths about consultants covered in this chapter. Identify the grain of truth in each of the myths.
9. If you were a consultant starting a relationship with a consultee, what consultee characteristics would you consider especially crucial for successful consultation?
10. With which response pattern to stress do you typically react? What information for guiding your behavior during consultation is gained by knowing your pattern in response to stress?

SUGGESTED SUPPLEMENTARY READINGS

Brown, D., Pryzwansky, W. B., & Schulte, A. C. (1987). *Psychological consultation: Introduction to theory and practice.* Boston: Allyn & Bacon. Chapter 7, "The Consultee as Variable," provides a lengthy review of the literature related to how consultee characteristics affect the consultation process. The authors end the chapter with a suggested method for "training" consultees to be more effective. Consult this chapter for details on what a consultant should look for in the way of consultee characteristics that might affect consultation.

Lippitt, G. & Lippitt, R. (1986). *The consulting process in action.* San Diego: University Associates. Chapter 3, "Multiple Roles of the Consultant," presents a comprehensive approach to categorizing the many roles that consultants can take on. The authors discuss each role and then speculate on the factors that influence when a given role will be taken on. Chapter 7, "The Consultant's Skills, Competencies, and Development," reflects a survey performed by the authors concerning the necessary components of an effective consultant. Skills, competencies, and attitudes are listed with sound rationales for their selection. These two chapters present a concise overview of the roles consultants can take on and the skills and attitudes necessary to fulfill them effectively.

A Generic Model of Consultation

THE STAGES OF CONSULTATION

Now that you have an idea of what consultation is, what consultants do, and the skills they need, let's examine a generic model of consultation. This model provides a framework for performing consultation. Because there is an increasing tendency to view consultation as a generic discipline (Mazade, 1985), a generic model is presented here. All consultation includes a relationship-building process, a time for definition of the problem, implementation of some plan, an evaluation component, and a termination phase. As you can see in the figure on page 39, consultation follows a problem-solving format consisting of four stages.

In practice these stages frequently overlap. For example, while a consultant and consultee are in the process of implementing a plan, a different aspect of the problem might emerge which would require returning to the diagnosis stage. Further, some experts in consultation consider the implementation stage to occur continuously; that is, each of the consultant's actions during the entire consultation process is viewed as an implementation.

Stage One of this model represents the "starting up" of the consultation process. It is called *entry* because during this stage the consultant enters the organization and/or enters into relationships with consultees. In this stage relationships are built, the parameters of the problem are examined, a contract is agreed upon, and contact is made with consultees within the organization. This stage lays the foundation upon which the remainder of the consultation rests.

Stage Two of this model is concerned with shedding light on the problem that was broadly examined during entry. In this stage the problem is understood more clearly and deeply. The consultant and consultee set goals based on this understanding, and they begin to think of ways to meet those goals. The term *diagnosis* is used instead of "problem definition" because the former term implies an ongoing process, whereas the latter connotes a task done only once.

Stage Three involves taking action to solve the problem that has been identified. This is the "action" stage in which a plan is formulated, implemented, and evaluated. This stage is called *implementation* in order to reflect its primary focus on action and its secondary emphasis on planning.

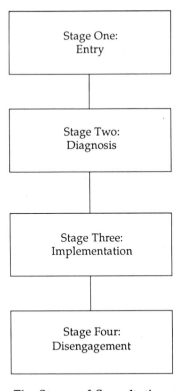

The Stages of Consultation

Stage Four "winds down" the process initiated in Stage One. This is the period of disengagement. Consultation is evaluated and consultant involvement is reduced. Good-byes are made, leave is taken. The term *disengagement* is used to imply that the process of consultation goes through a gradual reduction in activity. This term is used instead of "termination," which can imply a rather more abrupt ending of a process.

Each of the four stages in the consultation process consists of four phases. I have chosen the term *phase* because it implies process, whereas terms like "step" imply static entities and fail to acknowledge that consultation is a very human endeavor that goes through its own "life cycle." There is nothing magic in having four phases for each stage; four phases merely result from the way I choose to view the consultation process. Other authors (for example, Lippitt & Lippitt, 1986; Kurpius & Robinson, 1978; Stum, 1982) characterize the process in a variety of ways. The important thing to remember at this point is that consultation can be divided into certain stages and that each of these stages goes through different phases as consultation proceeds. The stages (and the phases within them as well) can overlap depending on what happens at a given point in the consultation process.

THE PHASES OF THE ENTRY STAGE

Stage One—entry—consists of the phases of exploring organizational needs, contracting, physically entering the system, and psychologically entering the system. *Exploring organizational needs* refers to the process in which the consultant, consultee, and perhaps other parties-at-interest discuss the concerns that brought them together and then determine whether consultation should proceed. *Contracting* refers to the process of formalizing the agreement that consultation should take place. Expectations for all parties involved are stated in the contract, as are fees for services rendered and deadlines to be met. When a consultant is *physically entering the system*, relationships are built, a work site obtained, the organization studied, and contact with the consultee begun. *Psychologically entering the system* entails the ongoing process in which the consultant gains acceptance as a temporary member of the organization in which consultation is to occur. This phase actually lasts the duration of the consultation process, and it is a task that requires continual attention if consultation is to be fully successful. The figure that follows illustrates the phases of the entry stage.

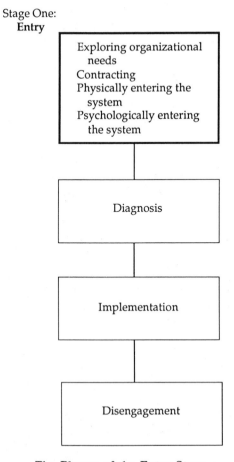

Stage One:
Entry

Exploring organizational
   needs
Contracting
Physically entering the
   system
Psychologically entering
   the system

Diagnosis

Implementation

Disengagement

The Phases of the Entry Stage

THE PHASES OF THE DIAGNOSIS STAGE

Once the entry stage is accomplished, the consultation process proceeds to the diagnosis stage, which consists of the phases gathering information, defining the problem, setting goals, and generating possible interventions. When *gathering information*, the consultant and consultee also attempt to increase the chances of understanding the problem by isolating factors that are precipitating it. Data can be gathered through a variety of means, including surveys, interviews, observations, and examination of records. When *defining the problem*, the consultant and consultee analyze and interpret the data that have been gathered. It is especially important for the consultant and consultee to remain objective during this phase. A biased interpretation of the data can lead to an erroneous definition of the problem. Once the problem has been defined to the satisfaction of the parties involved, *setting goals* to overcome the problem occurs. The consultant has the responsibility to make sure that any goal that is set meets the criteria of effective goals. Once goals have been set, the consultant and consultee move on to *generating possible interventions* that could have a beneficial effect on resolving the problem. The figure that follows illustrates the phases of the diagnosis stage.

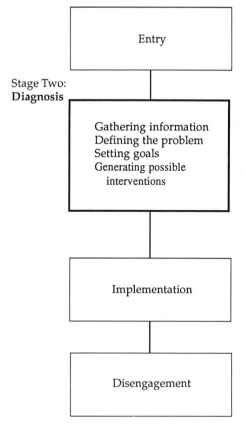

The Phases of the Diagnosis Stage

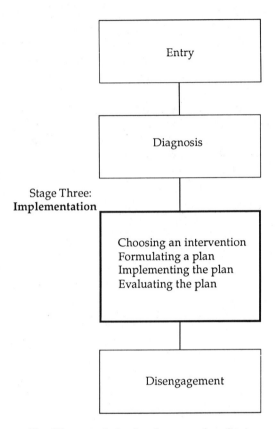

The Phases of the Implementation Stage

THE PHASES OF THE IMPLEMENTATION STAGE

Once a list of possible strategies has been generated, the consultation process moves to the implementation stage. Stage Three begins with *choosing an intervention* or group of interventions—activities the consultant and consultee think have the best chance of effectively solving the problem. Using these interventions, the consultant and consultee embark on *formulating a plan* that incorporates these interventions. The pros and cons of a variety of possible plans are carefully scrutinized until the best plan is chosen. The selected plan is tailored to the unique requirements of the client and/or the organization. The third phase is *implementing the plan,* and the consultant usually monitors the plan's progress once it has been implemented. The final phase is *evaluating the plan,* which occurs after implementation is complete. Based on the results of the evaluation, the consultation process either moves back to a previous phase of some stage (for example, defining the problem) or on to the stage of disengagement. The figure that follows illustrates the phases of the implementation stage.

THE PHASES OF THE DISENGAGEMENT STAGE

Stage Four—disengagement—consists of the following phases: evaluating the consultation process, planning postconsultation matters, reducing involvement and following up, and terminating. *Evaluating the consultation process* can range from assessing consultee satisfaction with consultation to measuring the impact of a systemwide intervention on the behavior of the members of an organization. Evaluation must be a planned event so that consultant and consultee alike will know what will be evaluated, by whom, how, and when. *Planning postconsultation matters* involves deciding how the effects of consultation are going to be maintained by the consultee and/or the organization. This phase is essential in increasing the probability that follow-through occurs after the consultant's involvement ends. *Reducing involvement* is the phase in which the consultant creates conditions of decreasing contact with the consultee and in which more and more responsibility for the results of consultation is taken on by the consultee.

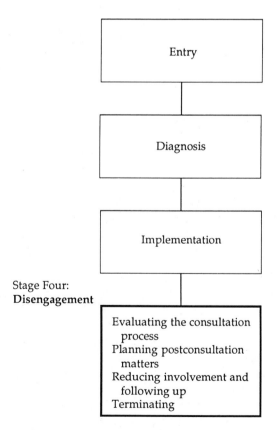

The Phases of the Disengagement Stage

Follow-up is the process in which the consultant monitors this transfer of responsibility in order to iron out any unforeseen problems. *Terminating* is the formal ending of the consultation process. It has professional aspects (for example, collecting final fees) and a personal side (for example, saying good-bye to people with whom the consultation has occurred). Effective consultants successfully accomplish both the professional and personal sides of termination. The figure on page 43 illustrates the phases of the disengagement stage.

AN EXAMPLE

The following example is designed to show how the consultation process generally works. Although oversimplified, it will provide a concrete example to which you can continue to refer as you read and study the next five chapters.

CASE STUDY:
Assume that you are a school counselor who is going to act in the role of a consultant. Your consultee is a school teacher and the client is a student of the teacher. You meet with the teacher, who discusses the behavior of the student, particularly the fact that the student rarely turns in homework. You help the teacher explore the problem, and at the same time you build rapport with him. You and the teacher agree that working on the homework problem is mutually agreeable, so you contract to meet three or four times to work on that problem. As the consultant you agree to observe the student in the teacher's classroom. You continue to use effective communication skills and to gain the teacher's acceptance of you as a person he can trust. At this point you have completed the entry stage.

You and the teacher now start to gather information on the student; together you examine the student's cumulative folder. The teacher keeps track of the times the student doesn't turn in homework and the conditions surrounding that behavior. Based on the data, you note that the student does not turn in homework on Tuesdays and Fridays but does on the other school days. An interview with the student's parents reveals that both parents attend school on Monday and Thursday nights and that the child is left with a babysitter. Based on this information you and the teacher redefine the problem as lack of parental supervision of homework completion on Monday and Thursday nights. You and the consultee set the goal of having the student turn in all homework every other Tuesday and Friday for the first month, and every Tuesday and Friday thereafter. When generating possible strategies you come up with several ideas, which include loss of recess when homework is not turned in and use of a parent-child contract for getting the homework done. You have now completed the diagnosis stage; you are ready to begin the implementation stage.

You and the teacher weigh the pros and cons of each possible intervention and determine that the parent-child contract is the best alternative. You then formulate a plan that consists of obtaining parental cooperation and assisting in the formulation of a parent-child contract for getting homework completed on the nights the parents are not home. When the parents agree to the plan, you and the teacher assist them in carrying it out. Strategies for appropriately reinforcing both the child and parents are included. The parents carry out the plan effectively; based on your evaluation, the goal has been met. The third stage, implementation, has just been accomplished. Now you go on to the fourth stage—disengagement.

In this final stage, you have the teacher rate his satisfaction with your efforts to assist him during each of the previous three stages. You then lay the groundwork concerning the way the teacher will carry on with the student after you cease consulting on this case. You check in with the teacher every two weeks or so to see how things are going with the student's homework. A month or so after your last contact you follow up to make sure that the homework is still being turned in. Toward the end of the next grading period you again check in about the student's performance. Because everything is proceeding well, you and the teacher agree to terminate consultation.

This overview of the consultation process is an idealized case; consultation, like any other human services activity, rarely proceeds so smoothly. But, nonetheless, the overview provides a rough outline of how the process works.

PERSONALIZING THE CONSULTATION PROCESS

Discussing consultation in terms of stages and phases leaves out the "human side" of the process. In order to include this human side, let's personalize the consultation process by showing the ways that "I as a consultant" can "be there" for my consultee. I developed this idea after reading Gerard Egan's book entitled *The Skilled Helper* (1986). In it Egan describes his counseling model as a series of steps for "being with" clients (Egan, 1986, pp. 54–55). Here is "how I can be there" for each consultee in each of the 16 phases in the consultation process:

1. I can be there for my consultee by listening well at the outset and by taking the time to build rapport.
2. I can be there for my consultee by assisting in formulating a contract that will make explicit the expectations we have for each other.
3. I can be there for my consultee by starting the consultation process on the consultee's turf as soon as possible.
4. I can be there for my consultee by proactively attempting to gain acceptance not only by the consultee, but also by the organization in which consultation is occurring.
5. I can be there for my consultee by doing my best to determine what information should be gathered on the problem and how it might best be gathered.
6. I can be there for my consultee by attempting to be unbiased as I assist in analyzing and interpreting the gathered data.
7. I can be there for my consultee by ensuring that the goals we set are effective goals that have a good probability of being successfully accomplished.

8. I can be there for my consultee by being as creative and "sharp" as I can be when it comes to generating possible interventions.
9. I can be there for my consultee by assisting in examining the pros and cons of each possible intervention we consider.
10. I can be there for my consultee by collaborating in putting together the best possible plan and considering the resources available to us.
11. I can be there for my consultee by being available to monitor the progress that is being made.
12. I can be there for my consultee by providing assistance and encouragement in evaluating the plan.
13. I can be there for my consultee by asking for evaluations of myself and my services.
14. I can be there for my consultee by assisting in planning what needs to be done regarding the consultation after I have left the scene.
15. I can be there for my consultee by avoiding consultee dependence through a gradual reduction in my involvement and by fostering consultee independence through intermittent follow-ups.
16. I can be there for my consultee by saying good-bye professionally and personally and by letting go of the relationship when that is in the consultee's best interest.

My main goal in this part of the book is to provide you with an understanding for how to go about the general process of conducting consultation. A second goal is for you to gain an appreciation of the complexity of the ethical, professional, and legal issues that surround the consultation process.

Chapter

3

Entry Stage

PREVIEW

Just like a good novel, the consultation process should have a beginning, a middle, and an end. The purpose of this chapter is to explain the beginning stage of the consultation process: the entry stage. Entry is both a distinct stage of consultation and a process in which the consultant begins to create relationships with the consultee organization and some of its members. The entry stage is complex and consists of four phases: exploring organizational needs, contracting, physically entering the organization's system, and psychologically entering the system.

To get a feel for the entry stage, consider the following:

CASE STUDY:

You are a professor of human services at a state university. A former student, now director of advising at a nearby community college, telephones and wants to come and talk with you about enhancing the quality of advising services at the community college. You set up an appointment, which will take place in your office.

During the appointment you assist the advising director in exploring the advising office's specific needs in regard to enhancing the quality of advising. You ask the director to make up a "wish list" to stimulate preliminary exploration. You ask what is going well and what is not going so well. You ask about the organizational environment in which advising occurs, and you ask for the advisors' views on the process of advising, its rewards, the level of administrative support for advising, and the advising director.

Based on this information, you agree to conduct two sessions with all the advisors. The first session is a workshop on effective advising; the second session is a troubleshooting meeting with the advisors to help them feel more "heard" by the parties involved in coordinating advising services. You and the advising director sign a contract to that effect.

The week before the workshop, you visit the community college and all of the workshop participants. You are supportive and ask them what things they would like to talk about. Next you arrange for the room at the community college in which the workshop is to occur. Then, when you open the first session, you ask the participants what they want and what they *do not* want out of the workshop.

Here are five questions to consider as you read this chapter:

1. In what ways is the entry stage a complex process?
2. Why is the entry stage both a critical and delicate stage of consultation?
3. How directive should a consultant be in guiding the course of consultation during the entry stage?
4. "There is more to a contract than what is written on the paper." What are the implications of this statement for consultants?
5. How can a consultant psychologically enter the consultation system effectively and efficiently?

INTRODUCTION

The entry stage can consist of one telephone call or can require several exploratory meetings (Bell & Nadler, 1979a). Throughout this stage the consultant and the organization's contact person continually attempt to determine how advantageous consultation can be. The activities of the entry stage are frequently referred to as "start-up" activities. The consultant should bear in mind that the success of the consultation depends in part on how well these start-up activities are accomplished (Brown & Kurpius, 1985).

ENTRY

Entry is the general process by which the consultant enters the system in which consultation is to occur. Glidewell (1959) defines entry of an external consultant as the attachment of a consultant to an existing social system through the creation of temporary membership in an organization for a person who is to help that system. This temporary membership is accomplished by creating relationships that assist in determining which functions a consultant should provide to best help the organization accomplish its ends (Glidewell, 1959). The consultant's functions should be temporary, should be needed by the system, should be within the consultant's capabilities, and should be currently unavailable within the system.

The consultant's external attachment is at once problematic and advantageous (Mann, 1983.) It is advantageous in that as an outsider, the consultant has flexibility in defining his or her role. This might mean, for example, that the consultant need not necessarily be constrained by the existing methods of communication within the system. The disadvantage is that the consultant needs to understand and accept unfamiliar roles within the organization. For example, the consultant may not be aware that consultees within the system see consultants primarily as advice givers.

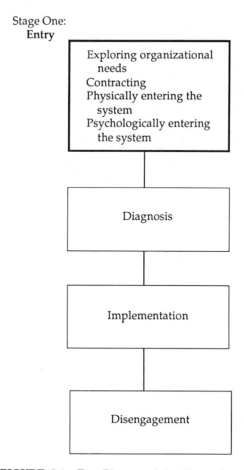

Stage One:
Entry

Exploring organizational
needs
Contracting
Physically entering the
system
Psychologically entering
the system

Diagnosis

Implementation

Disengagement

FIGURE 3.1   The Phases of the Entry Stage

The entry stage is very complex, so to aid our understanding of it we'll discuss the four phases of this stage: exploring organizational needs, contracting, physically entering the system, and psychologically entering the system (Gallessich, 1982). Figure 3.1 shows the four phases of the entry stage of consultation.

PHASE ONE: EXPLORING ORGANIZATIONAL NEEDS

Consultation typically begins when a representative of an organization contacts a consultant for the purpose of *exploring* the possibilities of initiating a consulting relationship. It is not unusual for an organization to contact a consultant without knowing the precise or even the appropriate reason why consultation is needed. In fact, the toughest aspect of entry is making a quick and accurate assessment of what is troubling the organization (Conoley & Conoley, 1982).

Some authors (Goodstein, 1978; Conoley & Conoley, 1982) note that rarely does an organization use refined techniques to determine its need for a consultant, and frequently the organization has misidentified its problem. Therefore, consultants should be cautious about moving too quickly into planning action during the beginning of the entry process.

Whether or not there is a firm grasp on what is needed in consultation, an organization typically contacts a consultant because it perceives it has a concern that cannot be solved within the organization or because there is an unfilled gap within the organization (Schein, 1969). For example, a school principal may contact a prospective consultant to perform in-service training for the school's staff. On the other hand, the process can also begin when a consultant contacts an organization and attempts to "sell" consultation services related to the typical concerns of organizations. For example, a consultant in private practice may approach a personnel manager in an industrial firm regarding the consultant's program for boosting morale.

Before actual physical and psychological entry into the organization occurs, the consultant must deal with certain preentry issues (Cherniss, 1976). One example of such an issue is whether the consultant appears to be the right person to help the organization get whatever it seeks from consultation. The process of considering these issues usually begins with an exploratory meeting referred to as the "first contact."

First contact may be initiated by either the prospective consultant or a contact person within an organization or agency. It usually involves the organization's contact person, perhaps some parties-at-interest, and the consultant. Ideally those involved should be knowledgeable about consultants and favorable toward their use (Schein, 1969).

The initial meeting for exploring organizational needs can occur either at the organization or in a neutral setting such as a restaurant (Gallessich, 1982). The advantage for meeting at the organization is that it allows the consultant on-site observations of the organization and the ways its personnel interact. There the serious nature of the consultation relationship is reinforced because the meeting is not in a social setting. The advantages of meeting in a neutral site are that it gives the organization's contact personnel a sense of more control and provides an informal setting that minimizes pressures to commit to a contract for consultation services. This more relaxed setting provides the organization's contact people an opportunity to ask the consultant to discuss his or her background so that they can ask the consultant more detailed questions (Gallessich, 1982). At their discretion, consultants may or may not charge for this initial meeting.

Determining Whether Consultation Should Take Place

The primary decision to be made during the preliminary exploration of organizational needs is whether or not consultation should be undertaken. There are six issues that relate to this decision:

1. the degree of congruence between the consultant and the consultee system (Gallessich, 1982; Matthews, 1983), for example, the degree of similarity between the consultant's and the organization's value systems;
2. the amount of resources the organization is willing to commit toward change (Lippitt & Lippitt, 1986), for example, the amount of administrative sanctioning for consultees' participation in consultation;
3. the appropriateness of the consultee's or the organization's characteristics (Pipes, 1981; Mann, 1983; Matthews, 1983), for example, the amount of flexibility within the organization with regard to the changes consultation may involve;
4. the ways in which the organization perceives the need for change (Mann, 1983), for example, the degree to which prospective consultees see consultation as important and needed;
5. mutual understanding of the expectations for consultation (Cherniss, 1976); for example, the consultant and consultees are able to agree on how consultation should proceed and on desirable outcomes for all parties involved; and
6. agreement on who constitutes the consultee system, the client system, and parties-at-interest (Matthews, 1983), for example, the consultant agrees to consult only with the crisis intervention team in a mental health center regarding approaches in counseling their clients.

Consultants usually deal with these issues by helping to identify and clarify the organization's need and readiness for change and by exploring the potential for working together (Lippitt & Lippitt, 1986). An excellent case study related to the exploration of the organization's needs is presented by Alpert (1982b).

Four questions shared by the consultant and the organization's contact person help to determine whether or not consultation is necessary and worthwhile: Why am I here? Who are you? What is likely to happen? What will be the result? (Bell & Nadler, 1985). The degree to which the four questions are answered to the satisfaction of both the consultant and the contact person eventually determines the success of the preliminary exploration of the organization's needs (Bell & Nadler, 1985). The most crucial of these questions is "Why am I here?"

Why am I Here?

The question "Why am I here?" is important to contact person and consultant alike. From the contact person's perspective, this question concerns perceived need. Put another way, the question is, "Is there a problem or concern in my organization with which a consultant might help?" From the consultant's perspective, the question involves assisting the consultee in defining an appropriate problem or concern and assessing whether the consultant is the right person for the job. In helping a contact person identify a problem, the prospective consultant must focus on using listening and clarifying skills. The answer to "Why am I here?" helps both the consultant and contact person know whether there is enough common ground to pursue further discussions.

The Task of Familiarization.   In order to create optimal conditions for successfully assisting the contact person's exploration of the organization's needs, the consultant must become familiar with the consultee system. This process is often referred to as the *task of familiarization* (Jarvis & Nelson, 1967).

During the task of familiarization consultants learn the ins and outs of the organization. Much of this task can be accomplished by becoming knowledgeable about the organization's history, mission, philosophy, and procedures. Consultants need to be willing to take the position of learner and allow their contact persons to share information about their organizations (Mann, 1983). Armed with such knowledge, consultants can raise their level of credibility and establish a common frame of reference with which to communicate with the organization's contact person (Parsons & Meyers, 1984).

Another part of the familiarization task is determining what the organization has done so far to solve its perceived problems, to what degree these activities were successful, and what factors prevented them from being more successful (Mann, 1983). Lippitt and Lippitt (1986) note that this step concerns helping contact persons to clearly express their concerns and needs. When no concrete needs or concerns have been identified, consultants frequently assist their contact persons in exploring potential problem areas.

Who Are You?

The question "Who are you?" concerns defining the roles taken on by the consultant, contact person, and others involved in consultation (Bell & Nadler, 1985). Answering this question involves identifying the roles and responsibilities of the consultant and the contact person (Cooper & Hodges, 1983). Is the consultant to help the contact person explore the organization's needs? Or is the consultant to "sell" himself or herself based on the contact person's assessment of the organization's needs? Is the contact person authorized to hire the consultant? Who constitutes the consultee system? Who constitutes the client system?

The answer to "Who are you?" allows the consultant and contact person to begin building a set of expectations for how each party will behave, and it puts into motion the creation of a mutually satisfying relationship. The prospective consultant is asking "Can I help?" and "How much help is wanted here?" The contact person is asking "Is this the right person for the job?" and "How will this person fit in?" By discussing views, attitudes, and perceptions pertinent to perceived organizational needs, values, and working styles, the consultant and contact person can determine the "goodness of fit" (Glidewell, 1959) between the perceived needs and the consultant's abilities pertinent to those needs. In determining their respective roles, both consultant and contact person need to remember that they represent their respective organizations as well as themselves (Caplan, 1970).

What is Likely to Happen?

The third question, "What is likely to happen?", really asks about means and ends: What is the goal of consultation? How will the goal be accomplished?

From the consultant's perspective the answer to this question involves determining the parameters of consultation. From the contact person's point of view, the answer to this question revolves around what can be expected from the consultant. For example, the contact person must determine the depth with which the consultant should be told about the organization's concerns and about such things as intraorganizational conflicts.

Preliminary exploration is the search for some common ground concerning the goals, objectives, and values of both the consultant and the organization (Beisser & Green, 1972). Thus, the consultant should assist the contact person in exploring the organization's needs as the organization's administrator sees them. Consultants should consider an organization's distribution of power when exploring organizational needs. To that end, consultants can suggest that they have contact with both the organization's upper echelon (Mann, 1983) and other personnel to ensure that the consultation process proceeds smoothly (Gallessich, 1982).

What Will be the Result?

The fourth question is "What will be the result?" From the consultant's perspective this question concerns how the impact of consultation will be assessed and evaluated. From the contact person's perspective, the answer to this question depends on how much change the consultation requires. Is the amount of change proposed worth the request for consultation? Are there other risks involved? This step of exploring the potential for working together is essential. Both parties ask "What's the payoff for engaging in consultation?" and "Do the rewards sufficiently outweigh the costs?"

In exploring the organization's readiness to change, the consultant must explore its willingness to devote the time, energy, and personnel needed to accomplish the determined goals of consultation (Lippitt & Lippitt, 1986); this assessment includes the contact person's impressions of the organization's commitment to the consultation process. The contact person, on the other hand, must assess the prospective consultant's suitability for helping the organization meet its perceived needs.

In summary, then, the answers to these four questions help to predict the success of consultation and provide a foundation upon which the remainder of the consultation process will be built.

What Can Go Wrong

The initial exploration of the organization's needs can go awry due to inadequacies in both the consultant's and the contact person's behavior. According to Ford (1979), several things a consultant might do during the entry phase can jeopardize the consultation relationship:

1. fail to identify the real problem,
2. promise too much,
3. fail to adequately specify consultant roles,
4. fail to recognize a lack of competence with respect to the identified problem, or
5. fail to adapt to the organization's particular problems and concerns.

By bearing these potential pitfalls in mind and by monitoring their own consulting behavior accordingly, consultants can frequently save the consultation process from difficulties.

Consultees can also prevent entry from proceeding smoothly. Among the many things a contact person can do during the entry phase to jeopardize the consultation relationship are:

1. fail to properly screen a prospective consultant,
2. neglect to seek clarification of how the consultant intends to operate within the system,
3. fail to clarify specific expectations for the consultant's role and behavior,
4. fail to accurately identify the organization's problem, or
5. fail to explain to the consultant how the organization's resource limitations might affect the potential consultation experience.

Consultants need to be aware of these potential pitfalls as they assist the organization's contact person to explore the organization's needs. Perhaps the best way to prevent these pitfalls is by allotting sufficient time to enable the parties to develop mutual understanding, which leads to open communication and discussions that are as specific and detailed as possible. Effective questioning by the consultant is particularly important in avoiding these pitfalls.

There are times, of course, when the best decision is not to consult. From the consultant's perspective, consultation is not recommended when any of the following conditions exist:

1. There is a lack of administrative or organizational support for consultation.
2. The organization in which consultation is to occur is in extreme crisis.
3. There is an alternative strategy that is better than consultation.
4. The consultant does not have the skill or knowledge to perform the required consultation.
5. There is not enough time to perform the consultation tasks selected.
6. The consultant is in some way unable to be objective or maintain a professional demeanor while providing services (Conoley & Conoley, 1982).

In summary, preliminary exploration of the organization's needs includes deciding who the consultees and client system will be, determining the consultant's role in the consultation process, and defining the organization's responsibility with regard to expectations held about the consultant (Weisbord, 1984). Once the preliminary exploration of the organization's needs has been adequately accomplished and it is determined that consultation should occur, the information gathered in this phase will be used extensively in the next phase—contracting.

PHASE TWO: CONTRACTING

If the preliminary exploration of organizational needs concludes with a decision that consultation is to take place, then the consultant and the contact person begin to discuss and negotiate the terms of consultation (Gallessich, 1982). This activity begins the phase of *contracting*.

What is a Contract?

Every relationship is based upon expectations. In consultation, the expectations concerning the consultation relationship are usually made explicit in formal contracts (Blake & Mouton, 1976; Kolb & Frohman, 1970). The term *contract* has a variety of meanings when used in the delivery of human services.

A contract in consultation is typically an oral or written agreement between the consultant and the organization that defines the parameters and character of the consultation relationship (Conoley & Conoley, 1982; Caplan, 1970; Argyris, 1970; French & Bell, 1973). In consultation relationships, the contract is an agreement ". . . spelling out the expectations and obligations of each party, the frequency of meetings, the scheduling of appointments and access to personnel in the consultee system, the data to be collected, the provisions for review and modification of the program and the amount and manner of payment of any fees involved" (Mann, 1983, p. 108). The contract, then, is an explicit exchange of expectations that can be expressed orally, in writing, or through a combination of the two. The contract reflects and clarifies the shared understanding between consultant and organization in three critical areas:

1. what each expects from the relationship;
2. how much time each will invest, as well as when and at what cost; and
3. ground rules under which the parties involved will operate (Weisbord, 1985, p. 306).

When adequately worded, a contract provides a general guide for the consultation process, clarifies the roles and expectations of the parties involved, and provides a form of self-protection for both the consultant and the organization (Kelley, 1981; Blake & Mouton, 1976).

The contract can be oral, can take the form of an exchange of letters, or can be a formal document. The consultant should bear in mind, however, that a detailed written contract has the advantages of framing participants' roles and providing a focus for evaluating consultation services. In fact, Kirby (1985) suggests that any oral contract be followed up with a letter that states what has been agreed upon. Whatever form a contract takes, its particulars must be clear (Conoley & Conoley, 1982).

The degree of specificity a contract needs depends on the precision with which the problem to be resolved during consultation has been defined. A contract can be quite explicit, as in an agreement between labor and management. Or a contract can be broad, such as a marriage contract (Blake & Mouton, 1976). To the degree that the contract is structured and specific, the consultant's role will be relatively constant. To the degree that the contract is general and loosely structured, the consultant's role may vary (Lippitt & Lippitt, 1986). Consultants should note that the matter of specificity can be an issue, and it must be agreed upon when the contract is being drawn up (Alpert, 1982).

A contract has both formal and psychological aspects (Schein, 1969). The formal aspect of a contract covers such things as services to be rendered, type and amount of payment, and the temporal duration of consultation (Bell &

Nadler, 1985). The psychological aspect of a contract refers to what each party hopes to gain from the relationship. The "psychological contract" is based on interpersonal trust, which cannot be put in writing, and it reflects a collaborative effort between the consultant and the organization's contact person concerning what each expects from the consultation process (Boss, 1985).

The Formal Aspects of a Contract

The formal aspects of contracting refer to the types of contracts used and their elements.

There are several types of contracts that can be used in consultation. Consultants should be willing to help the organization's contact person choose the type of contract that the nature of the consultation dictates. For an excellent discussion of the types of contracts, consult Matthews (1983).

Elements of a Contract

In order to develop and maintain a good working relationship between the consultant and the organization, certain key issues pertinent to the consultation should be covered in the contract (Matthews, 1983). All consultation contracts should cover the following elements (Gallessich, 1982, pp. 272–273):

1. general goals of consultation;
2. tentative time frame;
3. consultant's responsibilities:
   a) services to be provided,
   b) methods to be used,
   c) time to be committed to the agency,
   d) evaluation of the degree to which goals are achieved;
4. agency's responsibilities:
   a) nature and extent of staff contributions to consultation,
   b) fees to be paid to consultant, including expenses;
5. consultant's boundaries:
   a) the contact person to whom the consultant is to be responsible,
   b) people to whom the consultant is to have access (and those who are out of bounds),
   c) consultant's access to departments, meetings, and documents,
   d) conditions for bringing in other consultants or trainees,
   e) confidentiality rules regarding all information;
6. arrangements for periodic review and evaluation of the consultant's work; explication of freedom of either party to terminate the contract if consultation progress is unsatisfactory.

Figure 3.2 is a sample contract between a school system and a mental health consultant who is going to consult with school counselors and psychologists concerning ways of helping teachers to manage stress effectively. This sample represents a relatively informal, simple contract that contains only those elements pertinent to the nature of the consultation.

**Beach Town School System
Beach Town, USA**

Contract

This is a contract between the Beach Town School System, herein called the party of the first part, and Jan Clovis, herein referred to as the party of the second part. This contract is entered into on the sixth day of February, 1989 as follows:

The party of the second part agrees to serve as a consultant between March 6 and April 3, 1989, by providing education and training concerning stress management techniques for teachers to the counselors and psychologists employed by the party of the first part. Specifically, the party of the second part agrees to serve as a workshop leader and trainer for five days (each day from 9 A.M. to 4 P.M.): March 6, 13, 20, 27, and April 3 in the Beach Town School System workshop "Teaching Teachers Effective Stress Management Techniques." The party of the second part further agrees to conduct evaluations of the workshop participants' learning relative to the goals of the workshop and, with the permission of the participants, to share those evaluations with the contact person designated by the party of the first part. The party of the second part agrees to use Bernie Thompson, staff development director of the Beach Town School System, as the contact person for all matters pertaining to this consultation, including the possible use of additional consultants or the addition of other consultees as participants in the workshop.

The party of the first part agrees to pay the party of the second part a total of one thousand five hundred dollars ($1,500) plus expenses for travel and materials upon completion of the consultation services. The party of the second part also agrees to provide materials (including audiovisual) as long as the request for such is made by February 15, 1989.

This contract is subject to renegotiation at any time and either party is free to terminate it if either determines the consultation progress to be unsatisfactory.

For the Beach Town School System

_____

Party of the Second Part

_____

Signature _____

Address _____

_____

Social Security Number _____

Date _____

FIGURE 3.2 A Sample Contract

The Psychological Aspects of a Contract

Contracting has psychological as well as formal aspects. The psychological aspects of a contract refer to the set of expectations that govern the consultation relationship (Boss, 1985). These expectations are not always directly communicated, agreed upon, or written down; however, they are more crucial to the consultation process's success than a legal contract, and once broken they are difficult to repair (Kelley, 1981). Therefore, early in the relationship it is imperative that the consultant attempt to assess and shape any expectations deliberately or unwittingly withheld by the organization's contact person (Schein, 1969). In effect, the consultant must determine what psychological and business needs are to be met through consultation.

The following examples illustrate how psychological contracts were broken.

CASE ONE:
A consultant hired by a human services agency to assist in program development expected an office but was not provided one. The consultant's resultant resentment made it more difficult to objectively focus on the tasks to be accomplished.

CASE TWO:
In another instance, an organization's contact person wanted to be contacted by the consultant each time the consultant visited the organization. The contact person neither expressed this wish nor put it into the formal contract. When the consultant innocently restricted communication with the contact person, the contact person felt rejected and covertly began efforts to sabotage the consultant's activities.

To avoid unfortunate occurrences like those described above, consultants should be clear about what is expected from both the organization and themselves. By explaining their roles to contact persons and consultees, consultants can build trust with key members of the organization (Schein, 1969). Consultants should explain what behaviors will occur and the rationale behind these behaviors. Thus, a consultant who will observe the inner workings of an organization should clearly state that such observations will be made for the purpose of understanding organizational dynamics, not for gathering personal data about individuals.

In summary, if the consultant has effectively completed the preliminary exploration of organization needs, then the psychological aspects of contracting need less attention because mutual expectations have already been verbally expressed and agreed upon. The consultant's primary concern with regard to the psychological aspects of contracting is in involving the organization's contact person in mutual development of the formal contract. To the degree that the organization's contact person is directly involved in the formal aspects of contracting, the ground rules for the consultation process and mutual cooperation on future issues and problems will be established (Boss, 1985). Such involvement of the contact person, of course, requires the investment of more time at the outset of the entry stage (Boss, 1985). For an excellent case study of developing a contract, refer to Carner (1982).

Once a contract has been formalized, the consultant is ready for the next phase of the entry stage—physically entering the system.

PHASE THREE: PHYSICALLY ENTERING THE SYSTEM

Physically entering the system begins when the consultant first comes into contact with the members of the organization (Gallessich, 1982) and, where appropriate, creates consultant-consultee relationships. Physical entry is different from psychological entry, which is the ongoing process by which the consultant achieves increasing acceptance by the members of the organization.

A very important feature of physically entering the system is the consultant's work site within the organization. Should the consultant be assigned a private office? Or should the consultant move from place to place and meet in designated meeting rooms or the offices of other staff members? Although it is difficult to make a categorical answer to these questions, the reality of organizational life is that having one's own office is a sign of status and prestige. By providing the consultant with a temporary office, the organization makes a symbolic statement of strong support for the consultant, one that sanctions and demonstrates the administration's willingness to allocate the organizational resources needed to support the consultation process.

Having an office and always being in it are two different things. When beginning the physical entry process, consultants should consider moving about the work areas to begin building relationships with members of the organization. Consultees often feel most comfortable when the consultant is willing to meet them on their own turf. Thus, as soon as possible after entering the system, consultants should seek out everyone connected with the consultation. A specified time schedule that makes the consultant's comings and goings predictable is very useful in successfully accomplishing physical entry.

The consultant should proceed in a deliberate, cautious manner. Organizations are slow to change, and the consultant would do well to realize that appropriate physical entry will enhance the organizational members' acceptance so crucial to successful psychological entry. The consultant should adapt to the organization's schedules and thereby minimize any interruptions in the workday.

The consultant should remind the organization's contact person to inform the consultation's parties-at-interest of the consultant's upcoming entry into the organization. The members affected by consultation should be informed of the consultant's role and function, why that particular consultant was hired, what is to be accomplished within what time frame, and who is to be involved (Boss, 1985). Further, the work setting in which consultation services are to be delivered should be common knowledge (Schein, 1969). Such advance notification prepares the people involved for the consultant's entry. Finally, an open discussion concerning confidentiality and its limits is important, for it informs both administrators and consultees of what they can reveal to the consultant, and it can avoid problems later on (Conoley & Conoley, 1982).

In summary, effective physical entry requires that the consultant joins the system with a sanction that is publicly demonstrated by the organization's administration, makes a deliberate attempt to build relationships with all parties involved in the consultation, and develops a full understanding among all of what the consultant is to do and why.

PHASE FOUR: PSYCHOLOGICALLY ENTERING THE SYSTEM

In actual practice, physical and psychological entry cannot be separated. *Psychological entry* refers to the gradual acceptance of the consultant by members of the organization in which consultation is being performed. Effective accomplishment of the first three phases of entry can enhance the consultant's acceptance by the organization.

In gaining psychological acceptance in an organization, the consultant should consider the two levels of operation in any organization. The first level, referred to as the process level, concerns how an organization does what it does (Mann, 1978); that is, how an organization makes major decisions is a process level activity. The second level of operation within an organization involves the interpersonal interactions among the organization's members (Mann, 1978). An example of the functioning of this interpersonal level would be the way in which peers are encouraged to support each other on the job to build the organization's morale.

Consultants who achieve psychological entry relatively quickly can be said to be "working smart." Because they realize that organizations attempt to maintain a state of equilibrium and stability (Parsons & Meyers, 1984), the consultants create the conditions in which only minimal stress is placed on the organizational personnel involved in the consultation. They follow existing rules, regulations, and communication channels, and they ask to be judged on their deeds rather than on what they say.

The consultant's acceptance by the organization can be enhanced by keeping matters pertinent to consultation as simple as possible (Parsons & Meyers, 1984). The consultant should describe consultation interventions in concrete and specific terminology. Changes in the organization's structure that result from consultation should be minimized.

Psychological acceptance can be accomplished through the use of social influence. As related to consultation, social influence theory states that the people affected by consultation are more open to influence to the degree that they view the consultant as being attractive, trustworthy, and competent (Strong, 1968).

Consultants are seen as attractive when the people with whom they work perceive similarities between themselves and the consultant. Consultants can increase their attractiveness by identifying with and manifesting as many of the organization's values as are congruent with their own. To this end consultants can accept and abide by the organization's routines (Gallessich, 1982), use the terminology common within it (Gallessich, 1982), and abide by its dress codes (Steele, 1975).

Consultants are perceived as trustworthy when they demonstrate the following qualities: understanding, appropriate use of power, respect for confidentiality, and credibility (Egan, 1986). Consultants can create trustworthiness (Egan, 1986) by:

1. avoiding behaviors that imply ulterior motives,
2. using the power of social influence carefully,
3. promoting the best interest of the consultee or the organization, and
4. being realistic but optimistic about the ability of the consultee or organization to handle the demands of consultation.

Trustworthiness can also be gained by refusing to take sides, by avoiding issues not in the contract, and by staying away from off-limits areas in the organization (Gallessich, 1982).

One of the most valuable tools consultants have for obtaining acceptance is the effective use of questioning . During entry it is better if consultants ask good questions about the system (in order to obtain some understanding of how organization's members perceive consultation) than if they rattle off what they already know about the consultee or the organization (Caplan, 1970; Conoley & Conoley, 1982).

Ironically, consultants can become too accepted within the system; members of the organization may see them as permanent, rather than temporary, members. Consultants who become too accepted risk losing their objectivity and having members of the system wish to avoid imposing on them (Caplan, 1970).

No matter how many precautions consultants make to ease their physical and psychological entry into the system, some resistance to consultation is typical. Although such resistance is generally normal, this "lack of cooperation" in the consultation process can present significant challenges to consultants.

RESISTANCE TO CONSULTATION

Resistance is the failure of a consultee or organization to participate constructively in the consultation process. Although resistance can be encountered during any phase of the consultation process, it is most frequently encountered during the entry stage. Resistance can be minimized to the degree that the consultant successfully accomplishes psychological entry.

Resistance to consultation can be either healthy or unhealthy. In discussing healthy resistance, Gallessich (1982, p. 279) states that ". . . resistance to consultants is a natural phenomenon. The integration of any new person into an ongoing social structure unbalances it, creating reactions and forcing members to make adjustments." When people in organizations become established in certain roles and ways of behaving, they seek to maintain this operational status quo. The healthy forms of resistance include the ways an individual or organization attempts to cope with the implicit demands for change inherent in consultation.

Resistance to consultation is unhealthy when it results either from excessive rigidity in organizations or from consultees' psychological concerns (Caplan, 1970). All organizations exist in a changing environment to which they must adapt, and resistance is the innate tendency of organizations to avoid such changes. Whenever consultees lose their objectivity concerning their work-related problems and resist involvement in the consultation process, their resistance is considered unhealthy (Caplan, 1970).

Here are seven points the consultant should remember about resistance:

1. Resistance is a natural phenomenon in the consultation process and all consultants should learn to anticipate it.
2. Resistance typically occurs due to people's fear of change in their work settings.
3. Fear of consultants by consultees can be minimized by publicly clarifying the nature of the consultant's services and by developing strong consultant-consultee relationships.
4. The consultant must learn to cope effectively with resistance so that progress can be made in the consultation process.
5. Resistance can be minimized in proportion to the consultant's ability to build collaborative relationships with those involved in consultation.
6. Although the consultation relationship is collaborative in nature, the consultant must take the lead in dealing with and minimizing resistance.
7. Many means of handling resistance are effective in the consultation process.

Dealing Effectively with Resistance

Perhaps the best method of dealing with resistance in consultation is to prevent its occurrence in the first place. Two general ways of minimizing resistance are understanding and involvement (Kelley, 1981). Understanding refers to the consultant's ability to comprehend and appreciate the consultee's views of events. Involvement refers to consultants' use of collaboration to prevent them from overpowering consultees. Understanding and involvement can reduce resistance because they focus on listening and learning—the consultant becomes a student and learns about the skills and perceptions of the consultee.

Resistance is often engendered by consultee's perceptions of consultants—what they *think* about the consultant's behavior, not the actual behavior itself, is critical. Thus, the consultant should be concerned about creating within the consultee positive expectations about the experience and outcomes of consultation (Brown et al., 1987). Consultants should examine four activities related to consultees' perceptions and positive expectations:

1. maintaining objectivity,
2. getting appropriate support within the agency in which consultation is to take place,
3. being aware of organizational dynamics and relating to individuals, and
4. using social influence (Cohen, 1985).

SUMMARY

The entry process in consultation is a critical stage. When successfully completed, it increases the probability that the entire consultation process will turn out successfully. The success of the entry process relies heavily on the consultant's skills and how well these skills are used to accomplish the tasks of the entry stage. The most critical skills in the entry stage relate to exploring problems, contracting, relating, and communicating.

By effectively accomplishing the stage of entry, consultants can not only set the stage for successful consultation but also minimize the resistance that organizations and individual consultees can demonstrate.

Consultants should avoid the temptation to go quickly through the entry stage in order to get on with problem-solving activities. By effectively exploring the organization's needs, the consultant can help the organization determine its priorities for consultation. A well-designed contract makes the expectations of everyone involved explicit and prevents misunderstandings regarding consultation later in the process. Effective physical entry makes consultants less intrusive as they join in the organization's activities. By taking the time necessary for building relationships and gaining acceptance, consultants can become "insiders" and accomplish the difficult phase of psychological entry.

QUESTIONS FOR REFLECTION

1. What effects can resistance have on the consultant's performance?
2. Why is it important for the consultant to obtain sanctions for performing consultation from the organization's upper echelon?
3. Recall a situation in which an outsider entered your classroom. What were your immediate reactions? Relate your feelings to how members of an organization must feel when they encounter a consultant for the first time.
4. What characteristics would you look for in an organization or a consultee before you would agree to consultation?
5. Under what circumstances can resistance in consultation be seen as normal?
6. How can the power attributed to the consultant due to expertise or trustworthiness be useful in ameliorating resistance?
7. What are the key points consultants should consider in assessing their performance during the entry phase?
8. How would you as a consultant go about accomplishing psychological entry? That is, how would you go about the task of building relationships with and gaining acceptance by staff with whom you had no previous contact?
9. How would you go about the task of physically entering into consultation with an organization?
10. Under what circumstances do you think consultants should use formal contracts?

SUGGESTED SUPPLEMENTARY READINGS

If you are interested in reading in more depth and detail about the entry stage of consultation, here are some useful selected readings:

Cherniss, C. (1976). Preentry issues in consultation. *American Journal of Community Psychology, 4*(1), 13–24. In this article Cherniss provides an excellent overview of how a consultant should behave before physically entering the system. Cherniss poses several questions, such as "What will be the primary focus of consultation?", and then proceeds to answer these questions in a scholarly yet practical manner.

Gallessich, J. (1982). *The profession and practice of consultation.* San Francisco: Jossey-Bass. Chapter 12 of this book provides a nuts-and-bolts approach to the entry stage and makes some excellent suggestions for ways consultants can be effective in the process of contracting.

Glidewell, J. C. (1959). The entry problem in consultation. *Journal of Social Issues, 15*(2), 51–59. This article is a classic and well worth reading. Glidewell was one of the first authors to promote the idea of the consultant as a person who temporarily attaches to a social system. Glidewell also does an excellent job of pointing out that the process of entry can be accelerated or retarded by the perceptions of the members of the organization in which consultation is to occur.

Chapter
4

Diagnosis Stage

PREVIEW

Assume for the moment that you are the consultant described in the following example.

CASE STUDY:
You are a human services professional in private practice with a caseload of clients, and you perform consultation with other therapists and human services organizations. The director of a county social services agency requests that you assist in resolving some of the agency's problems. You have successfully completed the entry stage, and therefore you have a rough idea of what the agency's problems are, have contracted with it, have gotten to know the staff, and are set up in the office of a part-time staff member. The director is concerned about the morale within the agency: people work behind closed doors, "put-downs" of clients are frequently heard, backlogs of paperwork are large, and little camaraderie is apparent.

When consulting with the director you agree to design and conduct a survey about "what it is like to work in this place." You agree to interview a random number of the staff about their personal views of their professional work site. Based on the results of this information, you assist the director in determining "what's the matter." You divide the problem into three smaller problems: morale, high caseloads, and little administrative support and encouragement. You then assist the director in setting some goals to ameliorate these problems. These goals are then further broken down into more specific subgoals (for example, more oral and written praise and support from the director for jobs well done). Once goals have been set, you and the director come up with a variety of possible interventions that might be alternatives for meeting the set goals.

As this example illustrates, consultants are sometimes asked to assist in determining the nature of a problem prior to making some form of intervention. This stage of consultation—in which the consultant performs this assessment in the roles of information seeker and detective—is called the *diagnosis stage*. Recall that the diagnosis stage comprises four phases: gathering the information, defining the problem, setting goals, and generating possible interventions.

The consultant's relationship with the consultee is critical to the successful completion of this stage. Unless the consultant is able to obtain accurate, pertinent information and assist consultees in translating this data into a list of functional and viable alternate interventions, then it is likely that the wrong problem will be "solved."

As you read through this chapter, consider these questions:

1. How does a consultant determine the places within the organization from which to collect information?
2. How does a consultant determine who should gather the data needed to define the problem?
3. What factors should be considered in setting goals?
4. How can a consultant assist a consultee in developing a set of possible interventions?
5. In what ways is diagnosis an ongoing event?

INTRODUCTION

The preceding chapter discussed the entry process, in which the consultant engages in a preliminary exploration of organizational needs, formulates a contract, and physically and psychologically enters the system. The stage following entry is called the diagnosis stage. Within this second stage, the *gathering information phase* answers the question "What information do we need to find out where we are?"; the *defining the problem phase* answers the question "Where are we?"; the *goal-setting phase* answers the question "Where do we want to be?"; and the *generating possible interventions phase* answers the question "What are some of the things we can do that might help us get there?"

DIAGNOSIS

The nature of the diagnosis stage depends on the type of consultation being performed. A mental health consultant working with a therapist may assist in diagnosing the therapist's client's problem and in prescribing a treatment plan. A behavioral consultant may examine the antecedents and consequences of students' selected classroom behaviors and assist a teacher in implementing behavioral strategies to change those behaviors. An organizational consultant may assist an organization to improve its efficiency by focusing on an individual, a group, a subsystem, or the organization as a whole. The process of diagnosis remains the same for all consultation, although the types of data gathered in diagnosis depend on the type of consultation being performed.

The importance of defining and clarifying the problem in consultation cannot be overemphasized (Osterweil, 1987; Gutkin & Curtis, 1982). Because consultation is a problem-solving process, appropriate diagnosis is critical to its success.

Diagnosis is the identification of the forces underlying or precipitating the current way things are in a given situation (French, Bell, & Zawacki, 1978). "Diagnosis may pertain broadly to the present state of a system, including the many positive forces giving rise to desirable outcomes, or may be narrower in the sense of focusing on the dysfunctional forces that are producing undesirable outcomes, or may focus on changes in the state of the system over time" (French et al., 1978, pp. 115–116). A critical part of diagnosis is determining that part of the organization in which the problem is located. How the consultant approaches the diagnostic stage depends on the purpose of consultation, the complexity of the problem, and the time available (Argyris, 1970). For example, Tichy (1983) lists three types of organizational diagnosis based on complexity:

1. radar scan diagnosis, which involves a quick examination of the organization to locate problem areas;
2. symptom-focused diagnosis, in which information is examined relative to known problem areas; and
3. in-depth diagnosis, which involves a systematic, detailed organizational analysis.

Another important aspect of the diagnosis stage involves determining who constitutes the client system—an individual, a group, a subsystem of an organization, or the entire organization—for the nature of the client system affects diagnosis. As the client system increases in size, the complexity of the diagnostic stage usually increases as well: the more complex the diagnostic stage, the greater the need to use several data-gathering methods to collect data from a larger group of people.

The limits to the duration of diagnosis are quite indistinct (Bell & Nadler, 1985). The traditional view of diagnosis is that it is a one-time event: the consultant gathers pertinent information and makes a diagnosis. The current view considers diagnosis to be an ongoing event. For example, the consultant obtains some of the data used in diagnosis during the preliminary exploration of organizational needs. The very act of intervening at the very beginning of consultation yields information that can be used in diagnosis (Bell & Nadler, 1985).

Diagnosis, then, can be viewed as a continuous process intricately related to both data gathering and intervention (Gallessich, 1982). Figure 4.1 shows the interrelationships among diagnosis, data gathering, and intervention as determined by French (1972) and adapted by Gallessich (1982).

Purpose of Diagnosis

Diagnosis is important to the consultant as a means of determining what is needed in order to design appropriate interventions and obtain a picture of how the organization's members perceive the organization and its operation (Neilsen, 1984). This stage also facilitates awareness and growth in consultees and influences them to be responsible for pursuing a successful outcome of consultation (Furr, 1979). Consultants should create conditions such that the diagnostic stage yields valid and useful information, provides consultees a free

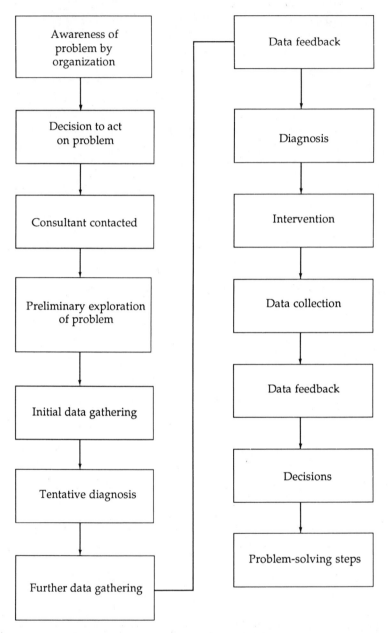

FIGURE 4.1   The Interrelationships Among Diagnosis, Data Gathering, and Intervention (French, 1972)

choice about what is desired as a result of obtaining the information, and results in an internal commitment to that choice (Argyris, 1970).

Diagnosis is important for consultees because they acquire the understanding necessary to obtain the desired outcomes for consultation. The diagnosis stage allows a consultee to "call the shots" concerning how the consultation process will proceed (Furr, 1979). Most models of consultation take a collaborative approach to diagnosis; the consultant leads the process, but the consultee has as much input as possible on defining content and making the diagnosis. A general rule of thumb for consultants: in involving consultees in the diagnostic stage, do not do anything for consultees that they can do for themselves. The collaborative model of diagnosis is based on the assumption that the consultee's diagnostic and problem-solving skills will be enhanced for future use as a result of participating in diagnosis (Schein, 1969).

Furr (1979) lists six interrelated aspects of the purpose of diagnosis:

1. to create change,
2. to assess the factors related to the desired changes,
3. to provide the conditions for growth and insight in the consultee,
4. to develop in the consultee a personal and professional regard for the consultation relationship,
5. to catalyze the undertaking of change, and
6. to assist the consultee in focusing on the factors related to the desired change.

As an example of the catalytic aspect of diagnosis, a counseling psychologist consulting with a social worker might suggest that the consultee consider the diagnostic results in terms of their implications for change. The "hard facts" of the diagnosis in this example might reinforce the social worker's momentum in changing the strategies used for assisting the client system.

Every consultant brings to and uses in the diagnostic process at least three theories (French et al., 1978). The first, descriptive and analytical in nature, is the theory by which the consultant attempts to understand the ins and outs of organizational events and behaviors. In this view, for example, behaviors might be considered rather more critical in understanding events than are attitudes. A second theory, one of change, consists of the consultant's views of how events influence one another and become different. For example, one view of this theory might state that structure, not people, determines change. Finally, consultants have a third diagnostic theory, which consists of a set of notions that assist in determining what is dysfunctional or "wrong." One example might be the viewpoint that a problem must be a long-standing one in order to be "severe."

The kind of information used for diagnosis depends on a given consultation model's view of what must be examined in order to find out what is wrong. Three major areas or domains that consultants may examine in their diagnoses are consultee characteristics, client system characteristics, and environmental characteristics (Brown et al., 1987). Consultants' theories of description-analysis, change, and dysfunction significantly affect which domains are examined and how a diagnosis is made. By being aware of their own theories, consultants can use them to accomplish accurate, effective diagnoses and avoid being unwittingly victimized by them during the diagnostic stage.

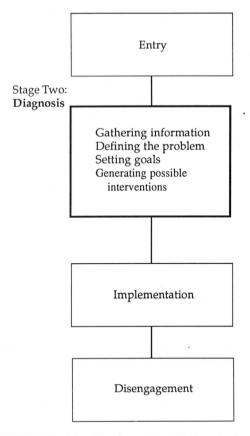

FIGURE 4.2   The Phases of the Diagnosis Stage

The diagnosis stage, like the entry stage, is very complex. It involves the four interrelated phases depicted in Figure 4.2: gathering information, defining the problem, setting goals, and developing possible interventions.

PHASE ONE: GATHERING INFORMATION

The Nature of Information Acquisition

An accurate diagnosis requires accurate information. The terms *data* and *information* are used interchangeably in this discussion. Although data gathering never ceases during the consultation process, there is a formal time for the process of gathering information.

The first step in the process is to conceptualize the problem. Some idea of the problem is obtained during the preliminary exploration of organizational needs, and a contract is made with regard to the findings of those explorations. The results of the preliminary exploration are, in part, determined by the model of consultation to be provided, for each model has its own view of human behavior, of what is necessary for change, and of what constitutes the client system. These factors in turn will determine the types of methods used to gather data.

Still, the consultant must assign some parameters to the task of consultation before diagnosis can begin (Goodstein, 1978). Perhaps it is best for the consultant to start with problems as they are perceived by the consultee (Huse, 1975); such action demonstrates the consultant's collaborative attitude (Goodstein, 1978).

In addition to conceptualizing the presenting problem, there are four additional steps in the information gathering phase (Block, 1981):

1. *Deciding to proceed.* This is a mutual decision by the consultant and the consultee to proceed based on the conclusion that the problem is worth solving and that further data concerning it are needed to make a more formal diagnosis. It is important for the consultant and consultee to have a clear idea about why the information is being gathered—about what relevant questions the data-gathering process will attempt to answer (Kilburg, 1978).

2. *Selecting dimensions.* This step is also a mutual decision by the consultant and the consultee. The dimensions of the data-collecting process are a function of how comprehensive the consultation is to be, the nature of the problem, and the type of consultation desired.

3. *Deciding who will be involved in the data collection.* Once the data collectors are identified, the parties from whom data are to be gathered are selected. An adequate sample of individuals from whom appropriate data are acquired is essential (Kilburg, 1978). A school psychologist consulting with a teacher about a student, for example, might decide to interview the student's parents and share that information with the teacher. Or an organizational consultant might decide to obtain data from organizational members directly related to a problem, some of those indirectly related, some personnel not related to the concern at all, and some people external but connected to the organization (for example, clients) (Dinkmeyer & Carlson, 1973).

4. *Selecting the data-collection methods.* The methods used are determined by the time available for the consultation process, the motivation for change within the organization (including the consultees involved), and the degree of need for consultation (Block, 1981). The procedure for selecting data-collection methods is discussed later in this section.

Like good detectives, consultants must gather and analyze data to understand what is going on; then they can use that understanding in assisting the consultee system to determine what changes it wants to make (Steele, 1975). Depending on the model of consultation in use, the consultant can draw from several data sources: genetic data, current descriptive data, process data, interpretive data, consultee-client system relationship data, and client system behavior data (Beer, 1980; Brown et al., 1987; Caplan, 1970; Bergan, 1977).

1. *Genetic data.* This type of data includes easily accessible, common information (for example, an organization's role and mission statement) and

historical information (for example, reports and memos). Example: a consultant might read the role and mission of a human services agency and decide to determine the degree to which the agency's members are aware of it.

2. *Current descriptive data.* As its name implies, this type of information describes an organization as it currently exists. The organization's physical layout and its command and salary structures are all descriptive information. Example: a human services agency asks for a consultant's help with its internal communication problems. The consultant examines the agency's organizational structure as a prelude to determining how superiors and subordinates within the agency communicate with one another.

3. *Process data.* Process data involves the organization's methods, including how decisions are made and how meetings are conducted. Example: a consultant acts as an observer at a crisis intervention team's staff meeting in order to determine who talks to whom about what.

4. *Interpretive data.* This kind of information tends to be subjective and have emotional aspects to it. Interpretive data include members' attitudes, beliefs, and perceptions about the organization, its means of functioning, and the ways members relate to one another. Example: a consultant gathers information about how school counselors perceive the support given them by the teachers in their school.

5. *Consultee-client system relationship data.* The dynamics between the consultee and the client system constitute this type of data, including the nature of interpersonal relationships, their direction, and how communication takes place. Example: a consultant watches a videotape of a consultee providing therapy to a client in order to help the consultee work more effectively with the client.

6. *Client system behavior data.* This type of information includes characteristics of the client system, such as level of intelligence, nature of the problem, levels of coping, the frequency of adaptive and maladaptive behaviors, and related environmental conditions. Example: a school psychologist consulting with a school counselor administers an individual intelligence test to the counselor's client in order to suggest some effective helping strategies the counselor can use with that client.

Great diversity of data sources is available to consultants. Depending on the nature of consultation, consultants may draw on one or more of these data sources. For example, consultants working with consultees whose client system is an organization may want to examine genetic data (for example, forms for writing up client reports from past years), current descriptive data (for example, current forms for writing up client reports), process data (for example, how the decision to use a given form for writing client reports was made), or interpretive data (for example, the results of a survey, which reveal how staff feel about the current form used to write up client reports). Consultants working with consultees who work with individual clients tend to rely on consultee-client system relationship data (for example, the theoretical approach the consultee is taking with the client) and client system behavior data (for example, the nature of the client's behaviors with which the consultee is having difficulty).

Scanning

Using the presenting problem as a starting point, it is a good idea for the consultant to "scan" the context in which the presenting problem is thought to occur (Gallessich, 1982). *Scanning* is the process of looking at the "big picture" in which the problem is thought to exist. The picture obtained includes information about events and relationships within the organization's internal and external environment (Aquilar, 1967). Scanning prevents a premature focus on the problem's more obvious major elements to the exclusion of new factors that may be more germane to the problem (Steele, 1975). Scanning procedures can provide data for determining the validity of the presenting problem, for identifying forces supporting or inhibiting effective change, and for detecting problems that are deeper than the ones identified in the preliminary exploration (Gallessich, 1982). In addition, scanning can prevent an a priori determination of the problem's nature and counteract the consultant's professional and personal biases (Gallessich, 1982).

Hypothetically, a consultant could scan the entire domain: consultee, client system, and environment; in practice, scanning must be cost effective. Therefore, consultants typically use their theories of description analysis, change, and dysfunction to scan these systems. To avoid biases, the consultant describes these theories and the results of scanning to the consultee, who can then add additional perspectives on the meaning of what is under examination during the diagnosis stage.

A consultant with a mental health perspective might pay close attention to consultees and their personal reasons for having problems with their cases. Some consultants with an organizational perspective examine the organization's reactions among its internal parts and with its external environment in order to determine how the organization could function more effectively. Such consultants frequently scan those parts of an organization related to the organization's effectiveness, efficiency, and health (Brown et al., 1987). A consultant with a behavioral perspective might look at behaviors to be changed in the client system, as well as the antecedents and consequences of those behaviors.

Once the entire context of the problem has been scanned and the results of the scanning interpreted, the consultant and consultee are ready to focus on more specific data.

Methods for Gathering Information

The information used in consultation is obtained by unobtrusive or obtrusive data-gathering devices. Unobtrusive devices include historical data (for example, memos), external data (for example, interviews with former clients of the organization), and observational data (for example, observing a meeting in action) (Bell & Nadler, 1985). Unobtrusive measures are not likely to interrupt the organization's normal flow of everyday activities or to be seen as threatening by the organization's members. Obtrusive data-gathering activities include those that in some way ask for a reaction from the members of the organization

(Bell & Nadler, 1985). Examples of this type of data gathering include questionnaires, surveys, and interviews with an organization's personnel (Bell & Nadler, 1985). Because these activities directly assess the organization through its members and may imply impending changes within the organization, they can be threatening and elicit resistance. Regardless of the method of data gathering used, the consultant can minimize resistance by ensuring that all appropriate personnel are informed of the data's anticipated uses.

Data can be "soft," such as subordinates' impressions of the organization's leadership, or "hard," such as statistical data on the number of clients who perceive that the organization has helped them in some way (Gallessich, 1982). A general rule for data gathering is to move from less to more structured methods (Parsons & Meyers, 1984). For example, concerning the morale of an entire organization, it is best to gather general information first, such as surveying a selected sample about the level of morale. Later, the consultant can gather more specific information, such as views concerning specific causes of the quality of morale. Instruments and procedures used to gather data should, whenever possible, be designed to take into consideration the uniqueness of the consultation situation (Argyris, 1970).

The methods used for gathering information in consultation depend on the nature of the client system and the perceived problem. A consultant working with a consultee who is a therapist experiencing difficulty with a case requires different information than would a consultant working with an organization suffering from poor morale. The most common information-gathering methods used in consultation include documents and records, questionnaires and surveys, interviews, and observation (Lippitt, Langseth, & Mossop, 1985).

Documents and Records

Consultants and consultees sometimes erroneously assume that they have to collect all of the data needed to make a diagnosis (Nadler, 1977). All organizations generate a wealth of information and keep some form of records. These documents are already in recorded form and include the organization's numerical data and written communications. Use of records is often considered unobtrusive because their examination does not interrupt the organization's normal flow of work. Records are frequently referred to as secondary data because the information in them has already been collected.

The consultation party who is responsible for data collection searches these documents without the aid of any structure or procedure (Nadler, 1977). A variety of documents supply the consultant with data for use in making a diagnosis, including (Gallessich, 1982, p. 234):

1. job descriptions,
2. agency policies and manuals of operating procedures,
3. historical records,
4. annual reports,
5. budgets,
6. audits,

7. personnel statistics,
8. orientation procedures,
9. promotion policies,
10. program descriptions,
11. grant proposals,
12. client demographic profiles,
13. surveys of client use of services,
14. public information brochures,
15. logs and appointment calendars, and
16. case records.

By comparing an organization's current and past records and documents, the consultant may be able to identify trends and forces influencing the organization (Brubaker, 1978). By noting current records, consultants can determine who corresponds in writing with whom, how critical information is disseminated throughout the agency, and so forth. Reviewing relevant documents is a data-gathering technique that is frequently underused by consultants (Egan, 1985).

Using records as an information-gathering technique has several strengths, including the use of existing information, cost efficiency, a wealth of relevant material, and the data's credibility with members of the organization (Fuqua & Newman, 1983). In addition, records are typically free from response bias and are nonreactive (Nadler, 1977).

The use of documents as an information-gathering device also has its weaknesses. Among these shortcomings are potential inaccuracy and incompleteness, limited availability, difficulties in data analysis, and the possibility of increasing resistance among consultees and the organization as a whole (Fuqua & Newman, 1983). Nadler (1977) corroborates these weaknesses by noting that records frequently have little relation to reality and that pertinent information is often difficult to retrieve. In addition, the consultant must frequently rely on the consultee's assistance in determining the validity of existing data and in identifying which data might be diagnostically useful.

Questionnaires and Surveys

Questionnaires and surveys are actually self-administered interviews (Nadler, 1977) that allow for simultaneous collection of information from several sources (Parsons & Meyers, 1984). There is a tremendous body of literature on conducting and interpreting questionnaires (Egan, 1985). The three types of questionnaires are the standardized, the modified, and the custom-made (Nadler, 1977).

Standardized questionnaires are those that are available either commercially or in research journals. Their validity and reliability have been demonstrated in the research literature. Modified questionnaires are usually standardized questionnaires that have been adapted in some way to meet some specific need or needs of the data-gathering process. For example, a school counselor might adapt a questionnaire used in a mental health center for use in a school setting. When a questionnaire is custom-made, it is developed by the consultant and consultee for a specific purpose. Thus, members of a university task force on teaching effectiveness might develop a questionnaire to measure faculty members' attitudes toward the teaching/learning process. Custom-made questionnaires require a substantial amount of time to construct and often lack high levels of validity and reliability. The type of questionnaire or survey a consultant chooses depends on the precise nature of the information the consultant and consultee feel is needed to make an adequate diagnosis (Goodstein, 1978).

Most questionnaires and surveys make use of fixed responses (Nadler, 1977). Respondents directly provide written information about their attitudes, perceptions, or points of view. A current trend toward incorporating some open-ended responses in questionnaires allows respondents to personalize their responses. However, open-ended responses are difficult to summarize and interpret (Burges, 1976).

Nadler (1977) discussed several advantages of using surveys and questionnaires as data-gathering techniques. Questionnaires allow sampling of large numbers of people simultaneously. Responses can be quickly and easily collated and statistically analyzed. Questionnaires are cost-effective and can be used for a variety of purposes. Questionnaires and surveys are probably the most powerful data-gathering tool for yielding maximum information in the most efficient manner (Greiner & Metzger, 1983).

Questionnaires and surveys also have disadvantages (Nadler, 1977). Questionnaires are nonempathic—the instrument does not interact with the respondent in a personal way—which can cause indifference toward the questionnaire on the part of the respondent. Questionnaires and surveys lack adaptability; that is, they are prestructured. If some questions are inappropriate for some respondents, nothing can be done about it. Questionnaires can also be difficult to interpret; different respondents may interpret the same question differently. Further, surveys and questionnaires can suffer from response bias, a situation in which the respondent answers items in a set way rather than answering each item on its own merit. Fordyce and Weil (1978) criticize questionnaires because they can produce "canned" results and because consultants frequently use them when direct human communication, such as interviews, is more appropriate.

Questionnaires and surveys are most useful when a large sample of people is needed to provide data. These common data-gathering techniques are among the most common because of the ease of collecting and analyzing the data they generate. They can be used to gather data for defining a problem, or they can provide clues about which data-gathering techniques (for example, interviews) should be used subsequently. Questionnaires and surveys are sometimes used in conjunction with interviews of a sample of the respondents (Nadler, 1977). For a detailed discussion of the use of questionnaires in data collection, consult Goode and Hatt (1972).

Interviews

One of the best ways to understand a client system or an organization is to ask the people in them what they think and feel (Nadler, 1977). Such a technique, the interview, is another commonly used form of data gathering (Gallessich, 1982). Even though interviews are used in all phases of the diagnostic process

(Parsons & Meyers, 1984), the nature of the interviewing process will depend on the type of model from which the consultant operates, the issues the interviews are to explore (Goodstein, 1978), and the consultant's earlier observations (Schein, 1969). Effective interviewing demands that the consultant be sufficiently skilled to note the interviewee's nonverbal and verbal behavior during the interview. Depending on how the interview is conducted, the consultant can uncover both positive and negative opinions and attitudes on a large number of relevant topics (Fordyce & Weil, 1978).

The interviewing process can be formal or informal, as can its setting (Egan, 1985), which can affect the type of information shared by the interviewee (Steele, 1975). Both groups and individuals can be interviewed. Interviewees are less likely to distort data in a group interview, but they are also less likely to share their true views and feelings (Greiner & Metzger , 1983). The process by which interviews take place is usually determined by such factors as cost and the data-gathering potential of the interviewing style (Nadler, 1977).

Different types of interviews produce different types of responses from different people (Egan, 1985). There are three common types of interviews: unstructured, structured and open-ended, and structured and fixed-response (Nadler, 1977).

Unstructured interviews have as one of their major characteristics minimal direction of their content by the interviewer (consultant). *Structured and open-ended interviews* consist of a set of preselected questions that the consultant asks the interviewee. *Structured and fixed-response interviews* provide both predetermined questions and responses from which to choose.

Interviews have several advantages (Nadler, 1977). They are adaptive—the interviewing process can be modified depending on the course of the interview. For example, if an interviewee provides an ambiguous response, the consultant can ask for clarification or an example of what the interviewee means. Interviews can be a source of detailed information on several topics and can provide "rich" sources of data about problems and their causes. Further, interviews allow the consultant to express empathy and understanding to the interviewee, and as a result, the interview process can be used to build rapport with some members of the organization.

Interviews also have their disadvantages. They are one of the most costly forms of data gathering in terms of both time and expense (Neilsen, 1984). The interviewee's responses can be affected by the consultant's biases to the degree that these biases dictate the types of questions asked during the interview. Interviewee bias can also affect the data obtained because the consultant gets not only the interviewee's perceptions but also observations of the consultee's behavior (Nadler, 1977). Consequently, the results of interviews should be carefully validated. Two additional potential disadvantages of interviews are the inaccessibility of interviewees and the perceived threat that what interviewees say could somehow later be used against them (Jones, 1973).

Interviewing is one of the most commonly used data-gathering devices, and it can provide the consultant very important data. The reasons for interviewing and the uses made of the interview data should be made known to all parties-at-interest prior to the onset of the interviewing process (Fordyce & Weil, 1978). For a detailed discussion of the use of interviewing to collect data, consult Cannell and Kahn (1972).

Observation

Data can be collected through observation—the deliberate viewing of events. This most obvious way to collect information puts the consultant in direct contact with the people, activities, and/or environment about which information is being collected (Nadler, 1977). Consultants must make choices about what, when, and how much to observe; such choices lend observations structure that can range from a strictly defined to a general framework. The consultant's basic question regarding observation is, "How can the observation be structured so that meaningful and useful data can be collected?" (Nadler, 1977, p. 133).

The three types of observation—structured, semi-structured, and unstructured (Nadler, 1977)—differ in the degree to which observers watch and record the observations.

Structured observations typically use specific procedures or instruments that specify what type of behavior is to be observed and how it is to be recorded (Nadler, 1977). *Semi-structured observations* have relatively unstructured observations but highly structured recording (Nadler, 1977). *Unstructured observations* have no strict guidelines for what is to be observed, what is to be recorded, or how recording should take place (Nadler, 1977).

Observation has several advantages (Nadler, 1977). It provides data on behavior rather than on reports of behavior and can note behaviors of which organization members or the client system are unaware. It can also be one of the more objective data-gathering methods. Observational data have strong face validity; that is, such data have concrete referents to back them up, whereas interviews and questionnaire data can be accused of being "overly subjective." Further, this type of data is also current, whereas questionnaires generally sample respondents' past perceptions. Finally, observation, like interviewing, is adaptive: the consultant can adjust what is to be observed as the situation demands.

Observation is not without its liabilities as a data-collection method (Nadler, 1977). Like interviewing, observation is expensive. The coding and interpretation that must be applied to observational data is subject to observer bias, and the less structured the observation, the more likely observer bias will enter into the observation process. As is the case with questionnaires, sampling is also an issue in observation. Observations require sampling with regard to people, time, space, and activities, and such intensive sampling can be costly in time and money. Finally, observation has the liability of potential observer effect.

Observer effect is the impact observers have on the behavior of those being observed. For example, counselors being observed by a consultant may be more empathic than usual with clients simply because they are under observation. For a detailed discussion of data collection by observation, consult Selltiz, Jahoda, Deutsch, and Cook (1972).

In summary, each data-collection method has its advantages and disadvantages. Selection of the appropriate data-collection method involves a trade-off of its advantages and disadvantages in the circumstances under which data gathering is to occur. Consultants should consider using multiple data-gathering methods as a way of both overcoming the liabilities of a given method and eliminating inaccurate or distorted data (Nadler, 1977).

PHASE TWO: DEFINING THE PROBLEM

After the data has been collected, it must be analyzed. In order to define a problem the consultant and the consultee should have a systematic, deliberate, and predetermined plan for analyzing the data (Nadler, 1977).

Data analysis is made up of two components: a conceptual model and a technical component composed of techniques for analyzing data (Nadler, 1977). The conceptual component—the diagnostic perspective described earlier—should have been agreed upon by the consultant and the consultee before data were gathered, as should the techniques for analysis. Analysis of the data may suggest new hypotheses concerning the problem that require collection of additional data and subsequent analysis.

As the consultant and consultee examine the data, a more complex conceptualization of the problem typically occurs (Brown et al., 1987). During the significant amount of time spent on analyzing and interpreting data, the consultant and consultee determine how a broad range of factors affects the problem (Brown et al., 1987). The problem may be analyzed in terms of how it develops over time, how past events are causing the present problem, or how future expectations are related to the problem (Osterweil, 1987). A clear, specific problem statement with corresponding objectives is crucial in making sure that the correct problem is attacked. Such a statement is helpful in setting specific goals for two reasons: all parties-at-interest have a clear understanding of how the problem is viewed, and such specificity suggests appropriate data collection techniques (Brown et al., 1987).

It is important that the problem statement be in language that is acceptable to the consultee (Dustin & Ehly, 1984). To this end, Osterweil (1987) suggests generating several alternative definitions of the problem from which the consultant and consultee can choose. Three criteria can be useful for selecting the most appropriate definition of the problem (Osterweil, 1987):

1. reasonability—the degree to which the definition seems reasonable to both consultant and consultee;
2. workability—the degree to which the definition seems practical and directed to new directions of action; and
3. motivation—the degree to which the consultee will be willing to take action on the defined problem.

The following illustrates the process of defining the problem:

CASE STUDY:
A school counselor was consulting with a school administrator about programs that the counseling department might sponsor. The administrator asked the counselor for assistance in determining which programs the school should implement.

The counselor interviewed a select group of administrators, teachers, parents, and students about the types of programs suitable for counseling department sponsorship. Based on these interviews the counseling department designed a set of four surveys. A separate survey was designed for and sent to a random sample of each group: administrators, parents, teachers, and students.

The counselor and administrator agreed to conceptualize the data analysis based on the common themes that emerged from each of the four surveys. In addition, they agreed to look for any program suggestions that were unique to any given set of responders. They asked themselves the following questions: Is there a consensus among the groups concerning the programs the counseling department should sponsor? What program suggestions are unique to each group? What are the implications of this information for planning programs?

Survey items were tallied and their relative ranks determined for each of the four groups. A given program would be seriously considered if it was ranked in the top four by two or more groups. The remainder of the data, though not given priority for the development of a particular program, was to be taken into account as the counseling department reviewed its entire set of activities.

In general, defining the problem involves collaboration between consultant and consultee in interpreting analyzed data according to some mutually accepted conceptual scheme (Lorsch & Lawrence, 1972). The consultant and the consultee determine the data's meanings and limitations (Lorsch & Lawrence, 1972). These efforts ideally result in both an appropriately defined problem and a cognitive map for the consultee's future use (Lorsch & Lawrence, 1972). Once the problem has been defined to the mutual satisfaction of consultant and consultee, they are ready to begin the next phase of the diagnostic process—setting goals.

PHASE THREE: SETTING GOALS

Setting goals is an important phase in the diagnostic stage. Consultants need to be experts in goal setting because it is likely that their consultees will not be (Egan, 1985). Goal setting is the process of designating what ends are to be achieved. In consultation, goal setting focuses on solving or ameliorating the identified problem or problems; that is, it determines which actions will effectively deal with the problem (Egan & Cowan, 1979).

The Process of Setting Goals

Goal setting is the central point in the diagnostic process (Egan, 1986). Empirical research (for example, Locke & Latham, 1984; Latham & Lee, 1986) supports the notion that, when properly performed, goal setting has positive benefits. Because choosing goals establishes what specific ends are to be accomplished, goal setting should not be rushed (Egan & Cowan, 1979), because inappropriate or poorly refined goals may be chosen.

Goal setting, then, is a process of shaping, a movement toward concreteness and specificity from a broader, more general perspective (Egan, 1985; Parsons & Meyers, 1984). If the problem is complex, the goal for resolving the problem will likely be complex, too (Egan, 1985).

The first step in goal setting is to "discover new goal possibilities" (Egan & Cowan, 1979, p. 143) related to the problem. To accomplish this end, Egan and Cowan (1979) suggest the following creative strategies:

1. divergent thinking,
2. brainstorming,
3. scenario writing, and
4. fantasy.

Once goal possibilities have been determined, the consultant and consultee engage in the following goal-setting steps (Locke & Latham, 1984):

1. specify the task or objective,
2. specify how the task or objective will be measured,
3. specify the target or standard to be reached,
4. specify the time span involved,
5. prioritize possible goals,
6. rate goals with respect to difficulty and importance, and
7. determine coordination requirements.

Based on these seven goal-setting steps, the consultant and consultee choose the most appropriate goal. The chosen goal is then evaluated and adjusted in light of the characteristics of effective goals.

Characteristics of Effective Goals

A *goal* is a specific outcome or accomplishment sought to solve or improve a problem; a *complex goal* is one that can be divided into subgoals (Egan, 1985). In the context of consultation, success is a complex goal that can be broken down into several subgoals: success in each of the stages of consultation. Further, each subgoal of success in each consultation stage can be broken down into still more subgoals: success in each phase of the process.

For goals to be effective, they must be (Egan & Cowan, 1979, p. 126):

1. *behavioral*—clear, concrete, specific, operational;
2. *measurable* (or in some way verifiable)—it is clear when they have been accomplished;

3. *realistic*—not set too high, capable of being accomplished with available resources;
4. *worthwhile*—not set too low, not petty or meaningless; and
5. *adequate*—they satisfy real needs and wants.

Additional characteristics of effective goals include (Egan, 1985):

1. *compatibility with the values* of the consultant, consultee, client system, and organization;
2. a reasonable *time frame* for accomplishment; and
3. clear *communication* about the goal to parties-at-interest.

For the goal-setting process to be successful, goals should be written in clear, specific, behavioral terms. Such specificity facilitates both selecting appropriate interventions to solve the problem and evaluating those interventions. Specific goals allow the consultant and consultee to regulate and evaluate the effectiveness of interventions designed to meet those goals (Latham & Lee, 1986). If, for example, a consultant and a consultee determine that the goal is "improved morale," this goal would be insufficient until they specified what they meant by "morale" and "improved."

Effective goals are verifiable in some way, preferably by measurement. Consultants and consultees must determine what should be measured, how it should be measured, and when measurement should take place. Accomplishment of goals can be verified either quantitatively or qualitatively. Measures of quantity include volume and rate, whereas measures of quality include accuracy and novelty (Egan, 1985). Cost effectiveness—whether the "expense" in meeting a goal was worth the benefits derived from accomplishing that goal—also should be taken into consideration in goal setting.

Three factors determine whether a goal is realistic: resources, control, and obstacles (Egan, 1985). The consultant and the consultee must determine the adequacy of available resources for accomplishing the goal. Thus, a mental health consultant whose consultee is a teacher may have to determine whether the school has the resources needed to help the teacher's emotionally disturbed student (client).

The consultant should ensure that the consultee has some control over whether or not the goal is met in this changing process (Egan, 1985). For example, a mental health consultant should assist a counselor (consultee) to set goals for the client's therapy in terms of the counselor's behavior, not the client's.

Obstacles to the accomplishment of any goal must be expected. Thus, for example, even though a consultant and consultee may have chosen as a goal the accomplishment of a treatment plan for the consultee's client, the client may not be willing to attend the number of counseling sessions required for effective implementation of the plan. The consultant and consultee should try to anticipate and neutralize any obstacles to the successful accomplishment of a goal.

Worthwhile goals are meaningful to the people involved in achieving them; they are considered to be worth the effort required to accomplish them.

The consultant and consultee must determine if the goal is adequate for achieving what is sought. Having a goal of improved communication among organizational members may not be adequate if a more appropriate goal is improved leadership by administrators. Adequate goals are relevant to the problem, and their accomplishment substantially alleviates or solves the problem.

Goals reflect the values of the people attempting to accomplish them, and they should conform to the values of the consultant, consultee, client system, and the organization. Consultants may occasionally need to help consultees clarify their values in order to set effective goals. Further, consultants may also need to reflect upon their own values so that they do not inadvertently impose them on their consultees during this phase of the diagnostic process.

All goals require a reasonable time frame for their accomplishment, contrary to the following familiar story:

Client: "I want to lose fifty pounds."
Counselor: "By when would you like to lose the weight?"
Client: "Tomorrow."

The consultant must frequently rely on the consultee's opinions concerning how much time is realistically required for a given goal to be accomplished. This is particularly true to the degree that the consultant is not familiar with the client system.

The consultant and consultee should determine who else needs to be informed about goals. Clear communication about goals to parties-at-interest is essential to receiving the cooperation so crucial to the accomplishment of the goals, especially when the accomplished goals will affect many of the organization's members.

Avoiding Problems in Setting Goals

Consultants can assist their consultees in avoiding some of the problems in setting goals by:

1. minimizing the stress of attempting to achieve goals,
2. ensuring goal acceptance,
3. discussing goals in terms of accomplishment, and
4. pointing out various pitfalls in the process of setting goals.

Consultants can minimize the stress on consultees of attempting to achieve a goal by ensuring that goals are clear and that the consultee's self-esteem is enhanced if the goal is accomplished (Locke & Latham, 1984).

Goal acceptance is critical for the goal-setting process to be effective. By providing support to the consultee, the consultant can be very instrumental in the consultee's acceptance of the goals (Locke & Latham, 1984).

Because goals are outcomes that are to be accomplished in the future and that provide direction for problem solving, it is desirable to talk about them in terms of accomplishment (Gilbert, 1978; Egan, 1985). An example of a goal stated in accomplishment terms is "successful change in client system behavior *made*."

To help their consultees avoid ineffective attempts to accomplish goals, consultants can point out the following ways to avoid the common pitfalls in setting goals (Locke & Latham, 1984):

1. Avoid taking excessive risks.
2. Avoid unnecessary stress.
3. View failure as an opportunity to learn.
4. Accomplish the goal beyond minimum standards when appropriate.
5. Consider important factors related to accomplishment of the goal (for example, how people affected by the goal's completion view that outcome).
6. If possible, relate the goal-setting process to long-term planning.
7. Create conditions such that personnel attempting to achieve the goal feel free to relate honestly progress toward the goal's accomplishment.

In summary, goal setting is the process of determining what ends are to be achieved during consultation; it is central to the diagnostic process. In the first step of setting goals, possible goals are determined through creative activities such as brainstorming and using fantasy. Then the possible goals are examined through several goal-setting activities like prioritizing goals and determining how factors affecting the accomplishment of goals may be coordinated. Finally, the selected goal is evaluated in terms of the characteristics of effective goals.

PHASE FOUR: GENERATING POSSIBLE INTERVENTIONS

Once the consultant and consultee have chosen an acceptable goal, they are ready to enter the last phase of the diagnosis stage—generating possible interventions to accomplish the goal.

Like goal setting, generating possible interventions is a critical step in the diagnostic stage. Whereas the goal suggests what the consultant and consultee want to accomplish, interventions are things they can do to accomplish that goal. An *intervention* is a force that attempts to modify some outcome. In consultation, interventions are the actions or activities that, when put together in a systematic manner, make up a plan to achieve a goal.

It would be a mistake for the consultant to assume that because consultees know what goals they want to accomplish, they also know all of the ways to go about accomplishing them. By discussing alternative interventions, consultants can ascertain both the consultee's knowledge of various types of interventions and what the consultee has tried so far to solve the problem.

Consultants can assist their consultees in generating possible interventions by using prompts (stimuli or reminders) that stimulate the consultee's creativity. These prompts include (Egan, 1986):

1. *people* who might assist the consultee in achieving goals, such as resource people or role models (for example, a program evaluator for a newly implemented program);

2. *places* that might be more appropriate for implementing a plan (for example, an off-campus location for a faculty retreat);
3. *things* that may lead to an easier way of accomplishing a goal (for example, computer technology for a proposed corporate reorganization);
4. *organizations* that could sponsor or assist the consultee in some way (for example, a private charitable foundation to provide funding for a pilot program);
5. *prepackaged programs* whose goals are similar to the consultee's (for example, a stress management program for teachers at a school); and
6. *consultee resources* that can be used to a large degree to generate possible interventions, particularly when the consultee is going to carry out the intervention that is ultimately selected (for example, the consultee is the counselor for a client about whom a goal has been set).

Brainstorming is a powerful strategy that consultants can use to help consultees generate a list of possible interventions (Maier, 1970; Pfeiffer & Jones, 1974; Summers & White, 1980). Such a technique assists the consultant and consultee to go beyond the usual consideration of only one or two alternatives in choosing an intervention (Carlisle, 1982). Whenever a consultee's work-related problem has some unknown factors and some uncertainty about the best way to solve it, it is appropriate to take the time necessary to generate and analyze a list of alternative interventions (Carlisle, 1982). By following the steps listed below, consultants can increase the probability that consultees will generate an adequate list of possible interventions. The rules of brainstorming include (Pfeiffer & Jones, 1974):

1. Do not evaluate strategies as they are being generated.
2. Generate as many interventions as possible.
3. Creativity and novelty are at a premium when generating a list of possible interventions.

Once the consultee understands the ground rules, the consultant and consultee brainstorm for an agreed-upon time period (for example, five minutes). The consultant and consultee should write down or tape-record interventions as they come to mind. After the brainstorming period, the consultant and consultee reconsider and clarify each item on the list. At the completion of this clarification process, a list of possible interventions has been generated.

If the consultee is unfamiliar with the brainstorming process, it is a good idea for the consultant to provide some practice sessions first. For example, the consultant and consultee could brainstorm ways people could stay dry after being caught out in the rain. Brainstorming does not replace the sound professional judgment of either the consultant or the consultee. Rather, it is simply a technique to enhance the quantity and quality of inputs into the decision-making process (Summers & White, 1980). Consultants should be aware that brainstorming is very demanding intellectually, for users of such techniques must consider the future, examine complex situations, recall previous experiences, and use creativity (Mitchell, 1978).

Consider the following example of a session for generating possible interventions:

CASE STUDY:
A school psychologist is consulting with a high school counselor. They have agreed that the goal of consultation is to alleviate the test anxiety of an international student. To bring to mind possible interventions, the school psychologist asks the school counselor questions, including the following:

> "Who do you think can assist you in your work with this student?"
> "What do you think is the best setting for working with the student?"
> "What things such as audiotapes and booklets might be available for you to use with the student?"
> "Are any organizations that work with international students available to be of help?"
> "Do you know of any companies who have prepackaged programs for test anxiety or for helping international students get acclimatized to American schools?"
> "What professional abilities do you have that you can use directly with the student?"

During the diagnostic stage, then, the consultant and consultee collect data, identify problems, set goals, and develop possible interventions. During the goal-setting phase, consultees can determine the relative importance of various potential goals by utilizing consultant feedback (Vroom, 1964). While developing possible interventions, consultees may experience conflict and uncertainty about having so many possible courses of action, typically because the majority of the possible interventions appear to be equally effective in reaching a desired goal (Ashford & Cummings, 1983). Therefore, the consultant may need to assist the consultee in selecting some of the better alternatives.

SUMMARY

Diagnosis is a critical stage in consultation. If the wrong problem is defined, then the wrong problem is solved! During this stage, the consultant and consultee collaborate in gathering information by various means, in defining a problem from that information, in setting a goal to resolve that problem, and then in generating some possible interventions to accomplish that goal. Diagnosis should not be rushed; consultants should encourage their consultees to remain patient and avoid the tendency to hastily define the problem.

This stage of consultation requires that the consultant and consultee gather the appropriate information necessary for defining the problem. To do this effectively, the consultant and consultee need to know both what information they seek and the methods by which they are going to gather it. Each method of data gathering—records, questionnaires and surveys, interviews, and observation—has its advantages and disadvantages. The consultant and consultee must weigh the pros and cons of each method in order to choose the best method for a given purpose. Further, the consultant and consultee need to analyze the data using some valid method that is consistent with the goal of consultation. Both quantitative and qualitative methods can be used in defining the problem.

Once the problem has been defined to the satisfaction of the parties involved, goal setting is initiated. Goal setting, like all phases of diagnosis, should be collaborative to enhance the likelihood that the consultee will obtain an effective set of diagnostic skills for future use.

Upon the completion of goal setting, the consultant and consultee generate a list of possible interventions. This is one of the more creative phases of diagnosis, and it is also one of the most difficult because consultees frequently consider several possible interventions to be equally effective. A major goal of the consultant during this phase is to assist the consultee in developing an adequate number of possible interventions.

QUESTIONS FOR REFLECTION

1. What do you envision as the most difficult phase of diagnosis for you to function in? Why?
2. Which ten skills are most needed by consultants to increase the chances that the diagnosis stage will be successful?
3. In which of the skills that you listed in question 2 above do you think most of your consultees will be deficient? Why?
4. What is the most practical way to scan a presenting problem? How would you determine what to scan?
5. How can you best teach consultees to enhance their skills in diagnosis?
6. Which methods of gathering information would you be most likely to use? Why?
7. Once the data have been collected, how does a consultant go about assisting a consultee in defining a problem?
8. Of the characteristics of effective goals mentioned in this chapter, which do you think are typically the most difficult to meet?
9. How would you assist a consultee in generating a list of several possible interventions?
10. You have now read about the entry and diagnosis stages of consultation. In what ways does the diagnosis stage build upon a successfully completed entry stage?

SUGGESTED SUPPLEMENTARY READINGS

Egan , G. (1985). *Change agent skills in helping and human service settings.* Pacific Grove, CA: Brooks/Cole. This is an excellent text that takes a systems approach to change agentry. Chapter 6, entitled "Clear and Realistic Goals," provides broad coverage of the topic of goal setting. I strongly recommend this chapter. Another excellent chapter is Chapter 3 on data gathering.

Margulies, N., & Raia, A. P. (Eds.). (1972). *Organizational development: Values, process, and technology.* New York : McGraw-Hill. Although somewhat dated, this is perhaps one of the most comprehensive texts on organizational development. A chapter each is provided on data gathering by questionnaire, survey, and observation. There is also an excellent chapter on diagnosis in organizations.

Nadler, D. A. (1977). *Feedback and organization development: Using data-based methods.* Reading, MA: Addison-Wesley. This book discusses the use of data as a tool for change in organizations. It provides coverage of the use of records, questionnaires, interviews, and observation in data gathering. This small book presents a wealth of information, including two chapters on feedback.

Chapter

5

Implementation Stage

PREVIEW

Consider for a moment the following:

CASE STUDY:
A staff development coordinator in a human services organization has been working with a consultant on some of the organization's concerns about improving the quality of the work environment within the organization. The coordinator's immediate superior calls the coordinator in and asks what progress has been made with the consultant. The coordinator indicates that the problem has been identified, explored, and analyzed. Further, several prospective interventions have been identified. The supervisor then asks what the next steps will be. The staff development coordinator replies that a plan will be formulated and the logistics of implementing it worked out. The plan will then be put into action and evaluated. The supervisor then asks for a time frame within which all of this will occur.

This sequence of events is quite common in consultation. Many times people within the organization in which consultation is occurring have relatively little idea about how complex and time-consuming effective consultation is. The staff development coordinator was in essence telling the supervisor that consultation had progressed to the implementation stage. She and the consultant had devised and were ready to choose among several possible interventions, formulate a plan, tailor it to the organization's needs, put it into action, and then evaluate the degree to which it worked.

This chapter covers the implementation stage of consultation. Clearly, good planning is essential to successful consultation, yet it is very easy to neglect. Because every plan has its advantages and disadvantages and possible glitches, there is no one best plan, but rather a plan that has the highest probability of succeeding.

As you read through this chapter, here are some questions to consider:

1. How does a consultant assist a consultee in choosing the most appropriate intervention or interventions from among those generated at the end of the diagnosis stage?

2. What are the pros and cons of the various types of interventions?
3. How do the consultant and consultee tailor the chosen plan to the organization in which it is to be implemented?
4. What is the consultant's role in implementing the plan?
5. How can the consultant and consultee determine the degree to which the plan was successful?

INTRODUCTION

Consultants need to assist their consultees in taking some action to solve the problem identified in the diagnosis stage. This "action stage" of consultation is implementation. The consultant often functions as a resource person and trainer during this stage. The various models of consultation (Chapters 9 through 11) may conceptualize the implementation process differently and use different types of interventions. An organizational consultant might spend a lot of time determining the level of the organization at which to intervene and then selecting an intervention appropriate to that level. A mental health consultant might carefully determine whether the problem in consultation is due to the consultee or to the client before identifying possible interventions. A behavioral consultant might determine which types of reinforcement are most effective with a given client and then choose an intervention that includes those types of reinforcements. Regardless of the model of consultation in use, however, the process of implementation remains the same.

IMPLEMENTATION

The implementation stage is composed of four phases: *choosing an intervention, formulating a plan, implementing the plan,* and *evaluating the plan.* Figure 5.1 illustrates the phases of the implementation stage.

In choosing an intervention, the consultant and consultee answer the question "What are we going to do?" In formulating a plan, they answer the question "How are we going to do it?" They actively try to solve the problem in the implementing the plan phase, and in evaluating the plan they ask "How did we do?"

As was the case in the entry and diagnosis stages, the implementation stage is critical in the consultation process: imagine the difficulties that would be encountered if an inappropriate plan were chosen for a given problem. The consultant and consultee would come up with the wrong solution for the right problem! Or if a proper plan were chosen but the wrong interventions were used, the consultant and consultee might have the right solution put together in the wrong way. (Even if the right solution were put together with the right interventions, the consultant and consultee might still make mistakes in implementing the plan.)

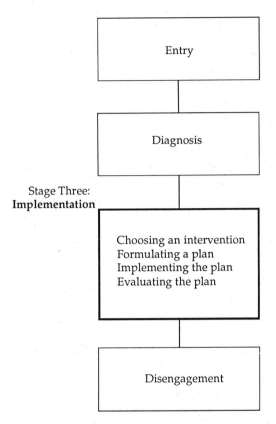

FIGURE 5.1 The Phases of the Implementation Stage

Now consider a situation in which the right plan, the right strategies, and correct implementation are combined, but the consultant and consultee failed to design an appropriate evaluation of the plan. In this situation, the consultant and consultee have the right plan, the right strategies, the correct implementation, but have no way of accurately determining the degree to which the plan actually worked. Clearly the implementation stage requires a large amount of effective planning by the consultant and consultee.

In the implementation stage the client or client system is now ready for some form of direct assistance from the consultee or indirect service from the consultant. The consultant must make sure that the consultee formulates an appropriate plan and correctly implements it; evaluating the plan is one of the consultant's highest priorities. The consultant may need to train the consultee in the interventions implemented during this stage; for example, a mental health consultant might need to train the consultee, a school psychologist, in a specific procedure for desensitizing a child with school phobia. As in other stages in the consultation process, consultants take a collaborative approach whenever possible and avoid doing anything for consultees that they can do for themselves.

The implementation stage is important to the consultee because it represents some action on the problem that prompted the consultee to request assistance in the first place. In this stage, the consultee either makes some intervention with a client system or benefits directly from some intervention by the consultant, who assumes that the experience will give the consultee useful skills for handling similar work-related concerns in the future.

PHASE ONE: CHOOSING AN INTERVENTION

The consultant and consultee have a large number of interventions available to them. As we noted in the previous chapter, consultees may experience conflict after several possible interventions have been generated because all of them look like "good" interventions. Therefore, the first phase of the implementation stage involves selecting one or more interventions that have a high probability of being successful.

One effective procedure the consultant can use in helping a consultee choose among possible interventions is decision counseling (Janis & Mann, 1977). Although developed for use in counseling and psychotherapy, this procedure is useful for ensuring that the consultee goes through the process of choosing an intervention in an appropriate manner. The process of *decision consultation*, which is based on effective decision making, consists of eight questions consultants can ask consultees. The following questions are adaptations of those developed by Janis and Mann (1977, p. 371):

1. To what degree has the consultee developed a wide range of alternative interventions?
2. To what degree has the consultee considered the objectives and related values of the possible interventions?
3. To what degree has the consultee weighed the potential negative consequences, risks, and potential payoffs of each possible intervention?
4. To what degree has the consultee searched for new information relative to each of the possible interventions?
5. To what degree has the consultee processed the consultant's comments about potential positive and negative factors related to the possible interventions?
6. To what degree has the consultee made a final determination of the possible interventions' potential positive and negative consequences, as well as the driving and inhibiting forces that affect their implementation?
7. To what degree does the consultee have the capacity to successfully execute the chosen intervention?
8. Which interventions have been set aside for use in contingency plans?

By engaging the consultee in the pursuit of answers to these questions, the consultant can help the consultee make a reasonably effective choice of interventions and can ascertain not only the degree to which the implementation appears satisfactory to the consultee, but also whether any adaptation of the intervention by the consultee will negatively affect its impact (Brown et al., 1987). The process involved in this kind of assistance can "rub off" on the consultee, who can then be more effective in choosing interventions for similar problems in the future.

Consultants should be aware of potential obstacles to the successful completion of this phase. First, the consultee and consultant must process a tremendous amount of information in selecting the intervention (Wheeler & Janis, 1980). Second, it is difficult to realistically predict the specific outcomes of various interventions due to the possibility of unforeseen events and potential human error (Wheeler & Janis, 1980). Therefore, the consultant should consider having the consultee keep a consistent, detailed set of notes concerning alternative interventions (to facilitate discussion about the possible impacts of given interventions).

Types of Interventions

CASE STUDY:
You are hungry, so you decide to go to a restaurant that offers a smorgasbord. As you walk through the smorgasbord, you have a very difficult time selecting from among the offerings because all of it looks so good! You decide that you should choose one item that is representative of each of the four food groups. So you choose one meat, one dairy product, one cereal product, and one green vegetable, and then you proceed to enjoy your meal.

You have, in effect, just classified all of your possible food choices into four categories and then chosen from each of these categories. By categorizing all your possible choices, you made your decision about what to eat much easier.

Indeed, consultants and consultees have a smorgasbord of interventions available to them. Therefore, consultants typically categorize all the possible interventions that might be put together in a plan. This categorization expedites the decision-making process by providing a framework into which to put possible interventions.

As we noted in the previous chapter, an intervention is a method through which change is sought in a problem situation. An intervention can be a single task, a series of related tasks, or a series of unrelated tasks organized around a common theme (French et al., 1978). One or more interventions can be put together systematically into a plan that is tailored to the unique problem that has been identified.

Effective consultants have a large number of interventions in their repertoire so that they can most effectively assist their consultees. Such expertise allows the consultant flexibility in combining programs to meet the goals of consultation. Hence, the effective consultant avoids approaching problems with a "pet" intervention. Do you know about the carpenter who could only use a hammer? He saw every problem as a nail to be hit! Consultants who do not have a knowledge of and skill in many types of interventions tend to conceptualize solutions in terms of what they know how to do instead of what is really needed.

A useful device for obtaining a broad perspective on interventions is a classification system (Kurpius, 1985). According to French and Bell (1984) and French and others (1978), interventions can be classified into the following categories:

1. families of interventions (for example, education/training activities);
2. types of interventions (for example, theory intervention);
3. mode of interventions (for example, problem-solving);
4. task vs. process interventions (for example, problem-solving vs. team-building);
5. target group of the intervention (for example, individual);
6. underlying causal mechanisms of the intervention that lead to change (for example, increased communication and interaction); and
7. depth of intervention (for example, anonymous questionnaire vs. personal interview).

A categorization of interventions based on target groups is a convenient one and is used in the following discussion. The target group is usually the client system. The following classification scheme, developed by French and Bell (1984), includes the following targets:

1. individuals,
2. dyads/triads,
3. teams and groups,
4. intergroup relations, and
5. total organization.

This classification scheme was developed for interventions in organizational consultation. However, it can easily be used as a generic classification system and can be useful to all consultants. Many interventions can focus on more than one target; some interventions, for example, can focus on both the individual and a team.

In summary, consultants and consultees can intervene at the individual level, at several group levels, or at the organizational level.

Individual Interventions

Because individual interventions can also be designed to assist the organization as a whole by improving the functioning of selected individual members of an organization (Kurpius, 1986), individual interventions can apply in a variety of consultation settings (Fuqua & Newman, 1985). The previous chapter discussed ways to determine when individual interventions are appropriate. Fuqua and Newman (1985) suggest that two general types of individual interventions are commonly used by consultants: consultee-focused intervention and educational/training interventions. In effect, all individual consultation interventions attempt to assist the consultee by alleviating one of four problem areas:

1. lack of knowledge,
2. lack of skill,
3. lack of confidence, and
4. lack of objectivity.

Consultee-focused interventions are used when the consultee is experiencing a work-related problem due to lack of objectivity or lack of confidence (Caplan, 1970), or lack of skill in problem solving and decision making (Fuqua & Newman, 1985). Educational/training methods are used when the consultee has a knowledge or skills deficit in a given area (Fuqua & Newman, 1985) or desires self-improvement in a given area (Parsons & Meyers, 1984).

Consultee-centered case consultation. This intervention is one approach to the mental health consultation model and is given in-depth coverage in Chapter 10. This approach suggests that the problem in consultation resides in the consultee (for example, some personal matter) rather than in the client and blocks any progress with the client (Caplan, 1970). Through use of indirect procedures, the consultant assists the consultee in regaining an objective view of the case. Once the consultee has gained objectivity with regard to the case, then the consultee-client helping relationship should proceed effectively.

Problem-solving/decision-making education/training. Because consultation is a problem-solving endeavor, consultees need at least marginal problem-solving skills if they are to generalize newly learned consultation skills to future work-related situations. Hence, consultants frequently must educate or train their consultees to approach work-related problems systematically through the enhancement of problem-solving and decision-making skills (Fuqua & Newman, 1985). For example, a human resource development specialist might assist a group of administrators in a community agency program deal with problems in the agency's strategic planning process.

Cognitive-restructuring. Consultees frequently need assistance from consultants because some work-related problem is due to erroneous cognitive functioning. That is, a problem exists because the consultee's thoughts about some event at work are "messed up." Consultants can assist consultees in recognizing and then modifying their cognitive distortions (McKay, Davis, & Fanning, 1981). Consider the following:

CASE STUDY:
The head of a substance abuse program at a mental health center erroneously assumes that the center's director is not adequately supporting the program. The resulting anger blocks the program head from adequately administering the program. The consultant attempts to change their erroneous thoughts and "cognitive distortions" so that the two can think more clearly about the work situation and engage in more productive problem solving.

Stress inoculation training. Another form of cognitive restructuring is stress inoculation training (Meichenbaum, 1977, 1985). In this approach, the consultee is taught to recognize debilitating "self-talk" about the work situation and to replace it with coping "self-talk." Through this process, consultants can assist their consultees to change their internal dialogue and create a more positive frame of reference concerning work-related concerns.

Stress inoculation training is analogous to the way vaccine inoculations build a person's medical defenses. Through exposure to mild doses of stressful situations and by rehearsing positive responses to these situations, consultees learn how to build more effective coping defenses to use with work-related concerns. Too frequently, consultees see stressful situations as all-or-nothing demands (for example, totally cure the client or no progress has occurred); through stress inoculation training, consultees learn to take a stressful situation and break it down into four phases (Meichenbaum, 1977):

1. preparing for a stressor,
2. confronting and handling a stressor,
3. coping with feelings of being overwhelmed, and
4. reinforcing self-statements.

Transactional analysis. Transactional analysis (TA) (Berne, 1961, 1964) is a frequently used intervention for individuals (French & Bell, 1978). TA is an educational approach that is designed to help consultees understand themselves, how they communicate with others, and the social roles they take on. TA is used as an intervention to assist consultees in learning to communicate and to analyze communications (that is, transactions among people) more effectively. TA can also assist consultees charged with management responsibilities to fulfill those responsibilities more effectively (James, 1975; Hunsaker & Alessandra, 1980).

Coaching and counseling. Coaching and counseling activities are interventions that help consultees define learning goals, become aware of how others perceive their behavior, and learn new behaviors that might help in achieving defined goals (French & Bell, 1978). The consultant makes these interventions only after the consultee has "owned" a work-related concern and is ready to improve his or her work-related performance (Schein, 1969). For example, a consultee might want to improve his or her listening skills at the work site. The consultant gathers feedback on the consultee from a variety of sources and, after providing the feedback, engages the consultee in a joint exploration of alternatives (French & Bell, 1978).

Lippitt (1982a) identifies five steps in the coaching/counseling process:

1. clarifying the functions, responsibilities, and authority of those involved in the coaching;
2. obtaining mutual agreement on what has just been clarified;
3. identifying the specific areas for coaching;
4. seeking out causes of the work-related concerns and developing alternatives; and
5. determining developmental activities that can be subjected to ongoing evaluation.

In the role of coach, a consultant assists consultees in deciding what they want to learn, helps them to learn those behaviors, and is instrumental in evaluating the degree to which those behaviors meet desired goals.

Life- and career-planning activities. Life- and career-planning activities are typically structured activities that help consultees examine courses of action in attempting to achieve their life and career goals (French & Bell, 1978).

Because career planning is part of life planning, both are typically performed concurrently. Aimed at the individual's development, these activities usually take place in workshops that last from one day to a week. Topics frequently examined in life- and career-planning include clarification of life goals, acceptance of the life cycle, acceptance of one's strengths and limitations, and how to contribute to the next generation (Lippitt, 1982b).

Sensitivity training. Sensitivity training is an intervention in which individual consultees are trained to become more aware of how they come across to others (Bradford, Gibb, & Benne, 1964). Sensitivity training occurs in groups, even though its focus is on individual development; individuals learn about themselves through the group process (Rudestam, 1982). The underlying assumption of sensitivity training is that people are in control of their ability to communicate, and they relate to others to the degree to which they are aware of interpersonal processes and how they come across to others. Sensitivity training is very powerful, and individuals learn the meaning and consequences of their behavior during the three-day to two-week life of the group (French & Bell, 1978).

You may have heard some of the "horror stories" about sensitivity training—instances in which group members' defenses were broken down without any attempt to provide more viable alternatives (House, 1978; Cohen, Fink, & Gadon, 1979). Some of these stories are undoubtably true. However, those group members who were casualties typically were not victims of sensitivity training, but rather of poor group leaders (Lieberman, Yalom, & Miles, 1973; Lakin, 1978).

Dyadic and Triadic Interventions

A dyad is a pair, a triad a group of three. Sometimes consultants are called upon to make interventions that are most effective with dyads or triads. Interventions aimed at these small groups are limited but popular due to frequent use of dyadic and triadic work groups in human services organizations. Some of the types of interventions that are useful with individuals (for example, TA) can be used to increase effectiveness of dyads and triads. Further, many of the interventions typically aimed at large groups, such as team building, are appropriate for use with these small groups. Next we'll consider third-party peacemaking, an intervention that is unique to dyads and triads.

Third-party peacemaking. Conflict is common in most organizations. Usually, conflict stems from parties' different perspectives on the same events. A strong cultural bias for avoidance of dealing with conflict exists in human services organizations (Carlisle, 1982). Differences between two consultees can be effectively dealt with in a variety of ways, including third-party peacemaking (Main & Roark, 1975; Eiseman, 1977), which, as its name implies, is used to resolve interpersonal conflict (Walton, 1969, 1978).

The consultant guides a process in which two or three consultees directly confront one another and use conflict resolution techniques (French & Bell, 1978; Fisher & Ury, 1981). The term *third party* refers to the consultant, who presumably is skilled and objective in terms of the conflict's resolution or management. (A consultant who helps the members of a triad resolve a conflict would be the "fourth party.")

Interventions for Groups and Teams

Organizations make extensive use of teams and groups (French & Bell, 1978), and consultants frequently are called on to make interventions to enhance the effectiveness of an intact group or a team. Interventions with groups or teams can be one of the most powerful of consultant interventions (Kurpius, 1985). The most common group or team interventions include:

1. the education/training approach (covered extensively in Chapter 9);
2. team-building procedures;
3. the nominal group technique (NGT) (Delbecq, Van de Ven, & Gustafson, 1975), a group decision-making techique for use with one or more groups; and
4. quality circles, a special type of work group that can be considered a group intervention (Kurpius, 1985).

Team building.   A team is a group of individuals working together in a coordinated effort (Dyer, 1977). Team building is the process by which a team's individuals attempt to improve the group's functioning through analyzing and evaluating their interactions (Beckhard, 1978; Lippitt, 1982a). The term *team building* came about because selected interventions lead to increases in team cohesiveness and effectiveness (French et al., 1978). The consultant is *not* a member of the team with which he or she is working (French & Bell, 1978).

During team building the consultant is typically a facilitator and a collaborator (Wigtil & Kelsey, 1978). The consultant can assist the team in determining how it should proceed, developing short- and long-term goals, creating teamwork, strengthening interpersonal relationships among members, and designing and using instruments to assess team performance and progress (Lippitt, 1982a). Special attention is paid to how the team's various members use power (Harrison, 1978b).

Nominal group technique.   The nominal group technique (NGT) (Delbecq et al., 1975) is a group problem-solving process designed specifically for engendering the members' involvement and creativity. The NGT is based on two assumptions: that all group members need only the proper encouragement to induce them to express their ideas and that the exchange of ideas and group decision making contribute to greater acceptance of decisions by the individuals involved.

The nominal group technique is a structured problem-solving meeting with a "one-person-one-vote" orientation; superiors and subordinates alike have equal status in the NGT. The technique yields a large quantity of high quality, specific ideas and encourages independent thinking by participants. The process is highly motivating, and participants experience the satisfaction of task accomplishment as well as the social reinforcement of having worked effectively together (Delbecq et al., 1975). The consultant acts as a facilitator of the problem-solving process, as well as a taskmaster who ensures that the steps of the NGT process are completed (Collison & Dunlap, 1978; Sandland & Dougherty, 1985).

Quality circles.   Quality circles are small problem-solving groups (Kurpius, 1985) whose members are typically from the same work area. The group meets for one to two hours per week to discuss concerns, investigate the sources of those concerns, make recommendations, and take authorized corrective action. The objective of quality circles is to create improvement in work quality, productivity, and motivation (Dewar, 1980).

The consultant's primary role with regard to quality circles is educating and training potential members and administrators in the ways quality circles work. In almost every case, the extent of the consultant's involvement is to recommend quality circles as ways administrators can help groups become more effective. For example, a human services consultant might suggest that a social services agency's chief administrator use a quality circle of staff members for the purpose of analyzing methods of outreach to the community.

Interventions for Use Between Groups

Human service organizations are made up of several groups that interact with and affect one another. One group frequently experiences tension or conflict with one or more other groups within the same organization. Consultants can assist groups in conflict to relate more effectively with one another by using strategies designed to alleviate group conflict. Two or more interdependent groups are put together as a single unit and engage in joint activities (French & Bell, 1978). Interventions between groups typically use analysis and discussion to confront the reasons for conflict (Ivancevich, Szilagyi, & Wallace, 1977).

The two major types of intergroup interventions—intergroup team building and organizational mirroring—work because the interactions between the groups are controlled and structured to maintain control (French & Bell, 1978). All information is shared between groups—there are no secrets—and the consultant engenders a spirit of constructive problem solving (French & Bell, 1978).

Intergroup team building.   Intergroup team building activities attempt to improve the communication and cooperation between two groups, reduce inappropriate group competition, and develop recognition of the interdependency of the groups (French & Bell, 1978; Kurpius, 1985). The accomplishment of these tasks can lead to more harmonious functioning within and between the groups (Goodstein, 1978).

The consultant's roles are primarily those of a process facilitator and a rule enforcer (Blake, Shepard, & Mouton, 1965). The consultant avoids adding content to the discussions between the two groups and refuses to make specific recommendations of a problem-solving nature. For example, a human services consultant might work with a mental health center to assist its crisis intervention team and its substance abuse team in deciding how clients are to be referred to either team.

Organizational mirroring. When the increased effectiveness of three or more groups is desired, organizational mirroring is frequently used (French & Bell, 1978). In this technique, one group, called the host group, receives feedback from other groups about the ways it is perceived; the technique's goal is change in the host group. To keep the number of participants manageable, representatives of each of the groups, rather than the entire membership of each group, are involved (Fordyce & Weil, 1971). As in intergroup team building, the consultant acts as the process's facilitator, enforcer of norms, and coordinator. As an example, a consultant might lead while a group of school counselors (host team) receives feedback from select groups of administrators and staff on their perceptions of the counseling department's programs.

Interventions for the Entire Organization

Interventions that attempt to enhance an entire organization's effectiveness are called *organizational interventions.* A large number of organizational interventions, ranging from culture-building activities and management by objectives to survey feedback and process consultation, are available to consultants. Many interventions used primarily at the organizational level also can be used as intergroup and team interventions. Consultants who intervene at the organizational level must be experts in organizational theory and dynamics, in addition to having the basic skills required of all consultants. The most common organizational interventions include:

1. process consultation,
2. survey feedback/action research,
3. collateral organization, and
4. management by objectives (MBO).

Process consultation. Because *process consultation* is covered in detail in Chapter 9, it will be described only briefly here. Process consultation was developed by Edgar Schein (1969) as a set of activities that help consultees recognize, comprehend, and act on the "process events" occurring within the organization. Process events include a variety of occurrences: how people communicate, who talks to whom and how frequently, how problems are solved and decisions made. The consultant's role is primarily that of facilitator (Schein, 1969). By assisting the consultee with a defined work-related problem, the consultant acts in such a manner that members of the organization learn the problem-solving skills necessary to solve its problems in the future.

Survey feedback/action research. *Survey feedback/action research* owes much of its development to the social psychologist Kurt Lewin (1945, 1951). Survey feedback/action research is an intervention designed to systematically collect data about some system (through surveys and/or interviews), analyze the data, and feed results back to appropriate personnel in workshop settings (Ivancevich et al., 1977). The problem is diagnosed and action steps planned during the workshop meetings (French & Bell, 1978). One underlying assumption of this approach is that whatever discrepancies are noted from interpreting the data will create the motivation to change things (Goodstein, 1978). Another underlying assumption is that ongoing feedback is necessary to keep the organization on course in terms of its role and mission (Gallessich, 1982).

The survey feedback/action research approach takes on a cyclical approach: research, data collection, feedback, planning, action, and evaluation (Frohman, Sashkin, & Kavanagh, 1978). Depending on the outcome of evaluation, the process may be repeated.

Collateral organization. One common organizational intervention consultants can recommend is the collateral organization. A *collateral organization* is a small organization within the existing organization. It is very much like a task force except that it is permitted to work outside the existing norms of the larger organization. This license to create its own norms allows the collateral organization the freedom necessary to attack problems that are "ill-structured" (Zand, 1978, p. 293) and thus difficult for the larger organization to solve. This intervention is used with high-priority, systemwide problems that involve people from more than one section of the organization (French et al., 1978). Its primary purpose is to increase the organization's flexibility in problem-solving endeavors (Zand, 1978).

The consultant's role with regard to collateral organizations is to act as a resource person to administrators considering their use and to the members of the collateral organization itself. Typically the consultant does not meet formally with the collateral group except on an as-needed basis.

Management by objectives (MBO). *Management by objectives* (MBO) is a structural intervention in which the focus is on work performance objectives and increased frequency of problem-solving discussions between subordinates and superiors (French & Bell, 1978; Levinson, 1978). MBO is an attempt to integrate individual and organizational goals while increasing the motivation levels of the organization's members (Kurpius, 1985). Because subordinates set goals and then review them with superiors, motivation is increased. Progress toward the goals is assessed at regularly designated times, which provides subordinates ongoing feedback. MBO works most effectively when it is used with teams rather than individuals because of the interdependence of group members' responsibilities (French & Bell, 1978).

In summary, consultants can assist entire organizations through interventions that focus on how things are done (as in process consultation) or that focus on changing the organization's structure (as in collateral organization). Regardless of the nature of the intervention, the goal is the same: increased effectiveness of the entire organization.

PHASE TWO: FORMULATING A PLAN

Once the consultant and consultee have been able to decide on one or more interventions that have a high probability of helping meet the goal that has been developed, they begin *formulating a plan.*

A *plan* refers to a detailed step-by-step method, formulated beforehand, for doing something. It is critical in this planning phase that the consultant emphasize the collaborative nature of consultation to ensure that the consultee has a ready-made commitment to the plan (Parsons & Meyers, 1984). It is usually best for the consultant and consultee to formulate a few possible plans and then choose the plan that appears to have the highest probability of succeeding.

Good plans shape successful consultation outcomes (Bittel, 1972). With the proper plan, the consultant and consultee can identify and gather the appropriate resources and dramatically increase the probability of successful consultation outcomes. When formulating a plan, the consultant and consultee should take the following into consideration (Bittel, 1972):

1. the what (that is, objectives);
2. the where (that is, locale of the implementation);
3. the when (that is, time frame for plan's steps);
4. the how (that is, methods, procedures, sequence); and
5. the who (that is, who is responsible for which things).

By considering the what, where, when, how, and who, the consultant and consultee can more effectively make a plan. The following lists the steps in plan formulation:

1. Determine the objectives;
2. Establish the procedure;
3. Set a timetable;
4. Assign responsibility;
5. Refine each step; and
6. Test for feasibility (for example, adequate resources), cost effectiveness (for example, weigh costs vs. payoffs), and capability (for example, the consultee's abilities).

Plan formulation is a complex activity that requires time to accomplish adequately. The consultant and consultee first determine the plan's objectives, choose its procedures and establish the time frame in which it is to be carried out. Next, they assign responsibility for carrying out each part of the plan. Each step is scrutinized again and adjusted as necessary. Finally, they assess the plan in terms of its feasibility, cost effectiveness, and capability of succeeding.

Consultants and consultees should adhere to several principles of formulating plans (Egan, 1985). Plans should be clearly linked to the established goals; a connection must exist between what the consultant and consultee want to accomplish and how they are going to accomplish it. A variety of plans to accomplish set goals should be constructed and examined. Brainstorming (Maier, 1970) is a helpful procedure for generating a variety of plans. Plans should be evaluated in terms of the criteria of effectiveness, efficiency, and ability to meet human needs. Steps in plans should be viewed as subgoals and measures taken to see that the subgoals meet the criteria of effective goals. The plans should each have a reasonable time frame for completion and be sufficiently detailed. Finally, plans should be examined in terms of their feasibility as contingency plans.

Once plans have been formulated, the consultant and consultee must choose a plan. One common way of choosing the best plan is force-field analysis. *Force-field analysis* is a method of determining the driving and restraining forces affecting the accomplishment of some goal (Lewin, 1951). Restraining forces inhibit movement toward a plan's successful implementation and driving forces support the plan's successful outcome. Force-field analysis helps consultees gain perspective on possible plans' pitfalls and strong points, and such awareness allows consultees to adapt plans to the specific settings in which clients are being served.

The several approaches to force-field analysis (for example, Lewin, 1951; Lippitt & Lippitt, 1986; Egan, 1986; Parsons & Meyers, 1984) are similar enough that consultants and consultees can use any of them to identify forces affecting each plan generated.

In using force-field analysis for assisting consultees in determining restraining and driving forces, the consultant has the consultee review each plan that has been generated. For each plan, the major restraining and driving forces, identified by brainstorming, are listed (Parsons & Meyers, 1984). The forces are then examined in detail and, depending on the plan, one or more restraining and driving forces are identified for modification. The forces chosen should be ones over which the consultee has some control. The consultee and consultant then brainstorm possible ways to minimize the selected restraining forces and maximize the selected driving forces. This force-field analysis process is repeated for each of the possible plans. The consultant and consultee then go over the plans and look at the relative weights of the restraining forces versus those of the driving forces. Those plans whose restraining forces outweigh their driving forces are discarded first. Then, from the remaining plans in which the driving forces outweigh the restraining forces, a plan along with a backup contingency plan is chosen. Specific adaptations of the plan to the unique needs of the client or client system are worked out.

In addition to using techniques such as force-field analysis, the consultant and consultee can work together to create a checklist (Bittel, 1972) in order to avoid the following pitfalls, which frequently contribute to the failure of plans (Kurpius, 1985):

1. trying to accomplish too much;
2. formulating too large a plan;
3. overanalyzing the plan, which causes disinterest and resistance;
4. underanalyzing the plan and failing to anticipate pertinent problems;
5. failing to consider the plan's systemwide impact;
6. inadequately defining the plan's desired outcomes; and
7. failing to consider the "human-side factors" (Kurpius, 1985, p. 385).

As a final safeguard the consultant and consultee may want to "walk through" the process one time to see who is affected in what ways by the plan. This technique is often referred to as "anticipatory rehearsal" (Lippitt & Lippitt, 1986, p. 21).

In summary, in helping the consultee to choose a plan, the consultant helps the consultee to consider each plan's comprehensiveness and positive and negative consequences, as well as the adequacy of the consultee's information about each plan. Further, the consultant assists the consultee to integrate the consultant's input regarding the plans, to make a final check of each plan's potential positive and negative consequences and driving and inhibiting forces (using force-field analysis), and to assess the consultee's capacity to carry out plans and develop contingencies successfully.

Consider the following example of plan formulation:

CASE STUDY:
A school psychologist is consulting with a school principal about what type of in-school suspension program would be most appropriate for the school. The school psychologist and the administrator develop three possible plans for operating the program: a punitive approach, a "time-out" approach, and a counseling approach. The pros and cons of each approach are weighed, and the consultant makes sure that the administrator possesses adequate knowledge of and the basis for each plan. The consultant's input into the various plans is clarified and a force-field analysis is applied to each plan. Together they decide that the in-school suspension plan with a counseling focus is the best plan; the "time-out" approach is chosen as a contingency.

Once the consultant and consultee have chosen a preferred plan and a contingency plan, they are ready to begin implementing the plan.

PHASE THREE: IMPLEMENTING THE PLAN

Now that the consultee and consultant have narrowed down the possibilities and formulated a plan, they are ready for action. The plan designed in the previous phase is now put into operation, and the focus of consultation now turns to making sure that the plan is put into action in such a way that it gets the desired results.

Although putting a plan into action seems quite straightforward on the surface, it is actually a very complex process. And because it is rare when there are not one or more unforeseen circumstances that arise when the plan is put into effect, the consultant and consultee should be flexible in adjusting the plan in light of unanticipated events (Bittel, 1972). The consultant should reassure the consultee that events sometimes get in the way of the plan's implementation and that most often this is due to factors in the complex environment in which all interventions must eventually be made.

The consultant can increase the probability of successful plan implementation by providing tactical assistance. *Tactics* is ". . . the art of adapting a plan (program) to the immediate situation" (Egan, 1985, p. 132). Tactics includes changing the plan on short notice, and therefore consultants should consider maintaining contact with consultees during the implementation phase so that they can provide needed tactical consultation.

Because the consultant and consultee made plans jointly, it is reasonable to assume that the consultee may welcome contact with the consultant during implementation (Conoley & Conoley, 1982). Such contact can be in the form of technical assistance (for example, plan revision) and/or emotional and cognitive support (for example, encouraging the consultee to take risks) (Brown et al., 1987).

Some consultants monitor the consultee's intervention efforts through a series of brief interviews and/or observations of the consultee during the implementation process (Bergan, 1977). When consultants have contact with consultees during plan implementation, they can obtain some data from the consultee concerning the effectiveness of the intervention; this data could range from a description of the consultee's and client's behavior during the intervention to measurements of changes in the client. A note of caution: during the implementation phase the consultant must exercise care to prevent excessive dependency in some consultees who may inadvertently rely too heavily on the consultant's expertise (Lippitt & Lippitt, 1986). For example, a school counselor consulting with a teacher might judiciously use questions to stimulate the teacher to take more responsibility for implementing the plan.

PHASE FOUR: EVALUATING THE PLAN

After the plan has been implemented, it must also be evaluated. *Evaluating the plan* is a part of a larger evaluation effort that assesses the effectiveness of the consultation process.

Although evaluation is frequently performed only toward the end of the consultation process, it is really an ongoing process. Pertinent data should be collected throughout implementation of the plan so that questions concerning evaluation can be accurately answered (Conoley & Conoley, 1982). Evaluation of the plan, like evaluation of the consultation process, is frequently considered to be out of the realm of expertise of the typical consultant and consultee (Parsons & Meyers, 1984). However, consultants are increasingly being held accountable for the quality of their services. Consultants must at least be able to evaluate their own interventions (Gallessich, 1982), and they should also assist in evaluating their consultees' plans.

Outcomes can be measured in terms of what happened to the client or client system as a result of some program. The consultant and consultee have a variety of instruments and techniques available for this purpose, but basically there are three ways to evaluate a plan's outcome (Anderson, Frieden, & Murphy, 1977):

1. individualized goal attainment measures,
2. standardized outcome assessment devices, and
3. consumer satisfaction surveys.

Individualized goal attainment measures are ". . . techniques whereby the efficacy of services is measured according to criteria that have been specifically tailored to the needs, capacities, and aspirations of the person(s) receiving services" (Anderson et al., 1977, p. 293). One example of an individualized goal attainment measure is concrete goal setting used with goal-oriented progress notes (Anderson et al., 1977). Ideally the consultant and consultee have already performed concrete goal setting during the diagnosis stage of consultation. Plan evaluation then becomes a simple procedure of determining the degree to which each goal was accomplished. For example, if the plan called for the client to reduce the number of cigarettes smoked from 40 to 6 a day, then it is relatively easy to monitor the degree to which this goal is being met.

Measurement of individualized goal attainment is often accomplished through goal attainment scaling. In this technique, the dimensions representing desired changes in client behavior are scaled (for example, from a "1" = minimally attained to a "5" = totally attained), expected levels of attainment set, and scores determined at the end of the plan's implementation.

Standardized outcome assessment devices measure the accomplishment of goals through some norm- or criterion-referenced device. Checklists and ratings scales are typically used in consultation (Anderson et al., 1977). For example, if a consultee assessed a client's career maturity on a standardized instrument and later retested the client on the same measure, the client's progress toward the goal of increased career maturity could be ascertained by the differences between the scores.

Consumer satisfaction surveys attempt to assess the opinions and attitudes of the client or client system regarding the services and effects of the plan provided to them (Anderson et al., 1977). These data, typically gathered through an interview or questionnaire, are quite subjective and of questionable validity if used as the only indicator of the plan's success. Yet, the client input regarding the plan's effectiveness can provide valuable assessment information.

SUMMARY

The implementation stage of consultation consists of choosing an intervention, formulating a plan, implementing the plan, and evaluating it. In this stage, the consultant provides the consultee with practical assistance to meet the goals set to help the client or client system. By asking a series of questions, the consultant assists the consultee in choosing an intervention that has a high probability of being successful.

A vast number of interventions are available for use in plans. Interventions can be categorized in a variety of ways, but classification by target level is the most common. Targets for these interventions include individuals, dyads/triads, groups and teams, and the entire organization. Interventions typically focus on improving the efficiency of the institution in which the consultees work by increasing the effectiveness of the level that is the target of intervention. Many interventions are effective with more than one level.

The role of the consultant in interventions can range from that of facilitator to that of trainer/educator. Consultants need to make sure that they have expertise in the interventions they are making and that they stay continually abreast of the burgeoning number of interventions available to them. The level at which a consultant intervenes depends upon the nature of the consultation problem, the resources the organization is willing to invest, and the organization's ability to effectively deal with the results of consultation.

A plan is a step-by-step method, determined beforehand, for accomplishing some goal. Once the appropriate intervention or interventions are chosen, consultants help consultees formulate and choose an appropriate plan. During plan implementation, the consultant provides the consultee tactical assistance and also monitors consultee procedures for implementing the plan. After the plan has been implemented, evaluation is performed to assess the degree to which the plan was effective in realizing its goals. Once the plan has been evaluated, the consultant and consultee determine whether consultation to work on the defined problem should continue. If the plan is considered to have worked satisfactorily, consultation moves to its next stage—disengagement.

QUESTIONS FOR REFLECTION

1. What is unique about the consultant's behavior during the implementation stage?
2. How would you as a consultant help a consultee choose an appropriate intervention?
3. Look over the interventions discussed in this chapter. How many of them could be used at more than one level?
4. Which of the interventions for individuals have the most danger of turning from consultation into counseling/psychotherapy? Why?
5. Which of the interventions described in this chapter could be most effectively implemented by a group of consultants rather than by one consultant? Why?
6. What are some ways in which consultants can learn new interventions?
7. Under what circumstances would you monitor a consultee's implementation of a plan?
8. What kinds of tactical assistance might most consultees require during plan implementation?
9. What are the basic differences between plan evaluation and evaluation of the process of consultation?
10. What should the consultant and consultee do if the evaluation of the plan indicates that little success in meeting the plan's goal was achieved?

SUGGESTED SUPPLEMENTARY READINGS

French, W. L., & Bell, C. H., Jr. (1984). *Organization development: Behavior science interventions for organization improvement* (3rd ed.). Englewood Cliffs, NJ:

Prentice-Hall. Chapters 9 through 14 of this book provide an interesting and practical overview of various interventions available to consultants. Of particular interest is the authors' discussion of the various ways in which interventions can be categorized. This book has become more or less a classic for consultants who work as "organizational consultants." Still, this book has a tremendous amount of information that any consultant in any setting will find invaluable.

French, W. L., Bell, C. H., Jr., & Zawacki, R. A. (Eds.). (1978). *Organization development: Theory, practice, and research*. Dallas, TX: Business Publications. Even though this book is written largely from the perspective of organization development, it provides a wealth of insight into and wisdom about the consultation process. Entire sections of the book are dedicated to specific interventions such as TA, collateral organizations, and many others. By reading some of the chapters in this book you can develop an increased appreciation for the complexity of organizations and the implications this complexity has for consultants who practice in organizations. In addition, you will benefit from a large number of practical case studies that demonstrate how interventions are used in "real-life situations." This is an excellent book for developing ideas on how to actually use various types of interventions.

Kurpius, D. J. (1985). Consultation interventions: Successes, failures, and proposals. *The Counseling Psychologist, 13*(3), 368–389. This article has two basic merits. The first is an updated summary of various intervention strategies available to consultants. Included are interventions aimed at individuals, groups, and organizations. The second merit of this article is its emphasis on the point that all interventions, regardless of their level of implementation, occur in some context, typically an organizational one. The author notes that interventions often fail because this organizational context is not properly taken into consideration. After reading this article you will be familiar with a broad range of possible consultant interventions and have some awareness of the time it takes to determine which intervention to choose in a given consultation problem.

Disengagement Stage

PREVIEW

If the entry stage is characterized by the question "Hello, what can I do for you?," then the disengagement stage is characterized by the question "What do we need to take care of before I say good-bye?"

Consider the following:

CASE STUDY:

You are a consultant who for two years has been working with a human services organization for an average of four hours a week. You have worked with several individual consultees, have done a lot of team building and organizational-level interventions, and have had your own office space and clerical assistance.

Leaving would not be as simple as packing your briefcase and walking out the door. What would you need to accomplish before you left? To whom would you say good-bye? How would you help the system plan to maintain the benefits of consultation after you have gone? How would you evaluate the process of consultation? What arrangements for follow-up would you make?

Consider this scenario in which disengagement is poorly done:

CASE STUDY:

You have worked very closely with a certain consultee who has assisted as your co-leader in many of the interventions you have made. Without any warning you announce to this consultee that, after two years of working together, today is your last day on the job and you wish the consultee the best of luck in the future. The consultee leaves the room in tears and slams the door. You wonder why the consultee is so upset, so you track the consultee down. As you discuss the situation you find out that the consultee has grown close to you over those two years and now resents being treated so impersonally; your decision to tell the consultee that you were leaving for good at the end of the day caused the resentment. The consultee feels that some weeks before you should have said when you were going to leave.

This situation—the process of taking leave—is called disengagement. It is saying "good-bye" to the consultee system and the people within it. Effective consultants consider both the human and the professional aspects of terminating the consultation process.

As you are reading the chapter, here are some questions to consider:

1. When does the process of disengagement really begin?
2. What kinds of things need to be taken into consideration during post-consultation planning?
3. What are the basic differences between evaluating the process of consultation and evaluating the plan in the implementation stage?
4. How would you arrange for follow-up with a consultee organization?
5. What effect does the length of time the consultant has spent with the consultee or organization have on what the consultant should do during the disengagement stage?

INTRODUCTION

Once the consultant and consultee have evaluated the plan, they must decide whether to continue or discontinue consultation. Typically, the decision to continue consultation results from an evaluation that indicates that the goal was not met satisfactorily. The consultant and consultee usually return to the end of the diagnostic stage and generate other possible interventions; occasionally, they may need to redefine the problem. In some other cases continued consultation may be needed because the consultee or organization has an additional work-related concern about which consultation is desired. In these cases, the consultation process typically reverts to exploring organizational needs in the entry stage.

DISENGAGEMENT

In the disengagement stage, the consultant and consultee *evaluate the consultation process, make plans for integrating the effects of consultation* into the system after the consultant leaves, go through a period of *reduced contact*, make provisions for *follow-up*, and *terminate* the consultation process itself. All decisions are made mutually by the consultant and consultee (Schein, 1969). In effect, the disengagement stage "winds down" what was "started up" in the entry stage.

In the first phase of the entry stage, exploring organizational needs, participants asked four basic questions:

1. Why am I here?
2. Who are you?
3. What will happen?
4. What will be the result?

Based on the answers to these questions, the consultant and consultee formulated a contract composed of formal and psychological aspects. Based on that contract, the consultant and consultee engaged in problem-solving activities such as formulating and implementing a plan. In order to participate in these activities, the consultant had to become a temporary part of the system.

In the disengagement stage the consultant proceeds to leave the system, and now these questions are phrased in the past tense and a new question is asked:

1. Why was I here?
2. Who were you?
3. What happened?
4. What were the results?
5. Given the answers to the above questions, what else needs to be done?

In answering the question "Why was I here?", the consultant and consultee review how they defined the problem and determined that the consultant was the right person for the job. The consultant reviews with the consultee the consultant's perceptions of the organization and describes any new perceptions that occurred as the consultation process progressed.

In responding to the question "Who were you?", the consultant and consultee review the roles played by the parties involved in or affected by the consultation process. The consultant and consultee review who engaged in what behaviors, who took responsibility for what, and how the resulting expectations were met.

In answering the question "What happened?", the consultant and consultee review the activities that occurred in the consultation process: how goals were set, how appropriate and adequate the goals were, and how they fit into the parameters of consultation.

In responding to the question "What were the results?", the consultant and consultee examine what changes occurred where, when, and under what circumstances, as well as the cost effectiveness of those changes. The resulting answers provide the basis for evaluating the consultation process.

The answer to "What else needs to be done?", the last question the consultant and consultee ask, provides the basis for postconsultation planning. By asking this question, the consultant makes it clear that he or she no longer will participate in this particular consultation process. This part of the process helps the consultee realize that the consultant is leaving and that it is the consultee's (and/or the consultee organization's) responsibility to follow through on the results of the consultation.

In summary, in the disengagement stage the consultant and consultee ask anew the questions they pondered early in the consultation process, and the answers to these questions provide a review of the consultation process. These questions are asked during this stage's four phases: evaluating the consultation process, planning postconsultation matters, reducing involvement and following up, and terminating (see Figure 6.1).

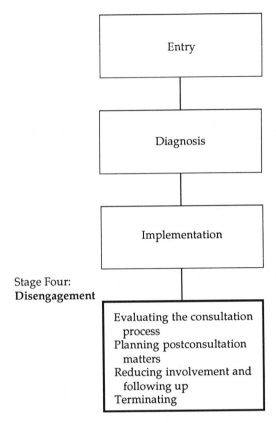

FIGURE 6.1   The Phases of the Disengagement Stage

PHASE ONE: EVALUATING THE CONSULTATION PROCESS

The Role of Evaluation

As it relates to consultation, *evaluation* might be defined as the systematic collection of information about the activities and outcomes of consultation for the purpose of making judgments and decisions about how consultation is proceeding and/or the effects it is having (Patton, 1977, p.26). A properly performed evaluation can provide the consultant

1. a quality-control device,
2. a learning device,
3. legal protection, and
4. a marketing tool (Kelley, 1981).

Frequently, consultation is evaluated only at the end of the process. However, many authors (for example, Swartz & Lippitt, 1975; Conoley & Conoley, 1982; Parsons & Meyers, 1984) note that evaluation is an *ongoing* process that should be performed throughout the consultation process.

Three steps are common to all evaluation processes (Anderson et al., 1977):

1. formation of criteria,
2. assessment of attainment of the criteria, and
3. utilization of results.

Formation of criteria refers to the creation or designation of the criteria (frequently goals) that will be used to assess those aspects of consultation under evaluation (Anderson et al., 1977). Developing evaluation criteria is one of the most difficult problems facing consultants (Lippitt, 1969). Systematically assessing the degree to which criteria have been met involves determining what information is to be gathered, how, by whom, and how it is to be analyzed. Utilization of results involves disseminating the results to appropriate parties, typically for some form of decision making (Anderson et al., 1977). For example, an organization might use the results of consultee satisfaction surveys to decide whether or not to retain a particular consultant.

Consultation is evaluated for three basic reasons (Brown et al., 1987):

1. to determine the processes and effects of a given consultation experience,
2. to assess accountability and improvements in service, and
3. to add knowledge to the field of consultation.

Such purposes as these make evaluation not only essential but unavoidable, and in this light evaluation is seen as constructive and mutually beneficial for the consultant and those affected by the consultation process (Parsons & Meyers, 1984).

Because the evaluation process is not always easy to perform, it is not unusual for consultants to consult others about how to evaluate both their services and the consultation process itself (Gallessich, 1982). Still, consultants and consultees should realize that they do not need to be experts in evaluation or research to adequately perform the practical evaluations required in consultation. Whereas merely going through the motions of evaluation is professionally inexcusable, a simple yet credible evaluation can be very informative (Caplan, 1970). Consultants need to be aware that at the opposite extreme they can spend so much of their time evaluating the consultation process that its human side can get lost in the volume of information collected and interpreted.

Consultants and consultees need two primary skills to effectively perform evaluation: the ability to identify the consequences of their actions and the ability to compare results to some standard. Although these skills were identified in the context of counseling skills clients need to effectively change their behavior (Heppner, 1978; Egan, 1986), they are certainly needed by the consultant and consultee as well.

Consultation is typically evaluated by examining pertinent data gathered from the following sources (Swartz & Lippitt, 1975):

1. observations,
2. questionnaires,
3. surveys,
4. interviews, and
5. the organization's documents.

Some authors (for example, Freedman, 1983) suggest that consultants and consultees use a multimethod approach to evaluation. Such an approach provides more than one perspective on the results obtained, may add information valuable in interpreting the data, and can reduce response bias. The use of devices for gathering data is discussed in Chapter 4 of this text.

When evaluating consultation, it is appropriate to gather data from the client system, the consultee, the consultant, and other parties-at-interest. In order to make evaluation manageable, the consultant and consultee should determine during the formation of the contract which kinds of evaluative information should be gathered from which parties.

Deciding who should conduct the evaluation of consultation is very difficult; perhaps the best rule of thumb is "it depends." Typically, the consultant and consultee make this decision during the contracting stage. Thus, in some cases the consultant helps the consultee to gather and make sense of the data; in other cases the consultee gathers the data and the consultant assists in its interpretation; in still other instances someone other than the consultee (for example, the organization's contact person) conducts some aspects of the evaluation. Some organizations even have special departments to evaluate services like consultation. So long as the people who perform the evaluation are qualified to do so and have no conflict of interest, it probably does not matter who conducts given aspects of it. Regardless of who performs it, consultants are responsible for arranging an evaluation of their services, and they should conduct a separate self-evaluation.

Pertinent evaluation information should be provided to the consultant, the consultee, administrators of the organization in which consultation has occurred, and (in some cases) the client. The consultant should take measures to see that the results of evaluation are *not* used in the following covert and inappropriate ways (Anderson et al., 1977):

1. for protection of an ineffective consultee or program,
2. as avoidance of decision making,
3. as a public relations tool, or
4. for getting rid of an effective but unpopular consultee or program.

Consultants may want to evaluate three general consultation topics: the plan that was carried out in the implementation stage, the overall effects of consultation and the consultant's behaviors, and the efficacy of certain stages and phases along the way. The decision concerning which topics to evaluate depends on the type of evaluation, the nature of the problem, and the level at which consultation occurs. For example, an organizational consultant might be interested in evaluating the impact of consultation on total organizational effectiveness, participants' attitudes toward the change process itself, or the efficacy of a specific intervention (Beer, 1980). It is very important that the consultant, consultee, and (if necessary) other parties-at-interest plan what is to be evaluated, how evaluation is to occur, who is going to perform it, and when, for such planning prevents evaluation procedures from becoming overwhelming. The contract that was developed during the entry stage provides a good basis for evaluating consultation (Conoley & Conoley, 1982).

The following questions provide a starting point for identifying the many things that can be evaluated at the end of consultation:

1. To what degree has behavior in the client or client system changed in the desired direction?
2. To what degree was the consultant able to psychologically enter the system?
3. In what ways has the organization changed as a result of consultation?
4. To what degree have the goals established in the contract been met?
5. To what degree have established timetables been met?
6. How successfully has a given intervention been carried out?
7. How effectively has the consultant established an effective working relationship with the consultee?
8. To what degree has consultation been worth the cost in time, effort, and money?

Some authors (for example, Goodstein, 1978; Parsons & Meyers, 1984; Brown et al., 1987) note specific items that can in some way be evaluated:

1. consultee preference for given models of consultation,
2. initial planning of the consultation process,
3. quantity and quality of consultee reports about the work-related problem,
4. progress made relative to each consultation stage,
5. organizational variables that affect the consultant process,
6. consultant behaviors at each consultation stage,
7. consultee behaviors throughout the consultation process,
8. client behaviors throughout the consultation process,
9. consultee satisfaction with consultation,
10. the degree to which goals are being attained,
11. adequacy of each consultation contact,
12. interpersonal behaviors of the consultant and consultee, and
13. institutionalization of change.

An examination of these evaluation questions and items evaluated in consultation show three criteria that typically are used in evaluating consultation: behavior change, cost effectiveness, and attitudes/opinions about consultation (Swartz & Lippitt, 1975). Changes in behavior are typically looked for in the client or client system (Dickinson & Adcox, 1984), but consultees can also be examined for such changes. For example, an evaluator could look for a reduction in the number of physically aggressive behaviors by a student (client) or an increase in the number of open-ended questions a consultee asks a client.

Cost effectiveness is a judgment call: were the costs in terms of time and resources needed for consultation "worth the returns"? Thus, the administer of a human services agency might calculate how much time and resources it took to have a consultant reorganize the agency and compare those costs to the perceived benefits of the consultation. Attitudes and opinions about consultation can range from indexes of consultee satisfaction with the consultant to views about the overall success of consultation. For example, a group of consultees might fill out a consultee satisfaction survey form after having six sessions with the consultant.

Consultants should make sure that they in some way receive an evaluation of their services, for this is frequently left out of the consultation evaluation process (Lundberg, 1985). Such feedback is essential in spite of the fact that it is ethical for the consultant *not* to perform evaluation if the organization cannot afford it or is unable to provide the needed necessary resources (Matuszek, 1981).

Consultation evaluation can be viewed from two time-related perspectives: evaluation of the consultation process as it proceeds and evaluation of consultation once it has run its course. Just as the consultant is continually entering the system, continually diagnosing, and continually intervening, so too should the consultant be continually evaluating. The evaluation performed along the way by the consultant and consultee is typically referred to as *formative evaluation* (Scriven, 1967). This type of evaluation is performed as progress in consultation is being "formed"; The *process* of consultation is evaluated without respect to the ultimate product. For example, a consultant and a consultee might use formative evaluation to investigate the degree of success of the diagnosis stage.

When the consultant and consultee evaluate the effects of the consultation process at its conclusion, such an evaluation is typically referred to as a *summative evaluation* (Scriven, 1967). The role of this form of evaluation is to determine the effects of outcomes of consultation; it "sums" things up at the end of the process and evaluates the *product* produced by it. For example, the consultant and consultee might decide to assess a training program's effects on the participants' morale.

Formative Evaluation

One of the best ways to conduct formative evaluation in consultation is to perform evaluations at the end of each phase of each stage. Such evaluations will assist the consultant and consultee in determining whether to stick to the current course of consultation or to modify the process in some alternative way. Evaluation can be formal (such as using written surveys or performing observations on some combination of consultant, consultee, and client behaviors) or informal (such as a discussion between the consultant and consultee or other parties-at-interest concerning how a given phase has progressed).

Human services professionals are familiar with and typically positive toward the use of surveys. Thus, consultants may want to develop questionnaires and surveys related to each of the phases of the consultation process. One good source for examples of questionnaires and surveys is Parsons & Meyers (1984), and sample evaluation questions for the phases of each stage of the consultation process are provided below. These questions can be helpful in developing a frame of reference whether evaluation is conducted by survey, observations, interviews, or examination of records.

Formative Evaluation Across the Consultation Process

Certain useful questions can be asked in the various stages of consultation; the answers obtained are helpful in evaluating each stage to make decisions concerning the progress and subsequent direction of consultation. The following questions are adapted from an evaluation form developed by Parsons & Meyers (1984):

How many contacts have been made with the consultee?
What is the average length of the contacts?
What is the average length of time between contacts?
What progress has been made so far?
What issues have come up that still need to be handled?
Who needs to be apprised of what has been done so far?
What does the consultee think about what has happened to date?
To what degree is the consultee satisfied about what has happened?
What does the consultee think about the consultant's style?
What details need to be worked out?
What does the consultant think about what has happened so far?
To what degree is the consultant satisfied with what has happened?
What are the consultant's impressions of the consultee?
Are there any changes needed in the way consultation is being conducted?

Among the innovative ways to conduct a formative evaluation is to use a metaphor in providing feedback to the consultant (Lundberg, 1985). The appropriate parties describe the consultant in terms of some metaphor (for example, "a perpetual-motion machine cranking out perpetually good ideas"). The metaphors are shared with the consultant in a group setting. Open discussion ensues and themes related to consultant effectiveness and ineffectiveness are elicited and explored. The consultant then summarizes the feedback and plans subsequent actions in the consultation process.

As noted earlier, consultants can evaluate their effectiveness in each phase of the consultation process. A set of questions consultants can use for evaluating their effectiveness in each phase is provided in this chapter. Consultants can convert these questions into surveys or checklists, use them for directing observations, or develop them as a basis for interviewing: Figure 6.2 is a survey for use in the formative evaluation of the exploring organizational needs phase, whereas Figure 6.3 is a sample checklist for evaluating the contracting phase of the entry stage.

Directions: Please rate each item according to the five-point scale listed below by circling the number that most accurately expresses your opinion on the following statements:

5 = strongly agree

4 = agree

3 = undecided

2 = disagree

1 = strongly disagree

1. The level of congruency between the consultant's abilities and the consultee system's needs was adequately determined.

       5   4   3   2   1

2. The amount of resources the organization was willing to commit to consultation was adequately defined.

       5   4   3   2   1

3. The identification and clarification of the need for change was adequately accomplished.

       5   4   3   2   1

4. The organization's readiness for change was adequately explored and defined.

       5   4   3   2   1

5. The potential of the parties involved for working together was adequately explored.

       5   4   3   2   1

6. Role expectations for those involved were made clear.

       5   4   3   2   1

7. The roles of the consultee and client system were adequately defined.

       5   4   3   2   1

FIGURE 6.2   Sample Survey for Evaluating the Exploring Organizational Needs Phase

Formative Evaluation of the Entry Stage

In the entry stage, the consultation process progressed through the phases of exploring organizational needs, contracting, physically entering the system, and psychologically entering the system. The consultant and consultee can evaluate each of these phases as a guide for conducting subsequent consultation phases.

Exploring organizational needs.   Some questions used in formative evaluation during this phase include:

> To what degree was the level of congruence between the consultant's abilities and consultee system's needs determined?

Directions: Please place a check mark on the line under the appropriate response.

	YES	NO
1. Were the professional expectations of the parties involved spelled out in the contract?	____	____
2. Were the personal expectations of the parties involved made explicit?	____	____
3. Were the conditions under which each party involved would invest time and other resources adequately defined?	____	____
4. Were ground rules under which the parties involved would operate specified clearly?	____	____
5. Were the boundaries of consultation defined?	____	____
6. Was the nature of the contract reviewed with all appropriate parties?	____	____
7. Were arrangements made for the periodic review and evaluation of consultation?	____	____

FIGURE 6.3   Sample Checklist for Evaluating the Contracting Phase of Consultation

Was the amount of resources the organization was willing to commit to consultation adequately defined?

To what extent was the identification and clarification of the need for change accomplished?

How well was the organization's readiness for change explored and defined?

How well was the potential for working together explored by the parties involved?

To what degree were role expectations made clear?

How well were the roles of consultee and client defined?

Contracting.   The questions that can be asked about contracting are more specific than those for the previous phase, which allows for greater specificity in the evaluation of this second phase:

How effectively were the professional expectations of the parties involved spelled out in the contract?

To what degree were the personal expectations of the parties involved made explicit?

Were the amount of time and other resources each party would invest, the times they would invest them, and the costs of those investments adequately defined?

How precisely specified were the ground rules under which the parties involved would operate?

How well were the boundaries of consultation defined?

To what degree was the nature of the contract reviewed with the appropriate parties?

Were arrangements made for the periodic review and evaluation of consultation?

Physically entering the system.   Evaluation of the physical entry into consultation is relatively straightforward—it deals with the creation of consultative relationships and the physical setup of consultation. Some questions useful in evaluating this phase include:

Is the selected work site conducive to effective consultation?

Is the selected work site strategically located?

Is the consultant appropriately balancing the amount of time spent at the work site with the time spent moving throughout the organization?

To what degree does the consultant adapt the schedule for consultation activities to the regular schedule of the organization?

To what degree have the parties affected by consultation been informed about the nature of consultation, its purpose, and its time frame?

Psychologically entering the system.   Even though psychological entry cannot be divorced from physical entry, the psychological aspects of entry can be evaluated by the judicious selection of questions. Some questions that can be used in evaluating this phase of consultation include:

To what degree has consultation placed minimal stress on the parties involved?

To what degree has consultation placed minimal stress on the organization's structure and processes?

To what degree has the consultant developed social influence within the organization?

How effectively has the consultant obtained some sanction for consultation from the organization's top-level administrators?

How effectively has the consultant built strong professional relationships with all parties affected by consultation?

In summary, the entry stage can best be evaluated by evaluating each of its phases. The consultant and consultee must agree on the most appropriate methods of evaluation and must limit the number of events that will be evaluated.

Formative Evaluation of the Diagnosis Stage

In the diagnosis stage , the consultation process progressed through the phases of gathering information, defining the problem, setting goals, and generating possible interventions. The consultant and consultee can evaluate each of these phases to help decide how best to approach the implementation stage that follows them.

Gathering information.   Some useful questions for the formative evaluation of this stage include:

How was the decision to proceed with data gathering made?
How was the degree of comprehensiveness of the data-gathering process determined?
How was it determined who would be involved in the data-gathering process?
What criteria were used in selecting the data-collecting methods?
How well were these criteria met when the data were collected?
Was the information collected useful in understanding the problem?
How thoroughly scanned was the context in which the problem was thought to occur?
How meaningful were the data that were collected?
To what degree were the advantages and disadvantages of the data-collecting methods taken into consideration?

Defining the problem.   Once the data have been collected they are analyzed and the problem defined. Questions helpful to consultants and consultees in their evaluation of this phase include:

How systematic was the plan for analyzing the data?
Did the plan for analyzing the data lead to a more complex conceptualization of the problem?
Were sufficiently large numbers of factors affecting the problem pinpointed?
Were the ways the problem developed over time determined?
Has a clear statement of the defined problem been put in writing and shared with parties-at-interest?
Was effective collaboration between the consultant and consultee apparent throughout this phase of consultation?
Was the problem statement's language satisfactory to everyone involved?

Setting goals.   In evaluating this process—that of designating what ends are to be met by the consultation process—consultants and consultees ask questions such as:

Was adequate time allocated to the goal-setting process?
To what extent was creativity used in setting goals?
Were the steps involved in setting goals properly followed?
To what degree did the selected goal conform to the characteristics of effective goals?
Was the accepted goal affected by efforts to achieve it?
Did the goal involve an adequate amount of risk?
Was a safe environment created in which people involved in achieving the goal could honestly report on progress toward it?

Generating possible interventions.   In evaluating this phase, during which possible ways to meet goals are developed, the consultant and consultee review previously used interventions (if any) and then collaboratively develop new ones. Questions helpful in evaluating this stage include:

How thoroughly were any previous interventions examined?

How effectively did the consultant use prompts to assist the consultee in creating new interventions?

To what degree was the consultee's skill in implementing interventions taken into consideration?

How productive were brainstorming activities?

How strictly were the rules for brainstorming adhered to?

How did the consultee handle confusion over the attractiveness of so many possible interventions?

In summary, by evaluating the phases of the diagnosis stage, the consultant and consultee can more effectively lay the groundwork for implementation. A rigorous, thorough evaluation of goals is a critical aspect of the evaluation of the diagnosis stage.

Formative Evaluation of the Implementation Stage

In the implementation stage, one or more interventions are selected, and then a plan is formulated, implemented, and evaluated. A multitude of events could be evaluated during this stage, including "an evaluation of the evaluation of the plan"! Evaluation of these phases must be kept manageable through judicious selection of the topics that are assessed.

Choosing an intervention. Evaluation of the process by which the consultant and consultee choose interventions is critical in preventing implementation of inappropriate plans. The following questions are useful in evaluating this phase:

How effective was the decision-making procedure used in choosing an intervention?

Were the potential positive and negative consequences of each possible intervention examined thoroughly?

To what degree has the consultee processed the consultant's contributions relative to the choice of intervention?

How were interventions selected for use in contingency plans?

To what degree were the objectives of each intervention considered?

How much new information was needed for implementing any given intervention and to what degree was that information obtained?

Formulating a plan. During the crucial process of formulating a plan the right intervention must be orchestrated in such a way that it effectively enables the goal of consultation to be met. Questions that can assist in evaluating formulation of the plan include:

To what degree was the "what," "where," "when," "how," and "who" of plan formulation taken into consideration?

Were enough plans constructed?
How effective was the method of plan selection?
To what degree was force-field analysis useful in the plan formulation process?
Were the objectives of the plan clearly stated?
Was a realistic timetable established?
Was each step of the plan sufficiently refined?
Was the plan tested for feasibility, cost effectiveness, and capability?

Implementing the plan. Even though during this phase—when the plan is put into action—contact between the consultant and consultee can be minimal, the consultant has a professional responsibility to the consultee to make sure that the plan is properly implemented. The following questions can be helpful in evaluating plan implementation:

To what degree was the plan adapted to the unique situation in which it was implemented?
In what ways was the consultant involved in tactical assistance?
How effective was the consultant's technical assistance?
Was dependence on the part of the consultee minimized?
How effectively did the consultant monitor the implementation process?
How effectively were unforeseen circumstances handled?

Evaluating the plan. It may seem a bit unusual to discuss an evaluation of an evaluation. However, consultants and consultees must determine how effective their procedures for evaluating the plan were. The following questions can assist in accomplishing this process:

To what degree were predetermined strategies for evaluating the plan effective?
Was the methodology for evaluating the plan sound?
Was the evaluation of the plan properly linked to the goals of the plan?
By what means and how effectively was the evaluation of the plan shared with parties-at-interest?
Were data in the plan's effectiveness gathered from a variety of sources?
Was more than one method of data collection used?

In summary, the evaluation of the implementation stage is a pivotal point in determining whether consultation will proceed toward disengagement or loop back to a previous stage and a different approach to the problem. Once proper evaluation of the plan has been accomplished, consultation is nearing its end.

Formative Evaluation of the Disengagement Stage

Like the other stages of consultation, the final stage—disengagement—should be evaluated phase by phase. Now let's consider the evaluation of this stage's phases: evaluating the consultation process (even though the entire process is not yet completed), planning postconsultation matters, reducing involvement and following up, and terminating.

Evaluating the consultation process.   The evaluation of the consultation process must take place before postconsultation planning, reduced involvement and follow-up, and termination occur. The results of the evaluation are used in determining the nature of postconsultation planning, as well as deciding whether or not the process should be terminated. The following questions are helpful in evaluating this phase:

Were the designs used in assessing the various facets of consultation appropriate?

To what degree did the consultant and consultee work together in planning and carrying out the evaluation?

Was the evaluation sufficiently comprehensive to evaluate what needed to be evaluated?

Were the results of the evaluation adequately disseminated?

Was a mechanism put into place for using the evaluation's results in post-consultation planning or for going back to repeat certain phases of the consultation process?

Were appropriate steps taken to ensure that confidentiality would be maintained concerning the evaluation's results?

Were efforts made to keep the evaluation free from distortion and bias?

Was the evaluation thorough yet cost-effective?

Were provisions made to allow evaluation of the consultant's services by the parties affected by the consultation?

Were both formative and summative types of evaluation used?

Planning postconsultation matters.   Once evaluation of the consultation has been achieved, consultation moves on to postconsultation planning. At this point the consultant and consultee make plans for integrating the results of consultation into the system after consultation has ended. The following questions can be helpful:

To what degree were the parties affected by consultation involved in the postconsultation planning process?

In what ways were the results of postconsultation planning disseminated?

Was agreement concerning postconsultation plans sought from appropriate parties?

How involved was the consultant in the postconsultation planning process?

Were postconsultation plans evaluated like any other types of plans?

Reducing involvement and following up.   Reduced involvement and follow-up, which should be conceived during postconsultation planning, can be evaluated by asking the following questions:

In what way did the consultant initiate reduced involvement?

Was the concept of fading satisfactorily applied in reducing involvement?

Was the independent functioning of both consultee and the organization given priority as the consultant's contact was being reduced?

Was the method of follow-up agreed on by the appropriate parties?

Was an appropriate timetable for follow-up procedures and activities set?
What plans were made for collecting information before follow-up?
What parties were designated to be contacted during follow-up?
What decisions were planned to be made as a result of the follow-up?
What measures did the consultant make to ensure that the follow-up process
  would be viewed as important by all parties affected by consultation?

Terminating.   Termination is the process of ending the consultation relationship. The following questions can be used in evaluating this final phase:

Did the consultant make plans to terminate gradually?
Were all parties informed about the ending of consultation in a timely manner?
Did the consultant deal with both the human and the professional sides of
  leave-taking?
Were all necessary reports written?
Were all bills for services rendered?
Was there a clearly defined termination meeting?
Were members of the consultee organization more independent upon termination of consultation than when the consultant first entered the system?

In summary, formative evaluation assesses the processes involved in consultation as they are occurring. Formative evaluation—also referred to as process evaluation—is frequently ongoing and is best accomplished by collecting data resulting from the judicious formulation and honest answering of questions. The data are used in making decisions about how well consultation is proceeding and what subsequent actions should be taken.

Summative Evaluation

Summative evaluation refers to the evaluation of outcomes or products (Scriven, 1967); indeed, it is often referred to as *product evaluation*. Consultants and consultees use summative evaluation to determine if the objectives of consultation were met. Sometimes consultants would benefit from consulting with experts in evaluation concerning the design of summative evaluation procedures.

An exhaustive treatment of the many possible designs used in summative evaluation are beyond the scope of this book. Excellent resources already available to consultants and consultees can provide guidance in designing evaluations of the consultation process, including *Research Methods for Counselors* (Goldman, 1978), *Experimental and Quasi-Experimental Designs for Research* (Campbell & Stanley, 1966), *Single Case Experimental Decisions* (Barlow & Hersen, 1984), and *The Scientist Practitioner* (Barlow, Hayes, & Nelson, 1984). A brief overview of some of the ways to perform summative evaluation is presented below.

The Pre-Post Method

The *pre-post method* attempts to assess changes that result from consultation by measuring variables related to desired changes before and after the consultation process. For example, a consultant might measure an organization's morale before and after an intervention designed to boost morale. The advantages of this evaluation method are that it is relatively simple and requires a minimum of time to perform.

The pre-post method is particularly valuable when the variables being measured are specific and observable (Swartz & Lippitt, 1975). Because there is no control group, however, this method is of limited value. Increases in the desired direction cannot be directly attributed to consultation because factors such as changes in the organization, life experiences, and other forces could just as well explain the results (Dougherty & Taylor, 1983). Still, this method is a step above nonstandardized observation and anecdotal accounts in that it provides more useful information and conclusive evidence.

The Group Comparison Method

The *group comparison method* adds clout to the evaluation by including a comparison group or control group, which strengthens the evaluation's validity (Dougherty & Taylor, 1983) by enabling comparison of a group that received consultation services with a group that did not receive such services. This method allows the consultant and consultee to be more confident that any changes found in the measurement are specifically attributable to consultation itself and not to extraneous variables. For example, a consultant might train half of an agency's crisis intervention team in cognitive therapy strategies for crisis situations. The other half of the team, which would receive no training, is used as a control group. The performance of both groups is assessed and compared on selected criteria.

Sometimes consultants use a no-contact control group or an attention-only control group. In using a *no-contact control group,* the only contact with the group occurs during the assessment of the dependent variables (measures of the factors to be changed by consultation). In an *attention-only control group,* the assessment of the dependent variables is made and the group is informed of the nature of consultation services without receiving these services directly. Attention-only control groups are useful in that they eliminate the possibility that the attention paid to the consultees and/or clients, not consultation itself, led to differences in the dependent variables. Several potential problems can be associated with the group comparison method of evaluation:

1. management of the control groups,
2. developmental complexity of the experimental design, and
3. required statistical knowledge beyond the expertise of consultant and consultee.

The group comparison method is particularly useful in a follow-up assessment using the same measurement(s) taken in posttesting. It is the method of choice when comparative performance data are particularly desirable (Swartz & Lippitt, 1975). Because of the complexity of the group comparison method, it is a desirable but relatively infrequently used method of consultation evaluation.

Time-Series Method

The *time-series method* involves establishing a series of measures on a given variable or variables over time (Barlow et al., 1984). The primary difference between this method and the group comparison and pre-post methods is that the time-series method uses more frequent assessments of designated variables. The effects of intervention are then assessed in terms of measured behaviors' variability, their level of occurrence, and possible trends (Barlow et al., 1984). Thus, pertinent information can be gathered on a measurement's changes over time (Barlow & Hersen, 1984). This method may or may not use a control group. As an example, a consultant and consultee might make a series of observations on how an imagery program affects a client's eating behavior at breakfast, lunch, and dinner.

Multiple baseline designs are one example of the time-series method. Multiple baselining reduces the effects of random influences on behavior change by replicating the change obtained in one time period in subsequent time periods; each subsequent time period serves as a control for the earlier time period (Barlow et al., 1984). Time-series methods are most effective when it is likely that a large number of variables are affecting the outcome of consultation (Swartz & Lippitt, 1975).

Case Study Method

A *case study* is ". . . a report of an intensive analytical and diagnostic intervention on an individual or other social unit, in which attention is focused on factors contributing to the development of personality patterns and/or behavior patterns" (Shertzer & Linden, 1979, p. 460). The case study method can be used to analyze the effects of consultation on the consultee and/or the client system; for example, a consultant might conduct a case study on the effects of quality circles on job satisfaction in a community service agency. Although it is descriptive in nature, the case study method does not excuse the consultant and consultee from identifying specific and behaviorally-defined goals at the outset of consultation (Ohlsen, 1974; Shertzer & Linden, 1979). It does, however, permit application of consultation evaluation to an individual consultee and/or client, with a minimum of statistical work (Goldman, 1978).

The case study can provide insight into previously unsuspected relationships affecting consultation (Ary, Jacobs, & Razavieh, 1985). The case study is, however, very susceptible to bias (Anton, 1978) and therefore users of this method must make careful judgments about the efficacy of consultation. Because of its uncontrolled nature, its users can have only limited confidence about the cause of any observed effects (Barlow et al., 1984). To the degree that a case study is comprehensive, it can be quite time-consuming (Shertzer & Linden, 1979). Case studies are often viewed as a lower-level evaluation tool, but they can be used to adequately evaluate consultation (Barlow et al., 1984; Barlow & Hersen, 1984).

Self-Report Assessment Method

The *self-report assessment method* is frequently used at the end of the consultation process to evaluate the effects of consultation. This method makes use of such instruments as rating scales, surveys, checklists, or questionnaires, which can be developed by the consultant and consultee or can be available in some standardized form.

In summative evaluation, self-assessment can be used in all of the previously mentioned methods, including a postconsultation assessment measure. The method tends to lack rigor in terms of experimental design and can easily provide inaccurate results if the precision of the instruments used is inadequate (Dougherty & Taylor, 1983). However, this is a very common method of evaluating consultation, and its use has been enhanced by significant improvements in the development of questionnaires and surveys in the past decade (for example, Birnbrauer, 1987; Quinn & Karp, 1986; Newstrom, 1987). The self-report method is particularly appropriate for evaluating consultation in terms of consultee satisfaction, consultant satisfaction, and perceived consultant effectiveness.

In summary, the evaluation of consultation effects moves the consultant into the realm of experimental design, which may require more sophistication in experimental design and statistics than the consultant and consultee possess. Under such circumstances they must either seek outside assistance or develop a suitable evaluation method that is within their levels of expertise. Because of the time, effort, and expense that outcome evaluation can require, the evaluation plan used must be cost-effective. The consultant must ensure that evaluation results are described completely and accurately and are disseminated to the appropriate parties, such as the consultee, organization contact person, administrators, and other appropriate parties-at-interest.

PHASE TWO: PLANNING POSTCONSULTATION MATTERS

The consultant can increase the chances that the results of consultation will be maintained after the consultant's departure by using effective postconsultation planning. During the *postconsultation planning phase*, plans are formulated to keep up the changes brought about by consultation. The plans produced for this purpose rely heavily on the resources available to the consultee and the organization.

The consultant and consultee can effectively plan postconsultation procedures by following many of the procedures used in the formulating a plan phase of the implementation stage of consultation. You may want to review the planning process in Chapter 5, including determining objectives, establishing procedures, defining steps, assigning responsibilities, and testing for feasibility, cost effectiveness, and capabilities (Bittel, 1972). Force-field analysis (Lewin, 1951) is a useful technique in assessing the forces that may aid or impede the accomplishment of plans. With the proper planning, then, the consultant can help the consultee and organization to effectively follow through on the results of consultation. Consider this brief example of postconsultation planning:

CASE STUDY:
A marriage and family therapist has been consulting with a counseling psychologist who is working with a couple on enhancing their relationship.

The family therapist has assisted the consultee in using therapeutic metaphors with the couple. Consultation has proceeded effectively. Together the consultant and consultee formulate a plan for how the consultee will proceed with the couple after consultation has ended. Part of the plan involves assisting the couple to write their own metaphors to enhance their emotional intimacy.

PHASE THREE: REDUCING INVOLVEMENT AND FOLLOWING UP

Once postconsultation plans have been formulated to the satisfaction of the parties involved, the consultant initiates a period of reduced involvement and enacts follow-up procedures.

Reducing Involvement

Reduced involvement refers to the gradual reduction in the consultant's contact with the consultee and the organization. The consultee and other appropriate parties begin to "pick up the slack" left by the consultant's declining involvement. Reduced involvement effectively prevents abrupt termination.

One method proven effective in reducing involvement is *fading*, a process in which the consultant reduces or "fades" contact and involvement with the consultee and the organization. For example, if a consultant has been meeting with a consultee on a weekly basis, contact might be faded to once every two weeks, then to once every three weeks, and so on. Similarly, the consultant's visits to the organization are reduced over time. As the consultant is fading the contact, the consultant's roles are gradually taken over by the consultee. The reduced involvement reinforces independence in the consultee and the organization.

Some authors (for example, Bell & Nadler, 1979b; 1979c) advocate that the consultant be available on an as-needed basis while the consultee and the organization try to manage the changes brought about by consultation. However reduced involvement is accomplished, it should be negotiated (Schein, 1969), for such a negotiation makes it clear to everyone involved that reduced involvement does not mean *no* involvement (Schein, 1969).

The following illustrates reduced involvement:

CASE STUDY:
A school counselor has been meeting weekly with a teacher regarding some classroom management problems the teacher has been having. As a result of consultation the teacher has made great strides in eliciting appropriate behavior from the students. The consultant has helped the teacher plan how the class will be managed for the entire term and how data on the students' behavior will be collected. To reduce the consultant's involvement, the consultant and consultee set two final meetings at three-week intervals before terminating the consultation.

Following Up

Planning follow-up procedures can reduce the stress that comes with winding down consultation. *Follow-up* refers to the process of periodically determining how well the results of consultation are being maintained over time and how well the consultee and organization are performing postconsultation efforts. Follow-up provides the consultee and organization with a regular "check up" (Kelley, 1981, p. 218). Follow-up is important because it provides (Kelley, 1981):

1. some indication of consultant availability,
2. an opportunity to salvage plans that have not been effectively carried out,
3. some assistance while promoting independence on the part of the consultee and the organization, and
4. some prevention of future problems.

When properly accomplished, reduced involvement and follow-up fill a gap between postconsultation planning and termination.

Here is a brief example of follow-up:

CASE STUDY:
A human resource development specialist has been training volunteers who work with incarcerates in a rehabilitation program. Three months after the training has concluded, the specialist calls the rehabilitation program director in order to check on how the volunteers are doing.

PHASE FOUR: TERMINATING

Like human relationships, consultation requires closure; *termination* provides that closure in a formal, ritualistic manner. Termination formally ends a process and ideally leads to a sense of satisfaction with whatever has been accomplished and a mutual sense of esteem for the parties involved (Bell & Nadler, 1979c). It also provides an appropriate time for celebrating whatever successes have been achieved.

Termination is a critical element in the consultation process; if performed inappropriately, it can result in dissatisfaction of the consultee and the organization in which consultation occurred. Inappropriate termination can affect the manner in which postconsultation planning and subsequent consultation experiences are perceived. Inappropriate termination procedures include:

1. a unilateral decision (by either the consultant or consultee) to terminate,
2. abrupt termination,
3. indefinite retention of consultation (no formal end point), and
4. unnecessary extension of the consultation process by any of the parties involved.

Abrupt termination is a shock and can be a distraction (Bell & Nadler, 1979c). Conversely, unnecessary extension of consultation is a particular danger to consultants in private practice and to consultants internal to the organization who feel they must always have "something to do." As the termination process is begun, consultants should maintain awareness of their "need to be needed" and avoid engendering dependence (Bell & Nadler, 1979c). The lingering of consultation prevents the human side of termination from receiving adequate consideration.

A meeting that concludes postconsultation planning is an excellent time to deal with any unresolved issues before the consultant's formal departure, and such a ritual can set the termination process in motion. A formal review of the consultant's final report is one proven method of effectively accomplishing termination (Bell & Nadler, 1979c). Here participants can discuss the progress made in consultation relative to the contract and the stated goals of consultation, and at this time a clearly defined point of termination can be set. This definite ending point can prevent unnecessary dependence on the part of the consultee or the organization (Parsons & Meyers, 1984). Finally, discussing future possibilities for consulting is another way of easing the stress of termination.

Two possible emotional issues can affect either consultants or consultees at termination time: dependence and depression (Kelley, 1981). No one wants a good and wholesome relationship to end; when the parties involved in such a relationship become aware of its imminent end, a sense of loss of the relationship begins to develop. Consultants, consultees, and other parties have grown accustomed to each other and consequently have come to need each other more than is readily apparent, and the possibility of mutual dependence exists. These phenomena can be minimized to the degree that the consultation process was properly implemented, and by being aware of these potential occurrences and by anticipating them, consultants can help the consultation process come to a personally and professionally satisfying conclusion. When consultants and consultees avoid these issues, the issues do not go away (Kelley, 1981). Rather, these unresolved feelings can lead to undesirable consequences such as anger among the parties involved or an unnecessary extension of the consultation process.

SUMMARY

The disengagement process in consultation is the winding down of the consultation process. It involves a sense of "letting go" on both professional and personal levels. During this stage the consultant and consultee engage in four phases: evaluating the consultation process, planning postconsultation matters, reducing involvement and following-up, and terminating.

Disengagement, which should be differentiated from termination, should not be rushed; it should be a well planned and executed procedure.

Evaluation of consultation is frequently done poorly and as a result does not provide any consultation participants a chance to examine how well they have done or how they have grown. Therefore, consultants need to be ready to assist their consultees in evaluating consultation and should ensure that evaluation of their services is part of the overall evaluation procedure. Consultants frequently need some consultation on how to evaluate the consultation process.

In postconsultation planning the consultant asks the consultee, "How are you going to follow through after I am gone?" This planning process places increased responsibility on the consultee and the organization to make effective use of the products of consultation. Postconsultation planning is an appropriate time for consultees to express their concerns about the consultant's leaving and for the consultant to encourage them to realize that they have the abilities to follow through.

The egos and self-esteem of everyone involved in consultation are affected during reduced involvement. Being needed as a consultant is gratifying to any consultant, and thus it is sometimes difficult to let others follow through on what the consultant has been instrumental in accomplishing. The consultant can more effectively reduce involvement by remembering that one goal of consultation is to help the consultee and the organization to continue to function without the consultant. Consultants can take pride in being instrumental in enabling consultees to use the new skills they learned from the consultants.

During follow-up the consultant takes on a trouble-shooting role in which help is provided to the consultee or organization on an "as-needed" basis. It is important to define what is meant by "as-needed" so that dependence is not fostered.

Termination is the formal ending of the consultation process. Saying good-bye is not always easy. Consequently, formal termination does not always occur or may be done in a stiff, artificial manner. Consultants can make termination easier for themselves and their consultees by being aware of their true feelings and by taking the risk of sharing their thoughts and feelings as they are taking leave.

By being perceived as fair, competent, human, and effective, consultants can take leave with an enhanced reputation, which can both be intrinsically satisfying and earn them subsequent consultation opportunities.

QUESTIONS FOR REFLECTION

1. How does the term *disengagement* differ from the term *termination*?
2. In what ways is disengagement a winding down of the consultation process?
3. For what purposes can evaluation of the effects of consultation be used?
4. As a consultant, when in the consultation process would you start to plan evaluation procedures?
5. How does a consultant proceed in determining what events to evaluate?
6. How would you handle evaluation of consultation if both you and your consultee lacked the expertise to perform sophisticated evaluation procedures?
7. What kinds of things should be accomplished in postconsultation planning?
8. What is the major difference between reduced involvement and follow-up?
9. How would you go about the process of psychologically terminating the consultation process?
10. What does the following statement mean: "The consultant begins termination upon entry into the consultation process"?

SUGGESTED SUPPLEMENTARY READINGS

Goldman, L. (Ed.). (1978). *Research methods for counselors.* New York: Wiley. This book provides invaluable evaluation information for consultants, whether or not they are trained as professional counselors. I recommend this book as a handbook for consultants to use when determining how to evaluate the effects of consultation. Even though the book's focus is on research, its concepts are easily translatable into evaluation procedures. The book discusses concepts like action research, individual change, program evaluation, and applications in field settings, and these topics are discussed in a very understandable manner without being "watered down." I recommend this book to consultants who feel that their evaluation skills need a boost.

Kelley, R. E. (1981). *Consulting: The complete guide to a profitable career.* New York: Scribner's. The 14th chapter of this book, "Terminating the Project" (pp. 216–221), provides valuable advice on how to terminate consultation. The author treats the topic of termination from administrative and psychological perspectives. Most noteworthy is the discussion of the human side of termination, which centers around consultee dependence and corresponding consultant depression as the consultation process winds down. The author makes some excellent suggestions for minimizing the negative effects of dependence and depression. This chapter provides coverage of a sensitive and important topic that is frequently overlooked by writers in the field.

Parsons, R. D., & Meyers, J. (1984). *Developing consultation skills.* San Fransisco: Jossey-Bass. The 11th chapter of this book, "Evaluating the Process and Impact of Consultation" (pp. 207–228), is an excellent resource for examples of questionnaires, surveys, and checklists that consultants can use in designing evaluations of consultation procedures. The authors provide an example of a formative evaluation checklist, a consultee satisfaction survey, a paper-and-pencil simulation to test the impact of training, and a program input checklist. These sample instruments are of great value in illustrating the kinds of consultation events that are evaluated and the methods by which evaluations are conducted.

Chapter

7

Ethical, Professional, and Legal Issues

PREVIEW

Consider the following scenario:

CASE STUDY:
You are a consultant working with a group of consultees in a human services organization. The consultees are all heads of sections within the organization, and you are providing training that will assist them in becoming more effective decision makers. It was clearly understood from the outset that the consultant was in no way to report to the organization's administration any opinions about any of the section heads' decision-making abilities. It was further understood by all the parties involved that the consultant was to maintain total confidentiality about all aspects of the consultation.

After two months of training, the chief administrator of the human services organization approaches you and asks you to evaluate the decision-making skills of a particular section head so that a personnel decision can be made about her. The administrator assures you that the information will not go beyond your conversation with her and that no one will know that you ever said anything about the section head's decision-making skills. When you remind the administrator that confidentiality was guaranteed at the outset of the training, the administrator becomes angry, demands that you share the requested information, and threatens to terminate consultation immediately if you do not cooperate.

What would you do if you were the consultant in the above case study? Would you be tempted to secretly share the information? What are your ethical obligations to the section head? What are your ethical obligations to the organization in which consultation is occurring? What is your ethical obligation to your profession?

As you can see from the above scenario, consultants must develop ethical standards; in fact, ethical principles and issues are a part of a consultant's professional practice. This chapter will examine ethical issues—how they may affect your consultation practice and how you make ethical decisions.

Several ethical, legal, and professional issues have arisen as consultation has become more widely practiced. Some authors (for example, Gross & Robinson, 1985) suggest that ethics is a neglected topic in consultation. Reading about the kinds of issues consultants encounter can allow a better understanding of the importance of ethics and can provide a deeper appreciation for consultation's complexity and human side.

There are few cut-and-dried answers when it comes to the ethics of consultation. Consultants frequently have to rely on their sound professional judgment when making ethical decisions. This chapter provides few "right answers," for in ethical decision making in consultation there are few categorical answers.

Here are some questions to consider as you read this chapter:

1. What professional and ethical obligations do consultants have beyond those to their consultees?
2. What are the basic legal issues that consultants encounter?
3. If consultation is just an emerging field and not yet a distinct profession, then how can there be a uniform code of ethics applicable to all consultants?
4. What are some professional and ethical issues related to consultant effectiveness?
5. What are some of the ethical issues related to the professional development of the consultant?

INTRODUCTION

Throughout their careers all consultants encounter professional and ethical issues about which they must make decisions. These decisions require sound judgment. Frequently, the problems these issues generate do not suggest clear and specific courses of action that the consultant can take to resolve them; this should not be surprising, for most issues in consultation are complex (Snow & Gersick, 1986).

When grappling with difficult issues, consultants need some form of guidelines that can help them to develop a sense of ethical responsibility. As human services professionals, consultants have an obligation to behave in such a way that they bring no harm to themselves, their consultees, the client system, the organizations involved, or society at large.

There are many reasons why now more than ever there is a need to stress the importance of ethical issues (Snow & Gersick, 1986). First, more and more professionals are practicing consultation, and more and more organizations and individuals recognize the need for consultation services. Because consultation is by nature complex, the consultant is frequently caught in ethical dilemmas. Finally, consulting is a prestigious activity that involves changing others.

Just as ethical issues are receiving more attention in consultation, so too are legal issues (Brown et al., 1987). Consultants can be sued for malpractice or breach of contract and can encounter a variety of other legal difficulties. Consultants need to learn about the laws affecting their practices and act in a manner that reflects that knowledge.

ETHICS AND PROFESSIONAL ISSUES

As it pertains to consultation, *ethics* refers to standards of moral and professional conduct. When a human services professional functions in the capacity of a consultant and follows broad, written ethical guidelines, such guidelines are typically referred to as a *code of ethics.*

A code of ethics serves to discourage inappropriate practice and protect the recipients of the services being rendered. In a positive sense, codes of ethics stress adherence to rigorous professional standards and promote exemplary behavior (George & Cristiani, 1986). Because codes of ethics tend to be general, they are unable to dictate specific courses of action (Tennyson & Strom, 1986). There is as yet no code of ethics specific to consultants (Gallessich, 1982), and one is needed. Each consultant can only apply the code of ethics of his or her profession and make the best possible professional decisions when applying the code to a particular situation (Corey et al., 1988). A situation in which a naive consultee is being served by a consultant who has no specific guidelines for behavior creates a high-risk situation to the consultation process (Robinson & Gross, 1985). One way to improve this situation is to develop more detailed case materials to serve as guides for making practical ethical decisions (Lowman, 1985).

Many consultants belong to various human services professional organizations. Most of these organizations—for example, the American Association for Counseling and Development (AACD), the American Psychological Association (APA), the American Society for Training and Development (ASTD), and the National Association of Social Workers (NASW)—have developed some sort of code of ethics. Thus, many consultants enjoy the privilege of having (and have the responsibility of following) some general guidelines that apply to the professional behavior of any human services professional.

By belonging to one of these organizations, the human services professional is agreeing to adhere to that organization's code of ethics. Some organizations, such as the AACD, have specific statements about the ethical conduct of consulting behavior. Other codes, such as that of the ASTD, make no explicit mention of consultation. The result is that there are some guidelines for acting as a human services professional in the general areas of competence (for example, not providing services for which one is not competent) and responsibility (for example, maintaining confidentiality) (Robinson & Gross, 1985). But there are a few guidelines specific to consulting behavior, such as applying principles of confidentiality in an organizational setting.

Part of the problem consultants in human services fields face with respect to ethics is that consultation is a relatively new function for human services providers. Consequently, many ethical issues are just beginning to be addressed across the human services professions (Brown et al., 1987). In addition, consultation is a very complex human enterprise in which many people are often affected (Gallessich, 1982).

In conclusion, consultants can use the ethical codes of their organizations only as general guidelines. The final decision for what constitutes a correct course of action in a given situation rests with the professional (Corey et al., 1988). Thus, developing personal methods for making ethical decisions is crucial to the consultant. In order for consultants to be more confident in their ethical behavior, more specific codes of ethics for consultants and deliberate training for consultants in ethical decision making are needed.

What kinds of professional and ethical issues face consultants in their practices? One issue all consultants must face is how their *values* affect their consulting behavior. Another issue concerns consultant *competence.* Consultants must be able to determine the boundaries and scope of their abilities. *Training* is another issue with which consultants must deal: to what degree do consultants require specific training to be able to consult in given areas? Due to its complexity, the *consultant-consultee-client relationship* generates several issues. Consider the difficulty a consultant might have in determining whether the consultee's problem with a client is due to a limitation in the client or to a limitation in the consultee. The *rights of consultees* is a very important issue for consultants. Although consultation is equal in terms of the status of the consultant and consultee, it is unequal in the sense that the consultee is in need due to a work-related problem. This "inequality due to need" raises issues related to how the consultant maintains the peer nature of the consultation relationship. Consultants are increasingly turning to *group work* as a method of working with consultees and organizations because of its cost effectiveness and other potential benefits. Issues related to group work frequently encountered by the consultant range from those related to confidentiality to those surrounding self-disclosure of group members.

Consultants can refer to the ethical codes of their professions for general guidance regarding these issues. But the bottom line remains that consultants, within those broad guidelines, need to make an ". . . informed, sound, and responsible judgment" (Corey et al., 1988, p. 3) on each issue they encounter.

Values and the Consultant

As in any helping relationship, values play an integral role in the consultation process. The consultant, the consultee, the members of the client system, and the parties-at-interest to consultation all have sets of values formed by their life experiences. The behavior of each party involved in or affected by consultation is in turn influenced by his or her values. It would be naive for consultants to think that their own values do not influence the consultation process while thinking that those of the other parties do.

A significant professional issue for consultants is the degree to which they let their values dictate their behavior in consultation. Consultants who impose their values on consultees or others involved in consultation are on very shaky ethical ground. When consultants impose their values on others, they deprive them of their due freedom. At the other extreme, when consultants are overly cautious about imposing their values on others involved in consultation, they risk rendering the consultation impotent. A middle-ground attitude appears to be one in which consultants are aware of their values, have a commitment not to impose those values on others, and go about the consultation process as effectively as they can. The ethical standards of the AACD explicitly state that consultants must remain well aware of their values in order to embark upon a consultation relationship (AACD, 1981).

Problem Areas

When consultants' and consultees' values conflict, effective progress in consultation can be blocked. The bottom-line choice for consultants is to determine whether or not to refer the consultee to another consultant. Just as when values conflicts arise in other helping relationships such as counseling (Corey et al., 1988), there are no easy conflict resolution solutions in consultation. Consultants experiencing values conflicts should be honest with themselves in determining whether they can remain objective enough to work with those with whom they disagree.

Consider the following example of a values conflict:

CASE STUDY:

A consultant is working with the administrator of a substance-abuse program in a human services agency. As consultation proceeds, it becomes apparent to the consultant that the consultee thinks the clients the program serves are all "welfare bums" who are "sponging off" society and the agency. The consultant, on the other hand, views the clients as sick and in need of rehabilitation.

How would you proceed if you were the consultant in the preceding example? How would you specifically deal with the values conflict in which you find yourself? Clearly, this situation has no easy answer. Perhaps the best method for handling values conflicts is to avoid them in the first place, or at least to diminish their potential danger by taking the time at the outset of the consultation process to explore some of the issues that emerged during the preliminary exploration of organizational needs. Such discussion can help make the consultant and consultee aware that some sensitive areas are involved in the consultation.

When values conflicts do occur, they are probably best met "head-on." The consultant can model effective conflict resolution skills for the consultee as they work through the conflict, and together they can determine whether consultation is still feasible, and if so, how next to proceed. Three areas in which values conflict issues are likely to arise are:

1. differences in philosophy of life,
2. differences in views of organizations, and
3. differences in views of the client or client system.

Again, conflicts in these areas can be minimized if the consultant and consultee mutually explore their values at the outset of consultation.

In summary, because values are connected to every important decision a consultant must make (Lippitt, 1983), consultants need to be aware of their values and make a commitment not to impose them on those with whom they work. The consultant's values can, however, be used to make appropriate decisions (Lippitt, 1983). Values issues concern the degree to which consultants should allow their values to influence their behavior in consultation and when they should reveal their values (Snow & Gersick, 1986). When values conflicts emerge, the consultant should deal with them in a nondefensive, professional manner. Because values conflicts occur relatively frequently in our diverse society, it is surprising that relatively little has been written about consultants and their values. Whereas the topic is given implicit attention throughout the literature, only a few authors (for example, Pfeiffer & Jones, 1977; Lippitt & Lippitt, 1986; and Gallessich, 1982) address it directly.

Consultant Competence

Whereas the ethical issues surrounding consultants and their values have received only minimal consideration, the issue of consultant competence has received much attention. The codes of ethics of the major organizations in which many consultants have membership (for example, the AACD, 1981; the APA, 1981; and the ASTD, 1987) all make statements to the effect that members should deliver only those services and accept only those positions for which they are qualified. These qualifications are usually determined by the consultant's training and experience.

The parameters of competence are the maintenance of high levels of professionalism, knowing one's professional limitations, knowing when to decline and refer, and avoiding consultation activities when personal concerns could affect professional performance (Lippitt & Lippitt, 1986).

Maintenance of High Levels of Professionalism

Consultants can do several things to maintain high levels of professional competence:

1. belong to and participate in professional organizations;
2. obtain the appropriate national and state credentials, certificates, and licenses for the profession in which the consultant is trained;
3. participate in continuing education activities in general;
4. participate in continuing education activities (both didactic and experiential) that pertain to the consultation services one delivers or wants to deliver;
5. co-consult with more experienced colleagues; and
6. consult under the supervision of a trusted colleague or a designated supervisor.

Underlying the maintenance of professionalism is consultants' desire to grow in their work. Consultants with such a growth orientation attempt to "stretch" themselves so that the depth and breadth of their knowledge and skills increase.

This willingness to grow professionally provides consultees a positive role model that stimulates their growth and desire to participate more fully in consultation.

Knowing One's Professional Limitations

Although it is easy to suggest ways of maintaining high levels of professionalism as a consultant, it is more difficult to suggest methods of knowing one's limitations. The ethical codes of the AACD (1981), the APA (1981), and the ASTD (1987) state that knowledge of limitations and/or abilities is essential. Probably the most important thing that consultants can do in recognizing their limitations is to make a commitment to maintain high levels of objectivity and integrity while placing the needs of the consultee and the organization above their own (Lippitt & Lippitt, 1986). By asking themselves the following four questions in order, consultants can stay focused on their limitations:

What can I do, given this situation?
What is the right thing to do in this situation?
Do I have the ability to do the right thing?
What is the right thing to do that is in the best interests of the consultee and the organization?

By carefully pondering these questions, consultants are less likely to make errors in judgment with respect to their limitations. There is no substitute for the combination of personal and professional self-awareness and the commitment to put forth one's best effort when consulting.

Knowing When to Decline and Refer

When consultants realize they are "in over their heads" in terms of what is expected of them, they need to decline providing consultation services and make an appropriate referral. The story we hear about a consultee walking up to a consultant and asking "Are you an expert in 'X'?", to which the consultant responds "Sure, just give me an hour" comes true all too often. Several professional organizations' ethical codes state that services should be delivered only if it is anticipated that the services provider can effectively manage the existing problem as well as any others that may arise.

A related issue involves the representation of oneself as a consultant. Consultants must state explicitly what they stand for, who they represent, and what they can and cannot do as consultants. This obligation to represent oneself honestly and accurately includes advertising. The AACD (1981), the APA (1981), and the ASTD (1987) all make explicit statements with regard to honest disclosure about oneself both in person and through advertising. In fact, the ethical code of the APA (1981) devotes more coverage to public statements than to any other ethical principle.

Closely tied to the issue of representing oneself honestly is the issue of remuneration. Consultants typically charge the "going fee" for a given type of consultation service with a given type of organization in a given geographic area. The AACD (1981) specifically states that its members must refuse any type of remuneration when consultation recipients are due those services through the member's organization. Consultants must consider for each potential consultation whether they are in a position to charge fees in the first place and, if so, how much.

How do consultants respond when they are asked to provide services for which they are not qualified? The answer lies in referral procedures. Consultants have the responsibility to determine at the outset of consultation (in exploring organizational needs) whether or not they can be of assistance. When consultants determine that they cannot be of assistance, they should consider making a referral to a qualified consultant; even if a referral is not possible, the provision of services should be declined anyway.

Consultants sometimes decline to offer their services when the time required for consultation is longer than the consultant has available. Thus, it would be unethical for consultants to take on a two-year project when at the outset they know they would be available for only six months.

In summary, consultants need to know when to make referrals; generally this is necessary when consultants have neither the skill nor the time required to provide adequate services.

When Personal Concerns Affect Professional Performance

Consultants of course have the same kinds of personal concerns and problems as anyone else, and these can negatively affect the consultant's professional performance to the degree that consultation services are not adequate. In this case the consultant should consider stopping the services and making an appropriate referral. In fact, APA's code of ethics (1981) states that when members suffer from personal concerns that affect professional functioning, they should seek out consultation regarding whether or not to continue providing services. Therefore, consultants who are experiencing high levels of stress should be particularly aware of their ability to provide adequate professional services.

Consultants need to be aware of their personal needs throughout each phase of the consultation process and should take measures so that those needs do not replace the needs of the consultee (Robinson & Gross, 1985). The following examples illustrate this issue at each stage of the consultation process:

Entry. The consultant is an expert in stress management; the consultee reports that morale in the organization is low and that previous stress management programs have not been successful in lifting morale. During preliminary exploration of organizational needs, the consultant must be wary of the need of "pushing" for a stress management program that will "really work."

Diagnosis. The consultant believes that for consultation to be effective the entire organization must be considered in the diagnosis, even when the focus of consultation is on the consultee's clients; the consultee prefers that diagnosis take place in terms of the client's problems only.

Implementation. The consultant adheres somewhat strictly to a behavioral perspective on interventions with the client; the consultee prefers a more humanistic approach to intervention.

Disengagement. The consultant believes that consultees should be "on their own" as soon as possible and that experiencing some anxiety is good for them; the consultee prefers to have a precise timetable for when reductions in consultant involvement will begin and wants it to occur only when the consultee is not feeling anxious about handling the case.

Consultants need to be honest with themselves in owning their needs; such awareness decreases the probability that the consultant will behave unethically.

Training of Consultants

Training is actually an aspect of consultant competence. Consultants must make sure they have the adequate training to perform the services for which they contract.

Training as an Ethical Issue

Consultation itself is not well enough developed to make any categorical statements about the subjects in which consultants should be trained and how this training should occur. The thinking about how consultants should be trained is in its infancy (Brown, 1985), but the topic is receiving increased attention (Dustin, 1985). Even the matter of when training in consultation should occur is being debated (Pryzwansky, 1985). In short, neither the actions of people engaged in consultation nor the skills required for effective consultation have been adequately defined (Gallessich, Long, & Jennings, 1986). This state of affairs relegates the issue of training of consultants to the realm of ethics.

Although there are some guidelines for the training of consultants, it is ultimately up to individual consultants to decide whether they have received sufficient training to allow delivery of competent services in a given consultation situation. The development of ethical behavior in consultants might be enhanced if they were required to engage in supervised, controlled consultation experiences during training (Crego, 1985).

Approaches to Training

Many authors (for example, Lippitt & Lippitt, 1986; Gallessich, 1982; Gallessich et al., 1986; Brown et al., 1987) have written about the training of consultants. Gallessich and others (1986) reported that historically consultants were trained in one of the following models:

1. *Clinical approaches:* The consultant typically observes (or meets with) and examines the consultee's client and then reports back to the consultee with a diagnosis and a recommended course of action;

2. *Consultee-centered approaches:* The main goal is to enhance the professional functioning of the consultee. The consultant collaborates with the consultee and provides needed support, education, and/or training;
3. *Behavioral approaches:* Techniques derived from learning theory are emphasized when consultants help consultees work with their clients; or
4. *Organizational approaches:* Consultants assist consultees in enhancing an organization's overall effectiveness by working with all or a part of that organization.

Today's training typically covers more than one of these approaches as the distinctions among these models becomes less clear.

The training of consultants is still haphazard, although training in interpersonal and communication skills (for example, Stum, 1982) and in design of consultation processes remains a consistent part of the training (Lippitt & Lippitt, 1986). Whereas most consultants received most of their training through on-the-job experiences (Gallessich, 1982), training opportunities are becoming increasingly available. Organizations such as the ASTD offer continuing education for consultants regardless of their professional discipline. More recently, colleges and universities have begun to offer prospective human services providers preservice training in the form of courses in consultation. No matter how consultants get their training, there appear to be five topics in which they should be trained (Gallessich, 1982):

1. the theoretical foundations of various models,
2. the range of possible consultant roles and functions,
3. a generic model of consultation,
4. organizational theory, and
5. knowledge/understanding of oneself as a consultant.

Gibbs (1985) has urged that consultants be trained in knowing about and using interventions appropriate for culturally different groups. Brown and others (1987) have developed an extensive list of competencies in which consultants should be trained based on a three-part schema that includes knowledge competencies, behavioral skills, and judgment competencies. Their list is basically an expansion and elaboration of the above list developed by Gallessich (1982).

Because of the paucity of empirical research that has been conducted on consultation, it is very difficult to categorically state how consultants can be adequately trained. The current state of affairs reflects a "shotgun approach" that provides widely divergent formal and informal training opportunities; the trend is toward training in a generic model (Gallessich et al., 1986). The solution to current needs may lie in supervised training conducted by experienced consultants who have been trained in supervision. Brown and others (1987) offer a model of supervision of consultants that may be helpful to experienced consultants who want to get training in supervision.

In summary, there are relatively few guidelines for training consultants. Still, regardless of how they receive training, consultants are ethically bound to determine whether they are adequately trained to provide services in each consultation situation as it arises.

The Consultant-Consultee-Client Relationship

The consultant-consultee-client relationship is very complex. What obligation, for example, does the consultant have to the consultee's client? What are the parameters of the consultation relationship as they relate to the consultant and consultee? Can the consultant-consultee-client relationship be examined only in the context of the organization in which consultation is occurring?

In general, the consultant-consultee-client relationship can be examined in isolation or within an organizational context; both views shed light on ethical issues. When considered in isolation, ethical issues concerning the relationship revolve around each party's obligations and how well those obligations were fulfilled. When examined in an organizational context, ethical issues involve matters that go beyond the isolated relationship. For example, when confidentiality is to be maintained, where within the organization do we set its limits?

Next we'll consider the ethical issues surrounding the complex consultant-consultee-client relationship in terms of work-related focus, dual relationships, and freedom of choice.

Work-Related Focus

The code of ethics of the AACD (1981) states that the focus of the consultation relationship should be on work-related problems and not on the parties involved (that is, a personal relationship); this work-related focus should be maintained from the outset. It can be inferred from this code that personal relationships with consultees and their clients is questionable ethical behavior. Further, this same code of ethics also implies that the consultation relationship should be contractual and based on well-defined, mutually agreed-upon expectations (for example, nature of the problem, goals of consultation, and desired results). This straightforward assumption must also be considered in light of the fact that the consultant and consultee represent their respective organizations (Snow & Gersick, 1986); either party may have obligations to others not directly involved in but directly affected by consultation. Attempting to sort out these obligations can be very difficult.

Dual Relationships

Consultants have obligations to consultees that are similar to those that therapists have to clients, although consultation focuses on work-related issues and counseling can address personal issues as well. In addition, because consultants provide indirect services to clients, they have some obligation to those clients. Indeed, there is some controversy with regard to whether the consultant's ultimate obligation is to the consultee or to the consultee's client (Snow & Gersick, 1986).

Consultants are obligated to avoid dual relationships with consultees. *Dual relationships* are those in which a professional has more than one role (usually one role is professional and the other is personal). As an extreme example, a consultant experiencing sexual intimacy with a consultee has a dual relationship with that consultee; one role of the relationship is professional—a consultant—and the other role is personal—sexual partner. Dual relationships frequently cause role conflict and conflicts of interest (Corey et al., 1988) and therefore they should be avoided (Conoley & Conoley, 1982).

A special type of dual relationship, one that is particularly hazardous to consultants and their consultees, occurs when a consultant maintains two professional roles in the consultation relationship. The two most common second roles in consultation relationships are counselor/psychotherapist and supervisor.

It is relatively easy for a consultant who is a trained counselor or therapist to move the consultation relationship into one that also provides counseling or therapy to the consultee. When this occurs, the act of counseling contaminates the consultation relationship by focusing on personal problems and by deemphasizing the work-related problems upon which consultation was contracted. The use of counseling or psychotherapy in the consultation relationship, when it occurs, usually results once the consultant has determined that the basis for the work-related problem resides more in the consultee than the client. Rather than providing direct counseling services to the consultee, consultants in such a situation should refer the consultee for assistance.

Another instance in which dual relationships occur is when supervision is somehow incorporated into the consultation relationship. It is relatively easy for the consultant who has had supervisory training and administrative experience to include supervisory activities in what should be an exclusively consultative relationship. Because supervision implies the use of evaluation, control, and power over someone, supervision violates the peer nature of the consultation relationship. Use of supervision in consultation allows the consultant to build an illegitimate power base, creates the potential for conflicts of interest, and violates the original consultation contract. Clearly such a dual relationship is to be avoided.

Freedom of Choice

Providing consultees and their clients freedom of choice is one of the major ethical obligations of consultants. Ethical issues related to freedom of choice concern:

1. assurance that the consultee is acting in the client's best interests,
2. the creation of dependence,
3. misuse of power, and
4. inappropriate manipulation of consultees by consultants.

Consultees should always perceive that they have the freedom to do whatever they wish with consultants' recommendations. This freedom of choice relieves the consultant from being responsible for the consultee's behavior, assuming that the consultee acts in a professionally responsible manner (Fanibanda, 1976). Such a view of freedom of choice requires consultants to take steps when they consider consultees' actions to be negative in some way (Snow & Gersick, 1986). The first step is to point out the inappropriate behavior to the consultee. Beyond this action, there is little consensus as to how the consultant should proceed (Snow & Gersick, 1986). The consultant may have the option of pointing out the consultee's behavior to the consultee's employer, or the consultant may terminate the consultation relationship, thereby placing the consultee's behavior under consideration beyond the consultation relationship.

Consultees cannot have complete freedom of choice if they are dependent on their consultant. This issue is also addressed by the AACD (1981), whose code of ethics specifically states that the consultation relationship should be such that the consultee does not become dependent on the consultant and learns increased self-direction. It is the consultant's responsibility to make sure that dependence does not occur. Because the very purpose of consultation is to assist consultees and their organizations to function more effectively and autonomously, it is unethical for consultants to create and maintain dependence on the part of consultees (Fanibanda, 1976).

Closely related to the issue of dependence is that of power. One of the most common abuses of power in the consultation relationship occurs when the consultant violates the peer nature of the relationship and pressures the consultee to get something accomplished. For example, a consultant might push a certain plan of action on the consultee. A second abuse of power involves misusing the relationship with the consulting organization's administrators to achieve something that should be accomplished through other channels (Glaser, 1981). For example, a consultant might ask an administrator to send through channels a memo concerning preferred action plans when it was agreed at the outset of consultation that consultees would develop action plans independent of the administration. A third misuse of power occurs when a consultee is forced to participate in consultation; because such coercion violates the voluntary nature of consultation, it is unethical behavior. In addition, consultants must ensure that their consultees are not receiving undue pressure to participate from their administrators.

Consultees cannot have freedom of choice if they are being manipulated by consultants (Hughes, 1986). Therefore, from the outset consultants should discuss with their consultees the ways in which consultants will attempt to influence them. Consultants can maintain their consultees' freedom of choice by discussing their own values and by helping consultees to critically consider consultants' suggestions on their own merits (Hughes, 1986).

In summary, the consultant-consultee-client relationship presents many ethical issues. Clear expectations concerning the relationship, avoidance of dual relationships, and freedom of choice for all parties involved contribute to maintaining ethical behavior on the part of consultants.

Rights of Consultees

Closely related to the issues concerning the consultant-consultee-client relationship are those surrounding the rights of consultees. Two major issues involving the rights of consultees are confidentiality and informed consent. As it applies to consultation, confidentiality can be viewed as an ethical responsibility (Corey et al., 1988) of the consultant to protect the consultee and the consultee's clients from inappropriate disclosure of information shared within the consultation relationship. The codes of ethics of the AACD (1981) and the

ASTD (1987) implicitly deal with confidentiality as it relates to consultation, while that of the APA (1981) mentions it explicitly. Informed consent refers to sharing with the consultee information pertinent to consultation in order for the consultee to know what is involved and to participate fully and effectively in the process. The codes of ethics of the AACD (1981), the APA (1981), and the ASTD (1987) all mention informed consent, although not specifically regarding the practice of consultation.

Confidentiality

The consultant is obligated to develop guidelines that safeguard the parties involved in consultation (Corey et al., 1988). These guidelines should be developed during the entry stage and put into the consultation contract. Guidelines should be structured to protect the consultee's oral and written communication and employee records (Robinson & Gross, 1985). Two aspects to confidentiality that should be considered in consultation are the tripartite nature of consultation and the limits on confidentiality (Snow & Gersick, 1986).

Consultation is by definition tripartite, which implies that at least three parties (and possibly more) can have knowledge of information that is disclosed during consultation. The simplest example is a consultee sharing information about a client to a consultant. In a more complex example, an external agency might require a report from a consultant about some aspect of consultation. The potential for several parties to acquire information may create trust issues in consultation and makes confidentiality a primary ethical concern for consultants. The consultant must create procedures for determining what information is to be shared with whom, when, how, for what reasons, and what the likely impact of sharing will be (Snow & Gersick, 1986).

Consultants can increase their awareness of the complexity of confidentiality by asking themselves the following questions:

What can I tell my own organization about what is said both in consultation and in the consultee organization?

With whom can I share information in the consultee organization?

What kinds of information can I share with external organizations such as funding agencies?

What should the consultee reveal to me about his/her client or organization?

How do I determine if my discussion of information obtained in consultation meets professional standards?

How do I determine which parties are sufficiently and appropriately concerned with the case such that they require or are entitled to information obtained in consultation?

Posing and answering such complex questions at the outset of consultation, getting consensus on the answers, and publicizing this consensus can prevent problems from occurring later on in the consultation process.

There is no such thing as pure confidentiality. Confidentiality has limits and it is up to the consultant to forge some agreement concerning those limits. The limits of confidentiality refer to those instances that would dictate that confidentiality be set aside.

The limits of confidentiality are commonly discussed in terms of weighing the individual's rights against the needs of society (Sheeley & Herlihy, 1986). It is usually assumed that consultants must get permission from their consultees or from members of the organization affected by the consultation before sharing information. But in cases in which permission is not granted, what do consultants do when they have what they feel are good reasons that the information should be revealed? Specifically, what should consultants do when they determine that a consultee is mistreating a client or that a program is counterproductive for the client system? There are no clear-cut answers in determining when confidentiality should be set aside in consultation (Snow & Gersick, 1986). This author is of the opinion that consultants should set aside confidentiality when they determine to the best of their ability that:

1. the best interests of society are not being met, or
2. the client system is being violated in some way.

When setting aside confidentiality, the consultant determines and takes responsibility for who is to be told, what they are to be told, and in what manner.

The second way in which the limits of confidentiality are discussed involves the concept of anonymity (Snow & Gersick, 1986). When maintaining confidentiality, the consultant can share information only with permission of the consultee or an appropriate member of the organization. When maintaining anonymity, the consultant can share the information but must protect its source. The use of anonymity has the advantage of facilitating a flow of information, which can be critical to the success of consultation that focuses on an organization as a whole. Using anonymity can be a very useful strategy for consultants: it prevents them from having "one helping hand tied behind their backs" when they have information that could be helpful if it were shared but are restrained from sharing by a lack of permission to do so.

Informed Consent

Informed consent is a second issue related to the rights of consultees. In order to determine whether they want to be involved in consultation in the first place, consultees need to be as fully informed as possible about the nature and goals of consultation, issues of confidentiality, their right to privacy, the voluntary nature of participation, and complete freedom in following or not following through on the consultant's recommendations (Hughes, 1986). The guidelines suggested by Corey and others (1988) for counselors and therapists who work with clients seem quite appropriate for consultants and their consultees.

Informed consent should be considered an ongoing process and not a one-time event (Corey et al., 1988). Such a conceptualization of informed consent prevents the consultant from making the mistake of overloading the consultee with too much information at the outset of consultation, and it permits candid discussion of the most critical information about which the consultee needs to be apprised.

Even though consultants should view informed consent as an ongoing process, they must still ask themselves what consultees need to know at the outset. A good practice for answering this question is for consultants to "place themselves in their consultees' shoes" and ascertain what they would like to know at the outset of consultation. The following questions may come to mind:

How long will consultation last?
What will a typical session be like?
What are you to do?
What am I to do?
Who else will know what we are doing?
To what degree will what we say here be private?
What are your goals for yourself and for me?
Who are you and what are your credentials?

These questions reinforce the idea that consultees come to consultation with many important, unanswered questions. By empathizing with their consultees, consultants are in a better position to patiently answer questions and provide information. Instead of merely being a routine exercise, the sharing of information to obtain informed consent can be a rapport-building event for consultant and consultee alike.

In summary, two important rights of consultees and their clients, confidentiality and informed consent, are complex issues due to the complexity of the consultation relationship itself. The keys to minimizing damage to consultation and the parties involved and to promoting ethical behavior are to define the limits of confidentiality at the outset of consultation and to view informed consent as an ongoing process.

The Consultant and the Group

Because of its cost effectiveness, an increasing amount of consultation is occurring between a consultant and a group of consultees or between a consultant and part or all of an organization. Due to this increase in such activities, ethical and professional issues related to consulting with groups are of increasing importance. Because consultation with groups raises unique ethical and professional issues, it is given separate consideration here.

Consulting with Groups with Caseloads

When a consultant considers working with the same group of consultees for some extended length of time, a basic issue that is raised is that of competence. To what degree is the consultant experienced and trained in group consultation? How aware is the consultant of group process and group dynamics? Because consulting with a group of consultees is much different from and more complex than working with an individual consultee, it is critical that consultants have some form of training in group consultation before embarking on such a venture.

Another issue that reemerges when consulting with a group of consultees is informed consent. To what degree have the consultees been made aware of the differences between individual and group consultation? Has participation been made voluntary? Have the consultees been made aware of what is expected of them within the group? As in individual consultation, informed consent should be an ongoing process.

A third issue that reemerges in group consultation is confidentiality. Clearly, the consultant cannot guarantee confidentiality for anyone in the group except himself or herself. Still, because most consultees are also professionals it is not unreasonable to expect them to live up to their obligation to respect confidentiality. Many authors (for example, Corey et al ., 1988) suggest that group leaders encourage confidentiality through such methods as providing a written policy statement at the outset and/or casually but seriously mentioning confidentiality throughout the life of the group.

A final issue that reemerges is that of dependence. Consultees can become dependent within a group more easily than when they experience consultation as individuals, especially if the consultation group is supportive and safe. The group can become a professional "family" and consultees can readily experience a sense of belonging and cohesiveness. Consultants can help reduce consultee dependence by moving especially cautiously into the disengagement stage and by placing special emphasis on consultees' independent functioning throughout the duration of consultation.

Consulting with Training Groups

Consultants are increasingly being retained to educate or train consultees. In their extensive treatment of the ethics of training groups, Pfeiffer and Jones (1977) list five basic issues of concern to consultants engaged in education or training:

1. deception,
2. co-optation,
3. inappropriate techniques,
4. inattention to application, and
5. rehashing.

In this context, *deception* refers to the willful misleading of consultees as a part of an educational or training strategy (Pfeiffer & Jones, 1977). Consultants are obligated to correct any misconceptions that may result from such deception and duly inform consultees of the goals and objectives of training activities by some form of debriefing.

Co-optation involves forcing a consultee to do something he or she does not want to do by such means as using excessive persuasion or group pressure. Such a practice, of course, violates informed consent and the right to privacy. Co-optation in any form is unethical and can be minimized by making the learning/training environment a safe one for all involved.

The use of *inappropriate techniques* frequently stems from the consultant's need to use some "pet" technique, from a lack of understanding among the consultant and consultees concerning what is to be accomplished, or possibly from poor planning by the consultant. A way to avoid this predicament in educational and training experiences is to take the norms of the consultee group into consideration during planning (Pfeiffer & Jones, 1977).

Inattention to the application of training refers to the state of affairs in which measures to apply the lessons of the educational experience are not taken (Pfeiffer & Jones, 1977). The consultant is ethically bound to assist consultees in applying what they have learned. The work of such authors as Kirkpatrick (1975) and Birnbrauer (1987) have provided guidance for consultants in determining consultees' reactions to education or training experiences, what they learned from those experiences, new behaviors that resulted from their new knowledge, and the results of those behaviors in terms of the consultees' professional growth.

Consultants have an ethical obligation not to repeat or *rehash* the same educational/training experience with the same consultees. In addition, consultants should keep their education and training offerings current and full of vitality (Pfeiffer & Jones, 1977). Consultants involved in education and training should take their own professional growth as seriously as they do that of their consultees; indeed, the ASTD code of ethics (1987) explicitly states that members should keep informed of pertinent knowledge in their fields.

THE CONSULTANT AND THE LAW

Relatively little has been written on the legal issues that concern consultants. Because consultation is still an emerging profession, relatively few guidelines on professional behavior exist to guide the court when consultants encounter legal entanglements. Still, as human services professionals consultants deliver their services in a sociolegal environment, and they need to be aware of legal matters that can affect them (Woody & Associates, 1984). The importance of attention to legal issues in the helping professions is emphasized by the fact that the AACD and the APA have set up legal defense funds for members involved in certain types of litigation (Hopkins & Anderson, 1985).

Those who have written about legal issues as they relate to consultants (for example, Brown et al., 1987) tend to extrapolate from legal issues encountered in counseling and psychotherapy. Others (for example, Cummings & Maxey, 1985) tend to write from the perspective of labor law. Next we'll consider a legal issue of paramount importance to consultants: malpractice.

Malpractice

Human services professionals are accountable for the quality of their services (Woody & Associates, 1984). In *malpractice* the service recipient is in some way damaged by improper services offered without good faith or through neglect or ignorance (Corey et al., 1988). Consultants can be sued for performing the wrong services or for failing to provide the correct services. How can the right or wrong type of service be determined? Applying what typically happens to professional counselors (that is, professionals with no well-defined professional identity in the eyes of the law) (Hopkins & Anderson, 1985) in a similar situation leads to this conclusion: the court would attempt to determine whether a "typical" professional consultant would act in a way similar to the way the consultant in question acted. An answer in the affirmative would likely lead to no liability, whereas a negative answer could lead to liability (Hopkins & Anderson, 1985).

In order to determine whether a consultant was guilty of malpractice, a court would seek answers to the following questions:

1. Did the defendant (consultant) have a professional obligation to the plaintiff?
2. Was that duty breached by the consultant?
3. Is there a causal link between the breach and the damage to the plaintiff?

To answer these questions, the court would probably attempt to determine whether the consultant showed "requisite skill and care" (Hopkins & Anderson, 1985, p. 25). However, because these terms are not yet adequately defined for consultants, courts typically rely on already-established standards for related professions that perform consultation for defining standards for appropriate professional consulting behavior (Hopkins & Anderson, 1985).

Malpractice suits can occur in just about any area of consultation practice. A recent literature review of the causes of malpractice (Corey et al., 1988, p. 23) cited several behaviors that could cause legal entanglement for consultants:

1. misrepresenting one's training and skills,
2. failing to respect integrity and privacy,
3. using improper diagnosis and assessment techniques,
4. using improper methods to collect fees,
5. making inappropriate public statements (libel and slander),
6. failing to honor agreements (breach of contract),
7. failing to keep adequate records,
8. failing to provide for informed consent, and
9. providing poor advice.

In summary, consultants can be sued for malpractice whenever there is the likelihood that they have provided services either without the proper skill or without the proper care.

Avoiding Legal Entanglements

It is safe to assume that the vast majority of consultants want to avoid legal entanglements. How should they go about doing this? It is most important that consultants learn about any state laws that may have implications for their practices. Ignorance of the law is not an excuse if a consultant is called into court.

Consultants should provide proper services—only those services in which they are skilled—with care and skill. The old adage "An ounce of prevention is worth a pound of cure" could not be more true when it comes to avoiding legal entanglements.

Consultants should consider joining a professional organization that has a code of ethics and should adhere to that code's principles and standards. Such adherence facilitates delivering consultation services with the proper skill and care and assists the consultant in determining standards of professional conduct.

Consultants need a personal and professional growth orientation based on a healthy and honest self-awareness. Knowledge of one's limitations and abilities as a person and a professional enhances a consultant's ability to make the correct decision concerning whether a given consultation service should be undertaken in the first place.

Consultants should do well each of the "little things" their profession demands of them:

1. use a written contract,
2. keep accurate records,
3. discuss fees at the outset of consultation,
4. discuss confidentiality and its limits as a matter of course at the outset of every consultation relationship,
5. make sure that any advertising or promotional activities provide current and accurate information,
6. seek consultation from a trusted colleague or a supervisor when in doubt about proper procedure, and
7. foster open communication at all times.

By taking such steps, consultants can dramatically reduce the likelihood of legal entanglement. Consultants who know what they are doing and why they are doing it have relatively little to fear, even though the boundaries of their professional behavior remain relatively indistinct in the eyes of the law.

SUMMARY

This chapter has presented an introduction to the closely related ethical, professional, and legal issues that pertain to consultation in the human services professions. Consultations can maintain professional standards by being aware of issues involving values, competence, training, the consultation relationship, the rights of consultees and their clients, and consultation in groups. Most legal issues that consultants encounter concern malpractice. Consultants can maintain a sense of ethical and professional responsibility and avoid legal entanglements by being committed to their own personal and professional growth.

QUESTIONS FOR REFLECTION

1. If ethical guidelines are by definition general in nature, how can consultants apply these guidelines in specific situations?
2. If there are no standards for professional behavior for consultants as a group, how can consultants be held accountable for their behavior?

3. As a consultant-in-training, how would you want to be trained in ethical decision making?
4. To what degree do consultants require specific training to be able to consult in a given area?
5. What are the consultant's professional and ethical obligations to the consultee?
6. What are the consultant's professional and ethical obligations to the consultee's client?
7. In what ways are consultants most likely to violate the rights of their consultees during consultation?
8. How does a consultant go about developing a personal and professional growth orientation?
9. If you were a judge in a court of law and a consultant was being sued for malpractice, what information would you want to know in order to determine whether malpractice had occurred?
10. How can there ever be a code of ethics for consultants when there are so many different professional groups whose members perform consultation as one of their primary functions?

SUGGESTED SUPPLEMENTARY READINGS

I hope you are interested in learning more about the ethical, professional, and legal issues that affect consultants. Here are a few readings that I strongly recommend for study and reflection.

Corey, G., Corey, M. S., & Callanan, P. (1988). *Issues and ethics in the helping professions* (3rd. ed.). Pacific Grove, CA: Brooks/Cole. This book provides a wealth of information for professionals and students in any of the human services professions. Although ethics and issues specifically related to consultation are given only brief coverage (pp. 276–279), many of the authors' ideas on several issues have relevance for consultants. Chapter 3, "Values and the Helping Relationship," provides excellent information that consultants can extrapolate and apply to their consultation practices. Chapter 7, "The Client/Therapist Relationship, Unethical Behavior, and Malpractice Issues," presents important information that consultants can use in developing their own standards of conduct. The appendix of this text contains the codes of ethics of the major helping professions, which can be useful resources and guides.

Robinson, S. E., & Gross, D. R. (1985). Ethics of consultation: The Canterville ghost. *The Counseling Psychologist*, 13(3), 444–465. This article presents an overview of the types of ethical issues that consultants encounter. The authors make the point that most ethical issues related to consultation concern consultant competence and responsibility. They then survey specific issues under these two areas, such as identifying the consultee and client systems, confidentiality, and knowing and respecting consultee and client rights. Organizational factors involved in ethical and professional issues are discussed relatively briefly.

Although written for counseling psychologists, professionals and students in other human services areas will benefit from reading this article.

Lippitt, G., & Lippitt, R. (1986). *The consulting process in action.* San Diego, CA: University Associates. Chapter 5, "Ethical Dilemmas and Guidelines for Consultants," is a particularly valuable reading for consultants. The merit of this chapter is its presentation of ethical dilemmas along with guidelines for ethical behavior. This chapter is written from the perspective of consultants who consult with organizations. Reading how the authors work through the selected ethical dilemmas is very rewarding exercise.

PART
3

Models of Consultation

Now that you have read about and studied the consultation process in general, we will consider some popular models of consultation. All models of consultation can assist consultees deal with a work-related concern through a problem-solving process. The ways problem solving is accomplished varies according to the model under consideration. In addition, most models can help consultees be more effective with similar or related problems in the future.

Some models of consultation are more structured than others. Depending on the model, the consultant acts in the role of technical expert, expert diagnostician, or expert facilitator. All models have a well defined approach to solving problems. But no model has developed a theoretical basis for the communication aspect of consultation (West & Idol, 1987); that is, no model of consultation is based on enough research to allow it to prescribe how the consultant and consultee should interact with each other.

Although tremendous progress has been made in the methods for performing consultation, little advancement has occurred in the development of theoretical models of consultation (Gallessich, 1985). In fact, some authors (for example, Gallessich, 1985) suggest that the practice of consultation is basically *atheoretical*. Three factors impede the development of adequate theories of consultation: an attitude among consultants that consultation is an atheoretical process, the rapidity of change in consultation practices, and problems in performing research on consultation and its effects (Gallessich, 1985). In order to overcome these obstacles, Gallessich (1985) suggests that consultation models be categorized by value structure, which results in three consultation models:

1. a scientific-technological model, which derives its primary value from the scientific method;
2. a human-development consultation model, which derives its primary value from belief in the desirability of human growth and development; and
3. a social/political consultation model, which derives its primary value from the social and/or political aspect of the consultee's work.

In spite of such suggestions as these, most authors still rely on the more traditional way of characterizing consultation models—in terms of their derivatives.

These models, which will be covered in this part of the book, include organizational, mental health, and behavioral consultation. The name associated with a given model of consultation serves to identify that model's primary focus.

Organizational consultation tends to consider the entire organization to be the client. *Mental health consultation* focuses on the mental health implications of human services professionals' mental health-related programs and their work with clients. *Behavioral consultation* typically focuses on specific changes in clients, client systems, and/or consultees.

Traditionally, models of consultation differ with respect to five dimensions:

1. conceptualization of the problem,
2. goals,
3. methods and assumptions,
4. consultant roles, and
5. professional values (Gallessich, 1982).

Organizational consultation conceptualizes the problem in terms of an organization's structure and processes. It has the goal of modifying those structures and processes to ameliorate some problem through carefully designed interventions that affect the organization's system. The consultant takes on one or more of a variety of roles to assist consultees. Those values are advocated that enhance the organization's overall effectiveness by helping its members become more satisfied and productive.

There is no one "organizational consultation," but rather a series of approaches that tend to consider the organization to be the client system. Program consultation and education/training consultation were included in the discussion of organizational consultation because of their similarities to other organizational approaches: both can improve the effectiveness of the organization in which consultation occurs, even though their roots are not specific to organizational consultation. For example, program consultation could assist an organization in determining the degree to which one of its programs was successful. In one example of education/training in the context of organizational consultation, a consultant might train teachers to communicate more effectively with their pupils, thereby enhancing the school's overall effectiveness.

Mental health consultation conceptualizes a problem in terms of mental health constructs. The goal of alleviating the mental health problem is accomplished by helping consultees work with their clients or with the mental health implications of their programs. The consultant acts either as facilitator or technical advisor in advocating the value of enhancing the mental health functioning of all involved in consultation. Mental health consultation focuses both on helping consultees help their clients and on helping consultees become more effective professionals.

Behavioral consultation conceptualizes the problem in terms of reducing the difference between the current frequency of some problem behavior and the desired frequency of that behavior. This behavioral goal is accomplished through the use of interventions based on the principles of learning. The consultant acts as both expert and guide and advocates that behavior be changed in a precise, scientific manner.

As the field of consultation has grown and developed, the differences among these three major models have become increasingly less distinct. All consultation is "organizational" in that it occurs within an organization of some kind. All consultation is "mental health" consultation in that the "psychological" well-being of the consultee and the client system is either directly or indirectly affected by consultation. All consultation is "behavioral" because by its very nature consultation implies change: when consultees, clients, and client systems such as organizations respond positively to consultation, they change their behavior.

Indeed, there are probably more similarities than differences among these models. Organizational consultation, for example, is becoming increasingly aware of mental health issues. Empirical research on organizations suggests that satisfied personnel work more productively than do dissatisfied personnel (Katz & Kahn, 1978). Behavioral consultation increasingly focuses on how behavioral technology can be used to help organizations more effectively meet their missions.

As noted above, some authors (for example, Gallessich, 1985; Dworkin & Dworkin, 1975) have suggested that consultation approaches be classified by their major goal or function rather than according to some model. However, most writers still categorize the models of consultation according to the primary focus of each. Hence, in the next few chapters we'll discuss the organizational, mental health, and behavioral models of consultation separately, all the while noting the rapidly disappearing differences among them.

Chapter

8

The Nature of Organizations

PREVIEW

Organizations are groups of people put together for a particular purpose. Each of these very complex entities has goals and objectives. When they have difficulty meeting goals and objectives, organizations frequently seek the help of consultants. Indeed, consultants are used so frequently by business, industry, and human services organizations that we now call many approaches "organizational consultation."

Consider this situation:

CASE STUDY:
In your job as chief administrator of a large human services agency, you notice an excessive turnover rate in two of your organization's six departments. You have made several unsuccessful attempts to rectify the problem; you know what is wrong, but you don't know "how to fix it." As a last resort, you decide to call in a consultant.

In preparing for the first meeting with the consultant, what exactly would you tell the consultant about your organization, the people in it, the problem, and the solutions you've tried? Where would you suggest the consultant should begin to try to help?

If you were the consultant in this situation, what information would you want to know? What values and biases about "how to fix things" would you bring into the consultation setting? Which personnel would you want to interview? How would you go about solving the problem? How would you know whether or not consultation had been successful? The answers to these and many other important questions depend on how well you (the consultant) and the human services agency's administrator understand the nature of organizations.

This chapter is intended to provide the working knowledge of organizations consultants need in order to be effective in consultation. Because consultation is one way to help organizations change so that they can function more effectively, consultants need to know what organizations are, how they develop, how they grow stagnant, how they change, and what the connection is between an organization's individuals and its ability to meet its goals and objectives. This chapter will explore these and other questions about organizations and the people in them and will serve as a foundation for the following chapter on the different kinds of organizational consultation.

As you read this chapter, keep the following questions in mind:

1. Which theory of organization seems most accurate to you?
2. If organizations are so complex, how can a consultant or group of consultants accomplish real changes in them?
3. How are organizations like live organisms?
4. What factors are involved in organizational change?
5. What things must come together to achieve excellence in an organization?

INTRODUCTION

Organizations can be defined in terms of what they do or how they are set up, and all of them have goals. Management is a specialty task in organizations that helps them meet those goals. How organizations are managed raises many values issues, and organizations are often criticized for their values and the ways they are run. For example, some human services organizations are criticized for valuing rules and regulations more than the clients they serve. An organization's values and behaviors become quite evident when it must face several, constantly changing issues. Regardless of the specific issues an organization faces at a given time, the basic issues remain constant: complexity, organizational size, and technology.

Organizational theories attempt to explain the whats, hows, and whys of organizations. Such theories tend to be based on different views of human nature: some positive views, some negative ones, and some neutral ones. An organizational theory that holds a positive view of human nature spawned what is known today as organization development. Organization development consultation is a part of the organization development movement, which attempts to help organizations increase their effectiveness.

When a consultant goes into an organization, the first step is to develop a basic definition of the organization. The theoretical frame of reference with which the consultant enters the organization determines what the consultant "sees." The consultant defines the organization by performing an assessment that attempts to clarify the organization's basic nature. Consultants usually have training in one of the four components of organizations: environment, people, structure, and process. Consultants also need a general perspective on organizations in order to be able to compare one organization with others.

DEFINITIONS OF ORGANIZATIONS

Organizations abound in our society: schools, businesses, human services agencies, and industries are all organizations. People organize because they think that is the best way to reach their goals. In order to be effective in organizational consultation, consultants need to know what prompts people to think and behave as they do within organizations, and in order to obtain this knowledge, consultants must first understand organizations themselves.

An organization has the following characteristics:

1. cooperation among many individuals,
2. certain common goals,
3. a division of labor, and
4. a hierarchy of authority (Jerrell & Jerrell, 1981, pp. 134–135).

Further, any definition of an organization should also include the following (Learned & Sproat, 1966, p. 2):

1. a purpose, goal, or goals;
2. activities designed to implement that purpose;
3. integration of jobs into units coordinated by various means, such as chains of command;
4. members' motivations, attitudes, values, and interactions;
5. processes such as decision making, control, communications, and rewards and punishments; and
6. an organizational pattern that lends internal harmony among all features.

In quoting W. G. Scott, Mitchell (1978) defines an organization as ". . . a system of coordinated activities of a group of people working cooperatively toward a common goal under authority and leadership" (p. 9).

Recent Changes in Organizations and Society

Some understanding of recent changes in organizations and society provides consultants a better grasp of the needs of the organizations in which they consult. During the last 50 years changes in organizational size and complexity and in technology have caused organizations to seek outside assistance, including consultation (Mitchell, 1978).

Organizations have become more complex; within them the number of different kinds of people performing different kinds of tasks has increased (Mitchell, 1978). This increased complexity and diversification makes it much more difficult for an organization to have a common purpose and adds to management difficulties caused by increased coordination problems (Mitchell, 1978).

As an organization increases in size, its members frequently do not know what others in the organization are doing; as in the old adage, "The left hand doesn't know what the right hand is doing." Administrators of such organizations have difficulty seeing the systemwide ramifications of their decisions, and because people within the organization often do not know or associate with one another, any consensus on common organizational goals is also difficult.

Increases in technology have had a greater impact on organizations than has any other change. Technological advances have created specialization and increased demands for retraining of staff in many organizations. This trend toward specialization makes it difficult for members of the organization to "speak the same language" and to feel confident that everyone is pulling together to achieve the same goals.

Not only has the nature of organizations changed; the environment in which they exist has also changed. According to Naisbitt (1982), ten societal "mega-trends" are altering the environment of organizations. These trends are changes:

1. from an industrial society to an information society,
2. from a forced technology to a high-tech/high-touch technology,
3. from a national economy to a world economy,
4. from management for the short term to management for the long term,
5. from centralization to decentralization,
6. from institutional help to self-help,
7. from representative democracy to participatory democracy,
8. from hierarchies to networking,
9. from the North to the South as the center of American life, and
10. from "either/or" to multiple options in terms of personal choices.

These trends are restructuring not only the personal lives of individuals, but their lives at work as well. Consultants who are aware of these structural changes can take them into account when helping organizations cope with change.

In recent years human services organizations have also undergone several environmental changes that reflect alterations in one or more of the strong, external forces of culture, politics, ecology, economics, and technology (Cooke, 1979). These changes, which have forced human services organizations to be more flexible, broad-spectrum, and adaptable, include (Gallessich, 1982):

1. a shift from the government to the individual as the major support for human services;
2. a shift in public attitude from the idea that society causes many human services problems and therefore should have a part in ameliorating them;
3. a change in the role of clients; they have become more demanding and less compliant;
4. some regulation in licensure by professional organizations such as the AACD and the APA, which can influence who can practice in certain human services agencies;
5. introduction of computers and data-processing procedures that require retraining of many personnel and open up new methods of working with clients;
6. overlap in services among agencies, which affects human service agencies' ability to serve client systems and causes some agencies to compete with and be counterproductive to the work of other agencies serving the same clients; and
7. increased scrutiny by the mass media of the work of human services agencies as representatives of the public; such pressure can force an agency to perform too rigidly "by the rules."

These environmental factors are both positive and negative, for "environmental tensions are the impetus for creating human services institutions. At the same time, these tensions greatly complicate the task of delivering services" (Gallessich, 1982, p. 61).

ORGANIZATIONAL THEORY

Consultants view each organization with which they work relative to some theory or theories of organizations, for knowledge of such organizational theories helps them develop a broad perspective on organizations. *Organizational theory* is the study of the structures and processes of organizations and the behavior of groups and individuals within organizations (Pugh, 1966). Because they attempt to explain these complex entities and how they are best designed, most theories of organizations must simplify organizations, and the way in which this simplification is accomplished depends on which factors are considered relevant (Argyris, 1970). A comprehensive coverage of different types of organizational theory is beyond the scope of this text; interested readers can gain in-depth information from such books as *The Social Psychology of Organizations* (Katz & Kahn, 1966). The following overview of different organizational theories highlights the many different perspectives from which organizations can be studied.

Historically, there are three types of organizational theory, each of which is based on a given philosophical approach to human nature. *Classical organizational theories* have a negative view of human nature, whereas *behavioral organizational theories* have a positive view of human nature. The behavioral approach should not be confused with the behavioral consultation model discussed in Chapter 11. "Behavioral" in this context refers to organizational theory that focuses on human behavior within organizations, rather than on the structure of organizations. The *contingency* and *systems organizational theories* have a neutral view of human nature. All three types of models are commonly espoused in today's world of organizations (Mitchell, 1978).

Classical Organizational Theories

Before the turn of the century, organizations were typically considered individual entities, such as church, government, and so forth. With the rise of capitalism in the late 19th century, organizations came to be viewed as a "class of collectivities" (Khandwalla, 1977). The classical model of organizations came into vogue near the beginning of the 20th century and was epitomized by Max Weber's model of bureaucracy (Mitchell, 1978). Frederick Taylor's model of scientific management is another classical theory, and it gained popularity in the 1920s (Khandwalla, 1977). Both of these models are considered machine theories. *Machine theory* is a generic term that implies that each organization is built according to a blueprint derived from its purpose, just as each machine is built according to a set of specifications (Katz & Kahn, 1966).

The Bureaucratic Model

Weber designed the *bureaucratic model* as the ideal of organizational effectiveness. The model's structural principles, which are "means to ends" in nature, include:

1. Rules and regulations are explicit and are needed to provide order and continuity. Rules and regulations allow standardization so that things are always done the same way and people can be treated equally.
2. Specific spheres of competence are required so that people have a well defined job and the authority to perform it. Put another way, the principle of division of labor is an integral part of this model.
3. The roots of authority are technical training, competence, and expertise. Objective standards are required to determine who is qualified or promoted to specific jobs.
4. Administrative staff members should be completely separated from the organization's ownership in order to make decision making rational and objective.
5. Lines of communication are vertical rather than horizontal. In this hierarchy each office is under the direct control and supervision of a higher office.
6. Acts, decisions, and rules are recorded in writing; thus, the organization's ongoing functioning is part of the public record (Mitchell, 1978, p. 17).

In this model work was to be unemotional, efficient, and clearly defined. Strong emphasis was placed on the structure and administration of organizations, but not on the human elements of the job (Mitchell, 1978).

According to this bureaucratic theory, organizations were meant to be efficient, effective, and equitable. However, the potentially counterproductive elements in this model can lead to red tape, rigidity, apathy, and resistance to change (Khandwalla, 1977).

The Principles of Management School

The *principles of management* orientation, also called the management process school, attempts to identify the principles that should govern organizations. This orientation focuses on the study of management and relies heavily on sociology and social psychology. Founded by Frederick Taylor, this school of thought requires studying an organization's operations with the goal of determining how those operations could be most effectively run. Mental work was differentiated from manual work: managers were to plan and workers were to do manual labor. Khandwalla (1977) lists four principles of scientific management advocated by Taylor:

1. Workers should be scientifically selected, trained, and given jobs for which they are best suited both physically and intellectually.
2. Work should be analyzed scientifically instead of by rules of thumb. Here, Taylor pointed to the need for technocracy and professionalism.

3. Close cooperation should exist between the planners and doers and between the managers and the workers so that work is done in accordance with scientific principles. Here, Taylor emphasized the interdependent nature of the organization's activities—that the whole can be greater than the sum of its parts only if the parts are properly integrated.
4. Managers and workers should share equal responsibility, with each group doing the work for which it is best equipped. Here, Taylor highlighted organizational ethics (Khandwalla, 1977, p. 146).

The scientific management school contributed two notions concerning organizations: that there are universal principles of management that should be heeded for efficient organizational functioning and that the act of managing is typified by planning, organizing, leading, controlling, and coordinating (Khandwalla, 1977). Critics of this school argue that there are no uniformly applied rules of management—that all rules are conditional—and that little, if any scientific evidence demonstrates that the rules of management actually work (Khandwalla, 1977).

The classical models of organizational theory emphasize specialization of tasks, standardized role performance, uniformity of function, and avoidance of duplication (Katz & Kahn, 1966). These models are inadequate in that they do not offer ways for the organization to adapt to change because they do not provide for interaction between the organization and its environment (Katz & Kahn, 1966).

Behavioral Organizational Theories

Both the bureaucratic and principles of management approaches emphasize the structure of organizations over their human elements. Although they do not ignore the structural aspects of organizations, behavioral approaches emphasize that human needs influence organizational structure, which in turn influences human behavior (Khandwalla, 1977). Therefore, organizational processes are given considerable attention in behavioral models of organizations.

There are three types of behavioral orientations to organizational theory. The *human relations* orientation gives primacy to individuals and their social needs within the organization. The *human resources* approach emphasizes full use of human potential in organizational behavior. The *"bounded rationality"* approach emphasizes humans' cognitive limitations and the consequent implications for the design and management of organizations (Khandwalla, 1977).

The Human Relations Approach

The human relations approach focuses on the concept that individuals' perceptions of their workplace, the work itself, and their co-workers are critical factors in understanding, designing, and running organizations. This approach is predicated on people's need for self-worth and meaningful social contact (Khandwalla, 1977). Important modern contributors to this school include Likert (1967) and Schein (1969, 1987). Major constructs related to this orientation include leadership styles and an informal power structure in organizations.

The human relations orientation has three major themes: the study of group dynamics, which investigates structure and process of groups; a focus on the informal organization, which examines how human processes arise spontaneously within the formal organization; and an emphasis on supervision styles, which relate to how managers and administrators work with subordinates and peers in formal settings.

The human relations school demonstrated that managers and administrators need a broad understanding of group behavior and motivation and that the "Hawthorne effect" (that is, positive social conditions affect worker satisfaction and productivity more than the physical conditions of work) needs to be taken seriously in any attempt to formulate an effective organizational theory (Gallessich, 1982). Among the contributions of the human relations orientation to organizational theory are an emphasis on the human factor and the fact that satisfied personnel are more productive (Khandwalla, 1977).

Critics of the human relations approach argue that it falsely assumes that there is always a solution to any problem and that the human relations tactics it emphasizes can easily be used to manipulate (Khandwalla, 1977).

The Human Resources Approach

The human resources orientation looks at the implications for organizations and their managers of people's need for self-actualization and a sense of competence. Key contributors to the human resources orientation include McGregor (1960), Argyris (1970), and Herzberg (1966). Management by objectives, participative management, enlargement of an individual's job, and the organization development and human resources development movements are all practical applications of this orientation to organizational theory (Khandwalla, 1977).

Some of the assumptions of a human resources orientation to organizational theory include (Beckhard, 1969):

1. Groups are the building blocks of the organization.
2. Cooperation is valued over competition within the organization.
3. Decisions are made on the basis of expertise rather than title.
4. Organizational behavior is determined by goals.
5. Open communication, trust, and confidence within and among all segments of the organization is highly desirable.
6. Active participation in and responsibility for what happens to the organization should be characteristic of all members of the organization.

The human resources orientation is criticized because there is little empirical research to support its validity, it tends to overemphasize motivation and underemphasize cognitive properties (Khandwalla, 1977), and it assumes one orientation—organization development—can be used as a "cure-all" for any organization or for any problem within an organization.

The "Bounded Rationality" Approach

The "bounded rationality" orientation, often referred to as the Carnegie approach, begins with the premise that human beings are imperfect problem solvers. The key figure associated with this approach, Herbert Simon, believed that organizations consist of people with limited rationality and information-processing skills working together to try to make decisions (Khandwalla, 1977). Simon assumed that individuals pursue goals serially, not simultaneously and that humans tend to have very selective perceptions and a limited capacity for processing information (Khandwalla, 1977). Consequently, humans often make decisions based on expediency rather than on long-term benefit (Khandwalla, 1977).

The Carnegie orientation makes the following assumptions about human nature and subsequent implications for running organizations (Khandwalla, 1977):

1. People are rational. Therefore, work should be structured to meet organizational goals.
2. People have limited information-processing capacities. Therefore, organizational information should be made as simple yet accurate as possible.
3. Human perception is selective in that it is determined by needs and preconceptions. Therefore, conflict, overspecialization, commitment to subsystem rather than organization-wide goals, and coalitions are normal organizational phenomena.
4. People tend to search for the "satisfactory" rather than the "best." Therefore, limited planning, mediocre decision making, and serial rather than simultaneous pursuit of organizational goals are typical in organizations.
5. People have "bounded rationality"; that is, they tend to search for simple and proximate rather than complex and long-term causes of behavior. As a result, organizations are reactive (not proactive), change by bits and pieces (not globally), and tend to become overly routinized.

The Carnegie orientation has been criticized for failing to answer the question, "Does the character of decision making vary from organization to organization, and if so, what factors account for the differences?" (Khandwalla, 1977). This model overemphasizes the cognitive at the expense of the affective and relegates human decision making to the mere processing of information (Khandwalla, 1977).

In summary, the behavioral type of organizational theory has three basic orientations: human relations, human resources, and "bounded rationality." In the human relations approach, effective organizations are those that produce a climate that fosters self-esteem, strong human connectedness, and strong support. The human resources orientation focuses on self-actualization; effective organizations are those that provide a climate that allows individuals to realize their potential within the organization. The "bounded rationality" orientation considers people to be guided by their limited cognitions; effective organizations take this limitation into consideration in decision making and in developing standard operating procedures (Khandwalla, 1977).

Contingency Theory

The contingency model of organizational theory stresses the interface between the organization and its environment (Khandwalla, 1977). The emphasis is not so much on the process of the organization's adaptation to the environment as it is on the end result of the organizational change. The theory examines organizations' structural adaptations to their task environments (Khandwalla, 1977). A *task environment* refers to the conditions, circumstances, and influences which affect a given job within an organization. The organization is seen as an open system—it and its environment can interact. Leading proponents of contingency theory include Lawrence and Lorsch (1967) and Perrow (1970).

According to Khandwalla (1977, p. 236),

> the basic idea of the contingency theorists is that the nature of the organization's technology, size, its legal incorporation, the character of its markets, and other factors confront the organization with some opportunities as well as constraints and problems and therefore set the tone of the organization's adaptation as revealed by its structure.

Contingency theory is based on a concept analogous to the biological adaptation of an organism to its environment. Thus, just as birds that feed in water typically have longer beaks than birds that feed on land, so too does the structure of an organization or a part of an organization depend a great deal on the demands of its environment.

Contingency theory is based on the following premises (Huse, 1975):

1. There is no "one best way" for designing an organization.
2. The design of an organization and its parts must be complementary with the organization's environment.
3. When an organization is properly designed, the needs of its members are well met.

Contingency theory, then, seeks to identify the kind of organizational structure that is most appropriate to the environmental context in which the organization exists. This match is achieved by identifying the factors that significantly contribute to the overall design of the organization, including its size and technology, and the nature of its environment. Contingency theory tries to predict how the variable efficiencies of organizations' operations and structures are due to differences in these factors (Khandwalla, 1977).

Lawrence and Lorsch (1967), major contributors to contingency theory, introduced the concept of *differentiation*: the development of a unique structure and identity, including values and behaviors, by some unit of the organization (Khandwalla, 1977). Differentiation is based on the idea that units of the organization will take their own forms depending on the type of environment in which they exist. In contingency theory this environment is referred to as task environment. For example, the administration of a mental health center might have one type of task environment based on managing and promotion, whereas the direct services personnel exist in an environment characterized by provision of services and supervision. The point is that the best type of structure for a part of an organization depends on its task environment (Mitchell, 1978).

In summary, contingency theory looks at organizations in a situational perspective (Khandwalla, 1977): the best way to design or manage an organization or a part of an organization depends on the demands of the situation (Mitchell, 1978). A criticism of contingency theory is that it tends to look at only one type of structure for a given type of task environment, whereas in reality many structures may be appropriate.

Systems Organizational Theories

One of the most popular models of organizational theory is *systems theory*, which provides a broadly based perspective on organizations developed from attempts to understand biological events (Gallessich, 1982).

A system can be defined as ". . . a set of interrelated elements or components" (Jerrell & Jerrell, 1981, p. 135). Kurpius (1985) defines a system as ". . . an entity made up of interconnected parts, with recognizable relationships that are systematically arranged to serve a perceived purpose" (p. 369). In systems theory, organizations can be defined as ". . . dynamic entities continually interacting with their environment, changing and adapting to develop congruence between people, process, structure, and external environment" (Beer, 1980, p. 15).

There are two types of systems: closed and open. Closed systems are those that are not affected by their environments: they have a finite amount of energy, and when that energy is used up, the system runs down. Open systems, on the other hand, have permeable boundaries and can obtain energy from the environment and send energy back to the environment (Katz & Kahn, 1966). As Jerrell & Jerrell (1981) note, "systems receive inputs from the environment and subject those inputs to a transformation process to produce outputs that are fed back into the environment" (Jerrell & Jerrell, 1981, p. 135). This phenomenon is called the input-throughput-output function of the system.

The systems view of organizations identifies four components that make up the organizational system (Kurpius, 1985):

1. a framework (pattern of activities),
2. goals,
3. methods and operations, and
4. people.

Like the contingency theory that it heavily influenced, the systems theory of organizations assumes that organizations are open systems; they are not isolated, closed entities, but instead are subject to influences from both inside and outside the organization (Jerrell & Jerrell, 1981). Also like contingency theory, systems theory considers the organization to be a totality, and it directly examines the interrelationships among an organization's subsystems and between the organization and its environment (Katz & Kahn, 1966).

The most fundamental property of a system is the interdependence among its parts (Kurpius, 1985). The systems approach is helpful in conceptualizing the multidimensional parts of a system as an integrated whole (Argyris, 1964), and it assumes that an organization is more than the sum of its parts (Mitchell, 1978). Organizations (and the people within them) are seen as adaptive (Mitchell, 1978) and as social systems operating within larger environments (Katz & Kahn, 1966). Organizational behavior is seen as dynamic and cyclical; the primary cycle in human services organizations consists of intake, treatment, and output of the client system (Gallessich, 1982).

Characteristics of Systems

When viewed as open systems, organizations have nine characteristics (Katz & Kahn, 1966):

1. *Importation of energy.* No social structure is self-sufficient: the organization must draw new energy from other organizations, from the material environment, and from people such as consultants.

2. *The throughput.* Energy is transformed as it goes through the organization. In a human services organization, throughput can be service to clients, training of existing personnel, addition of new staff, and so forth.

3. *The output.* The organization exports some product into the environment, such as some new service to the client system.

4. *Systems are cycles of events.* Organizations have an input-throughput-output cycle; the output product supplied to the environment provides energy for repetition of the cycle.

5. *Negative entropy.* Entropy is a law of nature that states that all organisms proceed toward death or disorganization. Organizations can arrest this entropy by importing more energy than they expend. This process of energy storage is called negative entropy.

6. *Information input, negative feedback, and the coding process.* Inputs into the organization can take the form of information that can give the organization signals about the environment and the organization's relationship to it. One type of information input is negative feedback, which allows the organization to stay on its chosen course or, if necessary, change course. The reception of inputs into the organization is selective; that is, the organization can attend to only so many inputs, and those inputs are the only ones among many that the organization tunes in. This selective mechanism is called coding, and the coding procedures of an organization are determined by the functions performed by the organization. For example, if a mental health center learns that the community would fund a dropout prevention program, it might make plans to develop and implement such a program.

7. *The steady state and dynamic homeostasis.* The importation of energy can serve to maintain some constancy in the flow of energy such that an organization is characterized by a steady state. Dynamic homeostasis refers to the basic preservation of the system's character. In preserving its character, the organization must import more energy than it exports. In adapting to its environment, an organization moves toward assimilating the external resources considered necessary for survival. Hence, organizations attempt to grow both quantitatively and qualitatively over time.

8. *Differentiation.* Organizations move in the direction of differentiation and elaboration: roles within the organization become specialized and the number of such roles tends to increase. For example, a mental health center might differentiate from a single team to consisting of a crisis-intervention team, a substance-abuse team, and any number of other specialized teams.

9. *Equifinality.* The principle of equifinality proposes that organizations can reach the same end by different means: this is the "There's more than one way to skin a cat" principle. For example, a single human services organization might use any of several methods to improve its public relations image.

Subsystems Within the Organization

The subsystems of an organization are integrated by means of the norms, roles, and values present within the system (Katz & Kahn, 1966, 1978). Role behavior is sanctioned by norms that are justified by values. Five subsystems within organizations are built around the organization's norms, roles, and values (Katz & Kahn, 1966, 1978):

1. the technological or production subsystem,
2. the support subsystem,
3. the maintenance subsystem,
4. the management subsystem, and
5. the adaptive subsystem.

The *technological subsystem* is concerned with the quantity and quality of the work accomplished within the organization (Katz & Kahn, 1966, 1978). For example, in a counseling center the direct delivery of services to the client system—the throughput—constitutes the technological subsystem. Organizations are often classified according to the type of product they provide, and the products of human services organizations are the clients they serve. (More precisely stated, the product of human services agencies is "better" people.) The technological subsystem is responsible for the input-throughput-output cycle.

The *support subsystem* is concerned with the procurement of inputs, the disposal of outputs, and the maintenance of an environment favorable to the organization (Katz & Kahn, 1966, 1978). For example, a university might seek funding (procurement of inputs) for a counseling program for learning-disabled college students. Upon termination of the program, a written report is submitted to the funding agency (disposal of outputs) and the program is widely publicized to attract students and strengthen its public image (maintenance of a favorable environment).

The *maintenance subsystem* is concerned with connecting people within the organization to their roles (Katz & Kahn, 1966, 1978). It is not concerned with the material being worked on (typically the client system in human services organizations), but rather with the equipment used to get the work done. In human services organizations, this concern relates to getting people who work for the organization into their proper roles—patterned human behavior (Katz & Kahn, 1966). This subsystem integrates people into the system through recruitment, socialization, training, rewarding, and sanctioning, and it is concerned with input with respect to the maintenance of the organization (for example, recruitment of personnel).

Because organizations exist in a changing environment, a subsystem is required to help the organization adjust as the environment changes. The subsystem that accomplishes this is the *adaptive subsystem*. The adaptive subsystem is specifically concerned with sensing and interpreting important changes in the external environment. Functions such as long-range planning, research and development, and market research are part of the adaptive subsystem.

The *managerial subsystem* controls, coordinates, and directs the other subsystems of the organization and adjusts the total system to its environment (Katz & Kahn, 1966, 1978). There are two major types of managerial subsystems: regulatory mechanisms and the authority structure.

Regulatory mechanisms gather and interpret data about the organization's input-throughput-output cycle and give feedback to the system about its output in relation to its input (Katz & Kahn, 1966, 1978). In a human services organization, a follow-up study of clients' perceived benefits from the organization would be an example of a regulatory function.

Organizations must have a defined and established decision-making framework called the *authority structure*. The authority structure describes the organization of the managerial system with regard to the positions at which decisions are made and the routes through which they are implemented (Katz & Kahn, 1966, 1978).

In summary, the open systems theory of organizations views organizations as dynamic entities that continually change and adapt as they interact with their environments through an input-throughput-output process. There are five subsystems: technological, supportive, maintenance, adaptive, and managerial. These subsystems are interactive—a change in one can create change in the others. A major criticism of the open systems model is that merely showing that subsystems are interactive is inadequate; what is needed is an understanding of how changes in any particular subsystem produce certain changes in the other subsystems (Khandwalla, 1977).

Summary of Organizational Theories

There is no one best organizational theory, and a good theory today may be inappropriate for tomorrow's world (Mitchell, 1978). The question is not "What are the effective organizational behaviors that result in effective organizations?" but rather "When should appropriate organizational behaviors be used?"

Now that we have examined several different theories of organizations, it should be clear that when consultants enter an organization they "see" and analyze that organization based on some theory of organizations. Whether you realize it or not, you have your own "theory" of organizations. The more you are aware of it, the more you will know what you are looking for and also what you are likely to overlook; you will also be in a better position to understand how your consultees view their organizations and the concomitant implications for your consultation.

Will you see the organization relative to the classical theory and assume that the members of the organization need to be controlled by certain highly regulated structures? Will you see the organization from the perspective of the behavioral theorists and consider the people in the organization and how their needs are being met, given their limitations and potential and those of the organization as well? Will you take a neutral view of human beings and look at the organization through the eyes of the contingency theorists? Will you look for a "goodness of fit" between the organization and its task environment to determine the best organizational structure? Will you adopt the position of the systems theorists and look at the interdependencies and interrelationships among the organization's subsystems to understand the organization? Whatever questions you ask, the variety of organizational theories available to consultants suggests that consultants should take a flexible view in analyzing organizations. Table 8.1 lists some questions that consultants subscribing to the various organizational theories might ask when analyzing an organization (adapted from a list developed by Khandwalla, 1977).

TABLE 8.1   Questions for Analyzing an Organization

Organizational Theory	*Questions*
Bureaucratic	What are the structural strengths and weaknesses of the organization?
	What kind of bureaucracy is the organization? What factors made it assume this form?
	What anticipated and unexpected consequences has this form of bureaucracy had?
Management process	What principles does the management of the organization try to use? Do they make sense?
	How does the organization's management fulfill its functions, and how well?
	Are there other principles or ways of discharging functions that might make better sense?
	What functions currently involve making managerial strategy?
	Which ones are likely to become strategic in the future?
Human relations	What is the organization's psychological climate? Does it vary from one part of the organization to another?
	How does the organization's psychological climate affect the motivation and productivity of groups and individuals functioning within it?
	What environmental, technological, or business factors make the climate what it is?
Human resources	How do the organization's structure and operating process affect the growth needs of the people working in it?
	How are employees' growth needs and the organization's requirements for efficiency, survival, and growth integrated? How should they be integrated?

(Cont.)

Table 8.1 (Cont.)

Organizational Theory	Questions
Carnegie	What are the information-processing and problem-solving capabilities of the organization's key administrators? How do these capabilities affect the development of routines and discretionary programs in the organization?
	How are decisions made in the organization?
	What coalition has the greatest influence? What rules of thumb, or *heuristics*, are being used in making decisions? How good are the decisions?
Contingency	What are the major dimensions of the organization's task environment? What contingencies, constraints, threats, and opportunities do they pose to the organization?
	What are the chief elements of the organization's structure, and how have they been shaped by the properties of the organization's task environment?
	Are there notable differences among the task environments of the organization's major departments? Have these differences caused significant structural differences among the departments?
	What integrative mechanisms is the organization using?
Systems	What are the organization's major subsystems? What are their properties? How do they interact?
	What are the properties of the organization as a whole? What kind of relationship does the organization have with its environment? How does the organization adjust to changes in its environment? Does it use multiple modes of adjustment?
	How do changes in the organization affect its various subsystems, and how do changes in any of its subsystems affect the organization as a whole?

ORGANIZATIONAL CHANGE

Consultants frequently assist organizations to change. The following discussions incorporate current thinking about effective organizations and the principles of organizational change.

Approaches to Change

Organizations change in response to pressure from internal or external forces. Depending on how well an organization monitors its internal and external environments, change may be either well planned or forced upon the organization through a crisis situation. The larger the organization, the more people, groups, and political constituencies are involved, and change must be planned with all of them in mind (Beer, 1980).

When an organization senses the need for change, it looks for new directions to proceed. Consultants—whether external consultants or internal consultants who are freed from traditional organizational constraints—can have a part in providing these new directions (Beer, 1980).

From a philosophical perspective, there are three views of planned change: the empirical-rational approach, the normative-reeducative approach, and the power-coercive approach (Chin & Benne, 1976).

The *empirical-rational approach* assumes that people are rational by nature and will follow their rational self-interests once these are made known. Thus, any proposed changes are presumed to be congruent with the self-interests of the organization and its members. Because the organization and its members presumably are rational and motivated by self-interest, changes will be adopted only if they can be rationally justified and gains are evident (Chin & Benne, 1976). In others words, according to this approach changes in cognitions produce changes in behavior (Gallessich, 1982). This approach's credibility is based on scientific research and the process of educating people for change.

The *normative-reeducative approach* does not deny the role of rationality in change but points out that change is supported by sociocultural norms based on attitudes and values. Change involves a shift in those attitudes and values away from old patterns and a commitment to new patterns (Chin & Benne, 1976). This approach views people as social by nature; their shifts in emotion about something will bring about change. Further, change is not only intellectual; it also involves feelings and attitudes (Chin & Benne, 1976).

The *power-coercive approach* to change focuses on the ingredients of power and the ways it is used in bringing about change. This approach relies on the use of political, economic, and moral sanctions in the exercise of power; it assumes that externally based sanctions are necessary for change to occur.

Change can also be examined in terms of the source from which the impetus to change comes. These "power structures" are top-down, bottom-up, and shared (Greiner, 1967).

In the *top-down approach,* change is implemented on authority of the organization's leadership, which also defines the problem and determines the solution (Beer, 1980). That change is to occur can be communicated in the following ways:

1. decree (for example, memorandum);
2. introduction of technology (for example, personal computers);
3. replacement (for example, changing key personnel); and
4. changes in structure (for example, reorganization of a subsystem).

Top-down changes are usually unilateral (Beer, 1980), are usually introduced rapidly, and involve only a few key, top-level administrators in the decision-making process.

The *bottom-up approach* to change is the opposite of the top-down approach. Because responsibility for change is delegated to members lower in the organization (Beer, 1980), administrators typically are not involved and know little about the changes (Beer, 1980). Bottom-up change can occur in the following contexts (Beer, 1980):

1. training sessions (for example, team building);
2. staff groups (for example, peer teaching and training in different managerial approaches); and
3. experimental units (for example, groups designed to take services to locations near the residences of the client systems' members).

In the bottom-up approach leadership in the organization relinquishes significant amounts of power and authority (Beer, 1980). Bottom-up changes are usually slow and subject to the influences of special-interest groups.

The *shared approach* involves personnel from all levels of the organization: continuous interaction among members of the organization's different levels and a process of mutual influence ensues (Beer, 1980). The shared approach to change can involve the following (Beer, 1980):

1. iterative communication (for example, a top-level administrator defines the problem and assigns staff to gather data and develop solutions. The process is reviewed frequently by members throughout the organization);
2. decision-making task forces (for example, top leadership defines the problem and the parameters of the solution, but has the task force generate solutions. Top leadership then makes the final selection of the most appropriate solution); and
3. diagnostic and problem-solving task forces (for example, a group composed of individuals from all levels of the organization defines the problem and generates and implements a solution).

Because they typically involve personnel from throughout the entire organization, shared approaches to change are usually slow, and because so many people are involved, ownership of changes is usually strong.

The Nature of Organizational Change

Change in an organization involves realignment, adaptation, alteration, or modification to any part of the tasks, technology, structures, or components of that organization (Cooke, 1979). Change is a part of the daily routine of any organization; it can be precipitated by internal or external forces and can be planned or unplanned (Lippitt, 1969). If these forces are adequately monitored, then change can occur in a planned and systematic way. If these forces are not adequately monitored, crises ensue and the organization is forced to cope in a less orderly, less effective manner. Pressure to change can be strong and can demand great adaptability from an organization. Nonprofit organizations frequently have a more difficult time coping with and planning for change because they are not subject to the marketplace forces that act on for-profit organizations.

Organizations are subject to the following principles of change (Cooke, 1979):

1. Change is likely to involve all facets of the organization.

2. Forces both inside and outside the organization can generate pressure for change.
3. The same forces that give rise to the need for change can also complicate the management of change in organizations.

As it relates to organizations, change has the following characteristics (Beckhard, 1979):

1. It must be "owned" by the key people in the organization—usually people at several levels.
2. It must be managed from the top.
3. It must be system-oriented—it must relate to the total organization or to significant parts or subsystems.
4. It must have an extended timetable.
5. It must be related to the organization's mission and goals. Organizational changes "for change's sake" or for improving internal conditions are not likely to be maintained. Efforts to achieve it must be responsive to organization/environmental interfaces; it is no longer practical to improve internal effectiveness without explicit attention to the relationship between an organization and its environment.
6. It must be implemented through the organization's leaders; facilitators can help in planning, but implementation must be managed by the organization's leadership.
7. Real organizational change will not take place and be maintained unless the following three conditions exist:
   a) There must be a sufficiently high level of dissatisfaction with the status quo to mobilize energy towards some change.
   b) The organization's leaders must have some vision of the desired result of change.
   c) The organization's leaders must envision and communicate some practical first steps towards this desired result if energy to begin change is to be mobilized (Beckhard, 1979, pp. 19–20).

In addition to these basic principles and characteristics of organizational change, organizations can experience some complications as a result of change (Cooke, 1979). First, change may be difficult to achieve because immediate results cannot be seen. Second, whether changes will be successful depends on their acceptance as necessities by all members of the organization. Finally, initiating change can be particularly difficult in organizations with highly specified roles and centralized systems for authority and communications; however, if the uncertainty involved in change cannot be reduced with well defined roles and clear lines of authority, members may become frustrated and abandon the effort to change.

Excellence in Organizations

Most organizations are willing to change in order to become more effective. In recent years, a great deal has been written about the qualities of effective organizations. Books such as *In Search of Excellence: Lessons from America's Best-run Companies* (Peters & Waterman, 1982) and *Re-inventing the Corporation: Transforming Your Job and Company for the New Information Society* (Naisbitt & Aburdene, 1985) have raised awareness of the need for change within organizations. Even though these books were written about corporations, they remain relevant for consultants working with human services organizations.

Peters and Waterman (1982) discussed eight attributes associated with excellent and innovative organizations:

1. a bias for action—for getting on with it;
2. the ability to learn from the people they serve;
3. autonomy and entrepreneurship engendered by encouraging creativity, taking practical risks, and supporting good efforts;
4. allowing employees the practical autonomy necessary to effectively perform their jobs;
5. a values-oriented philosophy, which is more important to the organization's success than either its technological goals or its economic resources;
6. the wisdom to do only those things they know how to do;
7. a simple structure and lean staffing at the top levels; and
8. an organizational scheme that is centralized with regard to the organization's few values and decentralized with respect to autonomy for workers.

Naisbitt and Aburdene (1985) point out that the present is historically unique in that two critical, interrelated elements for social (and hence organizational) change are upon us: new values and economic necessity. The number of talented people available to employers will decrease, and prospective organizational members will be able to choose to work for an organization that demonstrates respect for its employees and has a high economic status. Organizations can improve their positions by helping their members enjoy work for its own sake—by creating a work environment in which fun, profit, and productivity flow together—and by assisting members to see the connections between their work and the family, educational, and health aspects of their lives (Naisbitt & Aburdene, 1985). Clearly, consultants can effectively help organizations achieve these goals.

ORGANIZATION DEVELOPMENT

The organization development (OD) movement is related to organizational change and organizational consultation. OD is discussed here because it is a very popular model of organizational change; indeed, many of the change strategies discussed in Chapter 5 are derived from this movement.

Organization development can help consultants develop a frame of reference for assisting organizations to change. According to French and Bell (1984), OD is

a long-range effort to improve an organization's problem-solving and renewal processes, particularly through a more effective and collaborative diagnosis and

management of organization culture—with special emphasis on formal work teams
. . . with the assistance of a consultant–facilitator and the use of the theory and
technology of applied behavioral science, including action research (p. 17).

In other words, OD attempts to help organizations improve their effectiveness
and enhance the quality of work life for their members (French & Bell, 1984).
It offers organizations and their members a method of identifying and implementing organizational solutions that help the organization adapt to internal
and external forces while simultaneously increasing individual members' commitment to the organization (Beer, 1980). OD also provides a theory and a
method for expediting the process of change itself, whether that change is
related to organizational problems or organizational renewal (Beer, 1980).

The following basic assumptions underlie organization development (Huse,
1978):

1. Most people desire and need opportunities for growth and self-
   realization.
2. When their basic needs have been satisfied, most individuals will respond
   to interesting work, responsibility, and challenging opportunities.
3. Organizational efficiency and effectiveness are increased when work
   is organized to meet individuals' needs for challenge, growth, and
   responsibility.
4. Shifting the emphasis of conflict resolution from "smoothing over" and
   "making edicts" to open "confrontation" facilitates both personal growth
   and the accomplishment of organizational goals.
5. Organizational structure and job responsibilities can be modified to
   more effectively meet the needs of the organization, the group, and the
   individual.
6. Many "personality clashes" in organizations are the direct result of
   improper organizational design (Huse, 1978, p. 403).

These assumptions lead to several characteristics that differentiate OD from
other forms of organizational change:

1. emphasis (although not an exclusive one) on group and organizational
   processes rather than on substantive content;
2. emphasis on the work team as the key unit for learning more effective
   modes of organizational behavior;
3. emphasis on the collaborative management of a work-team culture;
4. emphasis on managing the culture of the total system;
5. attention to the management of system ramifications;
6. use of the action research model;
7. use of a behavioral scientist-change agent, sometimes referred to as a
   "catalyst" or "facilitator";
8. a view of the effort to change as an ongoing process; and
9. primary emphasis on human and social relationships (French & Bell, 1984,
   p. 22).

These characteristics result from OD's tenet that the health of an organization depends on effective exchanges between the individuals in an organization and the organization itself and between the organization and its environment. If the first exchange is faulty, then the psychological well-being of the organization's members is in jeopardy; if the second exchange is faulty, the survival of the organization is threatened (Beer, 1980). Because of these two relationships, OD focuses on both the formal and informal aspects of the organization (Friedlander & Brown, 1974). Formal aspects include goals, technology, structure, procedures, products, and financial resources; informal aspects include perceptions, attitudes, feelings, values, informal interactions, and group norms (French & Bell, 1984).

In conclusion, organization development is an optimistic, developmental, humanistic perspective on organizations. Much organizational consultation has been heavily influenced by OD; in fact, a major type of organizational consultation, "process consultation," is considered an OD intervention (Schein, 1969, 1987). Consultants who use OD need a breadth and depth of knowledge of organizational design, management practice, and interpersonal dynamics (Beer, 1980).

SUMMARY

Consultants need to be familiar with several aspects of organizations if they are to maximize the likelihood of providing effective organizational consultation. The more knowledgeable consultants are about organizations, the more likely they are to effectively consult with them.

How consultants view the broad range of organizational theories—from those that emphasize organizational structure to those that emphasize the human side of organizations—determines how they think organizational change should occur. Because the process of change within organizations is very complex, consultants can use a variety of approaches and many methods to assist organizations in the process. Organization development is a popular approach of assisting organizations to change such that the organization and its members are satisfied and in balance with their environment.

QUESTIONS FOR REFLECTION

1. Do you think that most members of a typical human services organization could explain how their organization really operates? Why or why not?
2. What is organizational theory?
3. Why is a firm understanding of organizational theory important for a consultant?
4. Why should a consultant have a "personal" theory of organizations that is carried into the consultation process?
5. How could a consultant teach members of an organization about their own organization?

6. What are the advantages for consultants of the systems model of organizational theory?
7. You are hired as a consultant to a human services organization. As you enter the organization for the first time, what types of things and activities would you look for? How would you find out more about these things and activities?
8. What are some of the ways that the adaptive subsystem of an organization can monitor its internal and external environments?
9. What are the implications of societal "megatrends" for organizations? For consultants?
10. To which approach to change do you hold most firmly: the rational-empirical, the normative-educative, or the power-coercive? Why?

SUGGESTED SUPPLEMENTARY READINGS

Bennis, W. G., Benne, K. D., Chin, R., & Corey, K. E. (Eds.). (1976). *The planning of change.* New York: Holt, Rinehart & Winston. This is *the* book on planned change. Although a few of the chapters are dated, this book is "must reading" for consultants who want to understand change in organizations. The diagnostics and interventions related to change are emphasized, and issues related to values in change are also discussed. A section entitled "General Strategies for Effecting Changes in Human Systems" by Chin and Benne is particularly informative.

Khandwalla, P. N. (1977). *The design of organizations.* New York: Harcourt Brace Jovanovich. This text provides broad coverage of organizational theory, design, operation, and behavior. The text provides the consultant with the basic ins and outs of organizational life. Reading this text can provide a broad overview of the concept we call "organization."

Peters, T. J., & Waterman, R. H., Jr. (1982). *In search of excellence: Lessons from America's best-run companies.* New York: Warner Books. In this book about management, Peters and Waterman devote a chapter to each of eight basic principles of management and provide a wealth of examples and anecdotes from several organizations. Consultants will find it helpful in understanding the kinds of skills necessary for administering any type of organization.

Organizational Consultation

PREVIEW

Now that you have a basic familiarity with organizations and the ways they operate, we'll examine how consultants operate in organizations. The main goal of organizational consultation is improvement in the organization's effectiveness, and it can take many forms and utilize a multitude of methods. Many types of organizational consultation originated in business and industry settings, whereas others have been influenced by the mental health movement.

Consider the following example, which covers just one of several approaches to organizational consultation:

CASE STUDY:
You are a human services professional who is asked to consult with a rehabilitation center staff. The center, which serves as a counseling facility for incarcerates nearing eligibility for parole, is having staff conflicts that are adversely affecting the success of its programs. The center's head administrator asks you to sit in on three of the regularly scheduled weekly staff meeting and provide the staff feedback concerning how they might resolve their conflicts.

As you observe the meetings, you take notes on such things as what is said, how things are said, and who talks to whom. You provide feedback to the staff at a special meeting and then help the group process that feedback. As a result, three areas of conflict are identified: some staff are perceived as being too "hard" on the clients, some staff are perceived as being too "soft" on the clients, and the center has no evaluation system in place to determine whether it really helps its clients.

You agree to spend an additional session with the staff to help them resolve their conflicts, and you agree to help a select group of staff develop procedures for evaluating the effectiveness of the center's services.

In this chapter we'll consider the historical development of organizational consultation and define some important terms. Then we'll examine a few of its key concepts, drawing from the discussion of the preceding chapter. We'll consider a general approach to organizational consultation developed by Blake and Mouton (1976); although this model of consultation is not exclusively an "organizational" one, its comprehensiveness and the great variety of activities it provides organizational consultants make it very appropriate in an organizational context.

We will also examine three specific models of organizational consultation: purchase of expertise, doctor/patient, and process consultation (Schein, 1969, 1978). In discussing the expertise model, we'll focus on education/training and program approaches. In the doctor/patient model, diagnosis is emphasized. In the section on the process model, Schein's (1969) model of process consultation is explored.

For each of these approaches we'll examine the goals, the roles, and functions of the consultant and the consultee's experience in consultation. We'll consider some applications of organizational consultation by discussing its techniques and procedures, and we'll note some arguments for and criticisms of this kind of consultation.

Here are some questions to consider as you read this chapter:

1. Why is consulting with organizations more complex than consulting with individuals?
2. Who or what makes up the client system in organizational consultation?
3. How can a consultant evaluate the effects of organizational consultation when the process is so complex?
4. How should a consultant select from among the multitude of available interventions?
5. What are the basic differences among the various approaches to organizational consultation?

INTRODUCTION

Organizational consultation is based on the concept that an organization can be made to function more effectively through the efforts of one or more consultants who work with some (or possibly all) the members of the organization. Thus, the organization itself or one of its parts becomes the "client," and the people with whom the consultant works are the consultees.

Organizational consultants can fulfill the following functions (Schein, 1987, p. 20):

1. provide information that is not otherwise available;
2. analyze information with sophisticated tools not available to clients or their subordinates;
3. diagnose complex organizational and business problems;
4. train clients or their subordinates to use diagnostic models that help them make better decisions;
5. listen and give support, comfort, and counsel during troubled times;
6. help implement difficult or unpopular decisions;
7. reward and punish certain kinds of behaviors, using status as an "outsider" as a special source of authority;
8. transmit information either up the normal chain of command or laterally as needed;

9. make decisions and give directives on how to proceed if for some reason line management cannot do so; and

10. take responsibility for decisions, allay anxiety that may attend the uncertainties of consultation, and in other ways provide the emotional strength to help others through difficult situations.

Historical Background

Organizational consultation first emerged in the 1890s in industrial settings. Consultants, experts who focused on manufacturing productivity, were called on to fix production problems (Heyel, 1973). In open systems terminology, the early organizational consultants dealt with the technological subsystem of the organization (Gallessich, 1982). At the outset of organizational consultation, consultants combined industrial engineering with time and motion studies and were often referred to as management engineers (Heyel, 1973).

During World War I, organizational consultants were often referred to as efficiency experts; they were concerned with functions such as input/output ratios and the relationships between humans and tools (Heyel, 1973). During the 1920s organizational consultation expanded into other subsystems of industrial organizations, particularly the management and maintenance subsystems.

The Great Depression of the 1930s created a crisis in which many businesses, industrial and nonindustrial alike, were forced to fight for survival. This financial crisis produced conditions conducive to a new consultant activity: helping "sick" organizations (Heyel, 1973). Although "sick" referred to finances during the Great Depression, the term has since come to refer to any aspect of an organization considered to have problems.

With the advent of group dynamics research and the call to improve work conditions during the 1940s and 1950s, psychology entered business settings, and motivation studies and leadership studies became quite popular (Chapiro, 1981). Organizations became increasingly aware that technological efficiency could be dehumanizing and that improved conditions could lead to greater productivity (Aplin, 1978). Organizations then no longer needed to be "sick" to benefit from the assistance of a consultant; rather, healthy organizations could become more efficient and effective in meeting their goals by obtaining consultant services in such areas as motivation and leadership. Thus, consultants became increasingly involved in delivering services to organizations in matters that related to how organizations were affected by such factors as lines of authority, types of leadership, and distribution of labor (Gallessich, 1982).

The national attention given to the concept of mental health and the emergence of mental health consultation (see Chapter 10) began to influence not only human services organizations but business and industrial organizations as well. Greater emphasis was placed on the psychological well-being of the worker on the job. Organizational leaders began to realize that satisfied workers were crucial to effective and productive organizations. Coincident to the national emphasis on mental health was the emergence of organization development (OD).

Organization development is the application of the behavioral sciences to an organization's internal workings in order to increase its efficiency and effectiveness (Huse, 1978). The organization development effort focuses "on the characteristics of the workplace as a whole, with the consultant attempting to use a variety of interventions that can integrate organizational and individual needs" (Lewis & Lewis, 1986, p. 202).

Organizational consultation developed under the influences of applied behavioral science and managerial science (Shultz, 1984): from behavioral science came laboratory training methods, the use of the survey research and feedback method, and autonomous work groups (Huse, 1978); from managerial science came quantitative analysis of business activities, particularly managerial decision making (Shultz, 1984).

The laboratory training methods are a series of experimental activities that focus on developing skills for more effective organizational functioning. Development occurs in a laboratory setting in which group members experiment with new behaviors and are given feedback. The new behaviors are then supposedly transferred to the work site (Rudestam, 1982).

In the survey research and feedback method, results of surveys about the organization are conveyed to the respondents (feedback) to further pinpoint problem areas (Huse, 1978) and to generate discussion (Gallessich, 1982). Such discussions are intended to improve relationships among the participants and help solve identified problems.

The Tavistock Institute of London, England developed a psychoanalytic theory of groups that influenced organization development (Rice, 1969; Goodstein, 1978). Much of this institute's work focused on study groups formed to examine how participants dealt with issues of authority, leadership, and norms (Goodstein, 1978). Participants were to take their newly acquired knowledge and apply it in their own organizations, which frequently led to the development of autonomous work groups within organizational settings (Huse, 1978).

Managerial science, which accompanied the development of management as a profession (Shultz, 1984), focuses on finances and quantitative analysis of all aspects of management. Unlike applied behavioral science, managerial science focuses almost exclusively on the tangible and the quantitative.

Organization development influenced and is frequently considered to be part of another field called human resources development (HRD), which developed during World War II out of military and industrial organizations' need for competent personnel (Chalofsky & Lincoln, 1983). The philosophical framework of HRD is the development of human potential (Chalofsky & Lincoln, 1983).

Whereas organizational consultation focuses on the workplace as an entity, HRD focuses on the individuals within the organization. HRD consists of the learning experiences "that are organized, for a specified time, and designed to bring about the possibility of behavioral change" (Nadler, 1980, p. 5). Craft (1979) offers a more comprehensive definition:

> Human Resources Development (HRD) is a planned approach to enhance the development and growth of employee skills, abilities, judgment, and maturity to

better meet overall organizational and individual goals. HRD programs are implemented to develop employee capabilities to carry out job functions more effectively and to meet projected staffing needs (p. 103).

HRD gained recognition when the American Society for Training and Development emerged and promoted HRD nationally. HRD can take place in educational as well as business and human services settings (Maher, Cook, & Kruger, 1987).

A current trend in organizations is to provide counseling for employees on the work site through, for example, employee assistance programs. This trend has led many counselors in organizational settings to become increasingly involved in organizational consultation activities (Lewis & Lewis, 1986).

The emergence of OD and HRD has given legitimacy to using either internal consultants (when present) or outside consultants (whenever internal ones were absent or unskilled in the area of service for which consultation was needed). The inclination to use organizational consultants in the private and public sectors has spread recently to the previously reluctant "third" sector of human services organizations (Goodstein, 1978).

ORGANIZATIONAL CONSULTATION DEFINED

In spite of the many attempts to define it, there is no agreement on the "one" definition of organizational consultation. What is clear is that there are many types of organizational consultation, and how it is performed depends on the theoretical orientation of the consultant, the nature of the organization, and the nature of the problem for which the consultant is sought (Lewis & Lewis, 1986).

The organization or some aspect of it became "the client" in organizational consultation because of its historical roots: consultants were retained to increase productivity, and one or more aspects of the organization were considered to be related to productivity (Brown et al., 1987).

Organizational consultation can be defined in terms of what the consultant does. Accordingly, Sinha (1979) provides the following definition:

> An organizational consultant is a professional, internal or external to the client system, who applies behavioral science knowledge in an ongoing organization with the explicit objectives of managing change and increasing its effectiveness. He engages in a wide variety of activities, often called interventions, such as organizational diagnosis, team building, intergroup activities, survey feedback, training for managerial effectiveness, restructuring organization, role negotiation, socio-technical system design, planning and goal setting, counseling and career planning, etc. The type and choice of interventions and relationship a consultant establishes with the client system often define the approach and style of consultants (p. 8).

In addition, all organizational consultants have as their goal the enhancement of the human and organizational capabilities of the client system through a process of collaboration between consultant and consultee (Sinha, 1979).

A synthesis of many authors' views on organizational consultation (for example, Schein, 1969; Goodstein, 1978; Lippitt & Lippitt, 1978; Sinha, 1979) might produce the following generic definition:

> *Organizational consultation* is the process in which a professional, functioning either internally or externally to an organization, provides assistance of a technical, diagnostic/prescriptive, or facilitative nature to an individual or group from that organization in order to enhance the organization's ability to deal with change and maintain or enhance its effectiveness in some designated way.

Some confusion surrounds the terms "consultee" and "client system" in organizational consultation. The consultees in organizational consultation are those people in the organization with whom the consultant works; frequently they are mid- to high-level managers or people who provide direct services to clients. In the consultation literature the term client often refers to the consultee, particularly when the discussion concerns the people in the organization with whom the consultant is working. With respect to organizational consultation in this text, the term *consultees* refers to the people with whom the consultant works directly; the *client system* is always the organization or some part of it.

KEY CONCEPTS IN ORGANIZATIONAL CONSULTATION

Most of the key concepts concerning organizational consultation were discussed in the preceding chapter. However, four concepts are sufficiently important to highlight: the organization as client, the cyclical nature of behavior, process is as important as content, and satisfied personnel are crucial to effective organizations.

The Organization as Client

The client system in organizational consultation is usually the organization or some part of an organization. In either case, the goal of organizational consultation is to enhance the overall effectiveness of the organization. Thus, the organization becomes the client system in organizational consultation. Many consultants are used to viewing the client system as either an individual client or a relatively small group of people. Consequently, it is sometimes difficult for consultants to envision the somewhat amorphous concept of the entire organization as the client (Brown et al., 1987).

The more complex the organization, the more complex the client system becomes. Organizations are systems made up of interactive and interdependent parts; consulting with one part of the organization can affect all of its parts. Organizations are made up of people, each of whom possesses a unique set of attitudes, values, beliefs, and behaviors. Individuals in an organization are affected not only by these attributes of their co-workers, but also by the social relationships that exist within the organization (Jerrell & Jerrell, 1981). When consultants provide services to one part of the organization, the potential impact of consultation on other parts of the organization must be considered.

Among the concepts important to understanding the complexity of viewing the organization as client is the principle of *synergy,* which states that the whole of a set of products is greater than the sum of its parts. For example, if you had some wooden dowels, a cylindrical piece of the same wood, and an iron hoop, you could, with a little luck in putting these items together, produce a wheel. The wheel is more than some dowels, a hub, and a rim; it consists of these things put together in a certain way so that they become something "new," namely, the wheel. When buildings, offices, people, and machines are put together in a certain way, they become more than the sum of their parts and become organizations. Because organizations are more than the sum of their parts, they are very complex. By viewing the entire organization as the client, consultants will understand the complexity of the potential ramifications of their interventions and avoid oversimplified consultation methods.

The Cyclical Nature of Behavior

Most models of consultation consider organizational behavior to be *cyclical.* Behavior is cyclical when ". . . a sequence of behavior repeats its main features, within specific time periods or within specifiable settings" (Blake & Mouton, 1976, p. 2). One example of cyclical behavior is a group of college professors who meet regularly as a task force but can never end their meetings on time, even when the time allocated for the meetings was increased.

Cyclical behavior becomes habitual—almost reflexive—and frequently the people, groups, or organizations involved are unaware that they are engaging in such behavior (Blake & Mouton, 1976). Cyclical behavior can be counterproductive—it's what gets people into "ruts"—and when organizations get into ruts, they behave in predictable patterns that tend to create stagnation and an inability either to cope with change or maintain effectiveness.

Many counterproductive cycles of behavior can promote organizational inefficiency. These cycles, referred to as *blockages* (Woodcock & Francis, 1979), are typically maintained by poor levels of communication within all or some part of the organization. Blockages can include such problems as low motivation and poor teamwork (Woodcock & Francis, 1979).

In a cyclical view of behavior, organizational consultation becomes a process in which cycles are broken by removing blockages to organizational effectiveness. Thus, organizational consultants assist organizations by helping them identify and change ineffective cycles of behavior (Blake & Mouton, 1976, 1978). For this reason organizational consultants are frequently referred to as *change agents* (Walz & Benjamin, 1978); they help change organizations' counterproductive cycles of behavior by energizing, by providing insight or resources, or by assisting processing behavior (Walz & Benjamin, 1978).

Process Is as Important as Content

An important underlying assumption of organizational consultation is that process is as important as content; That is, *how* something is done can be as important as *what* is done. Thus, how people communicate with one another in an organization is as important as what they communicate about, and how organizations go about solving a problem is as important as the nature of that problem. If the problem to be solved is considered to be the content, then the process is the method by which the problem is defined and solved (Schein, 1978). There is even a special kind of consultation, called process consultation, that focuses on the process of organizational behavior rather than on its content.

In organizations, process factors are distinguished from structural factors, such as departments and lines of authority. Structures are an organization's way of coordinating and controlling tasks in an efficient and timely manner (Jerrell & Jerrell, 1981). But the structure is surrounded by process factors, such as informal relationships, traditions, and culture (Schein, 1969). Further, how people perceive a structure (for example, their job's role) determines how they relate to others within the organization and how they act in that role (Schein, 1969). Only when its members are smoothly interacting with one another can the organization be functioning effectively. Consultants often help organizations become aware of the interactions between process factors and their members to assist them in functioning at optimal levels (Schein, 1969, 1978, 1987).

Although process and content are often considered separate entities, they are often subtly related (Schein, 1978); that is, there is a connection between an organization's problem (content) and how the problem is being worked on (process). Schein (1978) illustrates this connection by telling about a group that chose as its "topic" leadership (content) while it was experiencing a leadership struggle (process) among several of its members. Consultants frequently have the difficult task of deciding whether or not to focus on the interaction between process and content.

Satisfied Personnel Are Crucial to Effective Organizations

Organizations are made up of people; effective organizations are made up of satisfied people—those who perceive that their needs within the organization are being met satisfactorily. If personnel are not satisfied, the organization's efficiency and productivity suffer. For example, if an organization's decision-making structure does not allow for significant input from personnel who are parties-at-interest to the decision, decreases in morale, motivation, and commitment could result (Aplin, 1978).

Workers report greater job satisfaction when they have some sense of identity with and impact on the level of the organization in which they are functioning. Workers also feel more satisfied when they feel free to express both their emotions and their thoughts about work (French & Bell, 1978). What goes on during informal times on the job—coffee breaks, for example—directly affects levels of satisfaction and feelings of competence among workers. Organizational consultants help organizations to develop the skills and climates necessary for helping individuals experience greater satisfaction in their work.

THE ORGANIZATIONAL CONSULTATION PROCESS

The Consulcube

The most comprehensive approach to conceptualizing organizational consultation is the model developed by Blake & Mouton (1976, 1978). Its comprehensiveness and the great variety of strategies it makes available to organizational consultants make it excellent in organizational contexts. In this model, which organizes and systematizes the process of consultation, all behavior is cyclical in nature and consultation focuses on breaking inappropriate and counterproductive cycles.

Because consultation can be conceptualized in terms of three dimensions—kinds of cycle-breaking interventions, focal issues for interventions, and units of change—Blake and Mouton combined these three dimensions and produced the *"Consulcube,"* which is illustrated in Figure 9.1.

The Consulcube is a cube consisting of 100 cells. Each cell represents the characteristics of a certain type of intervention with a given type of consultee (unit of change) for breaking a cycle related to a given problem area (focal issue). The Consulcube provides framework for conceptualizing consultation in terms of what the consultant does, who receives the consultant's services, and what issue the consultation is intended to resolve. Put another way, it organizes consultation strategies so that their interrelatedness and underlying principles are apparent (Goodstein, 1978).

Each cell of the Consulcube is designated by a letter and subscript code. The front of the cube uses letters of the alphabet, each of which represents a combination of a kind of intervention and a focal issue. For example, the letter "M" on the Consulcube represents a prescriptive intervention on a power/authority focal issue, the letter "N" represents a prescriptive intervention on a morale/cohesion focal issue, and the letter "H" represents a catalytic intervention on a goals/objectives focal issue.

The numbers that are used as subscripts to the letters on the Consulcube represent the five units of change. When these numbers are combined with the letters on the cube, each of the 100 cells of the Consulcube has its own designation. For example, "A_2" represents an acceptant intervention to resolve a power/authority within a group situation, "K_5" represents a confrontation intervention to resolve a norms/standards problem within a larger social system, and "L_3" represents a confrontation intervention to resolve a goals/objectives problem in an intergroup situation.

Now we'll discuss the kinds of interventions, units of change, and focal issues that together constitute the Consulcube.

Kinds of Interventions

Interventions are those strategies used in attempts to break cycles. Interventions occur ". . . whenever someone does something to someone in the context of a cycle-breaking endeavor" (Blake & Mouton, 1978, p. 329).

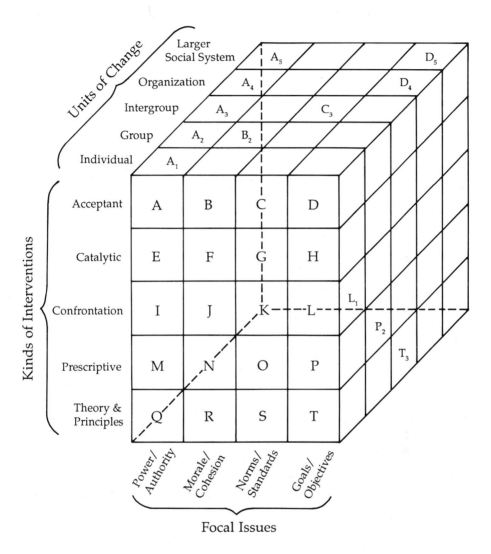

From Blake, R. R., Mouton, J. S. (1976), *Consultation.*
Reading, MA: Addison-Wesley. By permission of publisher.

FIGURE 9.1   The Consulcube

Many consultants use only those types of interventions with which they feel most comfortable (Blake & Mouton, 1978). Such a way of operating ignores the consultee's unique needs and each problem's particular situation. Consultants should therefore need to develop a broad repertoire of interventions in order to be fully effective. Blake and Mouton (1978) suggest that consultants match the different kinds of interventions—acceptant, catalytic, confrontation, prescriptive, and theories and principles—with the perceived problem and the consultee's needs and use them in a systematized, consistent manner.

Acceptant interventions.   Acceptant interventions are those that allow the consultee to feel accepted, safe, and competent in the consultation relationship and thereby permit an objective perspective on the problem. Examples of acceptant interventions are listening actively, avoiding judgments about the content of the consultee's expressions, making clarifying responses, reflecting the consultee's feelings, responding supportively, and being empathic. Acceptant interventions permit consultees to sort through their emotional reactions concerning the problem so that a greater sense of objectivity can be developed. As an example, a consultant might carefully listen to a therapist sharing feelings of incompetence in dealing with a difficult case.

Acceptant interventions are most appropriate when the consultee experiences emotional tension that blocks the problem-solving process (Blake & Mouton, 1976).

Catalytic interventions.   Catalytic interventions are designed to help consultees to better understand work-related situations either by corroborating existing information or by gathering new information (Goodstein, 1978). The resultant broadened awareness enables the consultee to take new and appropriate action on the problem.

The consultant—the catalyst—attempts to change the consultee's awareness of the problem such that the information needed to solve the problem can be acquired and processed more quickly. For example, a consultant might survey a client population in a mental health agency concerning clients' views of limited therapy services so that the agency's director can use the data to improve direct client services.

Catalytic interventions are best used when the consultee experiences an information deficit and a need to speed up the problem-solving process. When consultants notice that catalytic interventions upset the consultee, they frequently switch to acceptant interventions for a while and then return to catalytic ones.

Confrontation interventions.   Confrontation interventions challenge consultees to examine the values that underlie their thoughts about the problems addressed in consultation. Consultees' values can distort the way they view a problem; consultees' values might restrict their ability to see the range of potential solutions to certain problems. The major advantage of confrontation interventions is that if they were not made, consultees might never examine contradictions in their value systems that could result in less than effective job performance (Goodstein, 1978). For example, if a human services agency director talks about advocating democratic leadership but displays many autocratic tendencies, a consultant might point out the discrepancies in the agency director's values.

Confrontation interventions are most effective when discrepancies between a consultee's stated values and those that actually determine the consultee's behavior reduce effectiveness in consultation. The consultant must use confrontation interventions with caution because their use can damage the peer nature of the consultation relationship and may be perceived by the consultee as being judgmental or accusatory.

Prescriptive interventions. Prescriptive interventions, which are among the oldest approaches used by consultants (Blake & Mouton, 1976), use the consultant's expertise in diagnosing problem areas and in matching potential solutions to those problems. The basic premise of prescriptive interventions is that the consultant is the expert problem solver and that the consultee will accept and follow through on the course of action this expert recommends. For example, a consultant might suggest to a managerial staff that poor performance was the result of low morale and recommend a series of team-building exercises as a solution. An entire approach to consultation, the "doctor-patient" model, has developed around this concept.

A critical factor in prescriptive interventions is the consultant's ability to differentiate between the consultee's perceived and actual needs. A related underlying assumption is that the consultee does not possess the knowledge or objectivity needed to make an accurate diagnosis and engage in effective problem-solving activities. The most common types of prescriptive interventions include contracting, precision teaching, and "homework" assignments.

Prescriptive interventions work best when the consultee perceives that everything that can be done to solve a problem has been done and is experiencing some self-doubt and a lack of confidence.

Theory and principles interventions. In theories and principles interventions the consultant provides the consultee some theories and principles that are pertinent to the consultee's problem. Derived from the social sciences, theories and principles interventions are systematic and empirically tested (for example, behavior modification theory). The consultant helps the consultee internalize the theories and principles so that they become useful in viewing both current and similar future problems more analytically and objectively. For example, a consultant might assist a school teacher to deal with disruptive pupils by teaching him the theories and principles of behavior modification; the consultant would then monitor the teacher's effectiveness in using these principles to change the pupils' behavior.

The types of interventions, consultants' roles in each, and some indications for their use are summarized in Table 9.1, which is adapted from Blake & Mouton (1978, p. 465).

TABLE 9.1 Kinds of Interventions and Some Indications for Their Use

Interventions	Consultant's Primary Role(s)	Representative Indications For Use
Acceptant	Provide emotional release	Consultee's pent-up feelings are blocking thought and action so that needed initiatives cannot be taken.
Catalytic	Strengthen perception, quicken decision making	Consultee has obtained insufficient information, which slows progress or blocks effectiveness.

(Cont.)

Table 9.1 (Cont.)

Interventions	Consultant's Primary Role(s)	Representative Indications For Use
Confrontation	Clarify values	Consultee's values, often hidden, are contradictory or reduce effectiveness.
Prescriptive	Give answers	Consultee has "thrown up his hands" or is "on the ropes" and is unable to exercise sufficient initiative to proceed.
Theory and Principles	Provide insight	Consultee is ready to try or could benefit from a shift to a science-oriented approach to problem solving.

Units of Change

The various types of interventions consultants can use can be focused on one or more of the following units of change (Blake & Mouton, 1976, 1978):

1. individual,
2. group,
3. intergroup,
4. organization, and
5. larger social system.

Remember, the client and ultimate target in all cases of organizational consultation is the organization, even though the unit of change may be one of those listed above.

By consulting with an *individual* member of an organization, the overall effectiveness of the organization can be increased. For example, a consultant might assist a manager in developing staff evaluation skills.

Groups are common units of change in organizational consultation. Organizations frequently work with such groups as teams, quality circles, entire subsystems of the organization, and task forces. Again, consulting with groups is based on the assumption that the organization's overall effectiveness will be enhanced by successful consultation. For example, a consultant might help a task force write a grant proposal to an external funding agency.

The next level of change is *intergroup* change, in which consultants work with two or more groups within the organization for the benefit of the entire organization. For example, a school psychologist might consult with a school's teachers and its guidance counselors in determining the most effective way to implement a classroom-oriented substance-abuse prevention program.

The entire *organization* can be a unit of change. Consultants who work at this level typically use surveys and questionnaires and run meetings open to any member of the organization. For example, a team of consultants might assist a small, private human services agency in redefining its role and mission statement.

The largest unit of change is a *larger social system*, of which the organization is a part. Typically, "larger social system" refers to a community, city, region, or state. For example, a community (larger social system) might employ consultants to determine whether centralization of schools is the appropriate strategy for its school system (organization).

Focal Issues

The focal issues or "problems" about which consultants intervene with some unit of change fall into four categories (Blake & Mouton, 1976):

1. power/authority,
2. morale/cohesion,
3. norms/standards, and
4. goals/objectives.

These four categories are interdependent, and a change in one may result in a change in another. For example, a consultant might assist an organization by using team building and observe a subsequent increase in morale. The change in the organization's morale/cohesion might also produce a solidification of the organization's goals/objectives so that organization members work with more unity and direction.

Power refers to the capability of having an effect, and authority refers to the right to exercise power. *Power/authority issues* revolve around whether power and authority are used effectively in both formal and informal manners within the organization. Power/authority issues can arise over the ways power and authority are in fact used or over the ways their use is perceived by those who are not in positions of power within the organization. Power/authority issues are the most common focal issues and are best resolved with confrontational interventions.

Morale is a state of high, positive mental energy among members of an organization. Cohesion refers to the degree to which members of a group experience a positive sense of togetherness and unity. *Morale/cohesion issues* concern how members perceive the organization and its direction, as well as the degree to which members see themselves as part of a "team." Morale/cohesion issues are most effectively resolved by acceptant interventions.

Standards are the criteria organizations use for measuring quality. Norms are the "rules" that govern appropriate behavior by members of all or some part of the organization. *Standards/norms issues* are frequently raised when an organization is forced to cope with internal and/or external changes. Standards and norms are usually difficult to change; organizational consultants frequently use catalytic interventions when solving problems related to this issue.

Goals are the aims and purposes of an organization, and objectives are those things that are accomplished when goals are met. *Goals/objectives issues* are frequently related to standards and norms issues and typically arise when goals and objectives are either poorly defined or have not been achieved. Goals/objectives issues frequently surface during use of confrontation interventions on standards/norms issues, and prescriptive interventions are frequently necessary.

Although Blake & Mouton's (1976, 1978) model is the most comprehensive, it is not without its shortcomings. For example, Goodstein (1978) criticizes the model for not considering problems related to communications and worker roles as separate focal issues. Still, the Consulcube effectively reminds organizational consultants that their effectiveness depends on their skill in using a correct intervention with the appropriate individual or group concerning the pertinent focal issue.

Edgar Schein's Models of Consultation

Whereas the Consulcube provides a broad conceptual framework for organizational consultation, more specific conceptualizations have been developed.

Schein (1969, 1978, 1987) has conceived three models of consultation: the purchase of expertise model, the doctor-patient model, and the process model. Both the purchase of expertise and doctor-patient models are versions of "expert" consultation (Schein, 1978). In the *purchase of expertise model*, the consultee "purchases" a consultant who can provide expertise (knowledge or skill) to provide a solution to a previously determined problem. In the *doctor-patient model*, the consultee "purchases" the consultant's ability to both diagnose a problem and prescribe an appropriate set of solutions for it. The consultee retains control of defining the problem in the purchase of expertise model, but not in the doctor-patient model. In the purchase of expertise model, the consultee has already identified the solution (what the consultant does), whereas in the doctor-patient model neither the problem nor the solution was defined prior to consultation.

The *process model* views consultation as a ". . . set of activities on the part of the consultant which help the client to perceive, understand, and act upon process events which occur in the client's environment" (Schein, 1969, p. 9). (Note: Substitute the word "consultee" for the word "client" in this definition.) In process consultation, the consultee "purchases" the consultant's ability to help the consultee focus on process (as opposed to content) events; this approach focuses on how problems are solved, rather than on the content of problems.

There are two versions of the process model: the catalyst version and facilitator version. The *catalyst* version of process consultation occurs when the consultant does not know the solution to some problem but can help the consultee formulate his or her own solution. The *facilitator* version occurs when the consultant may have ideas (content) about solutions but withholds them in order to help the consultee to solve his or her own problem by going through a problem-solving process. Effective consultants use the version of process consultation that is most appropriate to the circumstances (Schein, 1987).

Schein's models form the basis of the following discussion of organization development consultation. First, education/training consultation and program consultation are discussed as examples of the purchase of expertise model. Next, the process of diagnosis is given special attention in the discussion of the doctor-patient model, and then the process model of consultation is considered last.

The Purchase of Expertise Model

When consultees request help from consultants, they are usually seeking some form of expertise. Expertise can take the form of knowledge, skill, or ability to find a solution to some problem. The essence of the purchase of expertise model is that the consultee knows what the problem is, what needs to be done to solve it, and who can be of help (Schein, 1969, 1978, 1987). The consultee is in effect saying to the consultant, "Here's the problem; fix it." This model is by its very nature content-oriented.

For the purchase of expertise model to be effective, the following four basic assumptions must be met (Schein, 1969, 1978, 1987):

1. The consultee has made a correct diagnosis of the problem,
2. The consultee has chosen the right consultant,
3. The consultee has correctly communicated the problem, and
4. The consultee has thought through and accepted the consequences of consultation.

If the consultee has not made the correct diagnosis, the entire consultation will be invalid: the right consultant might have been chosen, but the wrong problem will have been solved! If it becomes apparent that consultation is solving the wrong problem, the consultant is under no obligation to assist the consultee in making a new diagnosis.

It's the consultee's responsibility to ensure that the right consultant is chosen for the job. The burden is on the consultee to make sure that the consultant has the skills and abilities needed to meet the consultee's needs.

If the consultee does not correctly communicate the nature of the problem, then the consultant again may provide the correct solution to the wrong problem. By using effective communication skills such as clarifying responses, the consultant can assist the consultee in expressing the perceived problem in such a way that both parties agree about the exact nature of the problem. However, ultimately it is the consultee's responsibility to make sure that the problem has been correctly communicated to the consultant.

Inherent in the purchase of expertise model is the assumption that the consultee has thought through the consequences of consultation. Things happen when consultation takes place; a change in one part of an organization often affects other parts. Sometimes consultees are not fully aware of the potential long- and short-term impact of consultation. For example, polishing the communication skills of mid-level managers might have the unwanted impact of making them too assertive in trying to improve the entire organization. From the outset effective consultants help the consultee think through the consequences a consultant's activities could have.

In summary, the purchase of expertise model is often appropriate when a problem has been well defined, such as when a consultant can provide specific information or training or when a glitch arises in a human services program. It works best when the consultee has ascertained the consultant's suitability

for the job and has thoroughly thought through the consequences of consultation (Schein, 1978). Two of the most common forms of purchase of expertise
consultation provided by human services consultants are education/training
consultation and program consultation.

Education/training consultation. The education/training approach is the
most frequently used kind of purchase of expertise consultation. As its name
suggests, this approach emphasizes the two most common roles of the
consultant: educator and trainer (Gallessich, 1982). In this type of consultation, which is typically performed with groups and is cost effective, the
consultant shares expert knowledge and/or skills by some educational means,
such as a lecture, or through some kind of training, such as a workshop on
techniques for motivating supervisors. Gallessich (1982) defines the educa-
tion/training model as ". . . prearranged, organized services, in contrast to the
impromptu educational and training activities that are incidental to most forms
of consultation. This model, an exemplar of the technological approach to
consultation, is information-centered and emphasizes the dissemination of concepts, information, and skills rather than the formulation of a diagnosis" (pp.
109–110). Education/training consultation often takes the form of in-service or
staff development training, workshops, or on-the-job training (Conoley &
Conoley, 1982).

Consultation goals. The primary goal of the education/training consultation
is the increased effectiveness of the organization that results from the consultee's
improved professional functioning in the area upon which education and/or
training focuses. When consultation is educative in nature, some form of
information is being provided; when the consultant acts as a provider of training, however, the learning is usually experiential and focuses on "learning to
learn" (Lippitt & Nadler, 1979).

Whether a consultant uses an educational approach or a training approach
depends on whether the goal of consultation is to transmit knowledge to effect
cognitive learning or to change attitudes and behaviors (Beer, 1980). In an example of effecting cognitive learning, a consultant might provide a junior high
school faculty an in-service on the differences between a junior high school
and a middle school. In an experiential learning situation, a consultant might
have mid-level managers practice different types of leadership strategies in order
to strengthen their leadership skills.

Education and training can also be combined in consultation. For example,
a group of ministers might first be taught the characteristics of depression by
a mental health consultant and then participate in supervised counseling
sessions in which they attempt to detect these characteristics by role playing.
Whether the consultant emphasizes education, training, or both in the consultation depends primarily on what the consultee perceives the problem and
its solution to be.

Consultant function and roles. The consultant in education/training consultation functions as an expert that possesses information or skills that the consultee

needs and transmits that knowledge in one or more of the roles of advisor, educator, trainer, (Gallessich, 1982) or technical expert. The consultant's function is to provide the information and/or the training that best matches a consultee's interests and needs (Conoley & Conoley, 1982).

In order to provide accurate information and pertinent training, consultants must frequently determine (or have the organization's contact person determine) what prospective consultees perceive their needs to be. Such information can be invaluable in the consultee's preparation of an educational or training session. Some consultants may even train consultees in the best way to use a consultant before the educational or training intervention begins (Brown et al., 1987).

In addition to assisting in needs assessment and in planning and implementing education/training interventions, the consultant also assists in the evaluation of consultation. Although many organizations have standard evaluation forms to assist in this task, many consultants prefer to use their own forms, which can be specifically tailored to any particular evaluation. The purpose of evaluation is to determine whether consultees have learned the appropriate knowledge and/or skills required for the intervention in use.

The critical skills needed to function effectively as a consultant in education/training consultation include (Lippitt & Lippitt, 1986):

1. assessing the training needs related to the problem;
2. developing and stating measurable objectives for learning experiences;
3. understanding the learning and change process;
4. designing a learning experience;
5. planning and designing educational events;
6. going beyond traditional training and using heuristic laboratory methods;
7. using multiple learning stimuli, including multimedia presentations;
8. functioning as a group teacher or trainer; and
9. helping others learn how to learn (p. 36).

The consultee's experience in consultation. The major role of the consultee is to be "a good learner." Consultees are expected to learn the knowledge or skills they are taught, adapt them if necessary, and use them on the job to contribute to the organization's overall effectiveness. Consultees accomplish these tasks by giving the consultant honest and accurate information during needs assessment, being cooperative and motivated learners during the education/training process, and attempting to implement their new knowledge on the job.

During the needs assessment, the consultee is interviewed (or fills out a survey form) to identify topics for education/training, provide opinions on the nature of the problems of concern during the consultation, and to provide some idea of the consultee's willingness to participate in the consultation.

Cooperation and motivation can be enhanced during consultation if consultee participation is voluntary. Most consultants agree that if consultees must be coerced, however subtly, to participate, positive benefits will probably not accrue from consultation. Consultee cooperation and motivation can also be increased by providing them special incentives for participating. Consultees can also learn to be "good" consultees in general as well as in education/training consultation, if they are taught to:

1. understand that consultation as a process,
2. know how to initiate consultation,
3. understand that the timing of a request for consultation can affect both the process and the outcome, and
4. be able to determine when to choose consultation from among the available services (Brown et al., 1987, p. 228).

Consultees can be encouraged to implement what they have learned by education/training methodologies that help them to "personalize" the material. It is one thing to listen to a lecture on styles of management; it is another to be asked to consider how the different management styles match or contrast to a consultee's own style. Responding to consultees' perceived needs during the entire consultation process is an effective way to maximize the likelihood that consultees follow through on consultation activities.

Finally, as in all forms of consultation, it is up to consultees to decide whether or not they'll use the information and/or training received.

Application: consultant techniques and procedures. The education/training model consists of four steps:

1. needs assessment,
2. planning the educational and training activities,
3. performing the educational or training activities, and
4. evaluation.

Either the consultant or the organization's contact person conducts the *needs assessment*, which identifies the content of education or training sessions and occasionally the problems that consultation can help ameliorate. Needs assessment can be made by interviews to obtain in-depth information and opinions. This method is comprehensive, but very expensive and time-consuming as well. In other cases needs are assessed through questionnaires, which are cost effective and provide information that is relatively easy to collate. However, questionnaires frequently lack depth, and the framing of questions can affect the kinds of responses obtained. An example of a needs assessment form is provided in Figure 9.2.

Consultants should consider the nature of adult learners when *planning* activities (Cross, 1984; Knowles & Associates, 1984; Knox, 1986). Adults have learning behaviors that are influenced by past experience, current abilities and roles, and future aspirations (Knox, 1977). An understanding of these learner characteristics by the consultant can assist in organizing adult learners' activities around their backgrounds and aspirations (Knox, 1986). For example, although adult learners tend to be conservative in their educational outlook, they still enjoy innovative teaching methodologies. Many corporations and other organizations have applied modern concepts of adult learning in their education/ training consultation.

Our organization has set aside the week of April 10 for staff development training. Your frank and candid responses to the following items will assist the training division in arranging for training and development activities that coincide with your needs. In the next few weeks we will collate your responses and put them into a questionnaire that will help us to formulate specific training needs and activities. Please answer the following questions carefully and return them to the training division by the end of this week. All responses will be kept anonymous. Thank you for your participation.

1. I would benefit from knowing more about the following recent trends in my field:

2. I would benefit from discussing the following current issues in my field:

3. I would like to know more about the following new skills areas that are currently receiving much attention in my field:

4. List the needs within your part of the organization that you think that staff development should address.

5. List the needs within the entire organization that you think that staff development should address.

6. Add any suggestions you think are relevant to the week of staff development.

FIGURE 9.2 A Sample Needs Assessment Form

The term *andragogy,* which refers to a system of concepts about adult learners, is the art and science of helping adults learn (Knowles & Associates, 1984). There are several important points about andragogy that consultants should consider in their planning: adult learners are internally motivated, task-oriented, and rich resources for one another (Knowles & Associates, 1984).

In summary, proper planning is an essential ingredient in education/training consultation that should incorporate the needs of adult learners and needs of the particular group of consultees to be educated or trained.

In *performing the education or training,* the consultant should attempt to use methods that are appropriate to the consultees' characteristics and the objectives of the education/training. Many education/training consultants use designs that incorporate many methodologies, including (Gallessich, 1982):

1. lectures,
2. use of media and materials,
3. structured laboratory experiences,
4. small group discussions,
5. behavioral role modeling,
6. movement, and
7. feedback.

Further, the ways such methods as these are performed is critical to their success. For example, timing and the use of props and humor are very important to successful education/training activities (James & Dougherty, 1985).

How consultees respond to the consultant at the outset of education/training also affects the ultimate success of the consultation. Therefore, regardless of the methods used, the consultant should make an attempt to create a good working climate by (Conoley & Conoley, 1982):

1. using moderate levels of self-disclosure at the outset,
2. being open about any concerns that relate to how the education/training is proceeding,
3. treating consultees with respect,
4. being open to consultee feedback,
5. learning consultees' names as quickly as possible, and
6. being able to laugh at oneself when things go wrong.

During *evaluation* of the education/training consultants often use questionnaires and pre-post measures of pertinent material. Evaluations of education/training interventions are becoming increasingly sophisticated (Gallessich, 1982), including feedback loops that allow continuous adaptation of education/training procedures and methods for measuring the impact of education/training on the entire organization. There appears to be a trend from norm-referenced to criterion-referenced measures of learning in education/training evaluations (Gallessich, 1982). Chapters 5 and 6 of this text cover related points on evaluation in more detail and depth.

In summary, education/training is evaluated both formally and informally by participants who assess its usefulness, by consultants who assess "how it went," and by organizational administrators who decide how the organization might be affected (Knowles & Associates, 1984).

Here is an example of how education/training consultation proceeds:

CASE STUDY:

A human services professor at a university was asked by the director of personnel services of a large school district to conduct some workshops for the district's school counselors and psychologists. When the consultant asked the director what kind of workshops were desired, the director responded with, "You know, some of that new counseling stuff." The consultant advocated the use of a needs assessment instrument to give prospective participants input about the nature of the workshops. The director agreed to gather the information by using a needs assessment form developed by the consultant.

The needs assessment revealed that the participants desired information and training for dealing with AIDS, teenage pregnancy, and date rape. The consultant planned the activities by developing behavioral objectives to be accomplished through a variety of methods. A balance was struck between providing information and skills training. The consultant also took the needs of adult learners into consideration during the planning process.

One workshop was held on each topic. Additional input from the participants was obtained at the beginning of the first workshop. Several methods were used during the workshops, and a good working climate was developed and maintained throughout the duration of the workshops. At the conclusion of each workshop, the participants evaluated the consultant, the workshop content, and the usefulness of the session. The consultant's views concerning the workshop and its effects on the participants were sent to the personnel services director in a written report.

Program consultation. Most human service organizations have programs that frequently require programmatic consultative services. *Program consultation* is a form of purchase of expertise consultation in which the organization in some way uses the consultant to assist in planning a new program, revising an existing program, or dealing with factors that affect a current program. Program consultation differs from other forms of consultation in that it is restricted to a specific program and its goals (Gallessich, 1982).

In program consultation, the expertise the organization "purchases" is some kind of technical assistance. The organization perceives a need with respect to the program and hires a consultant to help fulfill that need. For example, a consultant might be hired to help design the evaluation of a program to determine whether it has met its goals; indeed, evaluation is the primary reason consultants are hired to assist with programs. Even though program consultation does not require any new skills on the part of the consultant, it clearly demonstrates how consultants can work with organizations to meet their goals (Gallessich, 1982).

Program consultation is becoming increasingly popular due to organizations' increased emphasis on programs, the increasingly complex technology related to programs, and the trend toward cost-effectiveness and accountability in organizations (Gallessich, 1982). In addition, the professional standards of organizations in which consultants work demand that evaluation of programs be performed (Kratochwill, Mace, & Bissel, 1987). Consultants frequently use program consultation as a way to "get their feet in the door" of an organization in order to be able to perform other types of consultation.

The primary goal of program consultation is to provide an organization technical assistance so that a given program is successful. Consultation services can be provided for any aspect of a program, including development and evaluation. Consultation is usually requested for some skill or knowledge that the organization neither possesses nor has time to use. Because program evaluation is the most frequently requested form of program consultation, we'll focus now on how program evaluation consultation is performed.

Consultation goals. *Program evaluation* is ". . . a systematic set of data collection and analysis activities undertaken to determine the value of a program to aid management, program planning, staff training, public accountability, and promotion" (Hagedorn, Beck, Nuebert, & Werlin, 1976, p. 3; quoted in Gibson & Mitchell, 1981). The goal of program evaluation is to improve current decision making in the program being evaluated (Matuszek, 1981) and thus improve the overall functioning of the organization. Organizations want to know if their programs are meeting their goals and objectives. When they are not sure how best to determine this, organizations frequently turn to program consultants who evaluate programs by a variety of methods and then transmit their findings to the organization so that decisions concerning the program can be made. For example, a consultant might assist in evaluating the effects of an employee assistance program in a large textile firm.

A secondary goal of evaluation in program consultation is increasing the consultee's ability to evaluate current and subsequent (similar) programs. If this goal is part of the consultation, the consultant might also function in the education/training consultation model described earlier in this chapter; in this case the consultant "gives away" the very skills that led to the need for a consultant in the first place.

Consultant function and roles.   In this model consultants act as experts in program development: they provide accurate, timely, and useful information to decision makers so that the program can be most effectively run.

The consultant conducts exploratory meetings with consultees to determine the needs of program evaluation, develops a program evaluation design, obtains consultee feedback on the design, and redesigns the evaluation (Matuszek, 1981). The consultant then carries out the evaluation by collecting and analyzing data and filing a report. The process of designing a program evaluation can be very time-consuming; much of the consultant's time is spent in preparation and planning.

Consultee experience in consultation.   The consultee's primary role in this model is to provide the consultant with as much accurate information as possible. This information is critical in the initial stages of program evaluation consultation because the consultant needs as much information as possible to develop the appropriate design. Therefore the consultee (or consultees) must make a commitment to spend whatever time and effort are required to be interviewed or to react to the consultant's progress in formulating a suitable evaluation design. Ideally the organization's administrative structure will sanction the consultees' participation so that they feel free to cooperate.

Consultees determine what, if anything, they will do with the results of program evaluation. Some typical uses of the results of program evaluations include (Matuszek, 1981):

1. making decisions about the program on a daily basis,
2. collecting data for reports required by the organization or by external agencies,
3. developing objectives for use in writing a proposal,
4. making decisions about modifying the program, and
5. making decisions regarding the program's continuation.

In addition to providing consultants accurate information, consultees should also do everything possible to ensure that consultants can function independently, particularly when internal consultants are asked to do program consultation that focuses on evaluation. Consultees should inform consultants before the evaluation what they will do if the results are positive, neutral, or negative to the program. Further, consultees can help consultants by determining the type of final report that will be submitted: Will the report be sent directly to a top administrator? Should the report be written in nontechnical language? Finally, consultees should inform consultants of any recent events within the organization that might effect the results of the evaluation.

Application: consultant techniques and procedures. Four steps in program consultation focus on evaluation:

1. hold ongoing meetings with consultees to design the evaluation,
2. collect data,
3. evaluate data, and
4. write a final report.

After program evaluation has been requested, the consultant completes the entry stage as in any other consultation situation. Once the consultant is given permission to consult, the parties to receive the report of the consultant's findings should be determined. The consultant is then ready to develop the program evaluation design, which involves a series of meetings with the consultees, typically called the *program staff*. During these meetings, the participants try to identify what decisions are to be made, determine who the organization's important decision makers are, and discuss how the program evaluation will tie into the decisions to be made (Matuszek, 1981).

The consultant meets with the consultees for as many meetings as necessary until both consultant and consultees are confident that all parties have an appropriate understanding of what is to occur and why. From all of this information, the consultant begins to put together an evaluation design that dictates the who, what, where, and when of the evaluation procedure (Fitz-Gibbon & Morris, 1978).

An in-depth discussion of the type of design a consultant should choose when evaluating a program is beyond the scope of this book. Interested readers may want to refer to *The Practice and Profession of Program Evaluation* (Anderson & Ball, 1978), which provides a comprehensive approach to program evaluation. Readers may also want to review Chapter 6 of this text for ways to evaluate the consultation process. Some of the evaluation models frequently used by program consultants include (Matuszek, 1981):

1. the formative-summative model (Scriven, 1967),
2. evaluation as information for decision makers model (Stufflebeam, Foley, Gephart, Guba, Hammond, Meriman, & Purvus, 1971),
3. the looking for discrepancies in a program model (Provus, 1971),
4. the actual effects model (Scriven, 1972), and
5. the adversary model (Owens, 1973).

Regardless of the model of evaluation the consultant uses, there are four evaluation standards to bear in mind: accuracy, utility, feasibility, and propriety (Matuszek, 1981). Accuracy standards are related to the methodological soundness of the evaluation. Utility standards relate to the concept that evaluation should have some practical application. Feasibility standards deal with whether the evaluation design is appropriate for the program in the first place. Propriety standards relate to any ethical or legal issues that are connected to the evaluation.

Once the consultant has put together the program evaluation design, a final review is held with the consultees and parties-at-interest. Any needed modifications in the design are made at this time.

The consultant is now ready to carry out the design. Data are collected and analyzed according to the design plan. Program consultants anticipate problem areas in carrying out the evaluation and stay in contact with all parties involved during data collection and analysis (Matuszek, 1981). After the data have been analyzed, the consultant writes and presents a formal report so that appropriate action can be taken.

Here is an example that illustrates program consultation:

CASE STUDY:
A psychologist in private practice is selected by a human services agency to help evaluate its "Big Sister-Big Brother" program, which has been in operation for three years. Although the agency thinks that the program is "doing okay," there appears to be a high turnover rate among its volunteers. The psychologist has had considerable experience with program evaluation and has worked with volunteer programs in the past.

The consultant starts out by holding a meeting with the program's staff to design an evaluation. Four other meetings are held to make sure that the parties involved are in agreement about what is going on and that the evaluation is proceeding smoothly.

The consultant and the program staff collect information on the volunteers and the children in the program, such as how long volunteers tend to stay with the program. Methods are determined for assessing the program's impact on the children. The consultant then analyzes the collected data and presents a report to the program staff. Among other things, the data show that volunteers last an average of nine months, receive little recognition or encouragement from the agency, and are not sure what is expected from them.

The consultant recommends a training program for the volunteers, more personal contact with the volunteers by the program's staff, and some form of recognition for service as a volunteer. The program's impact on the children was deemed to be positive. Parents reported that volunteers gave their children additional, desirable adult role models and helped "keep the kids off the streets," and the children liked the program because they "got to do a lot of extra things that were fun."

The Doctor-Patient Model

Sometimes consultees know something is wrong but don't know what it is. When consultation is requested, the consultant is given the power to make a diagnosis and prescribe a solution. It is as if the consultee is saying, "I don't know what's wrong. Find out and tell me how I can fix it." This type of consultation, called the doctor-patient model (Schein, 1969, 1987), is a type of expert consultation—the consultee is "purchasing" the consultant's expertise in diagnosing and prescribing.

In order for the doctor-patient model to be effective, the following assumptions must be met (Schein, 1969, 1987):

1. The diagnostic process itself is seen as helpful.
2. The consultee has correctly interpreted the organization's symptoms and has located the "sick" area.
3. The person or group defined as "sick" will provide the information needed to make a valid diagnosis; that is, they will neither hide data nor exaggerate symptoms.
4. The consultee understands and will correctly interpret the diagnosis provided by the consultant and will implement whatever prescription is offered.
5. The consultee can remain "effective" after the consultant leaves.

The very act of calling a consultant to perform a diagnosis is an intervention, and the consultant should make sure that the consultee is aware of this. If the consultee is unaware that diagnosis is an intervention or does not explain the consultant's presence adequately, then the consultant's efforts can meet considerable resistance that can adversely affect the results of consultation.

Because organizations are very complex entities, faith that the consultee has correctly interpreted the symptoms and knows where the organization is "sick" is a very large assumption (Schein, 1987). Consultees can easily misconstrue and misjudge events on the job. In addition, consultees and consultants can easily get caught in a cycle of incorrect diagnoses due to the consultee's desire to help and the consultant's desire to give it.

The doctor-patient model assumes that consultees and other members of the organization are straightforward and honest with the consultant about their perceptions of the organization's problems (Schein, 1987). The nature of this honesty is a function of the organizational climate: If the climate is one of mistrust, then the consultant is not likely to get the "real" story; if the climate is one of trust, the consultees and other organization members are likely to tell the consultant "everything" and could even exaggerate the problem. The consultant also needs to be cautious about creating dependence among consultees.

What will happen if the consultee doesn't like the consultant's diagnosis? Even if the diagnosis is accepted, what guarantees are there that the prescription is going to be implemented? To assume that consultees will in fact accept diagnosis and prescription from the consultant is a mistake.

The assumption that the consultee will remain "effective" after the consultant leaves may not be correct if the consultee did not learn any problem-solving skills during the consultation. If a similar problem arises for the consultee in the future, the consultant will have to be called in again.

Clearly, the relationship between the consultant and consultee is critical in the doctor-patient model of consultation. The consultant must be able to gain the trust of the consultee so that open communication can occur. If the consultee trusts the consultant, then real issues helpful to the diagnosis are more likely to emerge. In addition, if the consultant is able to create an effective relationship with the consultee and develop professional credibility, the prescription provided to the consultee also has more credibility.

In summary, the doctor-patient model works best when the consultee is willing to use a consultant, has observed and described the symptoms accurately, does not have the ability to perform the diagnosis and prescription, and is willing to follow through on the consultant's recommendations. A possible drawback of this model is that consultees might not enhance their problem-solving skills and may become dependent on the consultant (Schein, 1987).

Because many ideas in the doctor-patient model, including diagnosis, are covered in Chapter 4, only a brief overview of this model is given now.

Consultation goals. The consultant's primary goal in the doctor-patient model is to define the organization's problem and to recommend realistic interventions to ameliorate that problem. Enhancing the consultee's diagnostic skills is not a goal in this model.

Consultant functions and roles. The consultant functions as an expert who enters the system, interviews consultees and parties-at-interest, collects data, makes a diagnosis, and recommends a solution. The consultant may well be hired to implement the solution; in that case the consultant would change to the purchase of expertise model. Whereas the purchase of expertise model demands content expertise on the part of the consultant, the doctor-patient model demands expertise in diagnostic and prescriptive skills.

Consulting skills that are critical to the doctor-patient model include:

1. diagnostic skills,
2. a broad repertoire of prescriptive skills,
3. an in-depth knowledge of organizational theory,
4. the ability to "read" organizations,
5. data collection skills,
6. data interpretation skills, and
7. human relations skills.

Consultee experience in consultation. The main task of the consultee is to be a good "patient;" that is, to tell the consultant in as honest, objective, and accurate a way as possible the areas in which the organization has problems. The consultee should realize (and take into account) that asking a consultant for a diagnosis is also an intervention, that the very act of using a consultant affects the organization in some way. The consultee's tasks also include assisting the consultant in gathering additional data, ensuring that the consultant's diagnosis is fully and accurately understood, and advocating that the consultant's prescription be implemented.

Application: consultant techniques and procedures.   In the doctor-patient model consultants enter the system as they would in any other consultation model. The major step in this model is to determine how best to go about making a diagnosis; the choice of how to make a diagnosis is based on the situation, not the consultant's inclination to make diagnoses (Beer, 1980). Common problem areas in organizations include its purpose, its structure, its interpersonal relationships, its leadership, the informal devices it uses to build a sense of teamwork, and its reward structure (Weisbord, 1976). The method used to diagnose the organization's problems should obtain information about how its people see the organization's internal processes (Beer, 1980). It is crucial that the consultant ensure that people involved in the diagnosis feel free to express their true thoughts, opinions, and feelings.

After the data have been gathered, the consultant analyzes it and formulates a diagnosis. The diagnosis defines problems in the organization in terms that the consultee can both understand and utilize (Argyris, 1970).

In this model the consultant usually determines what is best for the consultee to do about the problem (Goodstein, 1978). However, consultants cannot necessarily help consultees make a commitment to change; they can only prescribe some solutions that the organization is capable of carrying out and tailor them to the unique aspects of the organization. Generalized prescriptions are rarely successful because they fail to consider the uniqueness of each organization.

Consider the following example of doctor-patient consultation:

CASE STUDY:

A counselor in a community counseling center was asked to be an internal consultant in order to improve the center's effectiveness in delivering services to its clients. The counselor was chosen because of her effective diagnostic skills, her solid working knowledge of organizations, and her trustworthiness. The consultant was given "free run" of the center and was charged with defining the center's problem areas and prescribing some ways to effectively manage them.

The consultant began by informing all staff members of the nature of consultation. Interviews and surveys were used to gather data from the center's administration and staff and from former clients. Complete confidentiality was guaranteed to all involved. Information was sought on such factors as interpersonal relationships, views of the center's organizational climate, and the center's role and mission. Based on the analysis of the data, the consultant concluded that there was little consensus concerning the center's overall role and mission, which led to a lack of understanding of how the center was run and what the staff and administration were supposed to do. In turn this lack of understanding led to inadequacies in the area of program development.

The consultant prescribed a review and subsequent modification of the center's role and mission statement. Further, the consultant recommended development of a five-year strategic plan based on the modified role and mission statement and suggested that all employees be involved in each of these recommended activities.

The Process Model

Sometimes a consultant is needed to supplement the consultee's problem-solving skills—the consultee knows something is wrong and wants to figure what it is and what to do about it. Process consultation is what the consultant does to help the consultee identify, understand, and change the process events that occur within an organization (Schein, 1969, 1978, 1987). The focus of consultation is not on the content of the problem, but rather on the process by which problems are solved. The consultee "owns" the problem (and continues to "own" it throughout the consultation process) and "purchases" the consultant's expertise in handling process events.

Process consultation is based on the premise that often things in an organization can be changed only if the consultee is involved in diagnosing the problem and generating solutions. Because of the complexity of problems in organizations and the consultees' familiarity with those problems, consultees' input into the diagnosis is crucial. In addition, advice given by consultants can be counterproductive in that it can cause resistance, power struggles, and resentment (Schein, 1987). Because organizations continually undergo change, there will always be problems to be diagnosed and solved. Thus, it is important that consultees "learn how to learn" to solve problems.

The relationship between the consultant and the consultee is extremely important. The consultant must both create an environment of trust and credibility and help the consultee feel safe enough to "own" the problem and work on it throughout the consultation process. Such tasks demand empathy, respect, and genuineness on the part of the consultant.

Process consultation works best when the following assumptions are met:

1. The consultee is distressed somehow but does not know the source of the distress or what to do about it.
2. The consultee does not know either what kind of help might be available or which consultant could provide the kind of help that may be needed.
3. The nature of the problem is such that the consultee not only needs help in figuring out what is wrong but would benefit from participation in the diagnostic process.
4. The consultee has "constructive intent," is motivated by goals and values that the consultant can accept, and has some capacity to enter into a helping relationship.
5. The consultee is ultimately the only one who knows what form of intervention will work best in the situation.
6. The consultee is capable of learning how to diagnose and solve his or her own organizational problems (Schein, 1987, pp. 32–33).

The process consultation model is most applicable when a consultee with some problem-solving ability is willing to learn how to work out solutions to a problem without seeking content assistance or giving the problem to the consultant for diagnosis. By focusing on the *how* rather than the *what* of problem solving, the consultant and consultee join in a collaborative effort to enable the consultee to solve current concerns and similar ones in the future.

Consultation goals. The primary goal of process consultation is to help consultees gain insight into the everyday events occurring within the organization. Process consultation attempts to teach consultees to act on those events so that consultees become more adept at identifying and modifying them in ways that achieve the consultees' goals (Schein, 1987). Process consultation helps consultees solve their own concerns and assists them in acquiring the skills required to be productive problem identifiers and problem solvers. If the consultant and consultee are successful, the ultimate goal of increasing the organization's overall effectiveness is also met.

Consultant functions and roles. The primary roles played by the process consultant are facilitator and catalyst (Schein, 1978). The consultant collaborates with the consultee such that consultation becomes a joint effort (Goodstein, 1978). Rather than providing content expertise, the consultant facilitates consultees' processes of self-discovery and self-exploration so that they are able to use their skills in identifying and addressing the problems at hand.

The consultant must be an expert in processes that occur at the individual, interpersonal, and intergroup levels; content expertise in the consultee institution's area of perceived difficulty is not required. The consultant helps the consultee obtain insight into the everyday human activities in an organization (for example, who talks to whom about what), which are viewed as critical to the appropriate diagnosis of an organizational problem (Schein, 1969). The process consultant provides less structure and direct input than would a consultant operating in either the purchase of expertise or doctor-patient model (Brown et al., 1987).

In addition to creating a climate conducive to consultee exploration and input, the process consultant assists in gathering data about the relationships within the organization and members' perceptions of organizational processes. The consultant then assists the consultee in making a diagnosis using these data, and process-oriented interventions, such as agenda setting and feedback, are made by the consultant and/or the consultee. Finally, the consultant helps the consultee evaluate the consultation by looking for changes in values and interpersonal behaviors within the organization (Schein, 1969). The consultant's success is measured by how effectively consultees define and achieve their goals and whether the changes produced remain effective in the long run (Schmuck, 1976). Once the evaluation has been concluded the consultant reduces involvement and terminates the consultation.

Consultee experience in consultation. The consultee, a person within the organization and perhaps a manager, senses that something is not quite right in the organization—that things could be better—and wants things to improve.

The consultee uses the consultant to translate vague feelings and perceptions into concrete actions to enhance the overall effectiveness of the organization (Bennis, Benne, Chin, & Corey, 1976).

The major role of the consultee in this model is that of an active collaborator. The consultee is assumed to have some problem-solving skills and be knowledgeable about the consultee organization. The consultee provides the content of the consultation and participates in the processes at issue as the consultee's process skills dictate. The consultee then discusses content issues and the nature of the perceived problems, sets goals, and attempts to make plans for action (Schmuck, 1976). The consultation process itself helps the consultee define diagnostic steps that lead to action plans or organizational change (Bennis et al., 1976).

Application: consultant techniques and procedures.   The premise of process consultation is that organizations are merely networks of people. If these networks are not functioning effectively, there will be extreme difficulty in accomplishing the tasks of the organization (Schein, 1969). Process consultation attempts to enhance the overall functioning of the organization by helping the consultee change values and develop skills. In effect, the consultee's development is accomplished when the consultant models the desired values and skills. Through collaboration, the consultee begins to take more and more responsibility for the diagnosis and implementation of procedures. As the desired skills and values become more evident in the consultee's behavior, the consultant gradually disengages from consultation.

There are seven overlapping steps to process consultation:

1. making initial contact with the consultee organization;
2. defining the relationship, formal contacting, and creating a psychological contract;
3. selecting a setting and method of work;
4. gathering data and making a diagnosis;
5. intervening;
6. reducing involvement; and
7. terminating (Schein, 1969).

The unique aspects of selecting a setting and a method of work, gathering data, intervening, and evaluating as they pertain to process consultation are discussed next.

Selecting a setting and method of work.   The final tasks of entry involve selecting a work setting, specifying a time schedule, and selecting a method of work (Schein, 1969).

The process consultant's work setting should be located so that the consultant can observe the "real work" within the organization. Such a setting helps diminish the consultant's image as an intrusive person and assures the consultant that everyone being observed has given their permission and wants feedback on interpersonal processes.

The method of work chosen by the consultant, although it may vary, should coincide as much as possible with the underlying values of process consultation. The process consultant favors approaches that suggest that the consultant doesn't have "the right answers" and is consistently available to consultees for questions and dialogue. Therefore, the process consultant favors the use of observation, informal interviews, and group discussions, which maximize opportunities for consultees and consultants to interact.

Gathering data. Although data gathering is itself an intervention and occurs throughout the entire consultation process, it is treated as a separate stage here for the sake of discussion. Consultants should bear in mind that data gathering is a crucial process that should be conducted in a manner that is consistent with the consultee's values. The very act of interviewing may stimulate the consultee to think of new things.

The process consultant believes that plans for gathering data should be general in nature because the only way to determine how to proceed is to use experiences resulting from initial data-gathering attempts. The common themes of all data-gathering strategies are the natural relationships within the organization, perceptions of organizational processes, and concern over organizational effectiveness (Schein, 1969).

Intervening. The way in which the process consultant gathers data provides the groundwork for effective intervention. As process consultation proceeds, the consultant can intervene in a variety of ways. Schein (1987, p. 146) categorized the interventions that process consultants can make in terms of their tactical goals—exploration, diagnosis, action alternatives, and confrontation—because the process consultant usually moves through these interventions in that order as the consultation process unfolds (Schein, 1987). This progression is based both on the interventions' power and the fact that the data one intervention produces enables the next intervention to be used. Which intervention is chosen is a matter of tactics and style. *Tactics* are skillful methods used to obtain goals, whereas *style* refers to how tactics are implemented. The consultant's major stylistic choices are whether to present interventions in the forms of assertions, declarative statements, or questions.

In summary, the consultant uses exploratory questions to stimulate the consultee's thinking and to determine how the consultee views things. Diagnostic interventions are used to involve the consultee in the diagnostic process, action alternative interventions help convince the consultee that something can be done about the situation, and confrontive interventions are used to test the consultee's motivation and willingness to act (Schein, 1987).

Evaluating. Interventions need to be evaluated in terms of whether they actually worked. The process consultant must consider what outcomes might occur as a result of consultation and how these outcomes are to be measured. As its ultimate goal process consultation attempts to produce improvements in organizational performance by changing values and interpersonal skills in key personnel.

Consider this example of process consultation:

CASE STUDY:
A group of teachers at a middle school were unsatisfied with the general quality of communication between the staff and students at the school and they wanted to improve the communication efforts of the staff as a whole. They asked the school counselor to sit in at their meetings and act as a "sounding board." The school counselor agreed to consult in this matter.

Time at the end of each meeting was allocated for the counselor to give feedback to the group. The counselor was also asked to help the group stay on task and get through the problem-solving process task at hand. During the consultation the counselor provided feedback to the group on its problem-solving skills, challenged the group to define its goals more precisely, and suggested that group members develop specific ways to evaluate their attempts to communicate better. All in all, the consultant helped the group members become more effective problem solvers. Finally, the consultant provided feedback on the group's ways of gathering information from students and the types of interventions it developed for improving communication. When everyone involved was satisfied with the way things were going, the consultant reduced involvement with the group and attended only every third meeting.

SUMMARY, TRENDS, AND CONCLUSIONS

Summary

Organizational consultation is a label for many types of consultation that are performed in an organization by a consultant who acts either internally or externally and who functions as a technical expert, a diagnostician, or a process expert. Regardless of the role of the consultant, organizational consultation is predicated on the notion that an organization can increase its overall effectiveness through consultation. The organization itself, or one of its parts, is the client, and consultees are people in the organization with whom the consultant works.

Organizational consultation has its roots in the fields of industrial technology, manufacturing productivity, the applied behavioral sciences, and managerial science. Important work in organizational consultation includes that of Blake & Mouton (1976, 1986, 1983), Schein (1969, 1978, 1987) and Lippitt and Lippitt (1986).

The basic assumptions of organizational consultation are that the organization can be viewed as the "client"; the process (the how) is as important as content (the what); the behavior of individuals, groups, and organizations is cyclical in nature; and satisfied personnel make for effective organizations.

Organizations suffer because their personnel lack the knowledge, skills, or values to function at optimum levels of effectiveness. Organizational consultants, armed with a broad repertoire of techniques grounded in organizational theory, attempt to help consultees deal with the complexities of organizational life in order to enhance organizational effectiveness.

Consulting with organizations is a little like feeding a hungry animal: In living its life, the organization uses up energy and becomes "hungry." If it doesn't get some food—consultation—it cannot function optimally and will eventually starve to death.

Trends

The major trends in organizational consulting are linked to several societal factors: a rapid movement toward an "information" society, the ever increasing pace of change in all aspects of life (Backer, 1985), the growing awareness that change requires systematic thinking, and the realization that change can be successfully accomplished only through influence, not by force (Goodstein, 1985). These factors in turn influence three themes that appear to underlie emerging trends in consultation (Backer, 1985, p. 20):

Professionalization in Consultation

1. more first-time/full-time career choices;
2. broader training opportunities;
3. growing knowledge base, including specialized publications;
4. more professional associations;
5. increasing opportunities for women and minorities; and
6. greater attention to professional practice issues, including ethics and evaluation.

Technology in Consulting

1. practice by telecommunications;
2. support by the microcomputer; and
3. competition from software consulting packages.

Impact of Consultation on Organizations

1. implementation of both information/expert and change/helper roles;
2. increasing breadth of topical areas of practice;
3. continued healthy growth;
4. enhanced policy influence; and
5. increasing prominence of organizational culture.

An additional trend, influenced by the mental health movement, is an increased involvement of organizational consultants in employee-assistance programs that have both preventative and remedial influences on organizational problems (Lewis & Lewis, 1986). A final trend is a movement toward specialization in both expert consultation and process consultation that has resulted from increases in organizational complexity (Aplin, 1985).

Conclusions

Because organizational consultation encompasses a variety of approaches, it is difficult to assess its major contributions. It is clear, however, that organizational consultation has contributed to improving workplace conditions (for example, through process consultation) and helping organizations become more diverse and accountable (for example, through program consultation).

Organizational consultation has emphasized the idea that meeting human needs and increasing productivity within the organization are interconnected (Brown et al., 1987). The specialized types of consultation available in organizational consultation have increased (Gallessich, 1982). Organizational consultation's concept of the organization-as-client has helped organizations understand the importance of organizational culture; indeed, most organizations now realize that much individual behavior is strongly influenced by organizational culture (French & Bell, 1978). Organizational consultation has also demonstrated that working with groups of consultees can be a cost-effective way to meet workers' needs and increase organizational effectiveness.

The criticisms of organizational consultation are frequently those directed at organizational development, including that it has not fulfilled its early promise to integrate or systematize its interventions. The following criticisms were adapted from a critique of organizational consultation by Gallessich (1982, pp. 221–222):

1. Organizational consultation is too preoccupied with interpersonal process to the detriment of problem-related factors such as budgeting and technology (Margulies & Raia, 1972; French & Bell, 1978).
2. Organizational consultation interventions are often "bandaids on an open wound" and hence are not effective in solving many organizational problems in the long run (Burke, 1980).
3. The results of organizational consultation are often "cosmetic" or only involve "fine-tuning" (Schein & Greiner, 1977).
4. Organizational consultants sometimes perform "dirty work" or "spy" for managers and other administrators (Friedlander & Brown, 1974).
5. Organizational consultants sometimes produce such grand designs that their interventions in effect are worse than the organization's problems were in the first place (Klein, 1969).
6. Organizational consultants sometimes try to apply methods of business and industry when providing organizational consultation to human services agencies (Golembiewski, 1969).

There are other criticisms of organizational consultation: some organizational consultants rely on one or two pet interventions (Huse, 1978). In addition, organizational consultants cannot always take into account administrators' deeply-rooted assumptions about administration and personnel, assumptions that may differ from those held by the consultant. Hence, there is at the outset of consultation tremendous potential for resistance that may never be overcome.

Schein (1969, 1978, 1987) noted that the purchase of expertise and doctor-patient types of organizational consultation are limited because they rely on basic assumptions that are rarely met in practice. Therefore, these types of consultation are at best superficial and, at worst, counterproductive. Because organizational consultation is complex and organizations themselves are slow to change, organizational consultation is likely to last a long time and be quite expensive (French & Bell, 1978).

Finally, organizational consultation frequently does not accurately take into account the external forces operating on the organization. Thus, performing consultation with an organization on Madison Avenue will require dealing with external forces quite different from those operating on an organization in the rural South.

These criticisms reflect more the imperfections of practicing organizational consultants than of the models of organizational consultation and their principles. Accordingly, better training procedures for organizational consultants are as likely to produce improvements as would refinements in organizational consultation models.

QUESTIONS FOR REFLECTION

1. What historical forces led to the development of organizational consultation?
2. How can an organization be a client?
3. Differentiate among the purchase of expertise, doctor-patient, and process models of consultation.
4. Why are the purchase of expertise and doctor-patient models particularly limited?
5. Explain how both education/training and program consultation are examples of purchase of expertise consultation.
6. Why is program evaluation the most common function of the program consultant?
7. Process consultation aims for changes in values and skills of the consultees involved. How are these values and skills related to organizational effectiveness?
8. Is it really possible for a consultant to produce an accurate diagnosis of an organization's problem? Why or why not?
9. Why do so few consultees follow through on the prescriptions made by organizational consultants?
10. Look at Blake and Mouton's (1976, 1983) Consulcube. Do you think that one consultant could be competent in implementing interventions for each of the focal issues? Why or why not?

SUGGESTED SUPPLEMENTARY READINGS

If you are interested in reading more about organizational consultation, you may want to read some or all of the articles and books listed below.

Bell, C. R., & Nadler, L. (Eds.). (1985). *Clients and consultants: Meeting and exceeding expectations* (2nd ed.). Houston: Gulf. Although some of the chapters in this text are dated, *Clients and Consultants* is an excellent resource on the consultation process. Topics covered include the consultant-consultee relationship and consultants' roles, the stages of consultation, and issues in organizational consultation. Although consultation in this text typically has business and industry settings, readers interested in consulting in human services settings can glean a wealth of pertinent information on consultation processes.

Schein, E. H. (1969). *Process consultation: Its role in organizational development.* Reading, MA: Addison-Wesley. This classic text on organizational consultation is must reading for anyone interested in consulting with organizations. Schein discusses process consultation in detail and in relation to the purchase of expertise and doctor-patient models.

Schein, E. H. (1987). *Process consultation: Lessons for managers and consultants.* Volume II. Reading, MA: Addison-Wesley. This is Schein's latest contribution to the field of process consultation. Filled with case studies, this text discusses advances in process consultation since his 1969 text. Of particular interest is Schein's discussion of new classifications of process consultation interventions. Its business and industry orientation should not diminish the wealth of applicable information in this book. Interested readers should note that this text was written for those who already possess a basic familiarity with process consultation.

Mental Health Consultation

PREVIEW

Mental health consultation, one of the most popular models of consultation, attempts to promote the mental health of the community through consultants' efforts to help direct caregivers, such as counselors, more effectively deliver their services. Clearly it is difficult to promote the mental health of society in a preventative way, as mental health consultation attempts to do. For example, how would you promote the unique mental health needs of each of the numerous subgroups in our culture?

Consider this relatively simple form of mental health consultation:

CASE STUDY:
You are a social worker who consults with psychiatric nurses concerning approaches to counsel the relatives of Alzheimer's disease victims. One of your consultees is having difficulty with a family of a certain patient. As you listen to the consultee describe the case, you get the impression that the patient's "Jekyll and Hyde" personality is keeping the family off balance. You suggest that the nurse teach the family some self-talk strategies they can use when the patient is acting out. You refer the nurse to several sources of information on self-talk strategies and agree to provide the consultee a training session on these kinds of strategies.

In this chapter we'll consider the historical development of the mental health consultation model and examine Caplan's (1970) model of mental health consultation. Included are the approaches the model can take, the approaches' respective goals, the consultant's role, the consultee's experience in consultation, and the techniques and procedures used. Finally, we'll examine some contributions and criticisms of the model and cite some trends in mental health consultation that have led to modifications of Caplan's model.

As you read this chapter, consider the following questions:

1. What are some of the differences and similarities between mental health consultation and the generic model we've already examined?

2. What difference would it make if a mental health consultant's primary goal in working with a human services worker was to make him or her a better worker in general, rather than to help the client under discussion?
3. For what reasons could human services providers have difficulties with their cases and programs that would require consultation services?
4. How would a consultant best determine the reasons that a human services worker or administrator is having difficulties with a work-related problem?
5. Are there really differences between work-related and personal problems? If so, what are they?

INTRODUCTION

Mental health consultation is based on the idea that society's mental health can be promoted through the efforts of consultants who work with deliverers of human services (such as counselors) or with administrators of human services programs (such as the director of a factory's employee assistance program). More specifically, mental health consultants assist their consultees with specific work-related problems, such as a difficult case or glitches in a mental health-related program. An important goal of mental health consultation is to help consultees cope not only with their specific work-related problems, but also to improve their general level of functioning so that they can be even more effective in the future. Mental health consultation has been used in schools (Berlin, 1977), welfare agencies (Rogawski, 1977), criminal justice agencies (Brodsky, 1977), churches (Mitchell, 1977), and many other settings.

Historical Background

Mental health consultation is a part of the community mental health concept that asserts that services should be available as needed within the community and should be integrated with other human services. Mental health consultation began in the late 1940s with the passage of the federal Mental Health Act of 1946 (Yolles, 1970), which created the National Institute of Mental Health (NIMH) and provided states federal monies for the purpose of supporting mental health services. Public acceptance for community-based mental health services increased in the 1950s; the idea that mental health services were limited to treating severely disturbed individuals in residential treatment centers waned. In 1963, Congress passed the Community Mental Health Centers Act, which provided federal funds for the construction of mental health facilities in local communities.

The concept of the prevention of mental illness became very important because there was a large discrepancy between the need for services and the ability to meet those needs (Caplan, 1970) and because the efficacy of psychotherapy in treating mental illness was under criticism (Meyers, 1981).

The ability of local mental health centers to provide preventative services thus became one of the criteria for being considered for these federal funds. Consultation services were seen as one type of preventative service to public and private human services professionals, who would become more effective as they attempted to meet the mental health needs of their clientele (Yolles, 1970).

A trend that paralleled public and federal interest in preventative services was a shift in the conceptualization of consultation. Before 1950, consultation in agencies was considered to be an extension of clinical psychiatric consultation (Beisser & Green, 1972). In other words, consultation was viewed in terms of the medical consultation model: the psychiatrist examines the patient, makes a diagnosis, and prescribes treatment to the professional in charge. Two trends emerged around 1950 to change this view: professionals other than psychiatrists came to be viewed as legitimate consultants, and it became clear that problems in treating cases could be due not only to lack of knowledge or skills on the part of those in charge of treatment, but also to the consultee's personal concerns or to organizational factors present in the consultee's work site (Beisser & Green, 1972). A few articles incorporating these trends began to appear in the early 1950s, and evidence increased substantially in the mid-1950s.

Around this time Gerald Caplan arrived on the scene. A psychiatrist by training, Caplan's name has become synonymous with "mental health consultation." In fact, mental health consultation is frequently referred to as the "Caplanian model" (Rogawski, 1978). Caplan is often credited with "discovering" the usefulness of mental health consultation and describing its various forms (Mazade, 1983).

Caplan's 1970 book, *The Theory and Practice of Mental Health Consultation*, reflects the development of his views based on his experiences as a consultant and his research in consultation. Caplan relates that his interest in mental health consultation began around 1949, when he was a member of a team of psychiatrists, social workers, and psychologists at a child guidance center in Israel. Part of the team's duties was to attend to the mental health needs of over 16,000 immigrant children who were cared for in about 100 residential centers. Referrals to the team far outweighed its ability to provide direct services to the children.

The operation of the team under these circumstances led to five discoveries by Caplan. First, the caretakers seemed to have a very restrictive perception of possible management strategies. Second, many of the caretakers had very stereotypic perceptions of the children and their difficulties. Third, the caretakers were frequently quite upset and their personal concerns affected their ability to be objective about the children with whom they were working. Fourth, the narrow perceptions, stereotypic attitudes, and personal issues of consultees could be ameliorated by particular consultant attitudes and interventions. Finally, the team could learn a substantial amount of relevant information about the children and caretakers by visiting the institution, rather than by bringing the caretakers and children to the team's central office.

Out of Caplan's experiences in Israel the basics rudiments of his model began to take shape. Consultation could be viewed as working with another person to help a client. Consultation typically would take place on the consultee's turf, and the consultee's perceptions of the client would be the basis for consultation. The consultant would need to be very observant of the consultee's perceptions and would look for possible distortions, stereotypes, and personal issues that might adversely affect working with the client. The consultant would be objective yet sympathetic and would focus on the client as a person with problems, not as a problem who happens to be a person.

After his experiences in Israel, Caplan continued to develop his model of consultation at Harvard's Schools of Public Health and Medicine, where he began to use the term *mental health consultation*. He formally developed the concept of the consultation as a collaborative relationship among equals. The idea that consultation need not occur in a crisis situation, but could also be used for preventative measures, also emerged, as did techniques of group consultation. Caplan has continued updating his views over the years (Caplan, 1974, 1977), but *The Theory and Practice of Mental Health Consultation* remains the primary source for readers interested in mental health consultation.

MENTAL HEALTH CONSULTATION DEFINED

Various attempts have been made to define mental health consultation (Hershenson & Power, 1987). The most consistently recognized definition of mental health consultation is Caplan's:

> . . . a process of interaction between two professional persons—the consultant, who is a specialist, and the consultee, who invokes the consultant's help in regard to a current work problem with which he is having some difficulty and which he has decided is within the other's area of specialized competence. The work problem involves the management or treatment of one or more clients of the consultee, or the planning or implementation of a program to cater to such clients (Caplan, 1970, p. 19).

Subsequent attempts at defining mental health consultation (Mannino, MacLennon, & Shore, 1975; Hodges & Cooper, 1983) have elaborated upon the type of "help" the consultant provides while holding to the basic ideas in Caplan's definition. Notice this emphasis in the following definition by MacLennon, Quinn, and Schroeder:

> Mental health consultation is the provision of technical assistance by an expert to individual and agency caregivers related to the mental health dimension of their work. Such assistance is directed to specific work-related problems, is advisory in nature, and the consultant has no direct responsibility for its acceptance or implementation (cited in Bloom, 1984, p. 155).

This definition suggests that the consultant will function as a technical expert who advises.

Hodges and Cooper (1983) expand on Caplan's definition by adding some of the specific role behaviors the consultant uses in helping consultees:

Community mental health consultation can be defined as the process by which a mental health professional interacts with community-based professionals and other service providers (the consultees) to supply information, skill training, and individual-process change or system change in order to help the consultee or the system better serve the mental health needs of the people in the community (Hodges & Cooper, 1983, pp. 19–20).

In summary, mental health consultation is a process in which a mental health professional interacts with another professional and assists him or her with the mental health aspects of a work-related problem that concerns either a client or a program. The consultant uses knowledge and skills to assist the consultee with the specific concern and, in addition, attempts to improve the consultee's ability to function in the future. The consultee has the freedom to choose whether or not to apply the assistance provided in consultation and remains responsible for the client or the program.

KEY CONCEPTS OF MENTAL HEALTH CONSULTATION

Basic Characteristics

From Caplan's (1970) point of view, mental health consultation has several basic characteristics, awareness of which is essential for understanding his view of mental health consultation:

1. Mental health consultation is a method used by two professionals in respect to a lay client or a program for such clients.

2. The consultee's work problem must be defined by him or her as being mental health-related, such as: a mental disorder or personality idiosyncracy of the client, the need to promote mental health in the client, or interpersonal aspects of the work situation. The consultant must have expert knowledge in these areas.

3. The consultant has neither administrative responsibility for the consultee's work nor professional responsibility for the outcome of the client's case. He is under no compulsion to modify the consultee's conduct of the case.

4. The consultee is under no compulsion to accept the consultant's ideas or suggestions.

5. The basic relationship between the two is coordinate; there is no built-in hierarchy or authority/subordinate tension, which in our culture potentiates the influence of ideas. The consultees' freedom to accept or reject what the consultant says enables them to take quickly as their own any ideas that appeal to them in their current situation.

6. The coordinate relationship is fostered by the consultant's membership (typically) in another profession and his or her arrival into the consultee's institution from the outside.

7. The coordinate relationship is further supported by the fact that consultation is usually given as a short series of interviews—two or three, on

the average—that take place intermittently in response to consultees' awareness of their current need for help with a work problem. The relationship in individual consultation is not maintained and dependence is not fostered by continuing contact. In group consultation there may be regular meetings, but dependence is reduced by peer support.

8. Consultation is expected to continue indefinitely, for consultees can be expected to encounter unusual work problems throughout their careers. Increasing competence and sophistication of consultees in their own profession increase the likelihood of their recognizing mental health complications and asking for consultation.

9. Consultants have no predetermined body of information that they intend to impart to a particular consultee. They respond only to the segment of the consultee's problems that the latter exposes in the current work difficulty. The consultant does not seek to remedy other areas of inadequacy in the consultee, but instead expects other issues to be raised in future consultation.

10. The twin goals of consultation are to help consultees improve their handling or understanding of the current work difficulty and through this to increase their capacity to master future problems of a similar type.

11. The aim of consultation is to improve consultees' job performance, not their sense of well-being. It is envisaged, however, that because the two are linked, consultees' feelings of personal worth will probably be increased by successful consultation, as will their capacity to deal in a reality-based socially acceptable way with certain life difficulties. In other words, successful consultation may have the secondary effect of being therapeutic to consultees.

12. Consultation does not focus overtly on personal problems and feelings of consultees; it respects their privacy. The consultant does not allow discussion of personal and private material in the consultation interview.

13. The exclusion of personal problems does not mean that consultants do not pay attention to the feelings of the consultees. They are particularly sensitive to the feelings and to the disturbance of task functioning produced by personal problems. Consultants deal with personal problems, however, in a special way, such as by discussing problems in the context in which they relate to the client's case and the work setting.

14. Consultation is usually only one of the professional functions of specialists, even if they have the formal title "consultant." Consultants should utilize consultation only when it is appropriate in the situation; at other times different methods should be used. Sometimes the demands of the situation will cause consultants to put aside their consultation in the middle. If, for instance, a consultant gets information during a consultation interview that leads to the judgment that the consultee's actions are seriously endangering the client (such as failing to prevent a suicide or to pursue treatment for a dangerous psychosis), the consultant should set aside the consultant role, revert to the basic role of a psychiatrist, psychologist, or social worker, and then give advice or take action that the consultee is not free to reject. Such action destroys the coordinate relationship and interrupts the consultation contact in favor of a

higher goal. Although such dramatic occasions are rare, consultants must constantly keep this possibility in mind as a realization of this method's realistic limits.

15. Finally, it is worth emphasizing that mental health consultation is a method of communication between a mental health specialist and another professional. It does not denote a new profession, but rather merely a special way in which existing professionals may operate. The process of this operation has been refined and analyzed and can be systematically taught and learned. The content of the consultation communication will naturally vary according to the specialized knowledge and experience of the consultant. Thus, although psychiatrists, psychologists, psychiatric social workers, and psychiatric nurses should use the same techniques of consultation with a particular consultee, the content of their specialized remarks about the client's case will differ. The consultant must have specialized knowledge about the topic on which the consultee needs help; the professional training and experience of the consultant will determine the detailed nature and form of this knowledge (Caplan, 1970, pp. 28–30). (Adapted from *The Theory and Practice of Mental Health Consultation* by Gerald Caplan. Copyright © 1970 by Basic Books, Inc. Reprinted by permission of the publisher.)

These fifteen characteristics represent the basis for the practice of mental health consultation from Caplan's (1970) perspective. Although the consultant is the expert, the relationship is an equal one. The nature of the consultant-consultee relationship is crucial: the consultant assists with work-related problems only and does not deal directly with the consultee's personal concerns. The consultee's work problems may be looked at from a psychodynamic perspective, and the goal of consultation is to enhance the consultee's current and future ability to function professionally.

Psychodynamic Orientation

The Caplan model uses a psychodynamic approach to consultation, for as a trained psychiatrist, Caplan was heavily influenced by the work of Sigmund Freud. The Caplan model relies on an intrapsychic view of behavior change (Meyers, 1981); this psychodynamic orientation makes the Caplan model one of the most complex consultation models (Conoley & Conoley, 1982). A detailed discussion of the psychodynamic approach is beyond the scope of this book. Those interested in reviewing Freud and his modifiers should consult a good text on theories of counseling and psychotherapy, such as Corey's *Theory and Practice of Counseling and Psychotherapy* (1986). A brief review of psychodynamic perspective follows. The *psychodynamic approach* fosters the concept that our behavior is a product of unconscious motivation and that most of our personal issues result from early childhood experiences. These issues often result in inner conflict that affects our behavior and causes us problems. Because these inner conflicts are usually unconscious, we are often unaware of the causes of our behavior. True behavior change must deal with these unresolved conflicts from the past; merely dealing with the behavioral manifestations of a person's problems only results in the emergence of another problem because the core problem has not been adequately addressed. This phenomenon is often referred to as symptom substitution.

Not every difficulty a consultee has with a case or program is due to inner conflict. A consultee may be having difficulty with a case or program because of a lack of appropriate professional knowledge about some aspect of the case. But from Caplan's perspective, when the consultee's inner conflicts are causing problems with a case or program, these inner conflicts must in some way be addressed to ensure the consultee's adequate functioning with the current case and with similar cases in the future. Changing overt behaviors will only provide temporary change. Because the consultant does not provide psychotherapy to the consultee, the consultee's inner conflicts must be dealt with indirectly.

Transfer of Effect

Transfer of effect refers to the concept that what is learned in one situation should be usable in similar, future situations. The transfer of effects is a key concept of the Caplanian model (Meyers, 1981). Thus, Caplan conceptualizes the goals of consultation based on the transfer of effect; that is, he views consultation as having "twin" goals: helping the consultee function more effectively in a current work problem and with future problems of a similar type.

One method the consultant can use to ensure this transfer of effect is for the consultant to use consultee-centered consultation to "improve the consultee's capacity to function effectively in this category of case, in order to benefit many similar clients in the future" (Caplan, 1970, p. 125). In effect, Caplan is suggesting that the transfer of effect occurs by having the consultant listen to the consultee's perceptions of the client or program, extrapolate from those perceptions the pertinent information concerning the consultee's difficulty, and then, by indirect means, help the consultee "straighten out" these misguided perceptions of the case in a more objective manner. This approach to transfer of effect is quite consistent with the psychodynamic view, which emphasizes the consultee's thoughts and feelings about a case rather than the specific behaviors of either the consultant or the client.

Critical Nature of the Relationship

The relationship that the consultant builds with both the consultee institution (the organization in which consultation is to take place) and the individual consultee should be strong.

Because of Caplan's (1970, 1974, 1977) prominence in the entire field of consultation, his views on consultation relationships have influenced most generic models of consultation, including the one discussed earlier in this text. Many of the significant points made concerning preliminary exploration of organizational needs, contracting, and physical and psychological entry discussed in Chapter 3 owe their origins to Caplan. When building relationships with a consultee institution, consultants can deal effectively with issues that arise by ensuring that clear, detailed communication concerning consultation and its nature is provided to all parties-at-interest, by keeping status issues at a minimum, and by being knowledgeable about the various types of consultee institutions and professions.

The relationship between the mental health consultant and the consultee is also crucial, for the effects of consultation are mediated through the relationship between the consultant and consultee; that is, in order for consultation to be effective, both the consultant and the consultee need to view the relationship as a "good" one. For their part, consultants can expedite the creation of a positive working relationship by providing conditions in which the consultee experiences acceptance, encouragement, and professional respect (Caplan, 1970; Conoley & Conoley, 1982).

The term *nonhierarchical coordinate interdependence* (Caplan, 1970, p. 28) is frequently used to describe the nature of the mental health relationship. Such a relationship is characterized by two professionals—one an expert in mental health, the other an expert in some area of training—sharing their views pertaining to a work-related problem. The relationship is between peers and the consultant avoids giving advice.

The consultation relationship is nonhierarchical. The consultant has no authority over the consultee from an administrative or supervisory perspective. The consultee is free to use the consultation process in any way seen fit and maintains responsibility for the outcome of any attempts to solve the work-related problem. Although the consultant is often seen by the consultee as an "expert," the creation of a nonhierarchical relationship reduces the possibility of consultee resistance due to perception of the consultant as an authority figure. Compliance based on dependence in which the consultee perceives the consultant's input as "ultimate truth" is avoided.

The nonhierarchical nature of the consultation relationship can be maintained through the use of "one-downsmanship" (Caplan, 1970, p. 96). One-downsmanship is a very valuable relationship-building technique the consultant can use to ensure that the relationship remains on an equal footing. This technique can be used when the consultee attempts to take an inferior stance relative to the consultant or attempts to manipulate the consultant into demonstrating superiority (Caplan, 1970). Consultees frequently use one-downsmanship to test the coordinate, nonhierarchical nature of the consultation relationship (Parsons & Meyers, 1984). Consultants should consider using one-downsmanship statements when a major, formal status differential exists between themselves and the consultees (Caplan, 1970). The following is an example of one-downsmanship:

Consultee: Dr. Jones, I am Jackie Smith.
Consultant: Please call me Leslie.

Types of Consultation

The manner in which mental health consultation is conceptualized is a very critical factor in terms of how it is practiced. The consultant should have a system to size up each consultation situation in order to anticipate what is likely to happen and to identify effective strategies with which to approach the consultation. In order to accomplish this end, Caplan (1970) devised a classification system with two major divisions. The first division is the primary *focus* of the consultant. There are two parts to this division: *focus on a case* (for example, a client at a halfway house) or *focus on an administrative problem* dealing with a mental health-related program (for example, helping a health science teacher implement a unit on substance abuse). Hence, the consultation's focus can be either on a case or administrative.

The second division used by Caplan concerns the consultant's primary goal. There are two parts to this division: "giving a specialized opinion and recommendation for a solution" (Caplan, 1970, p. 32) (for example, observing a client and recommending a specific therapeutic technique) or "attempting to improve the problem-solving capacity of the consultees and leaving them to work out their own way of solving it" (Caplan, 1970, p. 32) (for example, helping a parole officer be more objective about a case with a parolee). Thus, the primary goal may be to effect change in either the *client* (or *program*) or in the *consultee*.

These two divisions, each with two parts, make up four types of consultation: *client-centered case consultation, consultee-centered case consultation, program-centered administrative consultation,* and *consultee-centered administrative consultation* (Caplan, 1970). This classification of consultation formed the early organization of consultation types, and most reconceptualizations of consultation types are summaries of Caplan's work (Hodges & Cooper, 1983).

Each of the four types of consultation has a different level of intervention, an identifiable target, and an identifiable goal (Bloom, 1984). Table 10.1 presents Caplan's (1970) classification as defined by these three factors.

TABLE 10.1 Caplan's Consultation
Classification in Terms of Level, Target, and Goal

	Client-centered case	*Consultee-centered case*	*Program-centered administrative*	*Consultee-centered administrative*
Level	Case	Case	Administrative	Administrative
Target	Client	Consultee	Program	Consultee
Goal	Behavior change in client	Enhanced consultee performance in delivering services to clients	More effective delivery of program	Enhanced consultee performance in programing

THE CONSULTATION PROCESS

Next we'll examine these four types of mental health consultation in terms of their goals, the consultant's function and role, the consultee's experience in consultation, and the use of consultation techniques and procedures. Because of its unique nature and its impact on the development of mental health consultation, consultee-centered case consultation is covered in more depth than are the other three types.

The Client-Centered Case Consultation Process

Consultation Goals

Client-centered case consultation is the most commonly used form of mental health consultation. It typifies what most human services professionals think when they hear the word "consultation." The consultee presents a case in which a client has mental health problems that are causing the consultee some difficulty. The consultant investigates the case, either assesses or makes a diagnosis, and prescribes in writing possible interventions. The consultee adapts the consultant's recommendations as needed and then applies them.

The primary goal of this type of consultation is to develop a plan to help the client. Secondarily, the consultee is better able to handle similar cases alone in the future as a result of contact with the consultant. However, only limited educational benefit to the consultee is expected from this type of consultation because the consultant spends very little time with the consultee.

Consultant Function and Roles

The consultant functions primarily as an expert in assessing the situation, in diagnosing the client, and in making recommendations for the consultee's use in the case. Specifically, the consultant builds a relationship with the consultee, assesses the nature of the client's difficulty, determines the strengths and weaknesses of the consultee and the consultee's work environment with regard to effectively managing the case, and files a written report.

The consultant builds a relationship with the consultee in ways previously discussed. The client's difficulty is assessed by gathering information from the client and other sources. Assessment of the consultee's strengths, weaknesses, and work setting are best accomplished by visiting the consultee at the work site. The written report, usually a letter or a case record, should (if possible) be reviewed in a meeting with the consultee, which allows the consultant to help improve the consultee's functioning in similar cases in the future. It is the consultee's responsibility to use the written report and the conference with the consultant in dealing with the case. Finally, the consultant plans for a follow-up session with the consultee.

Consultee Experience in Consultation

Consultees in client-centered case consultation focus on providing the consultant with as much pertinent information and professional opinion as possible regarding the case. Even though the consultant is likely to observe, interview, or test the client, the consultant typically wants to know how the consultee views the case. The consultee, then, is not only a link between the consultant and client, but also a professional collaborator who knows the client better than the consultant and knows best how to deal with the client within the consultee institution.

The consultee's primary responsibility is to adapt and carry out the consultant's recommendations. The consultee is free to accept or reject any or all of the consultant's suggestions and opinions. The consultee may want to implement a given recommendation but may require the assistance of the consultant to do so; in this situation, the consultee must ask for such assistance. Finally, the consultee participates in a scheduled follow-up session with the consultant concerning the case at hand.

In summary, the consultee is a peer of the consultant who provides information and opinions concerning a case, collaborates with the consultant as much as possible, and adapts the consultant's recommendations to the client's situation within the consultee institution.

Application: Consultant Techniques and Procedures

Client-centered case consultation is structured around six steps (Caplan, 1970):

1. the request for consultation,
2. assessment of the client,
3. assessment of the consultee setting,
4. writing the consultation report,
5. implementation of the recommendations of the consultant, and
6. follow-up.

The request for consultation can come directly to the consultant (by personal contact or telephone) or indirectly (for example, through a secretary or administrative assistant). It is not unusual for a written note to accompany the request. Still, it is best for the consultant to respond to the consultee's request with some form of personal contact in order to build a relationship, clarify what the consultee desires from the consultant, and obtain more information on the client.

In assessing the client the consultant has two basic questions: Should the client be referred for specialized treatment? What can the consultee do to help the client in the consultee's work setting? These questions concerning the client are answered by listening to the consultee (and perhaps the client and the client's significant others when applicable).

It is quite risky to provide client-centered case consultation in the consultant's office. Without assessing the consultee and the consultee's work setting, the consultant can rely only on the client's report about the consultee and the work setting. Because the consultant needs to know about the strengths and weaknesses of the consultee and the consultee institution in order to make effective and realistic recommendations, the consultant should visit and perform consultation in the consultee institution.

One of the consultant's major tasks in client-centered case consultation is writing a report for the consultee. This report, typically supplemented by a face-to-face meeting with the consultee to clarify the report and answer questions related to it, should be written in language appropriate to the consultee's institution, should be practical, and should avoid condescending terminology. The main body of the report should focus on how the client is or is not coping in major areas of life and should include some recommendations as to how the consultee can facilitate improved client functioning in appropriate areas. Consider the following:

CASE STUDY:
The following is a portion of a report prepared by a mental health consultant. The consultant, a psychologist, is working with a teacher having difficulty with a third-grade student who steals from other children in the classroom.

> The stealing behavior is most likely caused by the child's need for security. The objects taken are usually food (for example, snacks) or school supplies (for example, pencils). The fact that the child makes little attempt not to get caught perhaps suggests that there is the perception on the child's part of too little attention. Stealing objects thus helps the child both feel more secure and gets the child attention.
>
> I recommend that the teacher make a deliberate attempt to praise the child throughout the school day for appropriate classroom behaviors. In addition, the child could be assigned some classroom responsibilities (for example, erasing the board) and then be reinforced for acting responsibly. The security of the child might be increased if the teacher frequently communicated to the child that the child belongs in the classroom and that the teacher takes care of all children in the classroom. Such verbalizations can reduce the insecurity of the child.

Implementation of the consultant's recommendations is the consultee's prerogative because the consultee has responsibility for the case. However, the consultant can help determine whether the consultee has the knowledge and skills required to perform the suggested interventions. Such a judgment is best achieved by having a history of sustained contact with the consultee so that an assessment of consultee strengths and weaknesses is possible before the formulation of recommendations.

Follow-up by the consultant is crucial: it provides the consultant a rough evaluation of the effects of consultation; it provides feedback on how the consultant's interventions affected the consultee in the case under discussion, which could be useful to the consultant in improving future interventions; and it conveys consultant interest to the consultee and improves the consultant-consultee relationship so that the consultee may actively seek additional consultation about this or some other case.

The following example shows how client-centered case consultation can be used:

CASE STUDY:
A psychologist, acting as an internal consultant, is consulting with an activity therapist concerning a patient in a residential psychiatric hospital. The activity

therapist reports that the patient, a fifteen-year-old, refuses to engage in any activity therapy. The client shows up on time but just sits and watches as the other patients engage in the therapy.

The consultant observes the patient in several hospital settings, including activity therapy, and interviews the patient's primary therapist concerning the case. The consultant determines that the patient appears to have few friends at the hospital but is friendly and approachable. The consultant also concludes that the consultee has the ability and motivation to assist the patient to begin participation in activity therapy.

The consultant writes a brief report suggesting a "buddy system" for the patient. The consultee would implement the program, in which one or two higher functioning patients could become friends with and accompany the patient to the activity therapy group, where they perform the activities together. The consultant shares this recommendation in a final consultation session with the consultee. The consultee agrees to the recommendation and takes steps to implement the program. The consultant follows up after two weeks to monitor the intervention.

The Consultee-Centered Case Consultation Process

Consultation Goals

The primary goal of consultee-centered case consultation is improvement of the consultee's ability to work effectively with a particular type of case so that the consultee can function more effectively with similar clients in the future. "In consultee-centered case consultation the consultant's primary focus is upon elucidating and remedying the shortcomings in the consultee's professional functioning that are responsible for his difficulties with the case with which he is seeking help" (Caplan, 1970, p. 125). Improvement of the client is the secondary goal. As in client-centered case consultation, the case is the focus of discussion, although usually the client is not seen by the consultant because the goal is to help the consultee. The way in which the consultant helps the consultee requires the consultant to hear the consultee's subjective view of the case.

Consultant Function and Role

In consultee-centered case consultation, the consultant plays the roles of detective, expert, and educator. In the role of detective, the consultant seeks out both the consultee's cognitive and emotional problems through active listening and judicious questioning. The consultant discusses the case with the consultee in the role of an expert mental health professional. As an educator, the consultant provides the consultee the information and/or training needed to solve problems with this and similar cases in the future (Caplan, 1970). Thus, the consultant builds a relationship with the consultee, assesses the consultee's problem with the case, and intervenes to alleviate the consultee's problem. The basic steps in consultee-centered case consultation are:

1. Build relationship with consultee;
2. Assess consultee's problem:
   a) lack of knowledge,
   b) lack of skill,
   c) lack of confidence,
   d) lack of objectivity; and
3. Intervene to alleviate the consultee's problem.

The consultant asks the consultee to discuss the case, and the remainder of the consultation relationship involves such discussions. The consultant, however, is more directive than in client-centered case consultation in that the consultee is asked to discuss selected aspects of the case, which provides the consultant information about the consultee's work difficulty. As the consultee discusses the case, the consultant categorizes the consultee's work difficulty as either a lack of knowledge, a lack of skill, a lack of confidence, or a lack of professional objectivity. Based on the category of the consultee's work problem, the consultant intervenes to resolve the problem. The so-called "grist for the mill" in consultation comes from the consultee's "subjectively determined story" (Caplan, 1970, p. 125), not from the real facts about the case.

Consultee Experience in Consultation

In consultee-centered case consultation, the consultee's task is to enter into the consultation relationship and discuss a case that is causing difficulty. Under the consultant's guidance, the consultee elaborates on the particulars of the case. When the consultant makes interventions designed to assist the consultee, it is up to the consultee to implement those recommendations, which often includes ways the consultee can improve professional functioning. The consultee maintains full responsibility for the case under discussion.

During the initial stages of consultation, the consultee may have a very narrow view of the case. Indeed, consultees often do not know why they are having difficulty with a case. In responding to the consultant's judicious questioning, the consultee's perceptions of the case are enriched and broadened so that the "cognitive grasp and emotional mastery" (Caplan, 1970, p. 125) of the particulars of the case are increased.

Application: Consultation Techniques and Procedures

There are four types of consultee-centered case consultation, one for each of the four reasons that consultees may have difficulty with cases: lack of knowledge, lack of skill, lack of self-confidence, and lack of professional objectivity. Now we'll consider each of these four types of consultation, which can be performed individually or in groups.

Lack of knowledge.   When the difficulty with a case is due to lack of knowledge, the consultee might not have sufficient understanding of the client's problem, some important client characteristics, or both. According to Caplan (1970), the consultee may lack either factual or theoretical knowledge needed to effectively deal with the case.

The consultant imparts the missing knowledge to the consultee in a manner conducive to the consultee's success in the case under discussion and in similar cases in the future. It is very important for the consultant to provide this information without violating the coordinate nature of the relationship, a task best accomplished by capitalizing on the consultee's motivation to learn information relevant to the case at hand. The consultee's education results from applying the needed knowledge to the current case, which also maintains the desired consultant-consultee relationship.

Lack of skill.   The consultee's lack of skill in solving the client's problem calls for another type of consultee-centered case consultation. The consultee may well have the knowledge required to understand the case but lacks only the skill to intervene effectively. In this situation, the consultant should avoid the temptation to supervise the consultee's conduct of the case.

Procedurally, the consultant and the consultee conduct a joint appraisal of the case: they explore the problems the case is causing, what the consultee has tried so far to help the client, and what the consultee could yet do to resolve the problems in the case. Such a procedure broadens the consultee's perspective on the case, provides a broader context for perceiving subsequent similar cases, maintains the coordinate nature of the relationship, and preserves the consultee's self-esteem. The consultant determines the degree of the consultee's skill deficit, describes what skills are needed to effectively deal with the case, and explores with the consultee the means to get the appropriate skills training within the consultee institution. If such training is not available within the consultee institution, the consultant can provide the training.

Lack of self-confidence.   Lack of self-confidence can cause confusion and uncertainty about how to handle a case. It can result from such factors as consultee inexperience (for example, being assigned a particular client problem for the first time or being a "beginner" on the job). Lack of confidence can also be a generalized trait within the consultee that manifests itself in reduced on-the-job functioning.

The goal of the consultant is to provide support and encouragement by fostering hope, confidence, and courage by affirming the consultee's strengths and capabilities. Reassurance, which damages the nonhierarchical nature of the relationship, should be avoided. The consultant's second goal is to help the consultee find a peer support group within the consultee institution.

Lack of objectivity.   Lack of objectivity is the most common problem among consultees who work in institutions that have a knowledgeable, skilled staff and a supervisory system. Hence, most consultee-centered case consultations are of this type. The consultee's lack of professional objectivity is due to "defective judgment" (Caplan, 1970, p. 131) based primarily on the inability to maintain an appropriate professional distance. In this situation the consultee's role functioning, perceptions, and judgments are impaired by subjective factors within the consultee, who is in turn unable to effectively apply existing knowledge and skills to the case.

By the time the consultee seeks out consultation, confusion, frustration, incompetence, and declining self-esteem are evident and cause a lack of professional poise. The coordinate nature of the consultant-consultee relationship is in greatest jeopardy in consultee-centered case consultation because the consultant appears to be in control of personal issues in the professional setting, whereas the consultee is not. Therefore, the consultant should *indirectly* help the consultee recapture professional objectivity by discussing the client, the consultant, or some fictitious client in a story or parable (Caplan, 1970). The consultee's problem should not be dealt with directly. Lack of objectivity in even the most knowledgeable and skilled consultees can result from five, rather connected reasons:

1. direct personal involvement,
2. simple identification,
3. transference,
4. characterological distortions, and
5. theme interference (Caplan, 1970, p. 132).

When a consultee loses professional objectivity due to *direct personal involvement,* the relationship changes from a professional to a personal one. An obvious example is when a consultee falls in love with a client. Because of the emotional nature of personal relationships, objectivity is lost. Professionals need to maintain a certain distance from their clients to maintain objectivity, and personal involvement alters the balance of that relationship by causing the consultee to be either too close or too distant from the client. A consultee who falls in love with a client clearly becomes too close to be objective, whereas a consultee who is prejudicial toward a client because of the client's ethnic identity becomes too distant to be objective. Consultees are frequently unaware of their personal involvement with their clients and do not realize they are fulfilling their own personal needs at the expense of those of the client.

Simple identification occurs when the consultee does not merely empathize with but instead identifies with the client (or some person in the client's life) and loses the sense of neutrality so essential to maintaining objectivity. The consultee identifies with some real characteristic of the client (or person in the client's life), such as race, gender, or some behavior pattern the consultee considers idiosyncratic to the client. For example, a consultee who is a minister might overidentify with a client who is also a minister. The client is then described in a positive, sympathetic manner, while others in the case are viewed in derogatory terms. The consultant can relatively easily identify simple identification because of the obvious similarities between the consultee and some person in the case.

Consultees frequently experience lack of objectivity with their cases due to *transference* distortions in relating to a given client (Caplan, 1970). A transference distortion occurs when the consultee transfers onto the client feelings and attitudes from key relationships in the past. Once the consultee's predetermined attitudes and feelings are imposed on the client and objectivity is lost, the consultee is unable to assess the client's real situation. For example, a consultee who has difficulty with authority figures due to her childhood relationship with her mother might have difficulty dealing with a client who is the head of a large company. The transference relationship tends to be repeated over time in similar cases (Caplan, 1970).

Minor disturbances in consultees, often referred to as *characterological distortions* of perception and behavior, can cause consultees to lose their professional objectivity. Caplan (1970) defines these distortions as personality problems most people have that interfere with the effective delivery of human services to the client. To illustrate this point, Caplan (1970) tells of a teacher with a tendency toward sexually acting out who anxiously attributed to several of her students harmful sexual behaviors that a consultant later described as quite normal.

Caplan's (1970) concept of *theme interference* is a special type of transference reaction that causes consultees to lose their professional objectivity. Theme interference becomes apparent to a consultant when the consultee is "blocked" from progressing with a case for no explicable reason. For example, a consultee who has difficulty dealing with anger might impose this trait on the client, in effect saying, "Unless this client deals with his anger during our sessions together, no progress can be made in this case."

According to Caplan, theme interference develops in the following manner: "A conflict related to actual life experiences or to fantasies in the consultee that have not been satisfactorily resolved is apt to persist in his preconscious or unconscious as an emotionally toned cognitive constellation which we call a 'theme' " (1970, p. 145). The theme is a recurring symbol of an unresolved problem and has a preemptory quality (Rogawski, 1978). Themes generally repeat themselves, carry a negative emotional valence, and take the form of a syllogism. This syllogism has two statements that constitute a prejudicial stereotyped notion (Rogawski, 1978) and are perceived by the consultee to be linked in such a way that they are inseparable. This stereotypical notion is composed of an "initial category" followed by an "inevitable outcome."

The initial category is a statement that signifies the condition that was characteristic of the original unresolved problem in the consultee's life. In reality, the client may or may not fit the stereotype, but still the consultee applies the stereotype to the client. The stereotype is imposed when consultees form their impressions of the client; certain pieces of information are put together and the initial category is formed. Placing the client in the initial category leads to expectations that are typified in the inevitable outcome.

The inevitable outcome, a statement that follows directly from the initial category, is a rigid assumption of an "inescapable failure" (Rogawski, 1978, p. 325).

When put together, the initial category and inevitable outcome take the form "If A (initial category) happens to anyone, then B (inevitable outcome) must occur." One example might be, "If my client doesn't deal with his anger, we will never make any progress in therapy." In this example the initial category is that the client is perceived to have a problem with anger; the inevitable outcome is that if this anger is not dealt with, there will be no progress in therapy. In such cases the consultant must assume that the consultee has a problem in dealing with anger and that the client may or may not have the same problem.

The problem with theme interference is that by losing objectivity, the consultee is unable to see that there are many possible outcomes to any problem and that several possible interventions are available to achieve those outcomes. This lack of objectivity causes inconsistent, sometimes panicky behavior in the consultee, and the subsequent lack of progress in the case reaffirms the belief in the inevitable outcome. Thus, a vicious cycle develops. There is, however, one source of consolation for the consultee: the inevitable outcome happens to the client, not the consultee. Theme interference tends to recur as long as the theme is manifest.

There are two basic methods the mental health consultant can use to relieve theme interference in consultees. First, the consultant can demonstrate that the consultee has placed the client in the wrong initial category. In this situation, the consultant helps the consultee reassess the cues in the client's case that led to placement in that initial category in the first place. Such a reevaluation permits the consultee to see that the original perceptions were erroneous, and the consultee's professional objectivity returns because the inevitable outcome is no longer pertinent. Caplan (1970) labels this technique "unlinking" (p. 148) because it unlinks the client from the consultee's theme. Although unlinking is likely to help the consultee with the case under consideration, Caplan (1970) considers it to be a "cardinal error" (p. 149) because the theme that caused the lack of objectivity remains intact so that the consultee is likely to experience theme interference again during the next similar case.

Whereas unlinking attempts to invalidate the initial category, the second approach, called theme interference reduction, attempts to invalidate the inevitable outcome. The consultant invalidates the "If A, then B" syllogism by assisting the consultee to reexamine the evidence on which the inevitability of the outcome is based. The consultee is then able to view the previously "inevitable" outcome as merely one of an array of possible outcomes (and not necessarily a very likely one at that). The influence of the consultee's theme then begins to wane.

Theme interference reduction affects the consultee on both cognitive and affective levels. Theme interference reduction techniques neither exacerbate resistance nor cause loss of face because the consultant "accepts" the consultee's view of the initial category: the consultant does not try to deal with the consultee's inner conflicts directly, but rather through their discussion of the case. When properly carried out, theme interference reduction helps consultees by lowering their level of tension, raising their level of objectivity, weakening the theme, and reducing the likelihood that the theme will be displaced on subsequent cases (Caplan, 1970).

Several techniques are effective in theme interference reduction, and all of them have the following steps in common:

1. assessment of the theme,
2. the consultant's intervention,
3. ending and follow-up, and
4. one to three sessions over a three- or four-week period (Caplan, 1970).

In assessing the theme, the consultant examines the consultee institution, the affective and cognitive reactions of the consultee to the case, indications of an initial category and inevitable outcome, and the possibility that there is more than one theme.

Once the existence of theme interference has been established, the consultant can make one or more of the following interventions:

1. verbal focus on the client;
2. verbal focus on an alternative object—the parable;
3. nonverbal focus on the case; and
4. nonverbal focus on the consultation relationship (Caplan, 1970).

A *verbal focus on the client* is the most commonly used technique in theme interference reduction. The consultant discusses with the consultee the evidence for the inevitable outcome by examining in significant detail the facts concerning the case. In examining the details of the case, the so-called inevitable outcome is seen instead as one possible outcome among many others. The likelihood of the inevitable outcome's occurrence is explored specifically and in depth to ensure that the consultee does not consider the consultant to be prejudiced against that outcome. By such a thorough examination, the consultee realizes that the inevitable outcome is not even among the most likely outcomes. For example, when a consultee thinks a client *must* deal with the issue of avoidance of competition, a consultant might help the consultee consider several other therapeutic approaches to pursue with the client.

Parables are used when the consultant thinks it important to create greater distance between the consultee's growing awareness of the theme and its connection to the personal issues in the consultee's life. It must be remembered that consultation is not psychotherapy; the consultee's personal issues are not to be discussed, even though they may be affecting the case. Once the consultant identifies the initial category and the inevitable outcome and decides that the case under consideration is not a good vehicle to break the connection between the two, a verbal focus on an alternative object is often used.

In using a parable, the consultant artistically creates a believable story concerning the identified theme but uses a fictitious client in a fictitious case. The details of the current case are used as a springboard for creating the anecdote, but details are changed significantly so that only basic similarities to the client and consultee remain. Discussion of the fictitious case then results in the realization that the so-called inevitable outcome was only one of many possible outcomes and that the fictitious case did indeed have a different outcome. Thus, for example, when a consultee suggests that a shy client *must* agree to assertive training to overcome the shyness, the consultant might relate a story about a fictitious shy client who overcame shyness by going through a cognitive behavioral form of counseling.

Because the consultee is likely to consider the consultant a role model, the ways the consultant responds nonverbally to the consultee's anxieties about the case can be a very powerful tool in theme interference reduction. When the consultant uses *a nonverbal focus on the case,* the consultant's nonverbal behavior communicates to the consultee that the consultant is not really worried that the inevitable outcome must occur. During their discussion of the case, the consultant strives to demonstrate for the consultee nonverbal behavior that communicates a relaxed state free from anxiety.

By using such nonverbal behavior while discussing the case, the consultant demonstrates that there is no rush to prevent the inevitable outcome. The consultee comes to realize that maybe the so-called inevitable outcome is not inevitable after all. This technique works only if the consultee perceives that the consultant has dealt with the case seriously and thoroughly and has appreciated both the consultee's concern for urgent action and the client's situation. In a simple example, when a consultee nervously relates the specifics of a case, the consultant would maintain a calm demeanor.

A *nonverbal focus on the consultation relationship* is needed when the consultee transfers themes not onto a case but onto the consultant, particularly when the consultation relationship is well developed and contains emotional connections between the two parties. If the consultee transfers a theme onto the consultant by ascribing a certain role to the consultant and then playing the complementary role, the consultant needs to show the usual acceptance of the initial category and then invalidate the inevitable outcome through discussion of the case. However, the expectation of the inevitable outcome should be dealt with in nonverbal manner; that is, by remaining calm, objective, and free from anxiety, the consultant prevents the inevitable outcome from happening within the consultation relationship. In other words, the consultant stays "cool, calm, and collected" both about the case and the transference occurring in the consultation relationship itself. It is as if the consultant is working on both of these planes simultaneously. For example, when a consultee suggests that the consultant should be as upset about the case as the consultee is, the consultant shows appreciation for the consultee's view but remains calm about what is happening in the consultation session.

Once theme interference reduction has taken place, the consultant proceeds to terminate the consultation relationship. The consultee will continue to work on the case with the realization that any successful outcome in the case is due to the efforts of consultee and client. Because theoretically the theme has been reduced, the consultee is more likely to be successful with similar cases in the future. The consultant offers to provide assistance with future cases and suggests that the consultee report on the outcome of the current case at that time (Caplan, 1970).

Consider this example of consultee-centered case consultation:

CASE STUDY:
A mental health consultant is working with a social worker whose caseload consists primarily of indigent families. The consultee brings up a case about a particular family the consultee thinks is "just plain lazy" and is becoming even lazier because of the welfare they are receiving. The consultee notes that the middle class is the ultimate loser. The consultant listens carefully to the consultee's subjective view of the case, notes the consultee's defective judgment, and determines that the consultee's difficulty in working effectively with the family is due to theme interference.

The consultee views hard work and effort as vehicles for achievement. The theme interference takes the form of the syllogism: "Unless the family overcomes its laziness (initial category), family members will never amount to much (inevitable outcome)." The consultant notes that the consultee appears to be fixated on the "laziness" of the family.

In attempts to reduce the theme interference, the consultant calls this case a tough one and suggests that three consultation sessions over a three-week period might help alleviate the problem. During the consultation sessions, the consultant listens and reacts calmly to the consultee's frustrations concerning the case. The consultant then describes two cases involving "lazy" families in which therapeutic benefits were attained, even though the families remained "lazy." As a result of these fictitious case examples, the consultee feels more comfortable about working on the case and begins to consider alternative approaches to the case, such as training in child-rearing practices. The consultant agrees to follow up at a later date concerning the consultee's progress with the case.

The Program-Centered Administrative Consultation Process

Consultation Goals

In program-centered administrative consultation, the consultant comes into an organization and consults with an administrator with regard to the mental health aspects of some program or the internal functioning of the organization. The consultant enters the organization, assesses and defines the problem, and makes a written report that includes a series of recommendations. It is up to the consultee to take the consultant's report and adapt and implement it within the organizational setting.

The specific goals of this type of consultation depend on the nature of the consultation request and could include recommendations to deal with problems in program development, in organizational planning, or in program functioning. A secondary goal is that the consultee will learn to be able to deal more effectively with similar program problems and issues in the future. Just as client-centered case consultation makes recommendations for working with a given client, administrative-centered program consultation makes recommendations for an administrative plan of action. As with client-centered consultation, a minimum of time is spent in direct contact with the consultee. The goals of program-centered administrative consultation are met in a relatively brief time, typically ranging from several hours to a few days. The consultant is seen as an expert who comes in, assesses the situation accurately, and writes knowledgeable recommendations.

Consultant Function and Roles

The consultant needs sufficient data-collecting, action-planning, and communication skills to be able to make findings and present recommendations in a form understandable to the principle consultee and other members of the consultee institution. The consultant should be a content expert; that is, the consultant should have a thorough knowledge of the problem area in which the program administrator (principle consultee) requests assistance. The consultant also should be knowledgeable and experienced in organizational theory and practice, program development, fiscal policy, administrative procedure, and personnel management.

It may be advantageous for an organization to hire a mental health consultant, rather than a generic management consultant of the "purchase of expertise" type discussed in Chapter 9, because the mental health consultant can assist more effectively with the mental health aspects of a program.

The consultant must be particularly careful to create effective relationships with staff members of the consultee institution because the staff's help might be needed in gathering data. For example, the consultant obtains significant amounts of information from individual and group interviews and may obtain additional information about the internal and external forces working on the organization from its members (Caplan, 1970).

The consultant must consider two issues when performing program-centered administrative consultation. The first issue is that the consultant is responsible for collecting and analyzing the data required to solve the problem and to make recommendations. Therefore, the consultant must do more than merely help the organization's staff determine what data they want to collect because the staff may lack the knowledge, skill, and confidence necessary to make that determination. Because of the responsibility for the content of the assessment and the recommendations, the amount, type, and timing of data collection should ultimately be based on the consultant's expert knowledge and objectivity.

The second issue relates to the consultant's authority with the organization's staff members affected by the consultation. In program-centered administrative consultation the consultee is the administrator who requested the consultant. This administrator, like any consultee, needs a coordinate relationship with the consultant and is free to accept or reject any or all of the consultant's report and recommendations. The consultant's relationship to the administrator's subordinates, however, is not coordinate. Therefore, in this type of consultation the sanctioning process should guarantee that the consultant's requests for information and cooperation will be honored by all involved.

Consultee Experience in Consultation

The consultee in program-centered administrative consultation is the program administrator who expedites the hiring of the consultant in the first place. (This may or may not be the person who initially contacts the consultant.) The administrator should be the principle consultee because of the power of that position to both sanction the consultation and to ensure that the consultant's recommendations are carried out at the end of consultation.

The consultee's task is to meet with the consultant to discuss the main reasons the consultant is being hired. The administrator discusses with the consultant any strategies for clarifying the problem that involve some of the organization's staff. The administrator must set the time frame for consultation and select methods of approving the consultant's activities throughout the organization.

Because the consultant needs considerable knowledge about the organization in order to determine which data to collect and to make realistic recommendations, the administrator should make available as much information as possible concerning the organization's nature and methods of operation. The administrator also produces a rank-ordered list of adminstrative problems about which the consultant's assistance is being requested.

During the consultation period the consultee should have as much contact with the consultant as the consultant deems necessary. The consultee has two primary tasks at this stage: to continually provide the consultant a broad view of the organization and the interactive nature of its subsystems, and to react to the consultant's tentative findings so that the consultant can modify the recommendations at key times during the consultation process.

After the consultant's report has been filed, the consultee is responsible for the degree to which the recommendations are accepted and implemented. Finally, during follow-up the consultee is expected to assist the consultant in assessing the impact of consultation.

Application: Consultant Techniques and Procedures

How does the consultant proceed in program-centered administrative consultation? In the beginning of consultation, needs are explored, the contract is negotiated, the administrator is identified as the principle consultee, and the approximate amount of time the consultant and the consultee will spend together is established. According to Caplan (1970), the consultant sets out on a path that results in a report containing recommendations concerning the program. The steps involved are as follow:

1. building the relationship,
2. exploring needs,
3. negotiating the contract,
4. establishing the time frame,
5. obtaining an overview of the problems and their ramifications,

6. conducting a fact-finding mission to understand the problems more clearly and generate more realistic solutions,
7. developing recommendations through repeated modification based on feedback from the principle consultee and other parties-at-interest,
8. maintaining contact with the principle consultee,
9. formulating recommendations,
10. filing a report, and
11. following up.

In obtaining an overview of the problems and their ramifications, the consultant makes a rapid initial assessment of the consultee institution's structure and culture and the nature of its problems. At this stage, the consultant is interested in forming general impressions and hunches that will provide a procedural blueprint for the remainder of the consultation. This process of obtaining a general overview is frequently referred to as "scanning" (Gallessich, 1982, p. 315).

Once the principle problems to be solved are identified, the consultant needs to gather additional information in order to shed light on them and to formulate potential solutions. Data are typically gathered by conducting formal and informal interviews with both individuals and groups, by observing the behavior of the organization's members in their routine work patterns, and occasionally by using questionnaires (Caplan, 1970).

Based on the information gathered, the consultant begins to develop interim recommendations, which are then provided to the principal consultee and other authorized parties-at-interest. The consultant incorporates the reactions received into progressively more detailed, complex, and sophisticated recommendations.

During assessment and the reformulation of interim recommendations, the consultant should maintain as much contact with the primary consultee as is feasible. Such contact provides the consultant reactions from the organization's administration, maintains the consultee's interest in the consultation, and increases the likelihood that some of the consultant's skills will "rub off" on the consultee.

By progressively modifying the recommendations made to solve the problem within the organization, the consultant has used a collaborative approach. The final recommendations should have both a short-term and a long-term focus and should indicate what the consultee institution needs to do to implement the recommendations.

Because the consultant's report is typically distributed widely and throughout several levels in the consultee institution, it should be written in a formal style and should cover the issues and problems investigated well enough to be understandable to parties-at-interest who had no direct contact with the consultant. It is up to the principle consultee to determine which, if any, of the recommendations will be implemented.

Finally, the consultant should set up a follow-up schedule before terminating the consultation and should arrange to receive the results of the implementation of the recommendations.

The following example shows how program-centered administrative consultation can proceed:

CASE STUDY:

A mental health consultant is working with an administrator, the head counselor, and the dropout prevention coordinator of a large urban secondary school. The focus of consultation is the school's dropout prevention program. The dropout rate for the school is one of the highest in the state and is still increasing in spite of the dropout prevention program, which has been in existence for three years. The consultant has been asked to make recommendations that could lead to a more effective program. Before the onset of consultation, the consultant made a thorough study of the dropout prevention programs in the state.

The consultant spent one day in the school to get a feel for a typical school day. During the next week, the consultant conducted in-depth interviews with the administrator, the head counselor, and the dropout prevention coordinator about their perceptions of the program. A few "high risk" students and some teachers were also interviewed about their perceptions of the program. The results of these interviews led the consultant to conclude that the program was viewed as a stigma or as "mickey mouse" by virtually everyone except the school's principal and the program coordinator. The dropout prevention coordinator was viewed as being inadequately trained for the job, as having a "cake" job, and as not sensitive enough to the needs of the students in the program.

Based on these findings, the consultant made some interim recommendations for changing the program's image and for getting the program coordinator additional training. These recommendations were shared with the appropriate staff members and were modified according to their input. The following is part of the consultant's final written report:

> Problem 1.1   The image of the dropout prevention program is poor among students and many staff members. The interviews conducted by the consultant suggest that most students view the dropout prevention program as "*not* a cool place to be." Students in general perceive students associated with the program as rejects. The school counselors see the program as a "dumping ground" for students who are having a difficult time adjusting to school. The teachers tend to think of the program as one more "nonacademic" activity at school. The administration and dropout prevention coordinator see the program as being adequate.
>
> The following suggestion is made: the administration of the school should appoint a Dropout Prevention Program Advisory Committee with representatives from the administration, the program, students, the counseling department, and teachers. The dropout prevention coordinator would present the committee an annual plan for working with potential dropouts as well as methods of promoting the program's image throughout the school. Special attention needs to be paid to student views of the program.

The consultant followed up three months later and found that the school was actively engaged in carrying out these recommendations. The dropout prevention coordinator was enrolled on a part-time basis in a masters degree program in counseling.

The Consultee-Centered Administrative Consultation Process

Consultation Goals

Consultee-centered administrative consultation is the most complicated, interesting, and demanding type of consultation. The consultant is hired to work with an organization's administrative-level personnel to help solve problems in personnel management or in the implementation of organizational policy. The consultant gathers information from within the organization to identify the organization's problems to help consultees overcome them.

The primary goal of consultee-centered administrative consultation is an increased level of consultees' professional functioning with regard to program development and organization so that they can develop effective plans and strategies to help the institution accomplish its mission in the future. A secondary goal is producing positive change in whatever program or programs the consultees discuss with the consultant.

Consultant Function and Role

In consultee-centered administrative consultation, the consultant may work with one or more administrators referred to as principal consultees. The consultation is expected to be long-term, ranging from a few months to more than a year. Depending on the size of the consultee institution and the nature of the requested consultation, more than one consultant may be used. The consultant needs the same skills required for program-centered administrative consultation, including expertise in group consultation and specialized knowledge of social systems, administrative procedures, and organizational theory. In particular, the consultee-centered administrative consultant must be able to understand how these skills relate to individuals and subgroups within the consultee institution, as well as to how the institution relates to the broader community. A final skill needed is the ability to scan the entire organization and to make quick judgments about portions of the organization to examine in more depth.

Upon determining who the consultees are, the consultant enters the organization and performs relationship-building activities. The consultant studies the social system of the consultee institution, plans an intervention, intervenes at the individual, group, or organization level, and then evaluates and follows up.

The consultant is more or less "free to roam" through the organization and assists in defining problems and gathering data. Consultants present ideas to consultees and encourage them to discuss and act on them.

Consultee Experience in Consultation

The principal consultee in this type of consultation is the administrator who hired the consultant. This administrator has the job of helping the consultant decide whether additional forms of consultation are required, whether there are to be other consultees, and how these consultees are to be involved in the consultation process. As in consultation of any kind, the principle consultee negotiates the contract, assists in getting sanctions from the top administrator, and provides the consultant logistical support for studying the organization's social structure.

The consultee must determine the extent of contact with the consultant and arrange meetings at which the consultant can present findings to all consultees involved. It is important that consultees know from the start that the consultant will discuss the findings with them for their consideration and input. Although the primary focus of consultation is on organizational problems, an important goal is for consultees to use the consultant's input to further develop their own skills. As in all consultation, the consultees take the consultant's contributions and do with them as they see fit.

Application: Consultant Techniques and Procedures

Next we'll consider the steps the consultant follows in consultee-centered administrative consultation:

1. building relationships,
2. exploring needs,
3. determining who the consultees will be,
4. ensuring that all parties involved know the scope of the consultant's work,
5. studying the organization's social system,
6. planning an intervention,
7. interviewing at various levels within the organization,
8. evaluating, and
9. following up.

The beginnings of consultation are the same as in the other types of mental health consultation and more or less follow the entry procedures discussed in Chapter 3. The consultant in consultee-centered administrative consultation, however, has two unique problems at the onset of consultation. The first is determining who in addition to the administrator will be consultees. The administrators may want the consultant to have contact with subordinates so that they can inform the consultant about the organization. The consultant would then use this information while consulting with the administrator. On the other hand, the administrator may want the consultant to actually consult with the subordinates concerning issues and problems within the organization. Whichever the case, it is very important for the consultant to be sure that everyone involved is aware of the nature of the consultant's role (Caplan, 1970).

The second problem is to ensure both that members of the consultee institution understand that the consultant is an agent of change who can move freely within the organization and that the threat they perceive in the consultant's position of power is minimized. Members of the organization may suspect that the consultant is a "spy" for the administrator, an agent who will use psychological influence to get them to do what the administrator wants, or an outsider who wants to mold the institution into some preconceived form. This perceived threat can be minimized by building proper relationships, including maintaining coordinate relationships, communicating openly, and proceeding cautiously when introducing interventions.

As the consultant studies the organization's social system, problems and issues are identified, which are then presented to the consultees concerned. The consultant's intervention is a neutral one that is restricted to ". . . increasing the range and depth of their [consultees'] understanding of the issues and to augmenting their emotional capacity to use such knowledge productively. It is then up to them to work out solutions in the light of their own personal and role-related choices" (Caplan, 1970, p. 275).

The most effective way for the consultant to remain neutral is to keep in mind the consultation processes of collecting information, making a consultation plan, and intervening to implement the plan.

Data collection has more constraints in consultee-centered administrative consultation than it does in program-centered consultation. First, staff participation in data collection is voluntary, even though it is administratively authorized. Second, because the people from whom the consultant is collecting data are potential consultees, relationship building must be accomplished as well. Third, although consultants have the freedom to collect data about any aspect of the organization, they would do well to focus on issues that are both important to the staff and related to changes the staff would like to make.

In planning the intervention, the consultant should avoid the temptation to intervene too quickly and should review the findings, set some goals, and determine how these goals are to be met. Each intervention targets an individual, a group, or an organization, has a time limit, and should be related to a problem the consultee thinks is important.

As in all of the other types of mental health consultation, the consultant schedules a follow-up session in which to evaluate consultation. If the consultation is ongoing, the consultant is then free to move on to another problem.

The following is a relatively simple example of consultee-centered administrative consultation:

CASE STUDY:
A community psychologist consulting with the staff of a community mental health center that was working with an increasing number of clients with special problems, including AIDS. A former staff member had in fact recently contracted the disease. The staff seemed familiar with the controversies surrounding AIDS, but were ill at ease about such problems as denial of the disease by some victims.

The consultant decided to use a consultee-centered approach but did not focus directly on the AIDS issue until it was brought up by some consultees. Once the subject was broached the consultant attempted to extend the consultees' "cognitive field"; in other words, the consultant attempted to increase the consultees' knowledge of denial in some AIDS victims.

The consultant met with the group of consultees for four sessions to discuss coping with the denial they might encounter. The consultant shared information on the feelings helpers often have when working with chronically ill patients. After the four sessions, the consultant evaluated the consultation process with the principal consultee and arranged for a follow-up in six months.

SUMMARY, TRENDS, AND CONCLUSIONS

Summary

Mental health consultation is a model of consultation in which a mental health expert (consultant) assists a human services worker or administrator (consultee) with a work-related problem. The approach is typically identified with Gerald Caplan (1970, 1974, 1977) and has its origins in the psychodynamic school of psychotherapy. This model stresses the importance of the consultant-consultee relationship and emphasizes enabling consultees to apply what they learned in consultation to similar situations in the future.

The combinations of two levels of mental health consultation (case and administrative) with the two possible targets of each level (the client or program and the consultee) produce the four possible types of mental health consultation: client-centered case, consultee-centered case, program-centered administrative, and consultee-centered administrative.

Consultees can have work-related concerns due to lack of knowledge, lack of skill, lack of confidence, or lack of objectivity. Depending on the type of consultation and the nature of the consultee's difficulty, consultants have at their disposal a broad array of techniques, including the most innovative as well as controversial of these techniques—theme interference reduction. All of these approaches to mental health consultation share the common goals of helping the consultee be more effective in the present and the future and benefiting the client or program addressed in consultation.

Trends

Several trends have occurred in mental health consultation since Caplan published his inaugural work on consultation in 1970. It is to Caplan's credit that the majority of these trends are primarily adaptations of his model, such as reconsiderations of who may qualify to be called a "consultee," reconceptualizations of his 1970 model, and innovations in methods of working with consultees.

One trend in mental health consultation is the inclusion of nonprofessionals as consultees (Altrocchi, 1972). Parents, volunteers such as hospice workers, and paraprofessionals such as mental health technicians all work with people in ways that can loosely be described as "providing human services." Consultants can help these workers deal more effectively with the people they serve by using essentially the same methods used with professionals (Altrocchi, 1972).

Mental health services are being delivered in school settings with increasing frequency. In recent years school consultation has accounted for over one-third of consultation services from mental health centers (Conoley, 1981; Bloom, 1984). Evidently because schools represent stable community organizations with a diversity of young clientele, they are excellent targets for primary prevention activities (Shaw & Goodyear, 1984).

Another trend is the increasing distinction between the terms *consultation* and *prevention* in mental health circles. Whereas these two terms were once synonymous, consultation is now considered to have prevention as its goal, for indeed ". . . mental health consultation is a process; prevention is an objective or goal" (Bloom, 1984, p. 188).

Some experts in the field of mental health consultation (Hodges & Cooper, 1983; Kuehnel & Kuehnel, 1983b; Heller & Monahan, 1983; Schmuck, 1983; Parsons & Meyers, 1984; Pryzwansky, 1977; Brown et al., 1987) have modified Caplan's original formulations.

Hodges and Cooper (1983) reconceptualized Caplan's model to include three models of consultation: the educational model, the individual-process model, and the system-process model.

In the educational model, the consultee's work-related problem is due to a lack of knowledge or skill. The consultant assists the consultee through modeling and/or providing information (Hodges & Cooper, 1983; Kuehnel & Kuehnel, 1983b). This model closely resembles client-centered case consultation.

The individual-process model assumes that the consultee's work-related problem is due to the consultee's attitudes, beliefs, personal issues, or personality characteristics. Consultant interventions attempt to diminish consultee defensiveness and theme interference and use personal growth strategies (Hodges & Cooper, 1983; Heller & Monahan, 1983). This model is similar to consultee-centered case and consultee-centered administrative consultation.

The systems-process model assumes that the consultee's work-related difficulties are due to "the characteristics of the organization or community to which the client and consultee belong" (Hodges & Cooper, 1983, p. 35). Consultant interventions attempt to influence organizational dynamics such as channels of communication and uses of power and influence (Hodges & Cooper, 1983; Schmuck, 1983). The basic difference between this model and Caplan's (1970) administrative models is that Caplan views organizational concerns in terms of program development, whereas the systems model utilizes system interventions (Hodges & Cooper, 1983). Systems approaches are needed because of the complex, increasingly unpredictable environments found within organizations (Hirschowitz, 1977a, 1977b).

Meyers, Parsons, and Martin (1979) and Parsons and Meyers (1984) have adapted Caplan's (1970) model to produce types of consultation, kind of service, and target: direct service to the client, indirect service to the client, service to the consultee, and service to the system. In direct service to the client, the consultant works with the client in such ways as observing, assessing, or interviewing (Parsons & Meyers, 1984). In indirect service to the client, the consultant collaborates with the consultee after data collection to plan a course of interventions (Parsons & Meyers, 1984). Service to the consultee, which is quite similar to Caplan's (1970) consultee-centered case consultation, involves assisting the organization as a whole to function more effectively. In service to the system, the consultant assists an organization to assess the effectiveness of its current level of functioning and to identify alternatives for enhancing that level of effectiveness (Schmuck, 1983; Parsons & Meyers, 1984).

Pryzwansky (1977) adapted the Caplanian model into what he calls "collaboration." In this model the consultant and consultee share mutual responsibility for all aspects of the consultation process. As with Caplan's (1970) model, the consultee maintains the responsibility of carrying out the results of consultation (Brown et al., 1987).

Finally, new models of mental health tend to examine the human/environment interface to a greater extent, which has led to increased emphasis on systems, behavior modification, and human ecology (Mannino et al., 1975). This trend implies less emphasis on case-oriented models and more on those concerned with ecology and events (Klein, 1983). In such models, the consultant becomes part of a community's ecology in efforts to change the ecological interactions to produce a milieu that promotes mental health (Klein, 1983).

Among the innovations in mental health consultation is the increased tendency of mental health consultants to collaborate with consultees in all the stages of the consultation process (Pryzwansky, 1977; Brown et al., 1987). In this model the consultant is free to be more involved than in the Caplanian model.

The issue of whether or not the consultant should directly confront consultee defenses has received some attention. Some authors (Meyers et al., 1979; Meyers, 1981) take a positive view of the consultant's use of direct confrontation with consultees. These authors disagree with Caplan's (1970) contention that direct confrontation takes away a consultee's defenses and that the time available in consultation for providing defensive coping strategies is too short. Proponents of direct confrontation argue that it is time-effective, much less dangerous than Caplan (1970) implies, and does not diminish self-esteem (Meyers, 1981).

Theme interference reduction has also received some modification. Heller and Monahan (1983) reconceptualized theme interference as being due to stereotypes and produced a method for alleviating these stereotypes without having to focus on manipulating the consultee or on the psychodynamic influence that originated the theme interference reduction methods.

Group consultation has received increasing positive attention because of its cost-effectiveness and the realization that it may not be less efficacious than individual consultation (Altrocchi, 1972; Caplan, 1974, 1977).

As for future trends, Brown and Fraser (1985) suggest that mental health consultants will increasingly move to organizational consultation in the following areas:

1. developing coping strategies for the continued rapidly paced changes in our society,
2. creating a systems perspective to understand environmental changes,
3. understanding that preparing for the future means understanding today and considering future scenarios, and
4. providing needed information and assisting in understanding how people and systems cope with change.

Conclusions

Mental health consultation has contributed significantly to the psychological well-being of our society. It has made possible more and better delivery of human services to client systems through the use of a pyramid structure in which consultants assist consultees working with clients or programs. Thus, a relatively large segment of the population can be served by a relatively small number of professionals.

Mental health consultation has promoted mental health and has helped to create positive public attitudes concerning delivery of human services. A significant portion of our society now views mental health as everyone's business.

In addition, mental health consultation has allowed untold thousands of human services professionals to improve and refine their skills, which has benefited the clients with whom they work.

Finally, mental health consultation has reemphasized the notion that personal issues can affect our work lives for better or worse. Indeed, deliverers of human services may bear the following dictum in mind throughout their careers: "Physician heal thyself."

Even though there is no doubt that mental health consultation has had a broad and positive impact, it is not without criticism. One of the basic criticisms is that even though mental health consultation has been defined, it has been done so more in terms of what consultants do than in terms of what the concept itself means. This has led to some controversy over the boundaries of consultation (Mazade, 1983). Mazade (1983) contends that the boundaries of mental health consultation are too broad: until there is a better definition of mental health consultation and a more consistent set of expectations concerning what mental health consultants do, research and attempts to define relevant and irrelevant delivery of services to consultees will suffer.

Bloom (1984) related several criticisms of mental health consultation made by Gottlieb (1974). First, because mental health consultation focuses on clients and their issues, consultees seek new cases rather than perform preventative measures. Hence, mental health case consultation may work at cross purposes with primary prevention. Second, the value of consultation is limited when the individual consultee (instead of the consultee institution) is the target for change. Third, mental health consultation can erroneously assume that consultees are not functioning effectively with their cases and programs when in fact they are (Gottlieb, 1974).

Most of the criticisms of mental health consultation have been directed at Caplan's (1970) model. For example, Beisser and Green (1972) criticize Caplan (1970) for creating a model that only works in an ideal situation that is rarely, if ever, obtained. Caplan's (1970) model has also been described as elitist (Beisser & Green, 1972), a vestige of a time when consultees had limited training in their field and few well-trained consultants were available to assist them.

Caplan also underestimates the amount of time needed to build relationships with individual consultees, particularly in consultee-centered approaches to consultation (Gallessich, 1982). Even the psychodynamic assumptions underlying theme interference reduction have been questioned, and theme reduction techniques have been criticized as being manipulative (Heller & Monahan, 1983; Zusman, 1972).

Further, consultants who are also therapists may have much more difficulty than Caplan suggests in avoiding direct therapeutic interventions to consultees who are too emotionally involved in their cases (Gallessich, 1982). The transfer of effect, discussed earlier as a key concept, has been increasingly questioned; only minimal research supports this concept's existence (Gallessich, 1982).

Finally, Caplan's view of a coordinate, nonhierarchical relationship is criticized because consultants, particularly in consultee-centered case consultation, do not always act as if the relationship were equal.

QUESTIONS FOR REFLECTION

1. How did the psychodynamic perspective influence Caplan?
2. Do you believe that the transfer of effect really takes place in mental health consultation? On what do you base your belief?
3. What difficulties would you anticipate if you were a mental health consultant attempting to build relationships with a consultee institution?
4. What does Caplan mean when he describes the consultation relationship as coordinate and nonhierarchical?
5. What are three basic differences between program-centered administrative consultation and consultee-centered administrative consultation?
6. What is theme interference? What themes in your life might block some of your effectiveness as a consultant?
7. What ethical issues are raised by use of techniques for reducing theme interference?
8. Is manipulation ever a legitimate consultant intervention? Why or why not?
9. Which of Caplan's four types of consultation would you feel most comfortable using? Why?
10. Do you feel that the consultee-centered case type demands too much skill on the part of the consultant to be used effectively by the majority of mental health consultants? Justify your position.

SUGGESTED SUPPLEMENTARY READINGS

If you are interested in reading in more detail and depth about mental health consultation, the following selected readings are recommended.

Caplan, G. (1970). *The theory and practice of mental health consultation.* New York: Basic Books. This book is "the book" on mental health consultation and was the primary source for this chapter. This work—a classic—presents a nice blend of theoretical and practical aspects. Of particular interest is Caplan's discussion of consultee-centered case consultation. Many of today's mental health professionals have used Caplan's ideas as a basis for developing their own particular style and approach to consultation.

Mazade, N. A. (1983). In conclusion the past, present, and future. In S. Cooper & W. F. Hodges (Eds.). *The mental health consultation field* (pp. 233–242). New York: Human Sciences Press. This excellent concluding chapter, which assumes a basic familiarity with the field of mental health consultation, presents various views of mental health consultation from the past and present, and looks to the future. In focusing on future trends, the author raises several generic issues in mental health consultation and discusses several methodological considerations.

Rogawski, A. S. (1978). The Caplanian model. *The Personnel and Guidance Journal, 56*(6), 324–327. This brief article is among the best of those that summarize Caplan's model. Although Rogawski focuses on consultee-centered case consultation, he suggests several general ways consultants can approach consultees and consultee organizations.

Chapter

11

Behavioral Consultation

PREVIEW

CASE STUDY:
You are a school teacher who asks a school psychologist to consult with you concerning one of your students, who causes disturbances by talking at inappropriate times throughout the school day. The school psychologist asks you to describe exactly those behaviors you consider to be "inappropriate," as well as your and the child's behaviors immediately before and after the undesirable behavior occurs. The school psychologist visits your classroom and observes the child. Based on your description and direct observations of the child, the school psychologist leads you through a problem-solving process designed to eliminate the child's inappropriate behavior. Strategies that you can implement and appropriate rewards and punishments are discussed. You agree to implement the program and the school psychologist agrees to help you measure the subsequent frequency of the child's inappropriate behavior.

Chances are excellent that the school psychologist in this example was using a model of behavioral consultation.

Behavioral consultation is a popular approach to consultation that applies behavioral technology to the consultation process. This chapter presents three models of behavioral consultation suggested by Vernberg & Reppucci (1986): behavioral case consultation, behavioral system consultation, and behavioral technology training.

In *behavioral case consultation* the consultant assists a consultee in applying behavioral principles to a case. This is perhaps the most typical form of behavioral consultation (Hawryluk & Smallwood, 1986). *Behavioral system consultation* analyzes and modifies an organization's processes and structures using behavioral technology principles (Vernberg & Reppucci, 1986). *Behavioral technology training* teaches specific behavioral technology skills to consultees (Vernberg & Reppucci, 1986).

As you read this chapter, consider the following questions:

1. What makes behavioral consultation "behavioral"?
2. What unique ethical issues, if any, might arise from the use of behavioral consultation?

3. Is this model's emphasis on measurement an asset or a liability?
4. What are the basic differences among the three approaches to behavioral consultation described in this chapter?
5. What special skills does a behavioral consultant need?

INTRODUCTION

Behavioral consultation is based on behavioral psychology, which has had a tremendous influence on all areas of human services. Behavioral psychology applies theory and research findings to behavior change techniques in systematic, problem-solving procedures. It stresses the principles of learning in order to understand how behavior is acquired and changed. Behavioral models of consultation are based on the idea that because most behavior is learned, it can be unlearned and new behavior can take its place. The result of consultation is some change in behavior in the consultee and/or the client system. Therefore, the principles of behavior change are combined with indirect service by the consultant to form the basis for consultation (Gutkin & Curtis, 1982).

When the behavioral consultant uses principles of learning to help consultees bring about desired changes in themselves or their clients, these principles of learning are translated into empirically-validated behavioral techniques (Tombari & Davis, 1979). Two key aspects of this type of consultation are a focus on *behavior change* and an extensive use of the *scientific method*.

Consultants who label themselves "behavioral consultants" specialize in a behavioral consultation approach. However, all consultants make occasional use of behavioral approaches to consultation (Gallessich, 1982). A consultant functioning within the behavioral framework needs to be skilled in behavioral theory and practice (Feld, Bergan, & Stone, 1987) and should become familiar with the work of such leaders in behavioral psychology as B. F. Skinner and Albert Bandura.

Behavioral consultation can be used in a variety of settings, including mental health centers, schools, and other human services organizations. In addition to its wide applicability, behavioral consultation is one of the most frequently practiced forms of consultation (Gutkin & Curtis, 1982); it is, for example, the most frequently reported method for working with other professionals in school classroom management (Meyers et al., 1979).

Historical Background

Behavioral consultation has its roots in behavior therapy, which in turn has its roots in experimental psychology. Experimental psychology encompasses not only operant and classical conditioning but also social, developmental, and cognitive psychology (Keller, 1981).

In the early 1900s, John Watson founded the behavioral school of psychology, which shunned "covert" events such as cognitions and restricted the parameters of psychology to observable behaviors only. As behaviorism became a strong force in experimental psychology, it was applied to the study of people's personal problems (Lutzker & Martin, 1981). Behaviorism strongly influenced operant conditioning, classical conditioning, modeling, behavioral ecology, and cognitive-behavior modification.

In the 1940s behaviorism became the dominating force in psychology under the guidance of Harvard psychologist B. F. Skinner. In developing the concept of operant conditioning, Skinner researched such principles of behavior change as reinforcement, punishment, and shaping and their applications to humans (Skinner, 1953). From the 1950s through today, many behaviorists have applied learning theory in developing treatment techniques for a variety of personal problems.

Psychotherapists such as Wolpe, Lazarus, and Eysenck were pioneers in applying the Pavlovian model of classical conditioning to the treatment of human psychological disorders (Lutzker & Martin, 1981). Their behavioral therapies were characterized by specific techniques that were validated by case histories (Rimm & Cunningham, 1985).

Until the 1960s, behavior therapy was based primarily on the learning principles known as operant and classical conditioning. In the late 1960s Albert Bandura popularized modeling, a powerful social learning theory based on observation and imitation of certain behaviors under conditions of reinforcement (Bandura, 1977; Matson, 1985; Perry & Furukawa, 1986).

In the 1970s, behavioral ecology (Willems, 1974) and systems theory (Morasky, 1982) began to receive attention. In behavioral ecology people are considered a part of a multilayered ecological environment. The settings in which people behave are interactive; a change in behavior for one setting could affect behavior in another setting. For example, the assertiveness behaviors a client learns in the workplace may produce different results when used in the home.

In the mid-1970s the cognitive-behavioral therapy movement became popular. This movement asserts that what we think or say to ourselves can affect our behavior for better or worse and that there is a connection between what a human thinks and whether or not a personal problem is likely to develop. Donald Meichenbaum (1977, 1985), a leader in this field, has shown that changing self-statements in an appropriate way can lead to desirable behavior change. For example, people who instruct themselves to cope with perceived stress are more likely to be able to effectively manage it than are people who engage in self-talk that expresses doubt in their ability to deal with stress.

Today, the behavior therapy movement has grown to include nationwide societies such as the Association for the Advancement of Behavior Therapy (Lutzker & Martin, 1981). At the same time, this growth and expansion have produced such diversity that it is more accurate to speak of behavior therapies rather than behavior therapy (Corey, 1986), and consequently behavior therapy has become a difficult concept to define (Patterson, 1980; Rimm & Cunningham, 1985). The unifying factor underlying behavioral therapy is its derivation from experimentally established principles and procedures (Keller, 1981, p. 62).

As the effectiveness of behavioral therapy became increasingly apparent, there occurred a parallel increase in requests from human services providers for assistance in the design and implementation of behavior-change programs (Russell, 1978). Hence the role of the behavioral therapist or counselor was expanded to include that of behavioral consultant. Behavioral consultation was first practiced in organizations that require high levels of client control, such as state mental hospitals (Gallessich, 1985). As behavior therapy came to be used in a variety of settings, behavioral consultation was increasingly used in such settings as mental health centers, schools, and other human services organizations. Most of the consultation provided by behavioral consultants consisted of case work; that is, the consultant helped a consultee apply behavioral principles to a specific problem in order to help a client or a group of clients. The influence of behavioral ecology and behavioral training models in the 1970s broadened the role of today's behavioral consultant to include behavioral system consultation and training in behavioral technology.

BEHAVIORAL CONSULTATION DEFINED

Behavioral consultation ". . . encompasses a wide variety of activities conducted in a broad range of settings with diverse populations" (Vernberg & Reppucci, 1986, p. 65). Because the conceptual framework that underlies behavioral consultation (behavior therapy) has become diffuse, behavioral consultation does not possess a central theory of consultation (Gallessich, 1985). According to Keller (1981), ". . . behavioral consultation is based upon a theory of change that is derived from a broad-based social learning model encompassing diverse streams of psychological and social science research and theory" (p. 64). When all these factors are taken into consideration, defining behavioral consultation clearly becomes a difficult task.

In its broadest sense behavioral consultation is ". . . a problem-solving endeavor that occurs within a behavioral framework" (Feld et al., 1987, p. 185). According to Keller (1981), behavioral consultation involves a ". . . relationship whereby services consistent with a behavioral orientation are provided to a client through the mediation of important others in that client's environment, that is, indirect service" (Keller, 1981, p. 65). Note that this actually defines behavioral case consultation because its major emphasis is on helping a consultee help a client. Keller's (1981) definition reflects a traditional classification scheme: mental health consultation focuses on the consultee so that the client will be helped; behavioral consultation focuses on the client so the client can be helped; and organizational consultation focuses on helping the "system" so that the client system can function better (Hawryluk & Smallwood, 1986).

Four characteristics typify behavioral consultation of any form:

1. use of indirect service delivery models;
2. a reliance on behavioral technology principles to design, implement, and assess consultative interventions;
3. a diversity of intervention goals ranging from solving problematic situations to enhancing competence to empowering; and

4. changes aimed at various targets (that is, individuals, groups, organizations, or communities) in different settings (that is, from single settings to multiple settings) (Vernberg & Reppucci, 1986, p. 50).

In effect, these characteristics broaden behavioral consultation from a case-oriented concept to a concept that includes the training and system forms.

Combining Keller's (1981) definition to ideas suggested by Vernberg and Reppucci (1986) produces the following definition of behavioral consultation: a relationship whereby services consistent with a behavioral orientation are provided either indirectly to a client or a system (through the mediation of important others in the client's environment or of those charged with the system's well-being) or directly by training consultees to enhance their skills with clients or systems.

Such a definition is consistent with nine characteristics or assumptions that typify behavioral consultation and account for its uniqueness (Keller, 1981, p. 64):

1. Problem and nonproblem behaviors are acquired and maintained, hence can be changed, through the action of social learning principles.
2. Behavior involves complex person-environment interactions.
3. A close relationship exists between assessment and consultation intervention.
4. A clear specification exists of variables and concepts.
5. Quantification is involved.
6. Environmental causality is assumed.
7. Individual differences in behavior and its determinants are recognized, which leads to idiosyncratic consultation and intervention.
8. Emphasis is placed on public events and direct observation of behavior in the natural environment.
9. The cybernetic, or self-correcting, nature of the behavioral construct system and its derived approaches is recognized.

These characteristics and assumptions reflect behavioral consultation's emphasis on quantification and measurement and its perspective regarding how behavior is learned and changed.

All three forms of behavioral consultation tend to follow a set problem-solving sequence (Zifferblatt & Hendricks, 1974; Lutzker & Martin, 1981), as follows:

1. description of the problem in behavioral terms,
2. a functional analysis of the problem's antecedents and consequences,
3. selection of a target behavior,
4. generation of behavioral objectives,
5. design and implementation of a behavior change program, and
6. evaluation of the behavior change program.

In behavior consultation the consultant and consultee use a problem-solving sequence that first uses behavioral terminology to describe the problem. Next, a functional analysis of the problem examines what happened before and after the problem occurred. Once a target for behavior change has been chosen, behavioral objectives are defined in terms of desired changes and a behavior change program is designed to achieve those objectives. The program is then implemented. Following (and sometimes during) the program's implementation, an evaluation of the program is made.

It might occur to some that the behavioral technology training form of behavioral consultation does not fit this sequence perfectly. In this form of consultation the implementation step of the sequence consists of the training sessions. (Steps one through four will already have been accomplished prior to the training.) Further, Lutzker & Martin (1981) note that the logic concerning behavior change principles that is used in training is the same as that used in any other application of behavior change.

KEY CONCEPTS OF BEHAVIORAL CONSULTATION

In the next part of our examination of the behavioral consultation process we'll discuss the following concepts: its scientific view of behavior, its emphasis on current influences on behavior, focus on change of overt behavior, and the principles of behavior change. An understanding of these key concepts will assist you in understanding why behavioral consultation proceeds as it does.

Scientific View of Behavior

Behavioral consultation, like the behavior therapy that spawned it, is grounded in a scientific view of human behavior, which implies use of a systematic and structured approach to the delivery of human services such as consultation (Corey, 1986). Because knowledge obtained from empirical research is valued so highly by behavioral consultants, such research is subjected to scientific validation. Put another way, behavioral consultation and its interventions are "put to the scientific test" in order to confirm their effectiveness. Such evaluation and subsequent validation are essential to the advancement of behavioral consultation beyond its current state of practice (Corey, 1986; Vernberg & Reppucci, 1986). This empirical testing process frequently involves controlled experiments (Rimm & Cunningham, 1985), a discussion of which is beyond the scope of this text. Interested readers can consult Lutzker and Martin (1981) for a concise discussion of experimental designs for behavior change strategies.

The emphasis on scientific investigation also leads behavioral consultants to use empirically validated consultation interventions because they believe that such a method of operation increases the likelihood that consultation will be successful (Bergan, 1977).

Focus on the Change of Overt Behaviors

Behavioral consultation tends to focus on *overt behaviors*—those that are observable in some way. Some examples include weight loss or gain, on-task behavior, and cigarette smoking. Overt behavior change is seen as the major criterion by which consultation should be judged: consultation is seen as a problem-solving process (Bergan, 1977; Kratochwill, 1985), and the problems to be solved are described in terms of observable, quantifiable behaviors (Lutzker & Martin, 1981). Karoly and Harris (1986) call this kind of description "precise specification." Many behavioral consultants insist on specificity, objectivity, and observability of behavior because these criteria allow continual, reliable reevaluation of interventions (Karoly & Harris, 1986). Attempts to objectify some types of covert events such as thoughts have been successful (Meichenbaum, 1977).

In addition to a focus on overt behavior and attempts to objectify covert behaviors, behavioral consultants tend to view behavior in terms of reciprocal determinism (Bandura, 1977); that is, humans not only are acted upon by their environments but they act on their environments as well. Humans are the producers as well as the products of their environments and ultimately of what they learn.

Emphasis on Current Influences on Behavior

Behavioral consultation focuses on current behavior as well. For the most part, behavioral consultation takes the position that because certain current behaviors constitute the problem in a particular situation (Patterson, 1980), behavioral consultation should focus on those certain behaviors. Behavioral consultation, as Bergan (1977, p. 26) notes: ". . . defines problems presented in consultation as being outside the skin of the client." It is the description of behavior, not the description of a person, that is essential. Thus, by the standards of behavioral consultation it is better to describe a client's hitting behavior in terms of its environmental antecedents and consequences than describe the client as "aggressive."

By focusing on current behaviors, behavioral consultation is better able to discriminate between existing and desired behavior (Bergan, 1977). Such discrimination allows defining the goals of consultation in behavioral terms. The consultant and consultee can mutually determine what behaviors currently exist and what alternative behaviors are desired; they then set behavioral goals, which create the conditions for more rigorous evaluation of the effects of consultation. Past behavior is viewed as important only to the degree that it assists in present interventions (Rimm & Cunningham, 1985). As a result, behavioral consultants do little to help consultees or the consultees' clients gain "insight" into their problems or concerns.

Principles of Behavior Change

Behaviorial consultation assumes that behavior is lawful (that is, orderly, following a set of rules) and that changing the consequences of behavior by using the principles of learning produces a change in behavior (Karoly and Harris, 1986). The consultant helps the consultee select these principles for use in the problem-solving process (Bergan, 1977). The consultant uses these principles of learning to examine and understand the client's behavior, to examine the consultee's behavior, and to determine how to proceed with the course of consultation (Russell, 1978).

Behavior consultants use many principles of behavior when assisting in the behavior change process, including reinforcement, punishment, extinction, shaping, and modeling. These principles can also be used by consultees in their work with their clients. For an excellent, detailed introduction to the principles of behavior, consult Kanfer and Goldstein's *Helping People Change* (1986). A valuable resource for locating techniques based on behavioral principles is Bellack and Hersen's *Dictionary of Behavior Therapy Techniques* (1985).

THE CONSULTATION PROCESS

Behavioral consultation can take three forms: behavioral case consultation, behavioral system consultation, and behavioral technology training consultation (Vernberg & Reppucci, 1986). All forms of behavioral consultation have the following characteristics: indirect service to the client system, use of behavioral technology principles throughout the consultation process, a problem-solving orientation, and empirical validation of interventions (Vernberg & Reppucci, 1986).

Next we'll examine each of the three forms of behavioral consultation in terms of goals, the consultant's function and role, the consultee's experience in consultation, and the use of consultation techniques and procedures.

Behavioral Case Consultation

In *behavioral case consultation* a consultant provides direct, behavior-based service to a consultee concerning the management of a client or group of clients assigned to the consultee.

Until recently the term "behavioral consultation" was identified with behavioral case consultation. Most case approaches to behavioral consultation (for example, Bergan, 1977; Russell, 1978; Keller, 1981; Gutkin & Curtis, 1982; Kuehnel & Kuehnel, 1983a, 1983b) still rely heavily on operant conditioning. However, a more recent model, that of Brown and others (1987), has relied on the social learning theory developed by Bandura (1977). By far the most comprehensive approach to behavioral case consultation is that of Bergan (1977); indeed, most other models, including that of Brown and others (1987), are basic variations of Bergan's model.

Behavioral case consultation has four sequential stages: problem identification, problem analysis, plan implementation, and problem evaluation (Bergan, 1977).

Consultation Goals

Behavioral case consultation is the most frequently used form of behavioral consultation. It is not, however, the only approach to behavioral consultation. In behavioral case consultation, the consultee presents a work-related concern with a client to the consultant, who uses expertise in the principles of learning to "manage the consultee's management of the case."

The typical, primary goal of behavioral case consultation is to help the consultee make positive changes in the client's environment (Feld et al., 1987); such changes lead to a desirable change in the client's behavior (Tombari & Davis, 1979). Recently, some authorities on behavioral consultation (for example, Hawryluk & Smallwood, 1986) have suggested that a second, complementary goal is to effect change in the consultee. Such a secondary goal is necessary because factors related to both the consultee and the client affect the identified problem (Russell, 1978; Hawryluk & Smallwood, 1986). Keller (1981) even suggests that behavioral case consultation can be consultee-centered; that is, that the primary goal of consultation can be enhancement of the consultee's professional functioning.

Consultant Function and Roles

Behavioral consultants use a systematic problem-solving process to assist consultees with their clients (Bergan, 1977; Tombari & Davis, 1979). Behavioral consultants frequently act in the role of expert and ensure that the stages of problem identification, problem analysis, plan implementation, and problem evaluation occur and are adequately accomplished.

Although the consultant is called upon to provide expertise, most behavioral consultants take a collaborative approach to the consultation relationship. Even though the content and process of consultation are under the consultant's control, the consultee is encouraged to become involved in content- and process-related decision making to the degree his or her knowledge and skill in the behavioral approach permit. The consultant helps the consultee determine the best course of action in the case and suggests an array of choices from which the consultee can choose (Tombari & Davis, 1979). Because the consultee is the primary instrument of change in the client, the consultant avoids giving direct advice or dictating the consultee's behavior (Tombari & Davis, 1979).

The consultant provides both knowledge concerning those principles of learning pertinent to the case and whatever knowledge is needed to help the consultee accomplish each of the stages in consultation. In some cases, the consultant must train the consultee in the use of strategies based on principles of learning. However, Bergan's model does not emphasize training of consultees to a great degree.

To ensure that the stages of consultation occur and are successfully accomplished, the consultant guides the consultee's behavior through the use of selected types of verbalizations. Thus, the consultant makes sure that problem identification occurs, but the consultee controls the process whereby identification of the problem occurs. The consultant must inform the consultee about the use of this form of management at the outset of consultation and be satisfied that the consultee is seeking services voluntarily. Management of the consultation process by using verbal skills in structuring the consultant-consultee interaction is, then, the major task of the consultant (Conoley & Conoley, 1982).

Verbal interaction techniques. Because consultation can be reduced to a series of verbal interactions between the consultant and the consultee, these verbal interactions must not be left to chance (Bergan, 1977). The consultant controls not only his or her own verbalizations, but also those of the consultee. The consultant does not attempt to control the specific content of the consultee's verbalizations during consultation, but rather attempts to encourage the consultee to produce the various types of verbalizations needed to achieve the task at hand in the consultation process.

Bergan produced a classification system to assist consultants in controlling the verbalizations in consultation (Table 11.1). Verbal interchanges can be classified in terms of message source, content, process, and control. Judicious use of this classification system can enable the consultant to successfully guide the consultee through the consultation process.

TABLE 11.1 Classification of Verbal Interchanges

Message source	Message content	Message process	Message control
Consultant	Background/environment	Specification	Elicitor
Consultee	Behavior-setting	Evaluation	Emitter
	Behavior	Inference	
	Individual characteristics	Summarization	
	Observation	Validation	
	Plan		
	Other		

Message source. The message source simply indicates whether the verbalization comes from the consultant or the consultee.

Message content. Message content refers to what is discussed by the consultant and the consultee. The consultant typically controls the content of verbalizations in consultation, which includes seven subcategories: background-environment, behavior-setting, behavior, individual characteristics, observation, plan, and other.

The *background/environment* subcategory of message content consists of verbalizations that concern historical factors or current environmental factors that are related to the behavior under discussion and might affect the client's behavior. For example, if the major focus of consultation is the client's adjustment at work, a consultant might ask for information on a client's home life or for a developmental history of the client's problem.

Behavior-setting verbalizations, which are among the most frequently used by behavioral consultants (Bergan, 1977), are used to analyze the client's behavior so that appropriate plans to change that behavior can be made. These verbalizations concern the conditions in the immediate environment that affect the client's behavior. Such environmental conditions are of three types: antecedent, consequent, and sequential.

Antecedent conditions are those that occur just before the behaviors under discussion. Thus, the consultant might ask the consultee to describe exactly what happens just before the client's behavior occurs. Consequent conditions are those that occur just after and may reinforce the behavior in question. Sequential conditions are those that reflect the patterns of antecedents and consequences or the timing of the client's behavior. For example, sequential conditions can become clear when the consultant asks about the events leading up to the client's behavior, when and how frequently the behavior tends to occur, and any special conditions that may be pertinent.

Behavior verbalizations allow precise specification of client behaviors so that they can be measured and discussed. Such verbalizations can also help identify which environmental factors affecting the client's behavior should be investigated. Verbalizations of this type include descriptions of the client's thoughts, feelings, overt behaviors, and their intensity, as well as discussions of written records concerning the client's behavior (for example, baseline behavior graphs). As an example, the consultant and consultee might discuss a client's written autobiographical statement, or the consultant might ask the consultee to describe as specifically as possible what happens when the client engages in a problem behavior.

The *individual characteristics* subcategory consists of verbalizations that describe the unique features or traits of the client. These verbalizations can help determine what is unique about the client and how that uniqueness is related to the client's problem. Consultant-consultee discussion of clients' attributes and traits can range from basic matters like age and weight to more complex personality characteristics and handicaps. For example, the consultant and the consultee might discuss the age, weight, and shyness of a teenage boy as it relates to his being the "class clown."

Often the consultant-consultee interaction produces a decision to obtain more information or data about the client's behavior. Verbalizations in this *observation* subcategory are related to observing and recording client behaviors. For example, a consultee might determine that data should be collected to compare the number of negative self-references a client makes in group therapy with the number made during individual therapy. In another example, a consultant might help a consultee determine the best way to record observations of a client's behavior.

The *plan* subcategory is broad and consists of those verbalizations related to attempts to solve the consultee's problems. Planning in this context typically refers either to general strategies for the consultee to consider or the tactics for intervening with some specific strategy. However, any verbalization about a plan—how it should be implemented, how it should be evaluated, or how well it worked—falls under this category. For example, the consultant and consultee might plan a strategy called a token economy system to help a child stay on task when doing school work, or the same consultant and consultee might discuss how well such a plan worked.

No classification can be fully comprehensive and concise, and in fact consultants and consultees make many other kinds of verbalizations during consultation. Therefore, a catchall subcategory, *other* verbalizations, is used for verbalizations that are not appropriate to the other six subcategories. For example, the consultant and consultee might "talk about the weather" or make statements only indirectly related to client behavior or to the consultation process.

In summary, the verbalizations that occur in behavioral case consultation are to be controlled by the consultant because what is talked about in consultation directly relates to the course and degree of success of the consultation. By determining what to discuss and when, the consultant can help the consultee work with the client more efficiently and effectively.

Message process.   Consultants not only select subcategories of verbalizations to control the topics discussed at any given time; they also control the *kinds* of verbal action that occur. In other words, the consultant controls not only the things that are talked about but also the way in which those things are discussed.

The verbal interchange between the consultant and consultee can be categorized by type of verbal process that occurs within a given content subcategory. As noted by Bergan (1977, p. 38), "The message-process category classifies verbal messages in accordance with the kinds of speaker actions they describe *vis-a-vis* the content of conversation." Process, then, refers to the type of verbal action conveyed in a message. The five message-process subcategories are specification, evaluation, inference, summarization, and validation.

Specification verbalizations ask for some detail or description concerning one of the content subcategories. Information about some behavior's background, its setting, its nature, or its occurrence could be specified. This subcategory is used when more precision or detail is needed to assist the consultee. For example, a consultant might ask a consultee to specify exactly how an intervention will be implemented, or a consultant might ask a consultee to describe the consequences of a given client behavior.

Evaluation verbalizations involve some sort of value judgment or reveal emotions and attitudes about some topic of discussion. For example, a consultee might judge a plan to be ineffective, or a consultant might praise the consultee's behavior in implementing a selected strategy.

Inference verbalizations concern making and playing "hunches" as compared to acting on known fact. Such verbalizations are frequently used to predict the effects of certain interventions on the client's behavior or to demonstrate the set of assumptions under which the consultant and consultee are acting. For example, a consultant might think or feel a certain plan will be effective and might tell this to a consultee, or a consultee might surmise that a client is acting out because of some kind of inappropriate child-rearing practice.

Summarization verbalizations are reviews or summaries of previously discussed information. Summaries can help the consultant and consultee remember what has been discussed previously, keep them focused on the task at hand, and provide a review of what has been agreed on. For example, a consultant might ask a consultee to review his or her perceptions of the client's problems, or a consultant might review what has been accomplished during a given consultation interview.

Validation verbalizations give or ask for a "yes" or a "no" response concerning the facts at hand. Validations are used primarily to develop and maintain consensus between the consultant and consultee concerning each stage in the consultation process. They can be used at any time to make sure that the consultant and consultee are on the same "wavelength." For example, a consultee might review some implementation strategy and ask the consultant if they agree about it, or a consultant might ask if there is agreement on the kind of observation that needs to be performed on a client's behavior.

Thus, there are five message processes that can describe what is occurring in each of the content subcategories. Consider the content subcategory "plan." By using each of the processes, the plan could be specified, evaluated, inferred about, summarized, or validated. The consultant, then, should know not only what to talk about, but the way in which it should be talked about.

Message control.   The consultant is charged with guiding the consultee through a successful consultation experience. To do this, the consultant must control the consultee's verbal behavior to guide the consultee through a successful consultation process (Bergan, 1977). To this end, the consultant must determine what is to be talked about (content), how those things are to be talked about (process), and who is going to talk about them (control). In effect, the consultant uses message control to either give input to or get input from the consultee. (The consultee can also use message control for the same purpose.)

In message-control behavior, the speaker's verbiage is classified in terms of whether or not it will have a direct effect on the receiver's response. If the speaker's message is intended to obtain a direct verbal response (and is thus considered controlling), it is called an *elicitor*. If the speaker's message is not intended to obtain a direct response (and thus does not control the receiver's response), it is termed an *emitter*.

Elicitors usually take the form of either direct or indirect questions that ask the consultee to engage in specification, evaluation, inference, summarization, or validation in one of the message content subcategories. The consultant could ask the consultee to use a verbal process about the conditions affecting the client's behavior, the behavior itself, related observations, or pertinent plans. Four examples of elicitors and their classifications in terms of content and process follow:

A consultant asks a consultee to describe the most problematic situation about the client's behavior (behavior–specification).

A consultant asks a consultee to validate a plan that is to be implemented (plan–validation).

A consultant asks a consultee how he or she feels about making a series of observations of a client's behavior (observation–evaluation).

A consultant asks a consultee for some hunches on why the client is acting in a certain way (background/environment–inference).

An emitter does not call for a reaction from the listener. When consultants use emitters, they provide both content and process information to consultees without attempting to control the consultee's response. Emitters usually take the form of declarative statements. Consider the following examples of emitters and their classifications according to content and process:

A consultant summarizes the individual characteristics of a client for the consultee (individual characteristics–summarization).

A consultant summarizes for the consultee some plan they have agreed to use to help the client (plan–summarization).

A consultant makes a statement agreeing with the consultee regarding the consequences of a given client behavior (behavior setting–validation).

A consultant shares hunches with the consultee about suspected traits and habits that the client might have (individual characteristics–inference).

In summary, the behavioral consultant controls the verbal communication in consultation in order to help the consultee use the consultation process with maximum effectiveness and efficiency by controlling who should talk, what should be discussed, and how the discussion should proceed.

Consultee Experience in Consultation

The consultee is expected to work with the consultant toward the successful completion of the consultation process. As in other forms of case consultation, such as Caplan's (1970) client-centered case consultation, the consultee is a link between the consultant and the client and functions as a professional collaborator. The consultee's four primary roles in the consultation process are:

1. specifier or describer,
2. evaluator or decision maker,
3. provider of direct services to the client, and
4. supervisor of the client's actions (Bergan, 1977).

The consultee should describe as specifically as possible the details of the case and the nature of the work-related problem. The consultee should respond to the consultant's prompts and probes as accurately as possible and provide the consultant with the most comprehensive, detailed picture of the work-related concern possible.

The consultee's role as evaluator or decision maker reflects the peer nature of all consultation: the consultant may make a recommendation concerning a case, but it is the consultee's task to determine what to do with that recommendation. Bergan (1977) relates an example of this consultee role in noting that the consultant might help the consultee select a method for measuring client behavior, but the consultee would have to evaluate that measurement's effectiveness in achieving desired outcomes.

Of course, a primary role of the consultee is to continue to work with the client. Such "work" can include performing a particular caregiving role the consultee has relative to the client (for example, teacher to student or counselor to client) and collecting data regarding the client's behavior. Frequently, the consultee's work with the client will be adaptations of the consultant's recommendations. A critical part of the consultee's work with the client is involving the client in the selection of the goals and processes of consultation; this task is frequently accomplished by having the consultee discuss with the client what the consultant and consultee are thinking about doing concerning the client.

A final (and relatively rare) consultee role is that of supervisor, as when a consultee is a teacher and the client is a student under that teacher's responsibility. However, the consultee may also supervise the involvement of other people involved in the client's treatment. For example, a teacher who is a consultee may supervise a teacher's aide who is collecting baseline data on a student's (the client's) behavior.

In summary, the consultee is a peer in the consultation relationship who frequently takes on the role of active problem solver. The consultee describes the case with detail and specificity, collects data on the client's behavior, makes the final decisions regarding how the case will be handled, works with the client, and if necessary supervises others involved in the client-related logistics of consultation.

Application: Consultant Techniques and Procedures

Each of the two types of behavioral case consultation—developmental and problem-centered—is concerned with changes in client behavior (Bergan, 1977). Developmental consultation deals with more or less long-term behavior change, whereas problem-centered consultation deals with problems that call for immediate attention (for example, crises). Most of the literature on behavioral case consultation refers to developmental consultation because it is by far the more extensively used, and thus our discussion of behavioral case consultation will be limited to developmental consultation.

Behavioral case consultation consists of four sequential, analytical stages (Bergan, 1977):

1. problem identification,
2. problem analysis,
3. plan implementation, and
4. problem evaluation.

Problem identification stage.   This stage provides the momentum for the entire consultation process (Tombari & Davis, 1979). The term *problem identification* sounds quite simple, but from a behavioral perspective defining the problem can be a complex and difficult matter (Vernberg & Reppucci, 1986). This stage is crucial because what occurs in it will determine the direction that consultation takes (Tombari & Davis, 1979) and affects whether or not consultation will be successful (Feld et al., 1987). Bergan and Tombari (1976) found that if the problem identification stage was not successfully completed, the entire consultation process might be irreversibly damaged.

During the problem identification process, the consultant helps the consultee accomplish the following steps:

Step One: designating the general and specific client performance goals to be achieved in consultation.

Step Two: determining how to measure the designated goals.

Step Three: assessing current client performance in terms of the designated goals.

Step Four: examining the results of the assessment.

Step Five: discerning the discrepancy between current and desired client performance (Bergan, 1977).

These steps are accomplished by means of a series of consultant-led interviews, which begins with the problem identification interview in which Steps One and Two are accomplished. Step Three is accomplished by the consultee after the problem identification interview and before a follow-up interview in which Steps Four and Five are accomplished. The problem identification stage ends once the discrepancy between current and desired client behavior has been specified (Feld et al., 1987).

In the problem identification stage, the consultant uses more elicitors than emitters; more specifications, validations, and summarizations than inferences and evaluations; and more verbalizations in the behavior, behavior setting, and observation categories than in other content categories.

When successfully accomplished, the problem identification stage results in a well specified problem defined by the discrepancy between current performance (as measured by collected data) and desired performance (as indicated by stated goals) (Feld et al., 1987). Successful problem identification sets the stage for problem analysis.

Problem analysis stage.   In this stage the consultant seeks to determine the conditions maintaining the client's problem behavior and formulate a plan to alleviate that problem behavior. The consultant jointly pursues these two tasks with the consultee. The problem analysis stage can thus be divided into two phases that contain a total of five steps:

Phase I. Problem analysis

Step One: choosing a procedure for analyzing the problem.

Step Two: conducting a conditions and/or skills analysis.

Phase II. Plan formulation

Step Three: developing plan strategies.

Step Four: developing plan tactics.

Step Five: establishing procedures for assessing the plan's effectiveness (Bergan, 1977).

These steps are accomplished by means of one or more problem analysis interviews. In the problem analysis phase, the client's problem behavior is examined from one of two perspectives:

1. internal and external conditions related to the behavior, or
2. a skills deficit in the client.

The consultant and consultee must first decide whether to conduct an analysis of the conditions surrounding the behavior, the skills of the client, or both. Bergan (1977) suggests that a conditions analysis be performed if the problem behavior tends to have variability over conditions; if the problem behavior remains constant over conditions, then a skills analysis is recommended. Skills analysis is also recommended when increased self-direction on the part of the client is desired. Once the consultant and consultee decide on which type of analysis to perform, Step One is accomplished.

In Step Two, conducting an analysis of the problem, the consultant and consultee work together to determine what conditions and/or skills need to be changed to successfully resolve the client's problem.

Once the consultant and consultee know what conditions or skills need to be altered, consultation enters the plan formulation phase. During this phase, consultation involves developing a systematic course of action to use with the client.

In Step Three the plan's strategies are developed. The consultant usually starts out by suggesting a broad strategy that seems promising based on the conditions or skills analysis performed earlier. In general, the consultant and consultee determine which principles of learning should be used and convert them into strategies designed to help the client. For example, a consultant might suggest using positive reinforcement as a strategy to change the client's behavior but allow the consultee flexibility in its use. Once the consultant and consultee agree on the use of a given strategy, they are ready to proceed to the next step.

In Step Four, the consultant and consultee consider the tactics involved in implementing the strategy. Put another way, now that the consultant and consultee have determined what to do, they now decide specifically how to do it. Next the consultant and consultee engage in Step Five, in which procedures for determining the plan's effectiveness are established. If a conditions analysis was performed, then those same techniques are used for assessment purposes. If a skills analysis was performed, then methods for measuring skill acquisition need to be used; Bergan (1977) suggests that items used in the skills analysis be adapted to measure skill acquisition. Once assessment procedures have been established, consultation moves to the plan implementation stage.

In the problem analysis stage, as in the problem identification stage, the consultant uses more elicitors than emitters and more specifications, validations, and summarizations than inferences and evaluations. Whereas the problem identification stage had a balance of verbalizations in the behavior, behavior-setting, and observation subcategories, the problem analysis stage has a balance of verbalizations in the behavior, behavior-setting, and plan subcategories.

Plan implementation stage.   Plan implementation is the third stage in the consultation process. In this stage, what was planned during the problem analysis stage is put into effect. Good planning does not necessarily lead to good implementation, and thus the consultant's major task in this stage is to make sure that the plan is adequately implemented. To this end, the consultant guides the consultee in accomplishing the two steps of this stage:

Step One: preparing for implementation.
Step Two: carrying out the implementation (Bergan, 1977).

This stage is different from the previous two stages in that there is no formal interview between the consultant and the consultee.

In preparing for plan implementation, roles related to the implementation are assigned, required materials are gathered, and skills necessary for implementation are affirmed.

The consultee generally takes the roles of the plan implementation director, plan executor, and observer of client behavior. The consultant is responsible for determining the need for and providing any training the consultee (or a designee of the consultee) needs to adequately perform these roles. Training can be very time-consuming, so any plans formulated should take the strengths of consultees into consideration (Tombari & Davis, 1979). Once the appropriate roles have been assigned and arrangements for use of materials made, the consultant and consultee proceed to implementing the plan. In this step, the consultee attempts to help the client with the consultant's guidance.

Problem evaluation stage.   Behavioral case consultation stresses evaluation of consultation more than any other model of consultation (Tombari & Davis, 1979). Considerable time is spent evaluating the goals of consultation and the effectiveness of the plan. The results of the evaluation determine what is to occur next in the consultation process. There are three steps in the problem evaluation stage:

Step One: evaluating goal attainment.
Step Two: evaluating plan effectiveness.
Step Three: planning activities based on these evaluations (Bergan, 1977).

Goal attainment is assessed by determining whether the client's behavior change adequately met previously set standards. Recall that the problem was defined in terms of a discrepancy between current and desired levels of behavior. In evaluation, the degree to which desired and observed behaviors coincide is judged to determine whether the goals of consultation have been met.

There are three possibilities in terms of goal attainment: no progress, some progress, and goal accomplishment. If there has been no progress, the consultant typically suggests a return to the problem analysis stage, or perhaps to the goal identification step within the problem identification stage. In some situations, consultation may be terminated and replaced by another type of service. If there is some progress in goal attainment, the consultant typically suggests a return to the problem analysis stage. On occasion, the consultant might suggest a return to the problem identification stage to reexamine goals; on rare occasions, the consultant might recommend termination. If the goals have been accomplished, the consultant and consultee proceed to evaluate the plan's effectiveness.

Behavioral consultants believe that even though the goals of consultation have been achieved, an appropriate design must be used in evaluating the plan in order to demonstrate that the plan was indeed responsible for the success of consultation (Feld et al., 1987). Plan evaluation has no direct bearing on the case at hand, but it can be used in solving similar concerns in the future (Bergan, 1977). Plan effectiveness is determined by applying an appropriate evaluation design that states when client behaviors are to be measured and when plan implementations are made relative to those measurements. Interested readers should consult Bergan (1977) for a discussion on evaluation design, for such a detailed discussion is beyond the scope of this book.

Step Three in problem evaluation is postimplementation planning. The consultant and consultee design a plan for use after consultation has formally been terminated. Such a plan prevents the problem from recurring and provides a way for the consultee to reestablish contact should the problem behavior return to undesirable levels. Sometimes the plan is left intact and is maintained, especially when the plan is relatively easy to implement and when there is some likelihood that the client's behavior would return were the plan eliminated. A new plan is often implemented when it is determined that it is as effective but more convenient than the first plan. Moving from tangible to nontangible reinforcers is a common example of this type of strategy. Finally, a program can be removed once it has been determined that it is no longer needed to maintain the performance levels desired of the client. Whatever the postimplementation plan, behavioral consultants suggest that consultees continue to monitor client behavior for some period of time.

When the goals of consultation and the implementation plan have been evaluated and postimplementation plans made, consultation is terminated.

During this stage, the consultant uses a balance of elicitors and emitters; more specifications, summarizations, validations, and inferences than evaluations; and more verbalizations in the behavior, plan, and observation subcategories.

In summary, behavioral case consultation is a form of behavioral consultation in which a consultant assists a consultee with a work-related problem with a client system. The process proceeds through the stages of problem identification, problem analysis, plan implementation, and problem evaluation. The following example illustrates how this approach to behavioral consultation can be used:

CASE STUDY:

A psychologist working as a mental health consultant is assisting a family therapist with a family. The consultant has expertise concerning youth who run away from home. Two of the family's three teenagers have run away. The family therapist wants to consult with the psychologist before using certain interventions with the family.

Together, the consultant and consultee define what is meant by "running away" behavior. They functionally analyze the behavior in terms of what occurs before and after its occurrence. Together, they devise a plan based on rewarding responsible behavior that has the goal of decreasing the target behavior. The consultee then implements the strategy with the family and evaluates it at its conclusion.

Behavioral System Consultation

In behavioral system consultation, behavioral technology principles are applied to a social system (Vernberg & Reppucci, 1986). Behavioral system consultants use behavior technology principles to analyze and change interactions among the various subsystems of a larger social system such as a school or mental health center. Behavioral system technology can also be used to examine and change relationships between two or more systems that affect one another. For example, a behavioral consultant might interact with the staff at a substance abuse clinic and the staff at a halfway house for substance abusers to assure proper coordination of treatment efforts.

The goal of behavioral system consultation is to enhance the efficiency and effectiveness of a system in terms of its stated functions (Vernberg & Reppucci, 1986). Whereas behavioral case consultation focuses on an individual client within a system, behavioral system consultation focuses on the process and structure of the system itself (Vernberg & Reppucci, 1986).

Behavioral system consultation is influenced by the research and theory of behavioral ecology and systems theory. Behavioral ecology, which states that humans are part of a multileveled system called an ecological environment (Willems, 1974), is a mix of individual approaches derived from traditional behavior modification and ecological approaches that study environments and social systems (Jeger & Slotnick, 1982c).

The settings in which individuals operate are interdependent. For example, what happens to people in their work can affect their home life. Behavioral ecology focuses on the interactions between individuals and their environments (Jeger & Slotnick, 1982a). People act on their environments just as their environments act on them; the interaction between a person and the environment is seen as a series of units, and a change in one unit effects change in the other units (Jeger & Slotnick, 1982b). The environment is seen as putting demands on individuals who have a variety of resources available to meet these demands. The "goodness of fit" between the demands and the resources (Jeger & Slotnick, 1982b, p. 10) determines whether or not there is a problem.

When a problem is perceived, consultants are one solution. Consultative interventions in the behavioral-ecological approach are typically adaptive in nature and systems-centered rather than individual-centered (Jeger & Slotnick, 1982b, 1982d). Interventions increase a person's ability to adapt by increasing access to information and autonomy and by improving internal organization (Jeger & Slotnick, 1982b). In addition, such interventions take both long-term and short-term perspectives. The goal of behavioral-ecological interventions is to match the demands of the system to the resources of the persons in that environment (Jeger & Slotnick, 1982b).

Because of its comprehensiveness, Maher's (1981) model of system consultation will be summarized here. Despite this model's development for use by school psychologists, its applicability is easily extended for use by other human services professionals. Readers might benefit from a review of systems theory (Chapter 8) before they read about Maher's model in the sections that follow.

Consultation Goals

The primary goal of behavioral system consultation is the more effective functioning of a social system in terms of its stated mission. This goal is accomplished through a combination of individual, group, and systemwide interventions; the majority of behavioral system interventions are systemwide in scope. The system itself is the "client" and the people with whom the consultant works are the consultees. Consultees' increased future functioning relative to their job duties within the system can be a secondary goal.

The consultant accomplishes the goal of consultation by guiding the consultee through the four stages of the behavioral system consultation process: system definition, system assessment, system intervention, and system evaluation.

Consultant Function and Role

As in behavioral case consultation, the consultant acts as an expert in behavioral technology, but in behavior system consultation the consultant must also be expert in systems theory and behavioral ecology. The consultant guides the consultee (referred to by Maher [1981] as the "referral agent") through a systematic problem-solving process and ensures that the steps of system definition, system assessment, system intervention, and system evaluation are accomplished.

Even though the consultant is an expert in behavioral technology, systems, and behavioral ecology, the nature of the consultation relationship is collaborative; consultees participate to the degree their skills and knowledge permit. Although Maher (1981) is vague about whether the consultant actually participates directly in implementing the intervention, the consultee remains the primary instrument of change in the system and the consultant provides the consultee with whatever assistance is deemed necessary. As in any other form of consultation, the consultant allows the consultee complete freedom of choice.

The consultant provides the consultee whatever knowledge about the behavioral technology, systems, and behavioral ecology is needed for successful consultation. Although Maher (1981) does not directly mention training of consultees, it can be assumed, as in Bergan's (1977) model, that some training of consultees may take place in topics crucial to the successful accomplishment of each stage of the consultation process.

In summary, the consultant guides the consultee through a collaborative consultation relationship in which the consultant uses his or her expertise while keeping all decisions joint and mutual.

Consultee Experience in Consultation

Maher (1981) makes no specific statement regarding the consultee's behavior except that in the role of collaborator in the consultation process. However, certain assumptions regarding consultee behavior can be made.

Perhaps the consultee's most important function is that of decision maker. Although the consultee participates in the consultation relationship as a peer with the consultant, in the end it is the consultee who decides how consultation is to proceed.

The consultee is charged with providing the consultant with fully accurate information, which can include descriptions of the problem within the system or of the system's parameters, suggestions for gathering data, or feedback on the feasibility of various possible interventions. Further, the consultee is responsible for carrying out the implementation. (As in behavioral case consultation, the consultee may designate another party to carry out the implementation.)

In summary, the consultee acts as an active problem solver who works in concert with the consultant by providing the consultant appropriate information concerning the problem and the system in which the problem exists. Other consultee roles include working with the consultant in data gathering and analysis, planning and implementing interventions, and evaluating consultation. The consultee reserves the right to make any and all decisions regarding the direction consultation takes.

Application: Consultation Techniques and Procedures

Behavioral system consultation assumes that all or part of some system is experiencing some functional difficulty; it consists of the following stages (Maher, 1981):

1. system definition,
2. system assessment,
3. system intervention, and
4. system evaluation.

System definition.   In order for consultation to be successful, information must be gathered about the behavior of members of the system relative to the system's goals and structures. There are two steps in this major task of the system definition stage:

Step One: defining the system structure.
Step Two: defining the system process.

In determining the *structure* of a system, the consultant and consultee define the system's parameters with regard to time and space. Variables related to understanding a system's structure include:

1. physical setting and boundaries (for example, where the system is located);
2. environmental design (for example, the system's physical plant);

3. number of system members (that is, demographic data); and
4. policies and procedures (for example, rules and regulations).

In determining the *process* of a system, the consultant and consultee define the system's parameters in terms of the behavior of the system's members. Variables related to understanding a system's process include:

1. assessment functions (that is, how behavior of various systems groups will be measured);
2. intervention functions (that is, how the system tries to change on its own);
3. evaluation functions (that is, how the quality of the system's functions is determined); and
4. communications functions (that is, who talks to whom, in what manner, and how often).

In defining both the structure and process of a system, the consultant and consultee rely on observations of the system's everyday functions, written records, and interviews of key members in the system.

System assessment.   Once the consultant and consultee have defined the system in terms of structural and process factors, they are ready to assess the system in terms of those factors. Assessment of the defined system is a joint effort of the consultant and consultee to gather appropriate information concerning the interrelationships among identified structures and processes. The consultant and consultee gather information through direct observation, interviews, and appropriate standardized instruments.

The system assessment provides information on the system's structure and process and the ways they influence behavior within the system. The consultant and consultee can then decide which parts of the system are operating adequately and which are "dysfunctional" (Maher, 1981, p. 502). The presence of dysfunctional parts of the system can point to problems that consultation might address.

Assessment of the structure includes gathering data about environmental restrictions and determining the degree to which the system's operating procedures are known and followed by the system's members.

Assessment of the system's process involves gathering information about specific behaviors of the system's members. The most and least productive system members are determined, as are those who either facilitate or block productive behavior. Based on this information, the consultant and consultee attempt to categorize aspects of both the system's structure and process as either functional or dysfunctional.

As a result of systems assessment, the consultant and consultee can determine the system's structural and process limitations, which are then used as the foundation for the next step in behavioral system consultation—system intervention.

System intervention.   The structural and process limitations of the system are considered areas of need, and the consultant and consultee develop a system program designed to eliminate those limitations. There are three steps in the system intervention stage:

Step One: prioritizing system needs.
Step Two: specifying behavioral outcomes goals.
Step Three: designing and implementing intervention programs.

The first step in the system intervention stage is to order perceived needs in terms of priority. The consultant and consultee come to an agreement concerning which need should be addressed first.

In the second step, specifying behavioral outcome goals based on the prioritizing activity in the first step, the goals are concrete, stated in behavioral terms, and measurable. Making these goals sets the direction of subsequent interventions and allows for rigorous evaluation of consultation efforts.

Once behavioral outcome goals have been set, the consultant and consultee engage in the third step—the design and implementation of a program designed to meet those goals. An array of programs is generated, and the advantages and disadvantages as well as the human, technological, informational, and financial resources required for each program are determined and evaluated. Based on the outcome of the evaluation of possible plans, the consultant and consultee choose and implement the most appropriate plan. The plan may target a subsystem of the organization or the entire system.

System evaluation. The system evaluation stage has two steps:

Step One: evaluating intervention program operations.
Step Two: evaluating system change.

In evaluating the operations of the intervention program, the consultant and consultee determine whether the program was implemented in the way intended and with the results expected. This information is in turn used to determine which activities were responsible for the outcome of the intervention and to modify the program for future use. Information is sought on the utilization of human resources involved in the program, the extent to which data has been collected according to plan, and the presence of positive and/or negative side effects. One method of evaluation is retrospective reporting, in which people involved in the program are interviewed to obtain their views of how things went. A second evaluation method is naturalistic observation, in which program participants are observed while they are engaged in the program.

Evaluating system change involves determining the degree to which the system changed relative to the goals of consultation. The consultant and consultee determine what structural and process changes occurred and how these changes influenced the system's operation relative to the goal that was set. The consultant and consultee also attempt to determine the degree to which observed changes were due to the intervention and not to extraneous factors. Typically, if behavior in the system changes in the desired direction, the change is attributed to the program.

The following example demonstrates how behavioral system consultation can be used:

CASE STUDY:
A human services professor from a university is consulting with a human services agency about enhancing its effectiveness. The consultant and the designated consultee first define the system in terms of its structure and process. They rather easily define the system in terms of its structure, but it takes them quite a bit longer to define the system's process. They examine each of the agency's subsystems (for example, the technological subsystem, which consists of the case workers) in terms of how communication takes place, how the behavior of the subsystem is measured and evaluated, and how the subsystem attempts to solve its own problems.

After defining the system, the consultant guides the consultee in assessing the interaction between the identified structural factors and process factors. The consultant and consultee determine that part of the system's limitations is due to poor "top-down" communication and lack of adequate autonomy for the agency's case workers.

In intervening to rectify the matter, the consultant and consultee make poor "top-down" communication the most important system problem. They set the objective of having a regular weekly staff meeting in which all participants are allowed to submit agenda items and all important information is discussed. In addition, the final ten minutes of the weekly meeting is to be allocated for discussion of any topic that an individual wants to bring up.

The consultant and consultee generate three possible programs and weigh advantages and disadvantages of each. They decide that the consultant will be a participant/observer at the first meeting and will provide feedback to the group concerning what the consultant observed. Based on this feedback, the group would decide how to modify procedures for conducting subsequent staff meetings. Following this intervention, the consultee agrees to monitor staff meetings on a regular basis to make sure the desired changes in "top-down" communication indeed occur. The changes in the system are evaluated six months later by surveying the staff regarding the nature of communication within the agency.

Behavioral Technology Training

This approach to behavioral consultation is used when consultees seek to increase general usage of behavioral technology principles when working with clients. Consultees are typically human services professionals such as teachers (Allen & Forman, 1984), caretakers such as paraprofessionals (Jeger & McClure, 1982; Liberman, Kuehnel, Kuehnel, Eckman, & Rosenstein, 1982), or parents (O'Dell, 1974; Gresham & Lemanek, 1987).

Consultants typically train consultees in general behavioral principles or specific behavioral technology skills (Bergan, 1977) or both (Vernberg & Reppucci, 1986). Behavioral technology training, which can be formal or informal (Bergan, 1977), can be given to individuals (for example, a consultant might train a therapist to perform systematic desensitization) or can be performed with groups (for example, a consultant might train special education teachers in token economy procedures). The education/training model of consultation discussed in Chapter 9 is similar to the process involved in behavioral technology training.

Behavioral technology training has several justifications for its existence (Vernberg & Reppucci, 1986):

1. Consultees who use behavioral technology are frequently successful.
2. An understanding of behavioral technology increases the likelihood that behavioral programs will be implemented appropriately.
3. Consultees who understand behavioral technology are likely to generalize it to new situations and thus enhance all aspects of their lives.
4. Behavioral technology is cost-effective and efficient.

The goal of behavioral technology training is increased consultee competence in the use of general and/or specific behavioral technology procedures. The consultant functions as a resource person and trainer. The consultee experiences consultation as a trainee expected to apply the training at appropriate times with work-related concerns. As is the case in most types of education/training consultation, the steps involved are conducting a needs assessment, planning the training, performing the training, and evaluating the training.

Behavioral technology training usually consists of training in behavior modification procedures and, more recently, in cognitive-behavioral approaches (Forman, 1984). Behavioral technology training has been provided to a variety of human services professions, especially school teachers. It has also been provided to a variety of nonprofessional caretaking roles such as parenting and paraprofessional services in human services settings (Tharp & Wetzel, 1969). There is strong empirical evidence that behavioral technology training of consultees leads to improved client behavior (Vernberg & Reppucci, 1986).

Problems encountered in evaluation of behavioral technology training revolve around whether the training is generalized to settings beyond the training setting and whether consultees continue to use the results of training in intended environments. Consultants who use behavioral technology training must decide what form of behavioral technology training is best for which type of consultee under what conditions (Vernberg & Reppucci, 1986).

In summary, behavioral technology training consultation utilizes the consultant's knowledge in behavioral technology and ability to train others in that technology. The principles and methods of the education/training model of consultation discussed in Chapter 9 apply to behavioral technology training, which has more support for its use than any other form of education/training consultation (Vernberg & Reppucci, 1986). The results of research indicate that behavioral technology training works.

The following example illustrates how behavioral technology training can be used:

CASE STUDY:
A school counselor acting as a consultant conducts a three-session workshop for teachers on "Catching Students Being Good." The focus of the workshop is on the effective use of the principles of extinction and positive reinforcement.

The consultant first presents the concepts of extinction and positive reinforcement and a realistic view of what to expect in using these principles. Situations from the classroom are used to illustrate how the principles can be used effectively. Following this, some general rules for using extinction and positive reinforcement are discussed. The teachers then practice using the principles in situations comparable to those they encounter in the classroom, receive feedback on their performances, and then receive hints for remembering to use the principles in the classroom. Finally, the consultant agrees to observe each teacher applying the principles in the classroom and to provide feedback.

SUMMARY, TRENDS, AND CONCLUSIONS

Summary

Behavioral consultation is a process in which a consultant uses the principles of learning to assist one or more consultees having a work-related problem with a client or a client system. Behavioral consultation owes its heritage primarily to behavior therapy and behavioral psychology. The boundaries of behavioral consultation tend to expand in direct relationship to advances in these two areas.

The result of all behavioral consultation is a change in behavior in the client, in the consultee, or in both. This change is accomplished through a systematic problem-solving process. The nature of the relationship between the consultant and consultee in this problem-solving process is a collaborative one in which the consultant is an expert who guides the consultee through the consultation process using the principles of learning.

Behavioral consultation can be performed in case, system, or training approaches. In the case approach, by far the most common approach of behavioral consultation, the consultant helps the consultee manage a client's case. In the system approach, a system or some part of it is modified through use of behavioral principles. Behavioral technology training consultation involves training the consultee in the use of general and/or specific behavioral principles for future use with clients and client systems.

The basic assumptions of behavioral consultation are that behavior can be viewed scientifically, overt and current behavior is the focus of change, and behavior is lawful and subject to systematic change.

Among the procedures advocated by behavioral consultants are use of direct assessment, operationalization of goals, objective measurement of target behaviors, and assessment of both the goals of consultation and the consultation plan.

Behavior consultation has been successfully applied in a variety of settings but is most frequently used when there are high levels of client or system control.

Trends

The major trends in behavioral consultation are linked to developments in behavior therapy and behavioral psychology. Because of the strong influence of these two areas on behavioral consultation, findings in these areas are quickly incorporated into the practices of behavioral consultants.

A major trend in the field is the expansion of behavioral consultation to include behavioral system and behavioral technology training approaches. This increase in the parameters of behavioral consultation has allowed it to move beyond traditional case consultation.

Another trend in behavioral consultation is an increased tendency to include other forms of behavioral technology in addition to those based on operant conditioning, classical conditioning, and observational learning. The cognitive-behavioral and behavioral ecology movements have made strong headway and now have a place in all behavioral consultation approaches (Tombari & Davis, 1979; Vernberg & Reppucci, 1986).

Behavioral consultants are becoming increasingly aware that the success of any approach to behavioral consultation is in part determined by the environment in which consultation occurs. Behavioral consultants now tend to more fully consider organizational issues such as the consultee institution's history and organizational structure (Reppucci, 1977; Hughes, 1980; Reppucci & Saunders, 1983; Forman, 1984). In educational settings behavioral consultants tend to work more closely with teachers in helping them enhance their instructional and behavioral management of their classrooms (Feld et al., 1987).

In terms of the consultant-consultee relationship, behavioral consultants are devoting more attention to the development of relationships based on rapport with their consultees and the consultee variables that may affect the success of consultation (Hawryluk & Smallwood, 1986).

Conclusions

The major contribution of behavioral consultation has been its emphasis on approaching consultation in a systematic way. Consultants can be taught to perform behavioral consultation in a straightforward, step-by-step manner. Such an emphasis on approaching consultation systematically has reinforced the view that consultation is a sequential process made up of identifiable stages.

A second major contribution of behavioral consultation, its emphasis on specifics, has contributed to more effective methods in setting the goals of consultation, gathering data on the perceived problem, and, most important, in evaluating the effects of consultation. Behavioral consultation's emphasis on specifics and measurement has encouraged consultants to be more accountable for their consultation efforts.

A third major contribution of behavioral consultation is the training of consultants in techniques from behavioral and cognitive-behavioral approaches to counseling and psychotherapy. Hence, school teachers are frequently able to use behavior modification procedures, and many counselors can use stress inoculation training.

A fourth major contribution of behavioral consultation is its leading role in research on consultation; no other form of consultation has been as well researched as behavioral consultation.

Behavioral consultation is not without its limitations and criticisms. One of its major criticisms surrounds the inappropriate control of client (and sometimes consultee) behavior. Vernberg & Reppucci (1986) note that behavioral consultants may be used inadvertently to control rather than treat consultees' clients and client systems. Behavioral consultation needs to better link program implementation with safeguards of client and client system rights (Vernberg & Reppucci, 1986).

A second criticism of behavioral consultation is that it does not adequately take into account consultees' thoughts and feelings regarding the use of behavioral principles with clients. Many times consultees have reservations about using behavioral interventions with clients because of perceived technical problems or manipulative behavioral procedures and because of concerns about their ability to satisfactorily implement the required procedures (Abidin, 1975).

Behavioral consultation is often criticized for the difficulties involved in applying behavioral procedures in "real life" or in natural environments (Gallessich, 1982). For example, it is one thing to help a teacher make a plan to control the behavior of a seventh-grade boy but quite another to implement the program in a classroom with 36 students.

Some consultants' neglect of a collaborative approach to consultation is frequently cited as a criticism of behavioral consultation (Conoley & Conoley, 1982). Because some work-related problems can be addressed simply by using behavioral interventions, some behavioral consultants adopt the role of expert and perform most of the consultation tasks except the intervention. The long-term positive effects on the consultee's future performance are likely to be negligible as a result. A closely related criticism is that some behavioral consultants rely too much on "pet" interventions (for example, on tangible reinforcers) when designing intervention programs with their consultees (Tombari & Davis, 1979).

Behavioral consultation is also criticized for not maintaining the "integrity of the treatment" (Vernberg & Reppucci, 1986). Frequently the agreed-upon treatment plan is implemented as planned due to a lack of adequate financial and/or human resources. Therefore, behavioral consultation does not always practice what it preaches: adequate monitoring of program implementation.

Each of these criticisms suggests that the shortcomings of behavioral consultation result from inadequacies of practicing behavioral consultants rather than from the failings of behavioral consultation as such. As with the other models of consultation covered in this text, the remedy to this situation may well be better training as well as refinement of approaches to behavioral consultation.

QUESTIONS FOR REFLECTION

1. Could any individual behavioral consultant incorporate the findings from operant conditioning, classical conditioning, observational learning, the cognitive-behavioral movement, and behavioral ecology into the practice of consultation? Justify your answer.
2. What are the essential characteristics of any approach to behavioral consultation?
3. To what degree are the underlying assumptions of each of the influences on behavioral consultation compatible with each other?
4. When would you as a behavioral consultant incorporate punishment into a treatment plan? Justify your answer.
5. How can a consultant using the behavioral case consultation approach avoid manipulating and excessively controlling the consultee's verbal behavior?
6. Which three of Bergan's subcategories of verbalizations would an organizational process consultant employ most frequently? How would this compare to a consultant employing behavioral case consultation?
7. Which three of Bergan's subcategories of verbalizations would a mental health consultant using consultee-centered case consultation employ most frequently? How would this compare to a consultant using behavioral case consultation?
8. What strengths does behavioral ecology add to behavioral system consultation?
9. Why does a consultant using behavioral technology training consultation need to be a "good teacher"?
10. When you consider both the contributions and criticisms of behavioral consultation, what conclusions do you draw?

SUGGESTED SUPPLEMENTARY READINGS

Those interested in reading further about behavioral consultation should consult the following suggested readings:

Bergan, J. R. (1977). *Behavioral consultation*. Columbus, OH: Charles E. Merrill. This is "the book" on behavioral case consultation. Although the author assumes consultants will be working in a school setting, readers can easily apply his ideas to any human-services setting. Bergan devotes at least a full chapter to each of the four stages of behavioral consultation, and extensive treatment of verbal interaction techniques is also provided. A case study section is provided to demonstrate precisely how a behavioral consultant would proceed. Be advised that this book is laborious reading but well worth the effort.

Keller, H. R. (1981). Behavioral consultation. In J. C. Conoley (Ed.), *Consultation in schools: Theory, research, and procedures* (pp. 59–99). New York: Academic Press. This is one of the most thorough reviews of behavioral consultation available. The discussion is both theoretical and practical. Keller provides a particularly scholarly presentation on the various principles of learning that influenced behavioral consultation. The literature related to the research on behavioral consultation is also discussed. Keller also describes an interesting variation of Bergan's (1977) model. This is must reading for people interested in behavioral consultation.

Vernberg, E. M. & Reppucci, N. D. (1986). Behavioral consultation. In F. V. Mannino, E. J. Trickett, M. F. Shore, M. G. Kidder, and G. Levin (Eds.), *Handbook of mental health consultation* (pp. 49–80). Rockville, MD: National Institute of Mental Health. This was the most current view of behavioral consultation when this textbook was in preparation. The authors argue that behavioral consultation should expand its boundaries beyond traditional case consultation to encompass behavioral system consultation and behavioral technology training. In addition to reviewing three types of behavioral consultation, it provides an excellent review of the challenges currently facing behavioral consultation.

Chapter

12

Case Study Illustrations

PREVIEW

This chapter illustrates how the various approaches to consultation could be applied within the same organizational setting to help you apply theory to practice and obtain a more realistic picture of what really transpires in consultation. It is important to remember that there are many different ways to implement a given approach to consultation.

Recall that some approaches deal with the entire organization as the client (for example, process consultation), whereas some work with consultees who are delivering direct services to clients (for example, client-centered case mental health consultation). Therefore, strict comparison among the various approaches to the three types of consultation are not possible because different approaches to consultation attempt to accomplish different things.

The next section describes a human services organization, Acme Human Services Center, in terms of its environment, people, structure, and activities, and the data concerning the organization that were gathered in a variety of ways and from a variety of sources. In order to accommodate the various approaches to consultation, this human services organization must deliver direct services to clients. Assume that for each approach the consultant has all the data mentioned for Acme Human Services Center. Each of the various approaches to consultation is then applied within this human services organization. Assume also that the contact persons in the organization know what kind of consultation is needed. (In reality, this happens only occasionally, and thus the overall context in which each consultation model is illustrated is somewhat unrealistic. However, the given illustration of each consultation approach will be very realistic.)

Each approach to consultation is discussed in terms of its goals, the consultant's role and function, the consultee's experience in consultation, and the application of the approach. The final case study, a composite of various approaches, illustrates how the ideas, goals, concepts, and techniques from various approaches can be synthesized and applied by a consultant in a given setting.

As you read the illustration of each approach, remember that:

285

1. There are several ways to go about expertly performing each approach to consultation.
2. The illustration reflects the author's style of consultation within the context of the approach.
3. Most of the approaches are highly flexible with regard to how a consultant might proceed.

Consider the following questions as you read through this chapter:

1. Are the various approaches to consultation more alike than they are different?
2. Based on the case studies in this chapter, are there any skills consultants need that are common to all the approaches discussed?
3. How can you use this chapter to help you develop your own personal model of consultation?
4. Which models seem most personally attractive to you?
5. In what ways would you apply the approaches presented in this chapter differently than the author did?

INTRODUCTION

Consider this situation:

CASE STUDY:
Assume that you are equally talented in each of the various approaches to organizational, mental health, and behavioral consultation. Imagine further that you are called into a human services organization and asked to perform, in turn, each approach to consultation. You would be asked to perform the education/training, program, doctor/patient, and process approaches to organizational consultation. You would then be asked to perform the client-centered case, consultee-centered case, program-centered administrative, and consultee-centered administrative approaches to mental health consultation. Finally, you would be asked to provide the behavioral case, behavioral system, and behavioral technology training approaches to behavioral consultation.

All this sounds like a pretty tall order! Of course, no consultant is going to be asked to provide such a broad array of services. In fact, no consultant would have the talents and abilities to provide the breadth of services that all the various approaches taken together would require.

Even if you were "super consultant" and were capable of such fantastic feats, you would still need to ask yourself several questions before proceeding with each approach:

1. What are the assumptions I need to make according to the approach I am about to use?
2. What are the goals of the approach to consultation I am about to use?

3. What are the consultant roles and functions that will be demanded of me?
4. What will my consultees experience during the consultation process?
5. In specific terms, how will I go about applying this particular approach?

Illustrations of each approach to consultation in more or less the same context can provide you several learning experiences, including:

1. a real-life "feel" for how the approaches work,
2. a deeper understanding of how the approaches converge and diverge in theory and practice,
3. a broader understanding of the similarities and differences across the approaches, and
4. an opportunity to begin developing personal preferences for some approaches over others.

These case studies can give you a starting point for proceeding with each of the approaches. In addition, the studies form a basis for comparing and contrasting the various approaches to consultation and provide material for thought and reflection in forming your own personal model of consultation. The development of your personal model of consultation is a lifelong process that will be continually modified based on your professional and personal experiences. The keys to a useful personal model of consultation are fourfold:

1. Know your own values about life in general and consultation in particular.
2. Know your personal and professional strengths and limitations.
3. Know and be able to practice as many approaches to consultation as possible.
4. Know what the organizations and consultees you are serving really need from you before you start.

THE CASE: ACME HUMAN SERVICES CENTER

A Description of the Organization

Acme Human Services Center is a large, private institution that provides a variety of counseling and psychological services in a wide portion of a rural southeastern state.

The Center is located in a city with a population of 90,000 and provides services to many of the small surrounding communities. The population base is 70% White, 20% Black, and 10% other minorities, including Hispanics and Asian-Americans. Textiles, furniture manufacturing, automobile assembly, and agriculture are the main industries of the area, which has been labeled economically depressed. It has a high unemployment rate and a moderate crime rate. Referendums for civic improvements such as schools and recreation centers are continually voted down by the populace. A four-year university in the area provides a variety of cultural, recreational, and social events. The casual observer would note the presence of modern churches, parks, music and drama organizations, and library facilities.

The Center competes with two other small, private practice corporations, a small number of individuals in private practice, and a local community mental health center that has been in existence for 20 years. Acme Human Services Center has been in operation for ten years under the same director.

The Center has a professional staff of 15: one psychiatrist, one nurse, two doctoral-level psychologists, two doctoral-level counselors, two masters-level school psychologists, two masters-level counselors, two masters-level clinical psychologists, and three masters-level social workers. Two clerical staff members and one mental health technician also work there.

The Center provides community-based services through a variety of outpatient programs. Clients are referred to the Center by schools, physicians, juvenile and adult court systems, the social services department, and occasionally the local mental health center. The basic realm of services is divided into several categories, including adult mental health services, child and adolescent mental health services, substance-abuse services, community consultation services, and employee assistance program services. Plans are being considered for providing mental retardation services.

The Center has no written role and mission statement. Its founder, a psychiatrist, feels that its mission is to help citizens develop and maintain an adequate level of social and personal well-being and dignity. The Center has dramatically increased in size over the last four years due to the addition of the substance-abuse and employee assistance programs; the organization's income doubled and five additional staff were added during that time.

The Organization's Problems

When the director of the organization last reviewed its progress, he listed problems that had emerged so that steps could be taken to solve them. He thought that such a procedure would help the organization maintain and perhaps enhance its financial position. As he reflected on the past four years, he listed the following problems:

1. an increase in referrals of cocaine-related substance abusers with no true "experts" on the staff to handle them,
2. a lack of knowledge about how to evaluate the effectiveness of the employee assistance programs,
3. increasing concern over the deteriorating relationship between the staffs of the child and adolescent program and the adult program,
4. too much of the decision-making responsibility in the hands of one leader for an increasingly complex organization,
5. insufficient time for program heads to consult on cases,
6. a lack of definite direction in the substance-abuse program,
7. an increase in the number of "acting out" adolescents as clients,
8. an increase in requests from schools for assistance in classroom management techniques,

9. the need for each program to clarify its own specific goals and objectives, and

10. growing concern over staff morale in general.

Although the director of the agency knew that he had a few staff people who could function as internal consultants, he felt that objectivity was at a premium and thus decided to seek outside consultation for each of the problem areas cited above. The director, himself a well-known consultant in the area, was easily able to identify an effective type of consultation that would be likely to solve each problem.

Because the staff had no true experts in cocaine-related substance abuse, an education/training organizational consultation was selected. The inability to evaluate the employee assistance programs could be resolved through program evaluation consultation. Because the deterioration of the relationships between the two staffs was a mystery as far as the director was concerned, a doctor/patient type of organizational consultation was in order. The centralization of leadership in an increasingly complex organization called for a review of how decisions are made and what other possibilities existed, and thus a process form of organizational consultation seemed in order.

Because program heads were increasingly taxed with other duties, they had little time to consult with the psychologists, counselors, and social workers who provided direct services to clients. Client-centered and possibly consultee-centered case mental health consultation seemed in order for this problem. The lack of definite direction in the substance-abuse program called for either program-centered administrative or consultee-centered program mental health consultation.

Because the increasing number of "acting out" adolescents required behavioral approaches, behavioral case consultation was selected. The increasing number of requests from schools for assistance in classroom management techniques required training the agency's staff, so behavioral technology training consultation was needed. Finally, each program could formulate its own specific goals and objectives with the assistance of behavioral system consultation.

Existing Data on the Organization

The organization's internal environment is frantically paced: everyone seems so busy that there is little time for social interaction at work. Office doors remain closed during the day, even when clients are not being seen. Paperwork appears to be backlogged in spite of computer-assisted office support. A trained observer would label the environment as unstable and heterogeneous.

The organization's personnel are cordial with one another, yet relationships tend to be superficial. Efficiency and productivity are high but come at a price, for little discussion occurs relative to the direction the Center should take. Although personnel feel secure about their jobs, it is evident that morale and a sense of teamwork are declining. The competition between the child and adolescent program and the adult program has caused some intense (but suppressed) negative feelings between some members of the programs.

The organization is bureaucratic: the director of the Center makes all decisions and only infrequently consults with program directors. Lines of communication follow a vertical chain of command, and thus the ideas of many of the therapists are not solicited. Employees were hired for specific purposes and are to work only to achieve those purposes. The rules of the organization, although explicitly stated in a manual, are never discussed. The director keeps a complete but disorganized set of records.

Change occurs at the Center in a "top-down" fashion. Typically, members of the organization are informed of changes through memoranda, although the nature of changes is described without any rationale. Clearly there is the assumption that each change will be acceptable and willingly carried out without discussion.

The Center does not place adequate emphasis on the personal or professional growth of its staff. It assumes that talented people have been hired and that they will take care of their own professional and personal needs. No attempts are made to include employees in the emotional "ownership" of the Center. An environment that nurtures employee growth is lacking at the Center, and networking is not used as a supplement to the director's leadership.

The Center is an organization in trouble. Although it and the demand for diversified services are growing rapidly, it is run as if it were still a small operation with a simple mission. The organization is still doing what it does well, but the price it is paying has alerted the director to the need for consultation.

THE APPROACHES TO CONSULTATION

In each illustration of the approaches below, you can assume that the consultant engages in all the appropriate behaviors expected of a highly professional, competent consultant. Most approaches to consultation adhere to some version of the generic model previously discussed. You can also assume that the consultant proceeds in the same sequence as the generic model. Thus, a good working relationship is established, a problem defined, a contract agreed upon, and entry accomplished. For the sake of brevity, I do not describe these "basics" of effective consultation behavior in each illustration. Rather, I attempt to provide the essence of each approach so that you can make appropriate comparisons and contrasts.

Organizational Consultation

Education/Training Approach

As I consult with Acme Human Services Center within the education/training framework, I attempt to enhance the overall effectiveness of the organization by improving the professional effectiveness of the members of the substance-abuse program with respect to cocaine-related substance-abuse counseling. I assume that a blend of didactic and experimental learning is the best approach.

The members of the substance-abuse team would probably need information related to cocaine abuse and some skills in working with abusers of the drug.

As a consultant using this approach, I function as an expert technological advisor, teacher, and trainer. Because I realize that the staff of the substance-abuse program is small and consists of skilled professionals, I tailor my consultation to their specific needs and am quite specific in the education and training I provide them.

The role of the consultees is that of learners. They have all volunteered for the consultation and meet my expectations that they will be interested and cooperative learners and will invest themselves in the consultation process. They realize that they need some assistance in working with cocaine abusers and are highly involved in the entire consultation process.

My first step is to conduct a needs assessment of the consultees. I want to make sure that they perceive a need for education and training in cocaine substance abuse. Further, I want to assess what they know and can already do related to working with cocaine abusers. Next, I want to determine what they need to learn to work more effectively with cocaine abusers. I construct a questionnaire to acquire this information and hold a brief meeting with each individual consultee. I then hold one meeting with the entire group to determine whether the information I received from them accurately reflects their perceptions of their needs.

Based on the results of the needs assessment, I plan the education/training. The results of the assessment indicate that the staff requires information and training in diagnosing cocaine abuse, particularly in determining patterns of pathological use, impairments of social and occupational functioning related to its use, determination of the duration of the disturbance, and determination of the probability of relapse into abuse. Utilizing the principles of adult learning, I assume that the participants are self-directing, can discuss many of their own experiences pertinent to the topic, and are ready to learn. For the primary tools of consultation, I plan a series of activities around the expressed needs of the consultees: lectures with audiovisual aids, several small group discussions, modeling and practice of diagnostic skills related to cocaine abuse, and feedback. I determine that four, two-hour sessions are needed to accomplish the goals of consultation.

As I implement the education/training consultation, I create a climate of mutual respect and am particularly careful not to "speak down" to the consultees or flaunt my knowledge of cocaine abuse. I am very open about what I know and don't know about the topic and about my experiences in working with cocaine abusers. During the course of consultation I include some of my own successes and failures with cocaine abusers. I remain flexible, keep a professional yet light atmosphere, and use humor when appropriate. I provide a great deal of time for practice of the skills required by the consultees, particularly during the last two sessions.

In evaluating the education/training, I use a pre-post questionnaire on the consultee's knowledge of cocaine abuse and behavioral checklists to determine their levels of functioning in applying their newly acquired skills. I have them evaluate the consultation in terms of its effect, adequacy, and value. Finally, I arrange for a follow-up meeting in 60 days to assess the impact of the training and for ironing out any unanticipated problems.

Program Approach

As a consultant with a program orientation, I am very much interested in working with the Acme Human Services Center in evaluating their employee assistance programs. In this case, the Center is purchasing my expertise in program evaluation so that it can determine the relative success of its employee assistance programs. The goal of program evaluation consultation is to improve current decision making about how a program should function. I have been hired to answer the question, "To what degree are the goals of the employee assistance programs being met?" In addition, I have been retained to assist the director of the Center and the program heads to be more effective program evaluators in their own rights.

My role is that of technological expert in program evaluation. I attempt to provide accurate, timely, and useful information to the director and program heads. I use as much of a collaborative approach as the skills of the consultees permit. I meet with the consultees to review the goals of the employee assistance program, develop a possible program evaluation design and present it to the consultees for their feedback, obtain their feedback, and redesign the evaluation accordingly. Much of my time is spent in preparing and planning the evaluation design.

The consultees provide me with as much information as possible about the employee assistance program, for such information is needed when I design the evaluation. I spend a lot of time with the consultees so that I can become very familiar with the program. I ask the director to give the head of the employee assistance program a great deal of free time so that she will feel free to cooperate, and I also discuss with the director what he intends to do with the results of the program evaluation. His reply indicates that my evaluation will be used for modifying the programs (if necessary) and for running the program on a day-to-day basis.

After preparing the program evaluation design, I collect some of the data and have consultees collect the rest of it. In evaluating the goals of the employee assistance program, I systematically collect data on the number of users of the services, the effects of the services on the users, attitudes of the users and the service providers toward the program, and attitudes of members of the organizations in which employee assistance programs are provided (including those who did not partake of the services). I collect this data by using questionnaires and surveys, by observing the programs (but not the direct delivery of services to clients), by conducting interviews of a few randomly selected volunteer service providers and clients, and by examining the programs' records on the number of clients for the various services offered and the duration of those services.

After collecting the data, I analyze it. I bear in mind the four standards of proper evaluation: accuracy, utility, feasibility, and propriety. I keep all the appropriate parties involved and apprised of my findings as they emerge. My findings indicate that only 3% of the employees use the employee assistance program for an average of three contacts. Reasons for this scant participation are the stigma of being seen going to a counselor at work and fear that confidentiality will somehow be broken. Attitudes of clients and service providers are quite positive in terms of the perceived effectiveness of the services provided. Nonusers of the program indicate that they would be more likely to use it if services were provided at the Center, not at the work site, and if the program did not have a reputation for serving only substance abusers. Measures that counselors took with their clients resulted in positive gains by the clients.

My final task is to present this data to the director and program head. I suggest that all personnel involved in the program be present at a "feedback meeting" in which I outline the results of the evaluation and facilitate a planning session based on the evaluation. At that meeting, I use graphics to explain the evaluation and what the data represent and mean. I avoid jargon but take care not to appear condescending. I then facilitate a planning session in which plans are made to publicize the program more thoroughly and promote it as a positive growth experience for the participants. Plans are also made to permit the employees the option of coming to the Center for services. I then summarize the evaluation, describe the next steps in which the consultees engage, and make arrangements for a follow-up visit.

Doctor-Patient Approach

The director had no idea why there was friction between the child and adolescent program and the adult program. When an organization knows that something is wrong but does not know exactly what, the doctor-patient model of consultation can be very helpful.

As a consultant using the doctor-patient approach, my job is to find out what is wrong and prescribe a solution. The organization is purchasing my expertise in diagnosis and prescription and expects me to determine what is precipitating the conflict between the two programs. I realize that my very presence is an intervention that affects how the problem will be diagnosed. Because of this, I spend time building effective relationships with the parties involved in and affected by the consultation. By taking the time to build such relationships, I increase the probability that the information obtained from the parties involved will be straightforward and honest.

My primary goal is to define the problem that is causing friction between the two programs and recommend a viable solution. I assume that the friction is merely a symptom of some broader problem. At this time I am not concerned about helping the organization enhance its diagnostic and prescriptive abilities.

In the doctor-patient approach, I function as an expert. I create relationships with the appropriate parties, collect and analyze information, make a diagnosis, and prescribe a solution. I must be able to "read" the organization and determine what data to obtain and how to obtain it.

The consultees are the "patients," and I need them to describe the symptoms of the problem as they see them. I attempt to create conditions in which they can provide truthful, complete information. I ask the consultees to be sure that they understand and are willing to implement my solution. I gather data about the organization's purpose, its structure, and the relationships, leadership, and reward structure within it. I gather this data by interviewing each member of each program, primarily asking them about their program and their perceptions of the other program. Confidentiality is assured to all involved.

From these interviews the child and adolescent program emerges as one that perceives itself to be out of favor with its director; the program members see themselves as "second class citizens" in his eyes and they question how they fit into the director's future plans. Some members of the child and adolescent team thought that the entire program would be scrapped so that the organization could become involved to a greater degree in the more profitable adult service area. In addition, the head of the adult program is seen as a favorite of the director who has undue influence in the day-to-day operation of the entire agency. These factors have caused the strain between the two programs.

Based on this analysis, I formulate some solutions that are tailored to the organization and its capability for solving its own problems. First, I recommend a series of group meetings between the members of the two programs using third-party conflict resolution. Second, I recommend that the director make a written statement concerning the short- and long-term future of each program. Third, I recommend that the director appoint all program heads to an advisory committee that he will chair. Finally, I encourage the director to implement these changes.

Process Approach

The Center's director knows that the leadership style of the organization must change. The director used to believe that an effective leader needed to control all the factors related to running an organization: employees' work-related behavior, record keeping, and decision making. This procedure worked relatively effectively until the Center started to grow in size and complexity. The director then continually found himself in a reactive posture he described in this way: "I feel like I am running from one brush fire to another. I am putting in 16-hour days. All the stress is affecting how I relate to clients and my employees. I think I need my own personal employee assistance program!"

As a process consultant, I realize that leadership is a process variable in managing any organization. The director already knows that leadership style changes are imperative, so I am confident that some substantial progress can be made in changing how the organization is managed. The director has asked me to observe him in action for one week to get a feel for how he manages, and he also asked me to observe each of the program heads for two days. Such observations give me some ideas about their decision-making styles and underlying assumptions about the nature of human beings that inevitably influence leadership style.

My goals as a process consultant are to help the director and the program heads become aware of their everyday leadership and decision-making behavior and to help them identify and modify them in ways that are consistent with their goals. I accomplish these outcomes by being a facilitator of self-discovery for each consultee. I assist in gathering data to shed light on leadership and decision-making procedures as they relate to the current state of affairs within the organization. In addition, I help the consultees diagnose what is being done and what yet needs to be done.

The director's goal is to delegate more authority, decision-making responsibility, and administrative tasks to the program heads. The program heads' goal is to develop leadership and decision-making skills that are necessary for their new responsibilities. Their roles are those of active collaborators; they must translate their vague perceptions into specific insights and then act on those insights.

I provide minimum structure in carrying out my assignment and use clarifying questions and probes to stimulate the consultees' thoughts on their own current behavior. As human service professionals with administrative experience, the consultees have decision-making and problem-solving skills on which I can capitalize. The consultees also assist me by suggesting interventions they think would be helpful. In this case, they ask for feedback on their leadership and decision-making skills from me.

I proceed by helping the consultees set goals and by observing them as they attempt to accomplish them. I help the consultees gather data concerning employees' perceptions of the leadership styles and decision-making procedures within the organization. Based on all this data, I help the consultees diagnose their problem—the need for practice in leadership and decision-making skills that involve input from all levels of the organization. I act as "director" and set up several role-playing situations in which the consultees practice the new skills. The director, for example, practices setting agendas for meetings, delegating authority, soliciting input from subordinates, and creating a strategic planning committee. The heads practice confrontation meetings, assertive behavior, and conflict resolution skills. After each role-playing segment, I coach the consultees in how they can increase their leadership and decision-making skills in an interpersonally effective manner. In addition, I make a few structural recommendations concerning how lines of authority can be set up within a small organization like the Center. I then help them develop ways to monitor their own progress in these areas.

Mental Health Consultation

Client-Centered Case Approach

Client-centered case consultation does not deal with issues residing within the consultee. Rather, the contract specifies that I, as a mental health consultant, would examine the consultee's client concerning some professional matter and write a report that includes recommendations. I operate in a fashion analogous to the doctor-patient approach to organizational consultation except the diagnosis and prescription are based on data concerning a client and not some aspect of an organization.

My focus is on the client, and my aim is to advise the consultee on how to "fix" some problem concerning the client under consideration. I examine the client, make some form of assessment and diagnosis, and provide the consultee with a report containing suggestions and recommendations to help the client. I spend very little time with the consultee.

A consultee from the Center seeks my help in determining how to go about getting a mother and teenage daughter to communicate openly during their counseling sessions. I function as an expert in parent-child interactions and use my expertise in diagnosing the causes of toxic relationships and in prescribing remedies for improving them.

The consultee is to provide me with as much pertinent information as possible regarding the difficulties the clients are having in communicating with each other in general and in the counseling sessions in particular. The consultee gathers additional information on the clients' family and relates it to me. The consultee is responsible for reading my report and determining whether to implement the recommendations I make.

I consult with the consultee for one session at the Center. During this time I build a relationship with her and get a feel for her perceptions of the particulars of the work-related problem. I assess the consultee's general abilities as she discusses the case and consider the strengths and weaknesses of the Center. As I do this, I come to the realization that my consultee is likely to get very little individual or group supervision on this case because of the very busy state of affairs at the Center. I realize that I need to devise a plan that is short-term and well within the consultee's level of expertise. My assessment is that the counselor is a talented professional but has had relatively little experience in helping parents and children work through communication difficulties during the counseling process.

Next I interview the mother and daughter, first together and then separately. My talk with the mother reveals that she had found out about and told her husband about a sexual experience of their daughter. According to the mother, the father had severely "beaten" the daughter. I pursue this topic in terms of the current state of affairs in the mother-daughter relationship.

Based on all the information I have gathered, I write up a report for the consultee and discuss it with her at our final meeting. After telling her that she is under no obligation to follow through on my recommendations, I proceed to share them with her. I suggest that the counselor see the mother and daughter on an individual basis for two or three sessions in order to get to know each of them better and to develop a more trusting relationship with each. Such a procedure would create the conditions that enable the mother and daughter to communicate more effectively in subsequent sessions together. I also suggest that she utilize a nondirective counseling style for the purpose of enhancing the relationship between the mother and daughter. These recommendations are well within the professional competencies of the counselor and have a high probability of being successful. No special training is necessary, nor were there any increased demands for supervision. As a final step, I arrange for a follow-up session in about six weeks.

Consultee-Centered Case Approach

When applying consultee-centered case consultation, my primary goal is to improve the ability of my consultee to work more effectively with the kind of case under consideration so that the consultee will function more effectively with similar clients in the future. The Center retains me as a consultant because no one at the Center has sufficient time for routine consultation. I am available to all staff. The case at hand involves a psychologist who is working with a female client who, in the words of the psychologist, "has a lot of anger inside of her that she needs to express." As I listen about the case, I develop a strong hunch that some of the unresolved needs of the consultee are blocking his effectiveness in the case.

I play the roles of detective, expert, and educator in this approach to mental health consultation. I determine what emotional and cognitive factors within the consultee are blocking progress in the case and give the consultee specific information he can use to help the client.

While discussing the case, the consultee mentions how much anger the client has and how important it is for the client to deal with that anger. The consultee discusses the case with some emotion and even a sense of desperation. He knows that I am going to make some recommendation to him, but he seems driven to convince me that I should recommend that anger be the central focus of the therapy.

As a matter of procedure, I do not interview or examine the client. Rather, I proceed by listening to my consultee's subjective view of the case. I determine that the consultee is suffering from a lack of professional objectivity about the case. I determine that there is little available supervisory assistance from members of the Center, so I decide to make some interventions designed to help the consultee regain more professional objectivity. I ask the consultee specific, detailed questions about the client's anger and the therapy interventions that have been used thus far. I am more interested in the consultee's version of the case than I am in the actual facts of the case. I am hoping that by discussing the client's need to express anger, the consultee will develop a broader, more objective perspective on the case.

I determine that theme interference is causing the lack of objectivity. It is as if the consultee is saying, "Unless she deals with the repressed anger in our therapy sessions, we will *never* make progress in therapy." The consultee cannot see that there are several ways to help the client besides helping her get in touch with and express her anger.

I attempt to use theme interference reduction through a combination of techniques. First, I keep the discussion on the client and remain calm in discussing the case. In addition, I remain very calm and objective about my relationship with the consultee. Finally, I tell the consultee a parable or "story" about a former client of mine who was similar to his. The client in my story never dealt with her repressed anger but still benefited tremendously from therapy. As I discuss the story, I notice a sense of reduced tension in the consultee about the case. He seems more objective and hopeful. I close the session by calmly scheduling a follow-up meeting. I express continued interest in the progress of the case and note that I am very hopeful that progress that can be made.

Program-Centered Administrative Approach

When applying program-centered administrative consultation, I work with the Center's director and the head of the substance-abuse program. They both want to develop a sense of direction for the program. My specific, primary goal is to help fix the program by helping these two consultees develop a sense of direction for the program. My general goals are to enhance the overall functioning of the program and increase the program development skills possessed by the director and the program head.

My role is that of an expert familiar with substance-abuse programs and how they operate. I collect information on the program and how it works, analyze that information, and recommend some solutions. I use my expertise in organizational theory in determining how to collect the information I need.

My consultees discuss with me why they hired me in the first place and what they think they want from consultation. They point out some of the organization's idiosyncracies and make suggestions about what staff I should contact in gathering information on the program. The administrators help me develop a timetable for consultation and the methods by which they will sanction my work throughout the Center. The director and program head provide me with as much information about the organization as possible and respond openly to my questions. The two administrators then develop a list of their reasons why the substance-abuse program has a lack of direction. Finally, they wish me good luck and let me know that they are available any time I have questions or need anything. They realize that they will have limited contact with me.

The program is a treatment program rather than a preventative one. I concentrate on looking at management and give some attention to the tasks that the program accomplishes. I examine agency records on information like unemployment rates, arrests for drug use and possession, and substance-use driving offenses. I interview key staff and administrators and find out that no one uses the information. Further, there are no records on the types of substances clients are abusing. No outcomes are recorded as a part of the program's objectives. Counselors and therapists in the program see clients as part of their caseloads but have little input into the overall workings of the program.

I proceed through the stages of formulating a simplistic solution, first becoming very confused about the entire situation and then getting a firm grasp of the consultation problem. Based on this information, I develop a set of tentative recommendations, which I feed back to all parties involved irrespective of their ranks within the organization. Based on the reactions I get, I modify those recommendations. The final list of recommendations looks something like this:

1. Use available data to determine community needs relative to substance abuse and, based on current staff, modify the program.
2. Set objectives and develop a philosophy for the program.

3. Point out that alcohol and cocaine abuse are on the rise in the community and that treatment of these illnesses could become the central focus of the program.
4. Keep detailed records of the contacts personnel have with substance-abuse cases.

These recommendations and the report that contains them are distributed to the appropriate people at the Center. It is up to the director to determine if and how my recommendations are to be implemented. I then set up a follow-up session to occur six months from the date of the report's distribution.

Consultee-Centered Administrative Approach

As a consultant applying consultee-centered administrative consultation, I am involved in the most complex and demanding type of mental health consultation. I am asked to work with the director and the head of the substance-abuse program regarding the program's lack of direction. The difference between this consultation and the example described under program-centered mental health consultation is that its main goal is to enhance the consultee's program development and maintenance skills, and its secondary goal is to improve specific programs.

My role is that of both expert and facilitator. I expect consultation to take a long time because I involve the consultees in every step along the way to help them improve their skills in developing plans and strategies related to the successful running of the substance-abuse program. I need the skills of knowing about organizations, how they are best managed, and how they change for the better. I also need the skill of "reading" an organization to pinpoint possible problem areas. I move about the Center as if I were a member and try to understand it from the employees' perspective. Because my role is complex, I need to make sure that the administrator lets everyone involved know precisely what my role is to be.

The director and program head are involved with me as much as possible in this collaborative effort. They lay the groundwork for my presence within the organization and provide the necessary sanctions for my presence. They arrange times for me to meet with everyone involved in the substance-abuse program so that I can present my findings.

As I begin to "float" through the Center, I make sure that no one sees me as a "spy" for the director. I want everyone in the program to see me as a helper and not a threat to their security. I am careful to build trusting relationships not only with the director and program head but also with all members of the substance-abuse program. I try to get them to gather the data they need to give the program a sense of direction. I know that their skills will be enhanced by discussing the data and the experience of gathering it. I help them use group meetings, interviews, and questionnaires as data collection devices and then help them discuss the data in meetings involving the entire program staff. As the consultees discuss the information, I notice that they think they know what is happening in the program and where the program is going but in fact do not.

I try to help them be more objective in analyzing the data by pointing out some key factors: there is no philosophy surrounding the program, there are no written objectives and goals for the program, and so forth. This information results in increased objectivity on their part. I am very patient and do not try to force my ideas on them. I take a relatively nondirective stance and ask them what they think various kinds of data mean.

Through my efforts the director and program head realize that if the substance-abuse program had a well-defined sense of direction, complete with philosophy, goals, objectives, and a strategic plan for the next five years, then a great deal of stress would be alleviated for all the parties involved. The director then appoints the head of the substance-abuse program to head a committee charged with developing the philosophy, goals, objectives, and strategic plan for the program. The committee consists of all substance-abuse program employees, and they are paid an honorarium beyond their normal salaries for their work. I agree to help the head of the substance-abuse program run this committee and to help him try out new leadership styles and techniques as the committee attempts to fulfill its charge.

Behavioral Consultation

Case Approach

As in client-centered case mental health consultation, my main objective in behavioral case consultation is to assist the consultee with a work-related problem in a given case. The difference between the two approaches is that in behavioral case consultation my work is within a behavioral framework. I work as a consultant in the Center and am available all day once a week.

My consultee is a masters-level social worker at the Center whose client is a male school teacher who wants to overcome his fear of flying in airplanes. My goal is to help the social worker create a positive outcome in this case.

I am an expert in behavioral technology and its application to counseling/therapy. I keep that role of expert throughout the consultation process, although I collaborate whenever possible with the consultee. I control the process of consultation, but the consultee determines the best course of action to take in regard to the case. I provide knowledge concerning the learning principles related to phobias about flying and make sure that all the stages of the consultation process are successfully accomplished.

As my link to the client, the consultee provides me with as much information as possible concerning the case. I get her to be as specific as possible about the case. Because she is my peer, she decides what course of action to take in helping the client with his phobia.

I lead the consultee through the stages of problem identification, problem analysis, plan implementation, and problem evaluation. First, we verify that a phobia about flying in airplanes exists. We next determine that the client does not possess "free floating" anxiety, but experiences only a few situation-specific anxieties. Then, we set a goal of having the client actually ride in an airplane with minimal anxiety. We determine that we can easily measure this by having the client use a checklist during the flight and by intermittently taking a pulse rate.

I illustrate how the process of classical conditioning has probably occurred and created the client's phobia. I then examine with the consultee how this conditioning maintains the client's phobia. Next, a plan is made in which the consultee will use systematic desensitization with the client.

Because the consultee does not know the procedure, I train her in it and monitor her handling of the case. I show her how to apply the general technique to the specific needs of the client by helping her develop a personalized strategy. I give her some books and videotapes so that she can do some independent studying. I role play systematic desensitization procedures with her, taking the role of her client. We design an evaluation that includes not only the successful completion of the desensitization strategy, but also whether or not the client actually flies in an airplane with acceptable levels of anxiety. We then arrange for a follow-up session in three months. When she feels ready, the consultee prepares to follow through on what she has learned.

Behavioral System Approach

Whereas when I consult from a behavioral case approach I focus on an individual client within a system, when I consult from a behavioral system approach I focus on the system itself.

My goal in this approach is to enhance the efficiency and effectiveness of the Center in terms of its stated function. The director invites me to "take a look at the Center" and then make some recommendations. He notes that the Center is growing very rapidly and that its affairs are in a constant state of disarray.

I function as an expert in the areas of behavioral technology and systems theory. I accomplish my goals by collaboratively guiding the director and program heads through defining and assessing the system, making selected interventions, and then evaluating the effects. I use behavioral technology to help the Center function more efficiently.

The consultees, who act as joint collaborators, determine what is to be done in consultation and how the results of consultation will be used. To accomplish this, they provide me with as much accurate information as they can. As the change agents within the Center, they have both the power and perspective to accomplish the goals of consultation.

I proceed by helping the consultees define the Center in terms of its structure and activities. We accomplish this by taking a week to observe what goes on in the Center's everyday routine. We then share our perceptions and come to a consensus on the Center's structure and activities. Once we have characterized the Center adequately, we are ready to assess it. We design questionnaires and arrange to observe the Center's various subsystems in order to evaluate the system. We try to answer the following question: What are the effects of the Center's structure and activities on the behavior of its members?

The major answer we obtain is that there is lack of direction among the Center's members because there are no defined goals and objectives for the various programs the Center offers. The consultees and I determine that the highest priority must be given to having each program develop, spell out, and adhere to a set of behavioral goals and objectives. We next set behavioral outcome goals that include what is to be accomplished, when, by whom, and under what conditions.

Criteria are set up to assess the quality of these goals, which are then evaluated. I suggest that the various programs modify their activities and structure to coincide with their newly written behavioral goals and objectives. The consultees agree. We then develop an evaluation to determine the degree to which each program behaves according to its specific goals and objectives. I arrange for a follow-up in six months to help the consultees discuss these evaluations and make appropriate adjustments.

Behavioral Technology Training Approach

When I consult from a behavioral technology training approach, I focus on enhancing my consultees' general and/or specific behavioral technology skills. The Center, particularly the child and adolescent program, was receiving more and more requests for classroom management strategies or "B-mod in the classroom" procedures from the local school system. None of the staff had professional experience with schools, but most had at least good general behavioral technology skills. Because of my expertise in behavioral technology and my many years of working with school systems and behavioral technology training, I was retained to train the entire staff of the child and adolescent program in behavioral classroom management skills.

My goal is to increase the consultees' skills in classroom management techniques so that they in turn can use behavior technology with school teachers concerned with classroom management. I make sure that the consultees have enough accurate information concerning classrooom management behavioral technology, have developed related competencies, and have a positive attitude toward the use of these skills.

The consultees should learn as best they can, integrate their knowledge about behavioral technology approaches to classroom management into their consultation skills, and attempt to create a positive attitude toward use of behavioral technology in the classroom.

I develop a training plan based on input from all the parties involved, including school personnel. I then implement that training plan using lectures, modeling, behavioral rehearsal, feedback, and reinforcement as my primary tools. Modeling that is followed by rehearsal and practice with feedback are stressed so that the consultee is able to perform the required skills well. I go to great lengths to demythologize behavior modification in the classroom. I provide rules of thumb for proceeding with classrooom management procedures, such as conducting observations and establishing token economies and "time-out" procedures. I have the Center's director come in and state specifically why this training is important to the consultees and the Center; he also comments on the types of rewards the consultees can expect from participation in the training.

I evaluate the training in several ways. First, I use a questionnaire that reveals attitudes toward the training itself. I administer a test that has the consultees specifically state what they think they have learned and their attitudes toward their newly-acquired knowledge and skills. A very important part of the evaluation comes six months later, when I observe while consultees consult with teachers on classroom management procedures derived from behavioral technology. At that time, I assess both the degree to which the consultees have transferred their knowledge and skills to actual school settings and the degree to which they effectively use the skills.

Blended Approach

In working in my own style, I become aware of my own values, strengths, and weaknesses and those of the Center as well. I spend a great deal of time building a good working relationship with the director because I know that he must sanction my presence and that he is an excellent resource for the duration of the consultation process. I not only build a relationship but ask several penetrating questions that help the director determine what he really wants from me and how that coincides with what I can offer.

I ask him about the lack of direction within the Center and what it means in terms of what it is like to work there, how it affects morale, and what it implies for leadership and other administrative functions. I ask about any unwritten rules and regulations and how they affect the quality of communication. I ask for his views about the human side of work and the process events that occur every day within the organization. Through this process of questioning and clarifying, I provide the director a more objective view of his organization. I then help him view the Center more realistically and assess its strengths and weaknesses.

We then come to a consensus about what two or three problem areas have the highest priority. Once we have identified these problem areas—lack of direction, inadequate leadership in a growing organization, and inadequate knowledge and skills to meet client demands—I help him select some desired outcomes. The director decides that the organization should increase its morale significantly, obtain the skills it needs to best serve its clients, and have an administrative structure that fosters better communication and understanding among the Center's employees.

I am introduced at a staff meeting attended by all the employees of the Center. I reassure them that I am there to help and that the director has assured me that confidentiality will be maintained. I tell them that there are neither sacred cows nor hidden agendas. I spend the next week observing various employees to get a feel for the Center's operation, and then I select five people to interview concerning their perceptions of the three major problem areas the director and I have identified. I design a questionnaire and send it to the remaining employees. I take a relatively quick look at past memos, the minutes of meetings, and similar records to assist my diagnosis of what specific problems the Center is having.

I next have a series of meetings with the entire staff to provide the results of my observations, my examination of the Center's records, my interviews, and the questionnaire. All of the results and subsequent discussion of them confirm my hypothesis that people at the Center are overworked and do not feel that they have any "ownership" of the organization. They feel like they are too busy to do anything about this problem except grumble and complain about the director. Many relate that although they are paid quite well, money alone does not compensate for their frustration as professionals with jobs in which they cannot affect anything or anyone except their clients.

I suggest that we hold a series of three meetings, one each on trying to solve each of the three problem areas identified. The meetings provide the staff a sense of ownership and importance. I conduct the three meetings, which I lead with each of the three program heads. I use the nominal group technique in each case.

The major solutions for the leadership problem are use of semiautonomous work groups, formation of a policy committee, design of an organizational chart, and in-service leadership training for all staff.

The major solutions for the morale problem are a limit on caseload numbers, weekly staff meeting, weekly group supervision for all staff that provide direct services, and development of a social committee with rotating membership.

The major solutions for the skills deficit in the staff relative to the needs of clients are a series of training sessions on cocaine abuse and its treatment, behavior management strategies for consulting with public school teachers, and a staff development program for all employees.

At the end of the third meeting we prioritize the solutions. I then take two weeks to put all the solutions into a feasible plan that the Center can implement. I also develop an evaluation scheme so the Center can determine the degree to which their goals are being met.

I present the plan and evaluation scheme to the Center's entire staff for their discussion, modification, and approval. I then arrange for four follow-up meetings at three-month intervals.

As I reflect on this consultation at a later date, I realize that many of my values were operating and that I maintained awareness of this during the entire consultation experience. I noticed that there were very few values conflicts with the Center's director or with anyone else at the Center. We all believed that the Center should deliver quality services to its clients and that when it couldn't do that, it should get the appropriate education and training. We all believed that old, autocratic ways of leadership don't work very well in leading talented professionals and in running complex organizations. We all believed that happy people make happy workers and that conditions at the work site profoundly affect workers' morale.

So this is how I would approach this situation. I examine my values and those of the Center and its staff. I determine what they need and the degree to which I can fulfill that need. Before I proceed, I ask myself a very important question: Am I willing to commit to seeing this consultation through to its successful conclusion?

SUMMARY

This chapter encourages you to begin to look at your own personal model of consultation. This chapter has applied the various approaches to organizational, mental health, and behavioral consultation to some work-related problem within a particular organization. Table 12.1 summarizes the major focus of each approach.

TABLE 12.1   The Major Focus of Several Consultation Approaches

Approach	Major Focus
Organizational	
Education/Training	Training or educating consultees to be more effective in some area
Program	Assisting organization with some aspect of a program, frequently evaluation
Doctor/Patient	Entering an organization, diagnosing a problem and prescribing a solution
Process	Assisting consultees to be better decision makers and problem solvers in the future
Mental Health	
Client-centered case	Helping a consultee with a client (with minimal contact with consultee)
Consultee-centered case	Considers work-related problem to reside in the consultee; helping consultee by focusing on case
Program-centered administrative	Helping administrator fix problem with some program
Consultee-centered administrative	Helping administrator and other consultees develop their skills to improve the mental-health aspects of the organization and its programs
Behavioral	
Case	Helping a consultee apply behavioral technology to a case
System	Assisting an organization to be more effective by using behavioral technology
Training	Training consultees to improve their skills in general and/or specific areas of behavioral technology

Each approach could have been applied in a variety of ways; each example merely illustrated how a consultant applying that approach might proceed. For each approach the goals of consultation were stated, the roles and functions of the consultant and consultees described, and application of the approach illustrated.

QUESTIONS FOR REFLECTION

1. Which of the approaches just described most emphasize the quality of the consultation relationship?
2. Of the cases just described, in which would consultation be the most difficult to adequately evaluate?
3. Do you see similarities among behavioral system consultation, doctor/patient consultation, and process consultation? Explain your answer.
4. Would you proceed in a manner different from mine if you were asked to perform process consultation? If so, how?
5. What similarities did you notice among all the different approaches?
6. What differences did you detect among the various approaches?
7. Which approach appeals to you the most, based on your reading of this chapter? Why?
8. Of the cases discussed, in which one would you most like to have been the consultant? Why?
9. With which approach would you have the most difficulty in the role of consultant? Why?
10. For which approaches would you actively seek out additional training?

SUGGESTED SUPPLEMENTARY READINGS

Alpert, J. L. (1982). *Psychological consultation in educational settings*. San Francisco: Jossey-Bass. This text consists of a series of detailed reports about consultation. Using a type of case-study format, each chapter emphasizes a different type of consultation in an educational setting. A final section of the book discusses issues such as the consultant's knowledge of the system, vested interests, and degree of accountability to the system. This book is limited in that it focuses only on consultation in educational settings; still, it provides the reader a wealth of anecdotes about consultation not found in journal articles or most texts. Read this book if you want to get a feel for the "hands-on" aspects of consultation.

Blake, R. R., & Mouton, J. S. (1976). *Consultation*. Reading, MA: Addison-Wesley. Every chapter in this text is filled with brief examples of consultation interventions with individuals, groups, and organizations. Problem areas addressed range from morale to leadership, and examples are provided across a variety of settings. A reading of this lengthy text will provide a wealth of information about the great diversity of consultation interventions.

EPILOGUE

I hope that you have enjoyed and benefited from this book. Functioning as a consultant can be one of the most enjoyable activities in which human services professionals engage. To feel the joy of helping another person or group of people become more effective in their work is truly an uplifting experience. Consultation is a relationship among humans—it needs to be performed with a personal touch. It is more than a science, more than an art, more than a craft: it is all of these together, plus a commitment—commitment to oneself as a consultant, to the people with whom one consults, and to the ever-challenging task of transmitting ideas and skills from the consultant to the consultee.

References

ABIDIN, R. R. (1975). Negative effects of behavioral consultation: "I know I ought to, but it hurts too much." *Journal of School Psychology, 13*(1), 51–57.

ALLEN, C. T., & FORMAN, S. G. (1984). Efficacy of methods of training teachers in behavior modification. *School Psychology Review, 13*(1), 26–32.

ALPERT, J. L. (1982a). (Ed.). *Psychological consultation in educational settings.* San Francisco: Jossey-Bass.

ALPERT, J. L. (1982b). Assessing problems and needs in an elementary school. In J. L. Alpert (Ed.), *Psychological consultation in educational settings* (pp. 33–54). San Francisco: Jossey-Bass.

ALPERT, J. L. (1982c). Conclusions: Issues and similarities across cases. In J. L. Alpert (Ed.), *Psychological consultation in educational settings* (pp. 304–316). San Francisco: Jossey-Bass.

ALPERT, J., & SILVERSTEIN, J. (1985). Mental health consultation: Historical, present and future perspectives. In J. R. Bergan (Ed.), *School psychology in contemporary society* (pp. 121–138). Columbus, Ohio: Merrill.

ALTROCCHI, J. (1972). Mental health consultation. In S. E. Golann & C. Eisdorfer (Eds.), *Handbook of community mental health* (pp. 477–508). New York: Appleton-Century-Crofts.

AMERICAN ASSOCIATION FOR COUNSELING AND DEVELOPMENT. (1981). *Ethical standards* (rev. ed.). Alexandria, Va: Author.

AMERICAN PSYCHOLOGICAL ASSOCIATION. (1981). Ethical principles of psychologists (rev. ed.). Washington, D.C.: Author.

ANDERSON, S. B., & BALL, S. (1978). *The profession and practice of program evaluation.* San Francisco: Jossey-Bass.

ANDERSON, W. F., FRIEDEN, B. J., & MURPHY, M. J. (Eds.). (1977). *Managing human services.* Washington, D.C.: The International City Management Association.

ANTON, J. L. (1978). Studying individual change. In L. Goldman (Ed.), *Research methods for counselors* (pp. 117–153). New York: Wiley.

APLIN, J. C. (1978). Structural change vs. behavioral change. *Personnel and Guidance Journal, 56*(7), 407–411.

APLIN, J. C. (1985). Business realities and organizational consultation. *Counseling psychologist, 13*(3), 396–402.

AQUILAR, J. F. (1967). *Scanning the business environment.* New York: Macmillan.

ARGYRIS, C. (1964). *Integrating the individual and the organization.* New York: Wiley.

ARGYRIS, C. (1970). *Intervention theory and method: A behavioral science view.* Reading, Mass.: Addison-Wesley.

ARGYRIS, C. (1976). Explorations in consulting-client relationships. In W. G. Bennis, K. D. Benne, R. Chin, & K. E. Corey (Eds.), *The planning of change* (3rd ed.) (pp. 331–352). New York: Holt, Rinehart & Winston.

ARY, D., JACOBS, L. C., & RAZAVIEH, A. (1985). *Introduction to research in education* (3rd ed.). New York: Holt, Rinehart & Winston.

ASHFORD, S. J., & CUMMINGS, L. L. (1983). Feedback as an individual resource: Personal strategies of creating information. *Organizational Behavior and Human Performance, 32,* 370–398.

ASTD (1987). *1987 who's who in training and development.* Alexandria, Va.: American Society for Training and Development.

BACKER, T. E. (1985). The future of organizational consulting. *Consultation, 4(1),* 17–29.

BANDURA, A. (1977). *Social learning theory.* Englewood Cliffs, N.J.: Prentice-Hall.

BARLOW, D. H., HAYES, S. C., & NELSON, R. O. (1984). *The scientist practitioner.* New York: Pergamon Press.

BARLOW, D. H., & HERSEN, M. (1984). *Single case experimental designs* (2nd ed.). New York: Pergamon Press.

BECKHARD, R. (1969). *Organization development: Strategies and models.* Reading, Mass.: Addison Wesley.

BECKHARD, R. (1978). Optimizing team-building efforts. In W. L. French, C. H. Bell, Jr., & R. A. Zawacki (Eds.), *Organization development: Theory, practice and research* (pp. 149–155). Dallas: Business Publications.

BECKHARD, R. (1979). Organization changing through consulting and training. In D. P. Sinha (Ed.), *Consultants and consultant styles* (pp. 17–44). New Delhi, India: Vision Books.

BEER, M. (1980). *Organization change and development: A systems view.* Glenview, Ill.: Scott, Foresman.

BEISSER, A. R., & GREEN, R. (1972). *Mental health consultation and education.* Palo Alto, Calif.: National Press Books.

BELL, C. R., & NADLER, L. (Eds.). (1979a). *The client-consultant handbook.* Houston: Gulf Publishing.

BELL, C. R., & NADLER, L. (1979b). Introduction to the client-consultant relationship. In C. R. Bell and L. Nadler (Eds.), *The client-consultant handbook* (pp. 1–7). Houston: Gulf Publishing.

BELL, C. R., & NADLER, L. (1979c). Disengagement and closure. In C. R. Bell and L. Nadler (Eds.), *The client-consultant handbook* (pp. 210–214). Houston: Gulf Publishing.

BELL, C. R., & NADLER, L. (1979d). Client-consultant roles. In C. R. Bell & L. Nadler (Eds.), *The client-consultant handbook* (pp. 39–43). Houston: Gulf Publishing.

BELL, C. R. & NADLER, L. (Eds.). (1985). *Clients and consultants: Meeting and exceeding expectations* (2nd ed.). Houston: Gulf Publishing.

BELLACK, A. S., & HERSEN, M. (Eds.). (1985). *Dictionary of behavior therapy techniques.* New York: Pergamon Press.

BENNIS, W. G., BENNE, K. D., CHIN, R., & COREY, K. E. (Eds.). (1976). *The planning of change.* New York: Holt, Rinehart & Winston.

BERGAN, J. R. (1977). *Behavioral consultation.* Columbus, Ohio: Merrill.

BERGAN, J. R. & TOMBARI, M. L. (1975). The analysis of verbal interactions occurring during consultation. *Journal of School Psychology, 13(3),* 209–226.

BERGAN, J. R. & TOMBARI, M. L. (1976). Consultant skill and efficiency and the implementation and outcomes of consultation. *Journal of School Psychology, 14(1),* 3–14.

BERLIN, I. N. (1977). Some lessons learned in 25 years of mental health consultation to schools. In S. C. Plog and P. I. Ahmed (Eds.), *Principles and techniques of mental health consultation* (pp. 23–48). New York: Plenum.

BERNE, E. (1961). *Transactional analysis in psychotherapy.* New York: Random House.

BERNE, E. (1964). *Games people play.* New York: Grove Press.

BIRNBRAUER, H. (1987). Evaluation techniques that work. *Training and Development Journal, 41(7),* 53–55.

BITTEL, L. R. (1972). *The nine master keys of management.* New York: McGraw-Hill.

BLAKE, R. R., & MOUTON, J. S. (1976). *Consultation.* Reading, Mass: Addison-Wesley.

BLAKE, R. R., & MOUTON, J. S. (1978). Toward a general theory of consultation. *Personnel and Guidance Journal, 56*(6), 328–330.

BLAKE, R. R., & MOUTON, J. S. (1983). *Consultation: A handbook for individual and organization development* (2nd ed.). Reading, Mass.: Addison-Wesley.

BLAKE, R. R., SHEPARD, H. A., & MOUTON, J. S. (1965). *Managing intergroup conflict in industry.* Houston: Gulf Publishing.

BLOCK, P. (1981). *Flawless consulting: A guide to getting your expertise used.* Austin, Tex.: Learning Concepts.

BLOOM, B. L. (1984). *Community mental health: A general introduction* (2nd ed.). Pacific Grove, Calif.: Brooks/Cole.

BOSS, R. W. (1985). The psychological contract: A key to effective organization development consultation. *Consultation, 4*(4), 284–304.

BRADFORD, L. P., GIBB, J. R., & BENNE, K. D. (Eds.). (1964). *T-group theory and the laboratory method.* New York: Wiley.

BRODSKY, S. L. (1977). The ambivalent consultee: The special problems of consultation to criminal justice agencies. In S. C. Plog and P. I. Ahmed (Eds.), *Principles and techniques of mental health consultation* (pp. 135–149). New York: Plenum.

BROWN, D. (1985). The preservice training and supervision of consultants. *The Counseling Psychologist, 13*(3), 410–425.

BROWN, D., PRYZWANSKY, W. B., & SCHULTE, A. C. (1987). *Psychological consultation: Introduction to theory and practice.* Boston: Allyn & Bacon.

BROWN, D. T., & KURPIUS, D. J. (1985). Guest editors' introduction. *The counseling psychologist, 13*(3), 333–335.

BROWN, D., WYNE, M. D., BLACKBURN, J. E., & POWELL, W. C. (1979). *Consultation.* Boston: Allyn & Bacon.

BROWN, V. B., & FRASER, M. (1985). Planning and shaping of the mental health delivery system of the future. *Consultation, 4*(3), 220–231.

BRUBAKER, J. C. (1978). Futures consultation: Designing desirable futures. *Personnel and Guidance Journal, 56,* 428–431.

BURGES, B. (1976). *Facts and figures: A layman's guide to conducting surveys.* Boston: Institute for Responsive Education.

BURKE, W. W. (1980). Organization development and bureaucracy in the 1980's. *Journal of applied behavioral science, 16*(3), 423–437.

CAMPBELL, D. T., & STANLEY, J. C. (1966). Experimental and quasi-experimental designs for research. Chicago: Rand McNally.

CANNELL, C. F., & KAHN, R. L. (1972). The collection of data by interviewing. In N. Margulies & A. P. Raia (Eds.), *Organizational development: Values, process, and technology* (pp. 135–162). New York: McGraw-Hill.

CAPLAN, G. (1970). *The theory and practice of mental health consultation.* New York: Basic Books.

CAPLAN, G. (1974). *Support systems and community health: Lectures in concept development.* New York: Behavioral Publications.

CAPLAN, G. (1977). Mental health consultation: Retrospect and prospect. In S. C. Plog & P. I. Ahmed (Eds.), *Principles and techniques of mental health consultation* (pp. 9–21). New York: Plenum.

CARLISLE, H. (1982). *Management: Concepts, methods, and applications* (2nd ed.). Chicago: S.R.A..

CARNER, L. A. (1982). Developing a consultative contract. In J. L. Alpert (Ed.), *Psychological consultation in educational settings* (pp. 8–32). San Francisco: Jossey-Bass.

CHALOFSKY, N. & LINCOLN, C. I. (1983). *Up the HRD ladder: A guide for professional growth.* Reading, Mass.: Addison-Wesley.

CHANDLER, L. A. (1985). *Children under stress* (2nd ed.). Springfield, Ill.: Charles C Thomas.

CHAPIRO, J. (1981). What kind of a system is an organization and with what metaphors do we describe it? In R. Lippitt & G. Lippitt (Eds.), *Systems thinking—a resource for organization diagnosis and intervention* (Vol. 3), (pp. 35–42). Washington, D.C.: International Consultants Foundation Series.

CHERNISS, C. (1976). Preentry issues in consultation. *American Journal of Community Psychology, 4*(1), 13–24.

CHERNISS, C. (1978). The consultation readiness scale: An attempt to improve consultation practice. *American Journal of Community Psychology, 6,* 15–21.

CHIN, R., & BENNE, K. D. (1976). General strategies for effecting changes in human systems. In W. G. Bennis, K. D. Benne, R. Chin, & K. E. Corey (Eds.), *The planning of change* (3rd ed.) (pp. 45–63). New York: Holt, Rinehart & Winston.

COHEN, W. A. (1985). *How to make it big as a consultant.* New York: AMACOM.

COHEN, A. R., FINK, S., & GADON, H. (1979). Key groups, not t-groups, for organization development. In D. P. Sinha (Ed.), *Consultants and consulting styles* (pp. 61–79). New Delhi, India: Vision Books.

COLLISON, B., & DUNLAP, D. (1978). Nominal group technique: A process for in-service and staff work. *School Counselor, 26,* 18–25.

CONOLEY, J. C. (Ed.). (1981). *Consultation in schools: Theory, research, procedures.* New York: Academic Press.

CONOLEY, J. C., & CONOLEY, C. W. (1982). *School consultation: A guide to practice and training.* New York: Pergamon Press.

COOKE, R. A. (1979). Managing change in organizations. In G. Zaltman (Ed.), *Management principles for nonprofit agencies and organizations* (pp. 154–209). New York: AMACOM.

COOPER, S., & HODGES, W. F. (Eds.). (1983). *The mental health consultation field.* New York: Human Sciences Press.

COREY, G. (1986). *Theory and practice of counseling and psychotherapy* (3rd ed.). Pacific Grove, Calif.: Brooks/Cole.

COREY, G., COREY, M. S., & CALLANAN, P. (1988). *Issues and ethics in the helping professions* (3rd ed.). Pacific Grove, Calif.: Brooks/Cole.

CORMIER, W. H., & CORMIER, L. S. (1985). *Interviewing strategies for helpers* (2nd ed.). Pacific Grove, Calif.: Brooks/Cole.

CRAFT, J. A. (1979). Managing human resources. In G. Zaltman (Ed.), *Management principles for nonprofit agencies and organizations.* New York: AMACOM.

CREGO, C. A. (1985). Ethics: The need for improved consultation training. *Counseling Psychologist, 13*(3), 473–476.

CROSS, P. (1984). *Adults as learners.* San Francisco: Jossey-Bass.

CUMMINGS, T., & MAXEY, C. (1985). Organization development and labor law: Implications for practice/malpractice. *Consultation, 4*(4), 331–342.

CYERT, R. M., & MARCH, J. G. (1972). *A behavioral theory of the firm.* Englewood Cliffs, N.J.: Prentice-Hall.

DEKOM, A. K. (1969). *The internal consultant.* New York: American Management Association.

DELBECQ, A. L., VAN DE VEN, A. H., & GUSTAFSON, D. H. (1975). *Group techniques for program planning: A guide to nominal group and delphi processes.* Glenview, Ill: Scott, Foresman.

DEWAR, D. L. (1980). *The quality circle guide to participation management.* Englewood Cliffs, N.J.: Prentice-Hall.

DICKINSON, D. J., & ADCOX, S. (1984). Program evaluation of a school consultation program. *Psychology in the Schools, 21,* 336–342.

DINKMEYER, D., & CARLSON, J. (1973). *Consulting: Facilitating human potential and change processes.* Columbus, Ohio: Merrill.

DOUGHERTY, A. M., & TAYLOR, B. L. B. (1983). Evaluation of peer helper programs. *Elementary School Guidance and Counseling, 18*(2), 130–136.

DUSTIN, D. (1985). On Brown's training and supervision of consultants. *The Counseling Psychologist, 13*(3), 436–440.

DUSTIN, D., & EHLY, S. (1984). Skills for effective consultation. *School Counselor, 32,* 23–29.

DWORKIN, A. L., & DWORKIN, E. P. (1975). A conceptual overview of selected consultation models. *American Journal of Community Psychology, 3*(2), 151–159.

DYER, W. G. (1977). *Team building: Issues and alternatives.* Reading, Mass.: Addison-Wesley.

EGAN, G. (1985). *Change agent skills in helping and human service settings.* Pacific Grove, Calif.: Brooks/Cole.

EGAN, G. (1986). *The skilled helper* (3rd ed.). Pacific Grove, Calif.: Brooks/Cole.

EGAN, G., & COWAN, M. A. (1979). *People in systems: A model for development in the human-service professions and education.* Pacific Grove, Calif.: Brooks/Cole.

EISEMAN, J. (1977). A third-party consultation model for resolving recurring conflicts collaboratively. *Journal of Applied Behavioral Science, 13,* 303–314.

FANIBANDA, D. K. (1976). Ethical issues of mental health consultation. *Professional Psychology, 7,* 547–552.

FELD, J. K., BERGAN, J. R., & STONE, C. A. (1987). Behavioral consultation. In C. A. Maher and S. G. Forman (Eds.), *A behavioral approach to education of children and youth* (pp. 183–219). Hillsdale, N.J.: Erlbaum.

FISHER, R., & URY, W. (1981). *Getting to yes: Negotiating without giving in.* New York: Penguin.

FITZ-GIBBON, C. T., & MORRIS, L. L. (1978). *How to design a program evaluation.* Beverly Hills, Calif.: Sage.

FORD, C. H. (1979). Developing a successful client-consultant relationship. In C. R. Bell & L. Nadler (Eds.), *The client-consultant handbook* (pp. 8–21). Houston: Gulf Publishing.

FORDYCE, J. K., & WEIL, R. (1971). *Managing with people.* Reading, Mass.: Addison-Wesley.

FORDYCE, J. K., & WEIL, R. (1978). Methods for finding out what is going on. In W. L. French, C. H. Bell, Jr., & R. A. Zawacki (Eds.), *Organization development: Theory, practice, and research* (pp. 121–129). Dallas: Business Publications.

FORMAN, S. G. (1984). Behavioral and cognitive-behavioral approaches to staff development. In C. A. Maher, R. J. Illback, and J. E. Zins (Eds.), *Organizational psychology in the schools: A handbook for professionals* (pp. 302–322). Springfield, Ill.: Charles C Thomas.

FREEDMAN, A. M. (1983). Evaluation of consultative services. In A. J. Lee and A. M. Freedman (Eds.), *Consultation skills reading* (pp. 87–88). Arlington, Va.: NTL Institute.

FRENCH, W. L. (1972). Organizational development: Objectives, assumptions and strategies. In N. Margulies & A. P. Raia (Eds.), *Organizational development values, process, and technology* (pp. 31–49). New York: McGraw-Hill.

FRENCH, W. L., & BELL, C. H., Jr. (1973). *Organization development: Behavioral science interventions for organizational improvement.* Englewood Cliffs, N.J.: Prentice-Hall.

FRENCH, W. L., & BELL, C. H., Jr. (1978). *Organization development: Behavioral science interventions for organizational improvement.* (2nd ed.). Englewood Cliffs, N.J.: Prentice-Hall.

FRENCH, W. L., & BELL, C. H., Jr. (1984). *Organization development: Behavioral science interventions for organization improvement* (3rd ed.). Englewood Cliffs, N.J.: Prentice-Hall.

FRENCH, W. L., BELL, C. H., Jr., & ZAWACKI, R. A. (Eds.). (1978). *Organization development: Theory, practice, and research.* Dallas: Business Publications.

FRIEDLANDER, F., & BROWN, L. D. (1974). Organization development. In M. R. Rosenzweig & L. W. Porter (Eds.), *Annual Review of Psychology, 25,* (pp. 219–340). Palo Alto, Calif.: Annual Reviews.

FROHMAN, M. A., SASHKIN, M., & KAVANAGH, M. J. (1978). Action-research as applied to organization development. In W. L. French, C. H. Bell, Jr., & R. A. Zawacki (Eds.), *Organization development: Theory, practice and research*. Dallas: Business Publications.

FUQUA, D. R., & NEWMAN, J. L. (1983). Models, principles, and methods of data utilization in organizational consultation. Paper presented at the American Personnel and Guidance Association Annual Convention, Washington, D.C.

FUQUA, D. R., & NEWMAN, J. L. (1985). Individual consultation. *The Counseling Psychologist, 13*(3), 390–395.

FURR, R. M. (1979). Surviving as a messenger: The client-consultant relationship during diagnosis. In C. R. Bell & L. Nadler (Eds.), *The client-consultant handbook* (pp. 119–128). Houston: Gulf Publishing.

GALLESSICH, J. (1982). *The profession and practice of consultation*. San Francisco: Jossey-Bass.

GALLESSICH, J. (1985). Toward a meta-theory of consultation. *Counseling Psychologist, 13*(3), 336–354.

GALLESSICH, J., LONG, K. M., & JENNINGS, S. (1986). Training of mental health consultants. In F. V. Mannino, E. J. Trickett, M. F. Shore, M. G. Kidder, & G. Levin (Eds.), *Handbook of mental health consultation* (pp. 279–317). Rockville, Md.: National Institute of Mental Health.

GATTIKER, U. E., & LARWOOD, L. (1985). Why do clients employ management consultants? *Consultation, 4*(2), 119–129.

GEORGE, R. L., & CRISTIANI, T. S. (1986). *Counseling: Theory and Practice* (2nd ed.). Englewood Cliffs, N.J.: Prentice-Hall.

GIBBS, J. T. (1980). The interpersonal orientation in mental health consultation: Toward a model of ethnic variations in consultation. *Journal of Community Psychology, 8,* 195–207.

GIBBS, J. T. (1985). Can we continue to be color-blind and class bound? *The Counseling Psychologist, 13*(3), 426–435.

GIBSON, R. L., & MITCHELL, M. H. (1981). *Introduction to guidance*. New York: Macmillan.

GILBERT, T. F. (1978). *Human competence: Engineering worthy performance*. New York: McGraw-Hill.

GLASER, E. M. (1981). Ethical issues in consultation practice with organizations. *Consultation, 1*(1) 12–16.

GLIDEWELL, J. C. (1959). The entry problem in consultation. *Journal of Social Issues, 15*(2), 51–59.

GOLDMAN, L. (Ed.). (1978). *Research methods for counselors*. New York: Wiley.

GOLEMBIEWSKI, R. T. (1969). Organization development in public agencies: Perspectives in theory and practice. *Public Administration Review 29,* 367–377.

GOODE, W. J., & HATT, P. K. (1972). The collection of data by questionnaire. In N. Margulies & A. P. Raia (Eds.), *Organizational development: Values, process, and technology* (pp. 163–185). New York: McGraw-Hill.

GOODSTEIN, L. D. (1978). *Consulting with human service systems*. Reading, Mass.: Addison-Wesley.

GOODSTEIN, L. D. (1985). Through a glass darkly: A commentary on Backer's "The future of organizational consulting." *Consultation, 4*(1), 30–33.

GOTTLIEB, B. H. (1974). Re-examining the preventive potential of mental health consultation. *Canada's Mental Health, 22,* 4–6.

GREINER, L. E. (1967). Patterns of organizational change. *Harvard Business Review,* (May-June), pp. 119–130.

GREINER, L. E., & METZGER, R. O. (1983). *Consulting to management: Insights to building and managing a successful practice*. Englewood Cliffs, N.J.: Prentice-Hall.

GRESHAM, F. M. & LEMANEK, K. L. (1987). Parent education. In C. A. Maher and S. G. Forman (Eds.), *A behavioral approach to education of children and youth* (pp. 153–181). Hillsdale, N.J.: Erlbaum.

GROSS, D. R., & ROBINSON, S. E. (1985). Ethics: The neglected issue in consultation. *Journal of Counseling and Development, 64*(1), 38–41.

GUTKIN, T. B., & CURTIS, M. J. (1982). School based consultation: Theory and techniques. In C. Reynolds & T. B. Gutkin. (Eds.), *The handbook of school psychology* (pp. 796–828). New York: Wiley.

HAGEDORN, H. J., BECK, K. J., NUEBERT, S. F., & WERLIN, S. H. (1976). *Working manual of simple program evaluation techniques for community mental health centers.* Rockville, Md.: Arthur D. Little, for the National Institute of Mental Health.

HANEY, C. H., and BOENISCH, E. W., Jr. (1982). *Stressmap: Finding your pressure points.* San Luis Obispo, Calif.: Impact Publishers.

HARRISON, R. (1978). When power conflicts trigger team spirit. In W. L. French, C. H. Bell, Jr., and R. A. Zawacki, (Eds.), *Organization development: Theory, practice, and research* (pp. 199–205). Dallas: Business Publications.

HAWRYLUK, M. K., & SMALLWOOD, D. L. (1986). Assessing and addressing consultee variables in school-based behavioral consultation. *School Psychology Review, 15*(4). 519–528.

HELLER, K. & MONAHAN, J. (1983). Individual-process consultation. In S. Cooper & W. F. Hodges (Eds.), *The mental health consultation field* (pp. 19–25). New York: Human Sciences Press.

HEPPNER, P. P. (1978). A review of the problem-solving literature and its relationship to the counseling process. *Journal of Counseling Psychology, 25*, 366–375.

HERSHENSON, D. B., & POWER, P. W. (1987). *Mental health counseling: Theory and practice.* New York: Pergamon Press.

HERZBERG, F. (1966). *Work and the nature of man.* Cleveland, Ohio: World.

HEYEL, C. (Ed.). (1973). *Encyclopedia of management* (2nd ed.). New York: Van Nostrand Reinhold.

HIRSCHOWITZ, R. G. (1977a). Consultation to complex organizations in transition: The dynamics of change and the principles of applied consultation. In S. C. Plog and P. I. Ahmed (Eds.), *Principles and techniques of mental health consultation* (pp. 169–197). New York: Plenum.

HIRSCHOWITZ, R. G. (1977b). Consultation to complex organizations in transition: The practical techniques of consultation. In S. C. Plog and R. I. Ahmed (Eds.), *Principles and techniques of mental health consultation* (pp. 199–219). New York: Plenum.

HODGES, W. F., & COOPER, S. (1983). General Introduction. In S. Cooper & W. F. Hodges (Eds.), *The mental health consultation field* (pp. 19–25). New York: Human Sciences Press.

HOPKINS, B. R., & ANDERSON, B. S. (1985). *The counselor and the law.* Alexandria, Va.: AACD Press.

HOUSE, R. J. (1978). T-group training: Good or bad? In W. L. French, C. H. Bell, Jr., & R. A. Zawacki (Eds.), *Organization development: Theory, practice and research* (pp. 199–205). Dallas: Business Publications.

HUGHES, J. (1980). Organizational issues consultants need to bear in mind. *School Psychology Review, 9*, 103–107.

HUGHES, J. N. (1986). Ethical issues in school consultation. *School Psychology Review, 15*(4), 489–499.

HUNSAKER, P. L., & ALESSANDRA, A. J. (1980). *The art of managing people.* Englewood Cliffs, N.J.: Prentice-Hall.

HUSE, E. F. (1975). *Organization development and change.* St. Paul, Minn.: West.

HUSE, E. F. (1978). Organization development. *Personnel and Guidance Journal, 56*(7), 403–406.

IVANCEVICH, A. L., SZILAGYI, D., Jr., & WALLACE, M. C., Jr. (1977). *Organizational behavior and performance.* Santa Monica, Calif.: Scott, Foresman.

JAMES, M. (1975). *The ok boss*. Reading, Mass.: Addison-Wesley.

JAMES, R. K., & DOUGHERTY, A. M. (1985). Doing your own dog and pony show: A guide for the perplexed school counselor. *School Counselor, 20*, 11–18.

JANIS, I. L., & MANN, L. (1977). *Decision making: A psychological analysis of conflict, choice, and commitment*. New York: Free Press.

JARVIS, P. E., & NELSON, S. (1967). Familiarization: A vital step in mental health consultation. *Community Mental Health Journal, 7*(3), 343–348.

JEGER, A. M., & McCLURE, G. (1982). An experiential evaluation and process analysis of a behavioral consultation program. In A. M. Jeger and R. S. Slotnick (Eds.), *Community mental health and behavioral-ecology: A handbook of theory, research, and practice* (pp. 389–401). New York: Plenum.

JEGER, A. M. & SLOTNICK, R. S. (1982a). Behavioral-ecology: Conceptualization, values, and knowledge bases. In A. M. Jeger and R. S. Slotnick (Eds.), *Community mental health and behavioral-ecology* (pp. 1–5). New York: Plenum.

JEGER, A. M. & SLOTNICK, R. S. (1982b). Community mental health: Toward a behavioral-ecological approach. In A. M. Jeger and R. S. Slotnick (Eds.), *Community mental health and behavioral-ecology* (pp. 7–26). New York: Plenum.

JEGER, A. M. & SLOTNICK, R. S. (1982c). Streams of behavioral ecology: A knowledge base for community mental health practice. In A. M. Jeger and R. S. Slotnick (Eds.), *Community mental health and behavior-ecology: A handbook of theory, research, and practice* (pp. 43–86). New York: Plenum.

JEGER, A. M. & SLOTNICK, R. S. (1982d). Consultation as indirect service. In A. M. Jeger and R. S. Slotnick (Eds.), *Community mental health and behavioral-ecology: A handbook of theory, research, and practice* (pp. 141–146). New York: Plenum.

JERRELL, J. M., & JERRELL, S. L. (1981). Organizational consultation in school systems. In J. C. Conoley (Ed.), *Consultation in schools* (pp. 133–156). New York: Academic Press.

JONES, J. E. (1973). The sensing interview. In J. W. Pfeiffer & J. E. Jones (Eds.), *The 1973 annual handbook for group facilitators* (pp. 213–234). La Jolla, Calif.: University Associates.

KANFER, F. H. & GOLDSTEIN, A. P. (Eds.). (1986). *Helping people change* (3rd ed.). New York: Pergamon Press.

KAROLY, P., & HARRIS, A. (1986). Operant methods. In F. H. Kanfer & A. P. Goldstein (Eds.), *Helping people change* (pp. 111–144). New York: Pergamon Press.

KATZ, D., & KAHN, R. L. (1966). *The social psychology of organizations*. New York: Wiley.

KATZ, D., & KAHN, R. L. (1978). *The social psychology of organizations* (2nd ed.). New York: Wiley.

KELLER, H. R. (1981). Behavioral consultation. In J. C. Conoley (Ed.), *Consultation in schools: Theory, research, and procedures* (pp. 59–99). New York: Academic Press.

KELLEY, R. E. (1981). *Consulting: The complete guide to a profitable career*. New York: Scribner's.

KHANDWALLA, P. N. (1977). *The design of organizations*. New York: Harcourt Brace Jovanovich.

KILBURG, R. (1978). Consumer survey as needs assessment method: A case study. *Evaluation and Program Planning, 1*, 285–292.

KIRBY, J. H. (1985). *Consultation: Practice and practitioner*. Muncie, Ind.: Accelerated Development.

KIRKPATRICK, D. L. (1975). *Evaluating training programs*. Madison, Wisc.: American Society for Training and Development.

KLEIN, D. (1969). Some notes on the dynamics of resistance to change: The defender role. In W. G. Bennis, K. D. Benne, R. Chin (Eds.), *The planning of change* (2nd. ed.) (pp. 498–507). New York: Holt, Rinehart & Winston.

KLEIN, D. C. (1983). Future directions for consultation by mental health systems. In S. Cooper & W. F. Hodges (Eds.), *The mental health consultation field* (pp. 221–229). New York: Human Sciences Press.

KNOWLES, M. S. & Associates. (1984). *Andragogy in action*. San Francisco: Jossey-Bass.

KNOX, A. B. (1977). *Adult development and learning: A handbook on individual growth and competence in the adult years*. San Francisco: Jossey-Bass.

KNOX, A. B. (1986). *Helping adults learn*. San Francisco: Jossey-Bass.

KOLB, D. A., & FROHMAN, A. L. (1970). An organization development approach to consulting. *Sloan Management Review, 12*(1), 51–65.

KRATOCHWILL, T. R. (1985). Behavioral consultation. In A. S. Bellack & M. Hersen (Eds.), *Dictionary of behavior therapy techniques* (pp. 22–24). New York: Pergamon Press.

KRATOCHWILL, T. R., MACE, F. C. & BISSEL, M. S. (1987). Program evaluation and research. In C. A. Maher & S. G. Foreman (Eds.), *A behavioral approach to education of children and youth* (pp. 253–288). Hillsdale, N.J.: Erlbaum.

KUEHNEL, T. G., & KUEHNEL, J. M. (1983a). Consultation training from a behavioral perspective. In J. L. Alpert and J. Meyers (Eds.), *Training in consultation* (pp. 85–103). Springfield, Ill.: Charles C Thomas.

KUEHNEL, T. G., & KUEHNEL, J. M. (1983b). Mental health consultation. In S. Cooper & W. F. Hodges (Eds.), *The mental health consultation field* (pp. 39–56). New York: Human Sciences Press.

KURPIUS, D. J. (1978). Consultation theory and process: An integrated model. *Personnel and Guidance Journal, 56*(6), 335–338.

KURPIUS, D. J. (1985). Consultation interventions: Successes, failures, and proposals. *The Journal of Counseling Psychology, 13*(3), 368–389.

KURPIUS, D. J. (1986). Consultation: An important human and organizational intervention. *Journal of Counseling and Human Service Professions, 1*(1), 58–66.

KURPIUS, D. J. (1987). Response to "Consultation in special education." *Journal of Learning Disabilities, 20*(8), 495.

KURPIUS, D. J., & ROBINSON, S. E. (1978). An overview of consultation. *Personnel and Guidance Journal, 56*(6), 321–323.

LAKIN, M. (1978). Some ethical issues in sensitivity training. In W. L. French, C. H. Bell, Jr., & R. A. Zawacki (Eds.), *Organization development: Theory, practice and research* (pp. 206–211). Dallas: Business Publications.

LATHAM, G. P., & LEE, T. W. (1986). Goal setting. In E. A. Locke (Ed.), *Generalizing from laboratory to field settings* (pp. 101–117). Lexington, Mass.: Lexington Books.

LAWRENCE, P., & LORSCH, J. (1967). *Organization and its environment*. Cambridge, Mass.: Harvard University Press.

LEARNED, E. P., & SPROAT, A. T. (1966). *Organizational theory and policy notes for analysis*. Homewood, Ill.: Richard D. Irwin.

LEVINSON, H. (1978). Management by whose objectives? In W. L. French, C. H. Bell, Jr., and R. A. Zawacki (Eds.), *Organization development: Theory, practice and research* (pp. 206-211). Dallas: Business Publication.

LEVINSON, H. (1985). Invited commentary: Consultation by cliche. *Consultation, 4*(2), 165-170.

LEWIN, K. (1945). Research center for group dynamics. *Sociometry, 8*(2), 9.

LEWIN, K. (1951). *Field theory in social sciences*. New York: Harper & Row.

LEWIS, J. A., & LEWIS, M. D. (1986). *Counseling programs for employees in the workplace*. Pacific Grove, Calif.: Brooks/Cole.

LIBERMAN, R. P., KUEHNEL, T. G., KUEHNEL, J. M., ECKMAN, T., & ROSENSTEIN, J. (1982). The behavioral analysis and modification project for community mental health. In A. M. Jeger and R. S. Slotnick (Eds.), *Community mental health and behavioral-ecology: A handbook of theory, research, and practice* (pp. 95-112). New York: Plenum.

LIEBERMAN, M. A., YALOM, I. D., & MILES, M. B. (1973). *Encounter groups: First facts*. New York: Basic Books.

LIKERT, R. (1967). *The human organization: Its management and value*. New York: McGraw-Hill.

LIPPITT, G. (1969). *Organizational renewal: Achieving viability in a changing world*. New York: Dutton.

LIPPITT, G. L. (1982a) *Organizational renewal: A holistic approach to organization development* (2nd ed.). Englewood Cliffs, N.J.: Prentice-Hall.

LIPPITT, G. L. (1982b). Managing conflict in today's organizations. *Training and Development Journal*, July, 1–5.

LIPPITT, G. L., LANGSETH, P., & MOSSOP, J. (1985). *Implementing organizational change*. San Francisco: Jossey-Bass.

LIPPITT, G., & LIPPITT, R. (1978). *The consulting process in action*. La Jolla, Calif.: University Associates.

LIPPITT, G. L., & NADLER, L. (1979). Emerging roles of the training director. In C. R. Bell & L. Nadler (Eds.), *The client-consultant handbook*. Houston: Gulf Publishing.

LIPPITT, R. (1983). Ethical issues and criteria in intervention decisions. In S. Cooper and W. F. Hodges (Eds.), *The mental health consultation field* (pp. 139–151). New York: Human Sciences Press.

LOCKE, E. A., & LATHAM, G. P. (1984). *Goal setting: A motivational technique that works.* Englewood Cliffs, N.J.: Prentice-Hall.

LORSCH, J. W., & LAWRENCE, P. (1972). The diagnosis of organizational problems. In N. Margulies & A. P. Raia (Eds.), *Organizational development: Values, process, and technology* (pp. 218–228). New York: McGraw-Hill.

LOWMAN, R. L. (1985). Ethical practice of psychological consultation: Not an impossible dream. *The Counseling Psychologist*, 13(3), 466–472.

LUNDBERG, C. C. (1985). Consultant feedback: A metaphor technique. *Consultation*, 4(2), 145–151.

LUTZKER, J. R., & MARTIN, J. A. (1981). *Behavior change*. Pacific Grove, Calif.: Brooks/Cole.

MACLENNAN, B. W. (1986). The organization and delivery of mental health consultation in changing times. In F. V. Mannino, E. J. Trickett, M. F. Shore, M. G. Kidder, and G. Levin (Eds.), *Handbook of mental health consultation* (pp. 319–345). Rockville, Md.: National Institute of Mental Health.

MACLENNAN, B. W., QUINN, R. D., & SCHROEDER, D. (1975). The scope of community health consultation. In F. V. Mannino, B. W. MacLennan, & M. F. Shore (Eds.), *The Practice of Mental Health Consultation* (pp. 3–24). Rockville, Md.: National Institute of Mental Health.

MAHER, C. A. (1981). Interventions with school social systems: A behavioral-systems approach. *School Psychology Review*, 10(4), 499–510.

MAHER, C. A., COOK, S. A., & KRUGER, L. J. (1987). Human resource development. In C. A. Maher & S. G. Forman (Eds.), *A behavioral approach to education of children and youth.* (pp. 221–252). Hillsdale, N.J.: Erlbaum.

MAIER, N. R. F. (1970). *Problem solving and creativity in groups*. Pacific Grove, Calif.: Brooks/Cole.

MAIN, A. P., & ROARK, A. E. (1975). A consensus method to reduce conflict. *Personnel and Guidance Journal*, 53, 754–759.

MANN, P. A. (1978). Mental health consultation in school settings. *Personnel and Guidance Journal*, 56(6), 369–373.

MANN, P. A. (1983). Transition points in consultation entry, transfer and termination. In S. Cooper & W. F. Hodges (Eds.), *The mental health consultation field* (pp. 99–105). New York: Human Sciences Press.

MANNINO, F. Y., MACLENNAN, B. W., & SHORE, M. F. (Eds.). (1975). *The practice of mental health consultation*. New York: Gardner Press.

MANNINO, F. V., & SHORE, M. F. (1986). Understanding consultation: Some orienting dimensions. *The Counseling Psychologist*, 13(3), 363–367.

MANNINO, F. V., TRICKETT, E. J., SHORE, M. F., KIDDER, M. G., LEVIN, G. (Eds.). (1986). *Handbook of mental health consultation*. Rockville, Md.: National Institute of Mental Health.

MARCH, J., & SIMON, H. (1958). *Organizations*. New York: Wiley.

MARGULIES, N., & RAIA, A. P. (Eds.). (1972). Emerging issues in organization development. In N. Margulies and A. P. Raia (Eds.), *Organizational development: Values, process, and technology* (pp. 475–478). New York: McGraw-Hill.

MARIS, T. L. (1985). Characteristics of successful management consultants. *Consultation, 4*(3) 258–263.

MATSON, J. (1985). Modeling. In A. S. Bellack & M. Hersen (Eds.), *Dictionary of behavior therapy techniques* (pp. 150–151). New York: Pergamon Press.

MATTHEWS, J. (1983). *The effective use of management consultants in higher education.* Boulder, Colo.: National Center for Higher Education Management Services.

MATUSZEK, P. A. (1981). Program evaluation as consultation. In J. C. Conoley (Ed.), *Consultation in schools* (pp. 179–200). New York: Academic Press.

MAZADE, N. A. (1983). In conclusion the past, present, and future in consultation. In S. Cooper & W. F. Hodges (Eds.), *The mental health consultation field* (pp. 233–242). New York: Human Sciences Press.

MAZADE, N. A. (1985). Issues in consultation. *Consultation, 4*(1), 7–16.

MCGREGOR, D. (1960). *The human side of enterprise.* New York: McGraw-Hill.

MCKAY, M., DAVIS, M., & FANNING, P. (1981). *Thoughts and feelings: The art of cognitive stress intervention.* Richmond, Calif.: New Harbinger Publications.

MCKEACHIE, W. J. (1986). *Teaching tips: A guidebook for the beginning teacher* (8th ed.). Boston: D. C. Heath.

MEDWAY, F. J. (1982). School consultation research: Past trends and future directions. *Professional Psychology, 13*(3), 422–429.

MEICHENBAUM, D. (1977). *Cognitive-behavior modification: An integrative approach.* New York: Plenum.

MEICHENBAUM, D. (1985). *Stress inoculation training.* New York: Pergamon Press.

MEYERS, J. (1981). Mental health consultation. In J. C. Conoley (Ed.), *Consultation in schools theory, research, procedures* (pp. 35–58). New York: Academic Press.

MEYERS, J., ALPERT, J. L., & FLEISHER, B. (1983). Models of consultation. In J. L. Alpert and J. Meyers (Eds.), *Training in consultation* (pp. 5–16). Springfield, Ill.: Charles C Thomas.

MEYERS, J., PARSONS, R. D., & MARTIN, R. (1979). *Mental health consultation in the schools.* San Francisco: Jossey-Bass.

MITCHELL, K. R. (1977). The special problems of consultation with local churches. In S. C. Plog and P. I. Ahmed (Eds.), *Principles and techniques of mental health consultation* (pp. 151–167). New York: Plenum.

MITCHELL, T. R. (1978). *People in organizations: Understanding their behavior.* New York: McGraw-Hill.

MORASKY, R. L. (1982). *Behavioral Systems.* New York: Praeger.

NADLER, D. A. (1977). *Feedback and organization development: Using data-based methods.* Reading, Mass.: Addison-Wesley.

NADLER, L. (1980). *Corporate human resources development: A managerial tool.* New York: Van Nostrand Reinhold.

NAISBITT, J. (1982). *Megatrends: Ten new directions transforming our lives.* New York: Warner Books.

NAISBITT, J. & ABURDENE, P. (1985). *Re-inventing the corporation: Transforming your job and company for the new information society.* New York: Warner Books.

NEILSEN, E. H. (1984). *Becoming an OD practitioner.* Englewood Cliffs, N.J.: Prentice-Hall.

NEWSTROM, J. W. (1987). Confronting anomalies in evaluation. *Training and Development Journal, 41*(7), 56–60.

O'DELL, S. (1974). Training parents in behavior modification: A review. *Psychological Bulletin, 81*, 418–433.

OHLSEN, M. M. (1974). *Guidance services in the modern school* (2nd ed.). New York: Harcourt Brace Jovanovich.

OKUN, B. F. (1976). *Effective helping: Interviewing and counseling techniques.* North Scituate, Mass.: Duxbury Press.

OSTERWEIL, Z. O. (1987). A structured process of problem definition in school consultation. *School Counselor, 34*(5), 345–352.

OWENS, T. R. (1973). Educational evaluation by adversary proceedings. In E. House (Ed.), *School evaluation: The politics and process*. Berkeley, Calif.: McCutchan.

PARSONS, R. D., & MEYERS, J. (1984). *Developing consultation skills*. San Francisco: Jossey-Bass.

PATTERSON, C. H. (1980). *Theories of counseling and psychotherapy* (3rd ed.). New York: Harper & Row.

PATTON, M. Q. (1977). *Utilization-focused evaluation*. Beverly Hills, Calif.: Sage.

PERROW, C. (1970). *Organizational analysis: A sociological view*. Belmont, Calif.: Wadsworth.

PERRY, M. A., & FURUKAWA, M. J. (1986). Modeling methods. In F. H. Kanfer & A. P. Goldstein (Eds.), *Helping people change* (pp. 66–110). New York: Pergamon Press.

PETERS, T. J., & WATERMAN, R. H., Jr. (1982). *In search of excellence: Lessons from America's best-run companies*. New York: Warner Books.

PFEIFFER, J. W., & JONES, J. E. (Eds.). (1974). *A handbook of structured experiences for human relations training* (Vol. 3). La Jolla, Calif.: University Associates.

PFEIFFER, J. W., & JONES, J. E. (Eds.). (1977). Ethical considerations in consulting. In J. E. Jones and J. W. Pfeiffer (Eds.), *The 1977 annual handbook for group facilitators* (pp. 217–224). La Jolla, Calif.: University Associates.

PIETROFESA, J. J., HOFFMAN, A., SPLETE, H. H., & PINTO, D. V. (1978). *Counseling: Theory, research, and practice*. Chicago: Rand McNally.

PIPES, R. B. (1981). Consulting in organizations: The entry problem. In J. C. Conoley (Ed.), *Consultation in schools theory, research, procedures* (pp. 11–33). New York: Academic Press.

PRYZWANSKY, W. B. (1977). Collaboration or consultation: Is there a difference? *Journal of Special Education, 11*, 179–182.

PRYZWANSKY, W. B. (1985). Challenges in consultation training. *The Counseling Psychologist, 13*(3), 441–443.

PRYZWANSKY, W. B. (1986). Indirect service delivery: Considerations for future research in consultation. *School Psychology Review, 15*(4), 479–488.

PUGH, D. S. (1966). Modern organizational theory: A psychological and sociological study. *Psychological Bulletin, 66*(4), 235–251.

QUINN, S. R., & KARP, S. (1986). Developing an objective evaluation tool. *Training and Development Journal, 40*(5), 90–92.

REPPUCCI, N. D. (1977). Implementation issues for the behavior modifier as institutional change agent. *Behavior Therapy, 8*, 594–605.

REPPUCCI, N. D., & SAUNDERS, J. T. (1983). Focal issues for institutional change. *Professional Psychology: Research and Practice, 14*, 514–528.

RICE, A. K. (1969). Individual, group, and intergroup process. *Human Relations, 22*, 565–584.

RIMM, D. C., & CUNNINGHAM, H. M. (1985). Behavior Therapies. In S. J. Lynn & J. P. Garske (Eds.), *Contemporary psychotherapies models and methods* (pp. 221–259). Columbus, Ohio: Charles E. Merrill.

ROBINSON, S. E., & GROSS, D. R. (1985). Ethics of consultation: The Canterville ghost. *The Counseling Psychologist, 13*(3), 444–465.

ROGAWSKI, A. S. (1977). Mental health consultations to welfare agencies. In S. C. Plog and P. I. Ahmed (Eds.), *Principles and techniques of mental health consultation* (pp. 119–133). New York: Plenum.

ROGAWSKI, A. S. (1978). The Caplanian model. *Personnel and Guidance Journal, 56*, 324–327.

ROGERS, C. R. (1961). *On becoming a person*. Boston: Houghton Mifflin.

RUDESTAM, K. E. (1982). *Experiential groups in theory and practice*. Pacific Grove, Calif.: Brooks/Cole.

RUSSELL, M. L. (1978). Behavioral consultation: Theory and process. *Personnel and Guidance Journal, 56*(6), 346–350.

SANDLAND, K., & DOUGHERTY, A. M. (1985). Using the nominal group technique with incarcerates. *Journal of Offender Counseling, 6*, 25–30.

SANDOVAL, J., LAMBERT, N. M., & DAVIS, J. M. (1977). Consultation from the consultee's perspective. *Journal of School Psychology, 15*(4), 334–342.

SCHEIN, E. H. (1969). *Process consultation: Its role in organization development.* Reading, Mass.: Addison-Wesley.

SCHEIN, E. H. (1978). The role of the consultant: Content expert or process facilitator? *Personnel and Guidance Journal, 56*(6), 339–343.

SCHEIN, E. H. (1987). *Process consultation: Lessons for managers and consultants* (Volume II). Reading, Mass.: Addison-Wesley.

SCHEIN, E. H. & GREINER, L. E. (1977). Can organization development be fine tuned to bureaucracies? *Organization Dynamics, 5*(3), 48–61.

SCHINDLER-RAINMAN, E. (1985). Invited commentary: The modern consultant—a renaissance person. *Consultation, 4*(3), 264–267.

SCHMIDT, J. J., & OSBORNE, W. L. (1981). Counseling and consulting: Separate processes or the same? *Personnel and Guidance Journal, 59*, 168–171.

SCHMUCK, R. A. (1976). Process consultation and organization development. *Professional Psychology, 7*, 626–635.

SCHMUCK, R. A. (1983). System-process mental health models. In S. Cooper & W. F. Hodges (Eds.), *The mental health consultation field* (pp. 71–90). New York: Human Sciences Press.

SCRIVEN, M. (1967). The methodology of evaluation. In R. Tyler, R. Gagne, & M. Scriven (Eds.), *Perspectives on curriculum evaluation* (AERA Monograph Series on Curriculum Evaluation). Chicago: Rand McNally.

SCRIVEN, M. (1972). Pros and cons about goal-free evaluation. *Evaluation Comment, 3*, 1–4.

SELLTIZ, C., JAHODA, M., DEUTSCH, M., & COOK, S. W. (1972). The collection of data by observation. In N. Margulies & A. P. Raia (Eds.), *Organizational development: Values, process, and technology* (pp. 186–214). New York: McGraw-Hill.

SELYE, H. (1975). *Stress without distress.* New York: New American Library.

SHAW, M. C. & GOODYEAR, R. K. (1984). Introduction to the special issues on primary prevention. *Personnel and Guidance Journal, 62*(8), 444–445.

SHEELEY, V. L., & HERLIHY, B. (1986). The ethics of confidentiality and privileged communication. *Journal of Counseling and Human Service Professions, 1*(1), 141–148.

SHERTZER, B., & LINDEN, J. D. (1979). *Fundamentals of individual appraisal.* Boston: Houghton Mifflin.

SHULTZ, J. (1984). Historical overview of OD consulting. In R. J. Lee & A. M. Freedman (Eds.), *Consultation skills reading* (pp. 1–3). Arlington, Va.: NTL Institute.

SINHA, D. P. (Ed.). (1979). *Consultants and consultant styles.* New Delhi, India: Vision Books.

SKINNER, B. F. (1953). *Science and human behavior.* New York: Macmillan.

SMITH, K. K., & CORSE, S. J. (1986). The process of consultation: Critical issues. In F. V. Mannino, E. J. Trickett, M. F. Shore, M. G. Kidder, and G. Levin (Eds.), *Handbook of mental health consultation* (pp. 247–278). Rockville, Md.: National Institute of Mental Health.

SNOW, D. L., & GERSICK, K. E. (1986). Ethical and professional issues in mental health consultation. In F. V. Mannino, E. J. Trickett, M. Shore, M. G. Kidder, and G. Levin (Eds.), *Handbook of mental health consultation* (pp. 393–431). Rockville, Md.: National Institute of Mental Health.

STEELE, F. (1975). *Consulting for organizational change.* Amherst, Mass.: University of Massachusetts Press.

STRONG, S. R. (1968). Counseling: An interpersonal influence process. *Journal of Counseling Psychology, 15*, 215–224.

STUFFLEBEAM, D., FOLEY, W., GEPHART, W., GUBA, E., HAMMOND, R., MERIMAN, H., & PURVUS, M. (1971). *Educational evaluation and decision making.* Itasca, Ill.: F. E. Peacock.

STUM, D. L. (1982). DIRECT: A consultation skills training model. *Personnel and Guidance Journal, 60,* 296–301.

SUMMERS, I., & WHITE, D. E. (1980). Creativity techniques: Toward improvement of the decision process. In S. Ferguson and S. Ferguson (Eds.), *Intercommunication: Readings in organizational communication* (pp. 338–348). Rochelle Park, N.J.: Hayden Books.

SWARTZ, D. (1975). Similarities and differences of internal and external consultants. *Journal of European Training, 4,* 258–262.

SWARTZ, D. & LIPPITT, G. (1975). Evaluating the consulting process. *Journal of European Training, 4,* 309–326.

SWIFT, C. F., & COOPER, S. (1986). Settings, consultees, and clients. In F. V. Mannino, E. J. Trickett, M. F. Shore, M. G. Kidder, and G. Levin (Eds.), *Handbook of mental health consultation* (pp. 347–392). Rockville, Md.: National Institute of Mental Health.

TENNYSON, W. W., & STROM, S. A. (1986). Beyond professional standards: Developing responsibleness. *Journal of Counseling and Development, 64*(5), 298–302.

THARP, R. G., & WETZEL, R. J. (1969). *Behavior modification in the natural environment.* New York: Academic Press.

TICHY, N. M. (1983). *Managing strategic change: Technical, political, and cultural dynamics.* New York: Wiley.

TOMBARI, M. & DAVIS, R. A. (1979). Behavioral consultation. In G. D. Phye & D. J. Reschly (Eds.), *School psychology perspectives and issues* (pp. 281–307). New York: Academic Press.

VERNBERG, E. M., & REPPUCCI, N. D. (1986). Behavioral consultation. In F. V. Mannino, E. J. Trickett, M. F. Shore, M. G. Kidder, and G. Levin (Eds.), *Handbook of mental health consultation* (pp. 49–80). Rockville, Md.: National Institute of Mental Health.

VROOM, V. H. (1964). *Work and motivation.* New York: Wiley.

WALTON, R. E. (1969). *Interpersonal peacemaking: Confrontations and third-party consultation.* Reading, Mass.: Addison-Wesley.

WALTON, R. E. (1978). Interpersonal confrontation and basic third-party functions: A case study. In W. L. French, C. H. Bell, Jr., & R. A. Zawacki (Eds.), *Organization development: Theory, practice, and research* (pp. 165–173). Dallas: Business Publications.

WALZ, G. R., & BENJAMIN, L. (1978). A change agent strategy for counselors functioning as consultants. *Personnel and Guidance Journal, 56*(6), 331–334.

WEISBORD, M. R. (1976). Organizational diagnosis: Six places to look for trouble with or without a theory. *Group and Organizational Studies, 1,* 430–447.

WEISBORD, M. R. (1984). Client contact: Entry and contract. In R. J. Lee & A. M. Freedman (Eds.), *Consultation skills readings* (pp. 63–66). Bethel, Maine: National Training Laboratories Institute.

WEISBORD, M. R. (1985). The organization development contract revisited. *Consultation, 4*(4), 305–315.

WEST, J. F. & IDOL, L. (1987). School consultation (Part I): An interdisciplinary perspective on theory, models, and research. *Journal of Learning Disabilities, 20*(7), 388–408.

WHEELER, D. D., & JANIS, I. J. (1980). *A practical guide for making decisions.* New York: Free Press.

WIGTIL, J. V., & KELSEY, R. C. (1978). Team building as a consulting intervention for influencing learning environments. *Personnel and Guidance Journal, 56*(7), 412–416.

WILLEMS, E. P. (1974). Behavioral technology and behavioral ecology. *Journal of Applied Behavioral Analysis, 7,* 151–156.

WOODCOCK, M., & FRANCIS, D. (1979). *Unblocking your organization.* La Jolla, Calif.: University Associates.

WOODY, R. H. & Associates. (1984) *The law and the practice of human services.* San Francisco: Jossey-Bass.

YOLLES, S. F. (1970). Foreward. In G. Caplan, *The theory and practice of mental health consultation*. New York: Basic Books.

ZAND, D. E. (1978). Collateral organization: A new change strategy. In W. L. French, C. H. Bell, Jr., & R. A. Zawacki (Eds.), *Organization development: Theory, practice, and research* (pp. 293–307). Dallas: Business Publications.

ZIFFERBLATT, S. M., & HENDRICKS, C. G. (1974). Applied behavioral analysis of societal problems: Population change, a case in point. *American Psychologist, 29,* 750–761.

ZUSMAN, J. (1972). Mental health consultation: Some theory and practice. In J. Zusman & D. L. Davidison (Eds.), *Practical aspects of mental health consultation*. Springfield, Ill.: Charles C Thomas.

Author Index

323

Subject Index

Acme Human Services Center, 287–290
Advocate role, 27
American Association for Counseling and Development (AACD), 136, 138, 139, 140, 144, 146, 147, 308
American Psychological Association (APA), 136, 139, 140, 141, 147, 308
American Society for Training and Development (ASTD), 136, 139, 140, 143, 147, 151, 309
Andragogy, 201

Behavioral case consultation, 254, 261–273
  application: consultant techniques and procedures, 268–272
  case study, 272–273, 300–301
  consultant function and roles, 262–267
  consultee's experience in, 267–268
  explained, 261
  goals of, 261–262
  major focus of, 305
  plan implementation stage, 271
  problem analysis stage, 269–270
  problem evaluation stage, 271–272
  problem identification stage, 268–269
  steps in, 268
  verbal interaction techniques, 263–267
Behavioral consultation, 254–283
  assumptions, 258
  behavioral case, 261–273
  behavioral system, 273–278
  behavioral technology training, 278–280
  changing overt behavior, 259–260
  characteristics of, 257–258, 261
  conclusions, 281–282
  consultation process, 261–280
  contributions, 281–282
  criticisms of, 282
  defined, 12, 257–259
  emphasis on current influences on behavior, 260
  focus of, 157
  focus on behavior change, 255
  historical background, 255–257

Behavioral consultation (continued)
  influence of behavior therapy, 255–256
  key concepts in, 259–261
  prejudice against, 9
  principles of behavior change, 260–261
  problem-solving sequence in, 258–259
  scientific view of behavior, 259
  trends, 281
Behavioral ecology, 256, 273
Behavioral system consultation, 254, 273–278
  application: consultation techniques and procedures, 275–278
  case study, 278, 301–302
  consultant function and roles, 274
  consultee's experience in consultation, 275
  goals of, 274
  major focus of, 305
  overview of, 273–274
  stages in, 275
  system assessment, 276
  system definition, 275–276
  system evaluation, 277
  system intervention, 276–277
Behavioral technology training, 254, 278–280
  application: consultation techniques and procedures, 279
  case study, 280, 302–303
  consultant function and roles, 279
  consultee's experience in consultation, 279
  goal of, 279
  major focus of, 305
  overview, 278–279
  rationale for, 279
  similarity to education/training model, 279
Being, with consultees, 45–46
Brainstorming, 81, 85

Change:
  in consultee and client system, 8
  exploring organization's commitment to, 53
  in organizations, 174–177
  organization development as one approach to, 178
  as part of consultant's growth orientation, 18

329

Credits

Chapter 1: 9, quotations from *The Profession and Practice of Consultation* by June Gallessich. Copyright 1982 by Jossey-Bass, Inc. Publishers. This and all other quotes from the same source are adaptations by permission of the publisher and the author.

Chapter 2: 26, quotations from *Psychological Consultation: Introduction to Theory and Practice*, by Brown, Pryzwansky, and Schulte. Copyright 1987 by Allyn & Bacon. This and all other quotes from the same source are used with permission.   **34,** paraphrasing of quotations from *Children Under Stress*, by L. A. Chandler. Copyright 1985 by Charles C Thomas. Courtesy of Charles C Thomas, Publishers, Springfield, IL.

Chapter 3: 49, quote from *School Consultation: A Guide to Practice and Training*, by J. C. Conoley and C. W. Conoley. This and all other quotes from the same source are reprinted with permission of Pergamon Journals Ltd.   **51,** quote from *Clients & Consultants*, Second Edition, by Chip R. Bell and Leonard Nadler, Editors. Copyright © 1985 by Gulf Publishing Company, Houston, TX. This and all other quotes from the same source are used with permission. All rights reserved. **51,** quote adapted from Gordon Lippitt and Ronald Lippitt, *The Consulting Process in Action* (2nd ed.). San Diego, CA: University Associates, Inc., 1986. This and all other quotes from the same source are used with permission.   **52,** quotes from *Developing Consultation Skills*, by R. D. Parsons and J. Meyers. Copyright 1984 by Jossey-Bass, Inc. Reprinted by permission of the publisher and author.   **53,** quotes from "Developing a Successful Client-Consultant Relationship," by C. R. Bell and L. Nadler. In *The Client-Consultant Handbook*, by Charles H. Ford. Copyright © 1974 by John Wiley and Sons, Inc. Reprinted by permission of John Wiley & Sons, Inc.   **54,** quote reprinted with permission from *School Consultation: A Guide to Practice and Training*, by J. A. Conoley and C. W. Conoley, Copyright 1982, Pergamon Journals, Ltd. **55,** quotations from S. Cooper and W. F. Hodges (Eds.) *The Mental Health Consultation Field.* Copyright 1983 by Human Sciences Press. Reprinted by permission.   **56,** paraphrase of a quote from "The Psychological Contract: A Key to Effective Organizational Development Consultation," by R. W. Boss. In *Consultation* 4(4), 1985. Copyright 1985 by Human Sciences Press. Used by permission.   **58, 62,** quotes excerpted from Robert E. Kelley, *Consulting: The Complete Guide to a Profitable Career.* Copyright © 1981 Robert E. Kelley. This and all other quotes from the same source are reprinted with the permission of Charles Scribner's Sons, an imprint of Macmillan Publishing Company.

Chapter 4: 68, Figure 4.1 adapted from "Organization Development: Objectives, Assumptions and Strategies," by W. French. In Margulies and Raia (Eds.), *Organizational Development: Values, Process and Technology.* Copyright 1972 by McGraw-Hill Book Company. Adapted by permission. **74,** quote from D. A. Nadler, *Feedback and Organization Development,* © 1977, Addison-Wesley Publishing Co., Inc., Reading, MA. Adapted excerpts. This and all other quotes from the same source are reprinted with permission.

Chapter 5: 94, quote from Wendell L. French/Cecil H. Bell, Jr., *Organization Development: Behavioral Science Interventions for Organization Improvement*, 3rd Edition, © 1984, p. 130. Adapted by permission of Prentice-Hall, Inc., Englewood Cliffs, NJ.   **103,** quote from "Consultation Interventions: Successes, Failures, and Proposals," by D. J. Kurpius, *The Consulting Psychologist*, 1984, 13(3), 368–389. Copyright © 1985 by The Consulting Psychologist. Reprinted by permission of Sage Publications, Inc.

Chapter 7: 150, 151, quotes and adaptations from: J. William Pfeiffer and John E. Jones (Eds.), *The 1977 Annual Handbook for Group Facilitators.* San Diego, CA: University Associates, Inc., 1977. Used with permission.   **162,** Chapter titles from *Megatrends: Ten New Directions Transforming Our Lives*, by J. Naisbett. Copyright © 1982 by Warner Books, Inc. Reprinted with permission.   **163, 164,** quotes from *People in Organizations and Understanding Their Behavior*, by T. R. Mitchell. Copyright 1978 by McGraw-Hill Book Company. Reprinted by permission.